The Humanity of Thucydides

The Humanity of Thucydides

Clifford Orwin

PRINCETON UNIVERSITY PRESS

PRINCETON, NEW JERSEY

Library of Congress Cataloging-in-Publication Data

Orwin, Clifford, 1947–
The humanity of Thucydides / Clifford Orwin.
p.   cm.
Includes bibliographical references and index.
ISBN 0-691-03449-4
ISBN 0-691-01726-3 (pbk.)
1. Thucydides. History of the Peloponnesian War.   2. Greece—
History—Peloponnesian War, 431–404 B.C.—Causes.
3. Human behavior.   I. Title.
DF229.T607 1994 938'.05—dc20 94-3111

This book has been composed in Galliard

Princeton University Press books are printed on acid-free paper
and meet the guidelines for permanence and durability of the
Committee on Production Guidelines for Book Longevity
of the Council on Library Resources

Third printing, and first paperback printing, 1997

Printed in the United States of America

3 5 7 9 10 8 6 4

To my parents

———————————————

CONTENTS

ACKNOWLEDGMENTS

IT HAS NOT taken me quite as long to write this book as it did for the Peloponnesian War to end. Over the twelve years that it has taken, however, I have incurred many debts. For financial and other institutional support, I am grateful to the University of Toronto and an unbroken succession of benevolent chairmen of its Department of Political Science, to the National Endowment for the Humanities, the Earhart Foundation, the Social Sciences and Humanities Research Council of Canada, the University of Chicago, and the Library of the American Academy in Rome and its former director, Dr. Rogers Scudder. In the final stages of preparation of the manuscript, I benefited greatly from the assistance of Randall B. Clark, my research assistant at the University of Chicago. The *American Political Science Review*, *The American Scholar*, the *Journal of Politics*, *Polis*, the *Review of Politics*, and the Carl Friedrich Siemens Stiftung of Munich have kindly permitted the use of revised versions of material originally published by them.

My thanks also to all to whom I owe invitations to lecture on Thucydides, and to Michigan State University, Harvard University, and the University of Chicago for visiting appointments, which enabled me to hone my views before their excellent students. To my equally excellent students at Toronto I owe a great deal.

I am grateful for encouragement and criticism from many teachers, friends, and colleagues, none of whom may be presumed to agree with the results; these include Edward C. Banfield, Saul Bellow, David Bolotin, Christopher Bruell, Marc Cogan, Lowell Edmunds, Joseph Epstein, J. Peter Euben, Helmut Flashar, Steven Forde, David Grene, Stephen T. Holmes, Donald Kagan, Robert P. Kraynak, David Leibowitz, Pierre Manent, Heinrich Meier, Arthur M. Melzer, Peter Nicholson, Thomas L. Pangle, Patrick F. Powers, David L. Schaefer, the late Judith N. Shklar, Joseph Solodow, Nathan S. Tarcov, and M. Richard Zinman. I owe special thanks to the philologists who humored my efforts to penetrate Thucydides' Greek, chief among them Malcolm B. Wallace. This book is better for the efforts of the readers for Princeton University Press, one of whom was Daniel Tompkins. Ann Himmelberger Wald, my editor at Princeton, was a model of encouragement, efficiency, and reassurance. My copy editor, Carol Roberts, suggested many improvements and saved me from many errors (and but for my obstinacy would have saved me from many more). Michael S. Rabieh composed the index, and Khalil Habib helped me with the corrections to the paperback edition.

To the late Allan Bloom, my teacher at Cornell and later my colleague at Toronto and (during the final year of his life) at Chicago, it is impossible to overstate my debt. He inspired my study of ancient (as well as modern) thought and continued to guide and nurture it. Although his seemed an impossible act to follow, Harvey C. Mansfield, Jr., who supervised my graduate studies at Harvard, proved capable of following it. I cannot think that anyone of my generation has been blessed with better teachers.

My wife Donna has been a tower of strength and support even as she somehow managed to pursue her own studies of Tolstoy, and our sons have acquiesced in this project even when they could think of better things for me to do. My primary debt I have acknowledged in my dedication.

A NOTE ON THE NOTES

THE NOTES in this work refer either to modern books or articles or to ancient works. I cite the latter by the conventional divisions by book and chapter (or by page) to be found in all editions of them, for example Herodotus 6.93, Aristotle *Nicomachean ethics* 2.8, Plato *Republic* 355a. Such works are not listed in the bibliography. The fragments of the pre-Socratic philosophers are referred to according to the standard enumeration of Diels/Kranz; English translations of these are available in Freeman's *Ancilla to the pre-Socratic philosophers*; these two works I have listed in the bibliography.

As regards modern works I have adopted the following practice. In order to save space while sparing the reader the necessity of searching back through the pages of the book for the original reference to an item, each work is cited throughout, from its first appearance to its last, by the very same abbreviation keyed to the bibliography. In the case of a book the citation consists of the author's name, a brief title, and the page number(s), for example Romilly *Imperialism* 231. In the case of an article in a journal, the citation consists of the author's name, the abbreviated title of the journal, the volume, the year, and the page number(s), for example Romilly *REG* 103 (1990) 376–78. In the case of an essay or chapter in a book, the forms are as follows: Stahl in Stadter ed. *Speeches* 64; Strauss in Strauss *Studies* 174. In every case the bibliography provides full information, including the unabbreviated title of the book or journal. For the sake of easy reference, items in the bibliography are alphabetized under the name of their author according to the following principle: books by the key word of the title (which is usually the first substantive word); articles by the name of the journal or the last name of the editor of the volume. Thus Lateiner's article in *Classical Philology* (abbreviated as *CP*) precedes in the bibliography his article in *Classical World* (abbreviated as *CW*), regardless of their respective dates and titles. Articles by the same author in the same journal are listed in chronological order.

A NOTE ON NARRATIVE STYLE

THE PRIMARY actors in Thucydides are not individuals but cities, and it seemed advisable for stylistic reasons to avoid unnecessary repetition of their names, whether in nominative, possessive, or adjectival form. Yet to describe a previously mentioned city as "it" and to employ "its" as its possessive form also poses problems, as the city then has to coexist with so many other matters with which it shares these pronouns that the reader cannot possibly assign each "it" to its respective referent. I have therefore availed myself of the traditional practice (inherited from Greek, Latin, and the Romance languages) of ascribing to cities the feminine gender. This permits a given city to glide neatly through a lengthy paragraph strewn with "hims" and "its," without repetition of the city's name and without the reader being left in doubt concerning the referent of any pronoun.

The gender of the city in the languages from which English has borrowed this usage is a matter of grammar rather than of sex (a distinction which English speakers with their overwhelmingly neuter language may not at first grasp): while spoons are of feminine gender in French, no Francophone thinks of them as female; while they are of masculine gender in German, no German speaker thinks of them as male. Similarly there is no reason to think that the Greek *polis* (etymologically akin to other Indo-European words the meaning of which is "fortress") or the Latin *urbs* (the etymology of which is probably "bounded area") originally expressed any sense of the femaleness of cities. It is true of course that the feminine *gender* of a sexless being suggests the possibility of the figurative or poetic ascription of feminine *characteristics* to that being. I, however, am not a poet. Readers should not suppose that in employing the same grammatical gender for both cities and women I mean to ascribe to the former any characteristics of the latter.

The Humanity of Thucydides

INTRODUCTION

> Thucydides is to my taste the true model of an
> historian. He reports the facts without judging them,
> but he omits none of the circumstances proper to make
> us judge them ourselves. He puts all he recounts before
> the reader's eyes. Far from putting himself between the
> events and his readers, he hides himself. The reader no
> longer believes he reads; he believes he sees.
> —Rousseau, *Emile*, Book 4.[1]

OF ALL WRITERS on politics, none stays closer than Thucydides to the world of the citizen and statesman. His work is surely not "academic"; this explains part of its attraction. In recording the emergence of the study of politics out of its practice, he shows us how the most political perspectives imply upon reflection a certain distance from political life. As an analyst, moreover, of societies, democratic and nondemocratic, subjected to the stress of a long and catastrophic war, he speaks more directly than any other ancient writer to our unquiet century.[2] Even so, some may find it surprising that a political scientist should write about him. He is, after all, usually called a historian, and custody of him has passed to our professors of classics and ancient history.

In fact Thucydides, who predates the division of intellectual life into disciplines, never calls himself a historian or anything else, except simply Thucydides an Athenian, who "wrote up" (*xynegrapse*) the war that we call Peloponnesian. We call him a historian because he limited himself to describing this particular series of events. As he makes clear, however, his aim is to expound their general and lasting significance (1.22.4; cf. 3.82.2). He seeks to display them *sub specie aeternitatis* (cf. 1.10), for the benefit of whoever might seek to understand the permanent contours of politics.

The greatest of Thucydides' English readers, Hobbes, extolled him for his success at this ambitious task. Hobbes saw Thucydides as of all ancient

---

[1] Rousseau *Emile* (tr. Bloom) 239.

[2] See Milosz *Witness of poetry* 81: "People always live within a certain order and are unable to visualize a time when [it] might cease to exist. The sudden crumbling of all current notions and criteria is a rare occurrence . . . characteristic of only the most stormy periods in history. . . . In general . . . the Nineteenth Century did not experience the rapid and violent changes of [our] century, whose only possible analogy may be the time of the Peloponnesian War, as we know it from Thucydides."

writers the one most worth reading, the political historian *par excellence*, "the most politic historiographer that ever writ." For Hobbes the difference between the political philosopher and the political historian was only that whereas the former instructed openly by means of precepts, the latter did so only implicitly or covertly: "[T]he narrative doth secretly instruct the reader, and more effectually than can possibly be done by precept." The reader may "from the narrations draw out lessons to himself." What Thucydides offers, through the unsurpassed artfulness of his narrative, is a vicarious experience of the events that he describes, for which no dogmatic presentation of the truths of political life could substitute. Yet we can benefit from his achievement only to the extent that we strive to "draw out lessons to ourselves," that we participate as readers of a great book must always participate.[3]

Thucydides thus belongs, according both to his own intention and to the judgment of such men as Hobbes and Rousseau, to students of political life of whatever time and place.[4] It is these whose possession for all time (1.22.4) his book was to be, and to whom I have addressed mine. My claim is not that Thucydides teaches how to get elected mayor of Chicago. Political astuteness always depends on knowledge of one's time that is available nowhere else, certainly not in books from other times. Thucydides aims to articulate the parameters of political life, its permanent patterns and thus also its permanent dilemmas. Despite the respect in which Marxist thinkers have always held him, nothing could be more alien to him than the view that mankind poses no problems that it cannot solve. Although he begins by stressing the unprecedented greatness of the war that is his theme, it proves to have surpassed all rivals above all in its calamitousness (1.23.1–4). It is a war of great plans, but the narrative stresses the recurrent discrepancies between plan and result, the limits of the perspectives of the participants, the salience of the unexpected and incalculable.[5] We cannot for this reason deny, however, that Thucydides intended the work to be of use to statesmen. Clear understanding does not confer mastery over (human or nonhuman) nature, but it does imply an awareness of both the means and the bounds of political accomplishment—and is useful to statesmen on both counts.[6]

---

[3] Hobbes *English Works* 8:viii, xvi–xvii, xxii, xxix, xxxii. For recent elaborations of the last point, see Adcock *Thucydides* 13; Connor *Thucydides*; Connor in *Greek historians* 1–17; Farrar *Origins* 135–36. For an updating of Hobbes's view of Thucydides (and a defense of political history), see Aron *History and Theory* 1 (1960–61) 103–28.

[4] See Regenbogen *Kleine Schriften* 224: "Thukydides schreibt als Politiker für die politischen Menschen." ("Thucydides writes as a politician for [the benefit of] political men.") Cf. Herter *RhM* 93 (1949) 133–53; Farrar *Origins* 126–31.

[5] Stahl *Thukydides*.

[6] Stahl's *Thukydides* denies that Thucydides' concerns are political and that he writes primarily for statesmen (cf. esp. 16–19, 29–30, 33–35). He fails to consider, however, that what a

Paradoxically, the deeds that Thucydides records are both unprecedented and paradigmatic, and are the latter because they are the former. Having achieved a grander scale than any previous (Greek) events, the Peloponnesian War displays with unprecedented clarity the limits of political life. Thucydides does not say that no larger war will ever succeed it. He does predict that whatever the magnitude of future events their structure or contours must resemble those of the sequence that he recounts. Whether such a claim is "naive" depends, as Thucydides is clearly aware, on the existence of a permanent human nature (3.82.2; cf. 1.22.4, 4.108.3) as well as on the plausibility of his claim to have comprehended it.[7]

Of course Hobbes is not the only modern reader to have noted Thucydides' intention of displaying permanent truths. To grant this intention, however, is not necessarily to welcome it. Of the most common reasons for slighting it, one has had to do with Thucydides in particular, while the other is much more general.

From F. W. Ulrich's *Beiträge zur Erklärung des Thukydides* (1845) through Romilly's *Thucydide et l'impérialisme athénien* (1947),[8] study of Thucydides was dominated by the so-called *Thukydidesfrage*. The "Thucydides question" was that of the stages of composition of his work. Here allegedly lay the key to explaining its difficulties: in a work composed over three decades which moreover remained unfinished, one could expect serious discrepancies. If Thucydides said one thing here and another there, that was because he wrote the first in (say) 427 B.C. and the second after the fall of Athens in 404.

The trouble with this approach was that its prophecy of rampant inconsistencies came in time to appear self-fulfilling. Interpretation—by which I mean the effort to display the coherence of the parts of a work and therefore its wholeness—fell from honor. As scholars busied themselves unearthing new evidence for this or that reduction of the work to fossil-bearing strata, its alleged inconsistencies multiplied. Thucydides practically ceased to exist, only Thucydideses remained, that of 431, that of 427, that of 411, et cetera.

---

statesman most requires is precisely knowledge of the "human" as such (1.22.4) or awareness of the limits of political action. In arguing, moreover, that Thucydides presents human beings as incapable of learning (147–48, 154), he overlooks the evidence that he himself cites that some are capable of learning—men like Thucydides and such of his characters as Demosthenes and Diodotus (154; cf. also Thucydides' praise of Themistocles [1.138]).

The question of the "utility" of Thucydides' work has aroused much debate. The obvious fact is that the work contains much of use to a statesman in analyzing the dilemmas that he confronts, both foreign and domestic. It is advisable to begin from obvious facts. For a recent review of the literature and some sensible conclusions, see Euben *Tragedy* 195–99; also good on this question is Farrar *Origins* 128–37, 187–91.

[7] Cf. 1.10 and Orwin *RevPol* 51 (1989) 348–51.

[8] Cited hereafter as *Imperialism* in the translation of P. Thody, 1963.

The author had been replaced by a series of his phases of development. Yet there was never a consensus as to which passages to assign to which epoch (or as to how much of each passage to assign to what epoch). A century of scholars' quarrels led only to further such quarrels.[9] Jacqueline de Romilly's landmark study established beyond reasonable doubt the essential unity of Thucydides' work and the distinctly secondary importance of such development as she still discerned in it.[10]

Recently W. R. Connor has gone further.[11] Meeting the separatists on their own ground, he has focused on the many perplexities in Thucydides' work: the shifts of perspective, the glaring omissions, the repetitions with a difference, the withholding or postponement of important facts, the fostering of expectations that are not met, the odd anecdotes and seeming digressions. According to Connor, these supposed blemishes are aspects of the work's perfection. Far from detracting from its unity, they evince the supreme artfulness of the means by which Thucydides achieves it. For upon scrutiny these "inconsistencies" further a consistent, if highly complex, intention. Previous "unitarian" readings have tended to be one-dimensional, precisely because they have not done justice to the features invoked by the "separatists." The unity that Connor defends in Thucydides is subtler and richer than that perceived by most critics. It defies reduction to nostrums. Connor's deservedly influential work has done much to restore Thucydides' reputation as a first-rate writer whose work is a masterpiece of world literature.

Even prior to Connor's work, Leo Strauss had stressed in *The city and man*, first published in 1964, the centrality for Thucydides of a number of crucial problems and antitheses, above all that stated in the title of Strauss's book. Strauss too had argued that the seeming contradictions in the text represented the articulation of different perspectives on these problems, which furthered the education of the reader. More than Connor, moreover, Strauss emphasized the importance of the issues of justice and piety in the work. It was he who first persuaded me that Thucydides spoke to my own deepest concerns. Strauss stands apart from the usual critical schools, and his work on Thucydides, while widely influential among political theorists, is little known among classicists. Those readers who do know Strauss's work will recognize the pervasiveness of my debt to it.

[9] Romilly *Imperialism* 3–10; so also von Fritz *GG* 1:565–75. For a recent restatement of the compositionalist view, see Dover *HCT* 5:384–444.

[10] J. H. Finley (*Three essays* 118–69) had argued powerfully in 1940 that the work was unified in the sense that the version we possess had been composed during a single epoch; Romilly's contribution was rather to demonstrate that even if this were not the case, the inconsistencies were minor in comparison with the book's overall consistency.

[11] Connor *Thucydides*. I discuss this remarkable book at greater length in *The American Scholar*, vol. 55 (winter 1985–86) 128–30.

Thanks, then, to the efforts of scholars like Romilly, Strauss, and Connor, it is once more respectable to concede the basic unity of Thucydides' work. Like every decisive scholarly action, however, this has provoked a heated reaction. Many now hold the unity of Thucydides' intention against him, as if nothing were so detrimental to his craft as a historian. He stands accused of having treated events as Procrustes did his guests, clipping or stretching them to make them fit his interpretive pattern, of having squeezed the particular dry without succeeding in presenting us with a fresh glass of the general.[12]

Other more sympathetic critics, such as Connor himself, who may call their Thucydides "postmodernist,"[13] agree with the detractors that histori-cal interpretation is inevitably a subjective matter. They manage, however, to praise Thucydides without crediting him with Truth with a capital T; as one of them has put it, "[Thucydides'] *History* of the Peloponnesian War is not the truth, it is Thucydides' truth."[14] Much of what they praise is his masterfulness as a writer (in particular the acumen with which he com-mands the responses of his readers), which, however, they cannot expound without conveying also his subtlety and depth as a thinker. The best of these critics, moreover, appear to take such pains with Thucydides largely because they find him so compelling. It seems that his Truth largely jibes with their own—with *the* truth in the self-deprecating light that their "postmoder-nism" leads them to view it.[15]

This book presents an unapologetic case for studying Thucydides. I do not blush to say that I have learned more from him about the issues here discussed than from any other writer. Typically my undergraduates marvel at how daring and "modern" he is. Such, however, is not my claim, as if "modern" (or for that matter "postmodern") implied all necessary approba-

---

[12] The patron saint of such critics is Collingwood; see his *Idea of history* 28–31. See more recently Wallace *Phoenix* 18 (1964) 251–61 and M. I. Finley in Finley *Aspects* 44–58 and *Use and abuse* 31–32.

[13] Connor *CJ* 72 (1977) 289–98.

[14] Rawlings *Structure* 272.

[15] For example, Connor (*Thucydides* 231–50), who both does and does not want to say that we can draw from Thucydides practical conclusions for our own day. In effect, the postmoder-nists claim that Thucydides' work has stood the test of time because it teaches that there can be no dogmatic teaching; Thucydides is the great enemy of systems. Cf. also Farrar's highly intelligent defense of Thucydides' claim to generality (*Origins* 128–37); although she surely asserts that we can draw conclusions from Thucydides for our own day, she appears to vacillate on the central question of the status of nature (cf. 135 and n.18 with her repeated cautions against interpreting him as the expounder of "static [human] nature"). These questions relate to that of the "utility" of the work; cf. Euben *Tragedy* 195–99 (especially good is 198–99). It is worth noting with Romilly (*La construction* 7) that Thucydides' selectivity and the artfulness of his arrangement of the facts do not preclude its objectivity. (Romilly explains what she means by objectivity at 52–54.)

tion. I found that undeniably modern though I was, I had much to learn from Thucydides and he little to learn from me.

Such respect as Thucydides enjoys among political scientists is due to his reputation as the father of political realism. This is one variety of his reputation for modernity: he is praised for having presented politics stripped almost naked. "Even in Thucydides," Stanley Hoffmann has noted, "when statesmen, in their speeches, argue about their respective positions and ambitions, they reason in moral terms of rights and wrongs."[16] "Even" salutes the prevailing view that Thucydides and his characters display as little genuine concern with justice as one can find anywhere. Among classicists and historians, too, Thucydides' prevailing reputation, at least until very recently, has been that of an exponent of "power politics" or of "Sophistic skepticism" or of "ethical positivism."[17]

In recent years other views have emerged to challenge this "realist" one. Critics now hold that Thucydides' "ethical" views are in fact conventional, much what we would expect from a wealthy Athenian gentleman. Whatever these views (for here there is disagreement), they are neither searching nor original. The morality of cities is one thing, that of citizens is another; he questions neither, nor does he draw conclusions from either for the other. Perhaps he is even pious, in a perfectly traditional Greek way. His virtues as a thinker lie elsewhere.[18]

Thucydides indeed evinces sympathy with ordinary decency and piety. It remains unconvincing, however, to portray him as merely conventional. Certain speeches in his work as well as leading aspects of the narrative point far beyond the opinions of the citizen or the gentleman. The perspective that finally emerges is neither democratic nor oligarchic/aristocratic, neither Athenian nor Spartan, neither sophistic nor tragic, neither Periclean and innovative nor pious and conservative—in short, it cannot be assigned to any conventional milieu.[19]

[16] Hoffmann *Justice beyond borders* 40.

[17] Cf. Shorey *TAPA* 24 (1893) 66–88; Nestle *NJbb* 17 (1914) 649–85; Gomperz *Greek thinkers* 1:502–19 and 2:25–26; Regenbogen *Kleine Schriften* 219–47; Kiechle *Gymnasium* 70:4 (1963) 289–312.

[18] Romilly *Imperialism* 98–100 and 210 n.4; McGregor *Phoenix* 10 (1956) 93–102 (Thucydides as a confirmed oligarch); Grant *Phoenix* 28 (1974) 92–94 (Thucydides as a conservative); Luschnat *RE* suppl. 12 (1971) 1251; Adcock *Thucydides* 50–57; Schneider *Information und Absicht* 122; Hornblower *Thucydides*; Ostwald *Ananke* 53–61, 66. On Thucydides as pious (wittingly or not), see Steup in Classen and Steup *Thukydides* 1:lx–lxiii; De Sanctis *RendLinc* ser. 6 vol. 7 (1930) 299–308; Lloyd-Jones *Justice of Zeus* 137–44; Marinatos *JHS* 101 (1981) 138–40 and *Thucydides and religion*. Edmunds (*HSCP* 79 [1975] 73–92) and Loraux (*QS* 23 [1986] 95–134) (Loraux with some qualifications) present Thucydides as an adherent of that "archaic pessimism" the classic of which is Hesiod. Cornford (*Thucydides mythistoricus*) claims that Thucydides is so completely under the spell of tragic poetry that his work is so to speak nothing but a document of Greek piety.

[19] Ostwald's highly useful monograph on ἀνάγκη in Thucydides (*Ananke*) provides a particularly sharp foil to the present work. When he turns to consider "ἀνάγκη (i.e., necessity

According to yet a third view, the "ethical" element is not absent from Thucydides, nor are his views conventional. Complex and elusive, they are most clearly manifest in his sympathy for the victims of power and chance. Thucydides combines an unflinching presentation of the harshness of political life with an element that transcends this presentation. We may describe this last as "humanity." To this combination the work owes its power—but the relationship of the elements remains obscure.[20]

I doubt that any reader of the present volume will accuse me of minimizing the harshness of Thucydides' teaching. At the same time I have sought to do justice to those elements in his work that have evoked the competing interpretations. Thucydides' "realism" is not quite the same as what goes by that name today.[21] And while he does not exaggerate the power of justice, neither does he come close to denying it. As his characters take justice more seriously than is usually recognized,[22] so does he. The case for justice gains a sympathetic hearing in his pages.

---

or compulsion) and morality," he argues (57) that "the fact that [compulsions] constrain agents to act in a way that they do not desire, foresee, or intend, should enable us to discover the considerations that [these compulsions] frustrate or override [and thereby to] get a glimpse of the moral values Thucydides' contemporaries regarded as desirable." These last prove to be the "moral values" that Ostwald ascribes to Thucydides himself.

Ostwald here makes two crucial assumptions. The first, that Thucydides' "moral values" do not differ from those of his contemporaries, poses obvious problems. We cannot infer Thucydides' views simply by canvassing those of his characters, for these disagree among themselves, as his contemporaries outside his pages may also be presumed to have done. As for his explicit judgments, these prove partial and ambiguous, and subject to interpretation within their particular contexts and that of the narrative as a whole.

Ostwald's second assumption is that "moral values" are wholly insulated from considerations of necessity, that while necessity may frustrate them it does not affect their substance. This implies of the crucial "moral" case (that of justice) that what may justly be demanded of human beings does not depend on what reason establishes as possible for them. The present work will contend the opposite.

[20] The classic articulations of this view are Reinhardt *Vermächtnis* 184–218 (esp. 207–17), Grene *Greek political theory*, and Stahl *Thukydides*, all works of great merit. One might include Connor in this company (cf. *Thucydides* 246–50) as well as the late Colin Macleod, all of whose articles on Thucydides repay close attention. (Macleod's friends have republished these in his *Collected essays*). Cf. also Paronzi *Aevum* 20 (1946) 231; Topitsch *WS* 61–62 (1943–47) 64–67; Barbu *Studii Clasice* 8 (1966) 35–44; Parry *YCS* 22 (1973) 49–50; and, much earlier, Girard *Essai*, for whom Thucydides is a moralist whose moralism is elusive. Lloyd-Jones (*Justice of Zeus* 137–44) asserts Thucydides' humanity and links it with his residual piety. Conflenti *Tucidide* goes so far as to insist on Thucydides' pacifism. I am indebted to Carnes Lord for long ago calling my attention to the works of Reinhardt and Grene.

[21] Noting Thucydides' kinship with contemporary "realism" while also seeking to distinguish him from it are Garst *ISQ* 33 (1989) 3–27; Donnelly *Thucydides*; Forde *JPol* 54 (1992) 372–93. Especially useful on this question is Johnson, *Thucydides, Hobbes, and the interpretation of realism.*

[22] Creed *CQ* NS 23 (1973) 213–31. Cf. Ferrara *Parola del Passato* 11 (1956) 341–43; Barbu *Studii Clasice* 8 (1966) 35–44; Farrar *Origins* 153–54; and Heath *Historia* 39 (1990) 389–91.

Taking justice seriously, however, implies attention to the problems it poses, the experience of which is inseparable from that of justice itself. The first of these problems is of course that of what justice requires. It is characteristic of political life that without being able to articulate a comprehensive understanding of justice each party to a dispute claims to grasp (and to honor) the demands of justice in the given case. Thucydides' treatment is true to this phenomenon, and I in turn have tried to remain true to both by leaving each facet of the question of justice to disclose itself concretely rather than abstractly. It is for this reason that I do not begin by offering any sort of working definition of justice.

A second crucial difficulty finds expression in the "realist" insight that justice however understood is much weaker in the world than we would wish. Again and again in political life we confront injustice (or what is angrily alleged to be such). Usually we note this prevalence of injustice and deplore it, without reflecting further on the matter; that justice is so weak does not move us to doubt whether injustice is so blameworthy. There is, however, a real problem here. If, when the shoe pinches, so few are persuaded by the case for justice, might that case be unpersuasive? If it is, can we blame those who remain unpersuaded? Thucydides explores the relation of the weakness of justice to the question of its goodness, and thereby also of its substance, for it is at least doubtful whether what is bad for us can justly be required of us.[23]

Nor does Thucydides merely raise these questions: he offers a compelling articulation of them. (This must be distinguished from "providing solutions" to them.) He does so, moreover, within the context of what was to become the great question for classical political philosophy, that of the regime. As the true antagonists of Herodotus' *Histories* are not individuals but what most today would call "cultures"—Greece and Persia, Egypt and Scythia—so those of Thucydides are the two preeminent regimes, Athens and Sparta, each a constellation of particular virtues and their obverse vices. To grasp that human nature expresses itself *politically* is to grasp that its manifestations are shaped above all by the regime.[24] At the same time,

---

[23] "Our ability to interpret . . . the history of political philosophy has been greatly impeded by the influence in our time of an unexamined . . . Kantian moralism that makes us insist, as previous ages had not, that the eudaemonistic or heteronomous consideration of 'sanctions' not be relevant to the issue of moral obligation. Thus, we no longer raise or understand the question of whether morality is supported by nature, or by the state, or by God. This explains the three most striking characteristics of contemporary moral philosophy as compared with the thought of the past: it is indifferent to the issue of morality's 'naturalness'. . . , it is extremely unpolitical, and it sees no philosophical need to raise the religious question." Melzer *Natural goodness* 131 n.25.

[24] Regenbogen *Kleine Schriften* 230–36; Chatelet *La naissance* 134–35; Strauss *City and man* 145–63, 209–26; Barel *La quête du sens* 221–23: "La nature humaine est ce qu'elle est, mais elle ne produit pas *partout* et *toujours* les *mêmes* effets. Ce qu'elle produit est fonction, entre

Thucydides seeks to articulate an understanding of human affairs that transcends that fostered by any regime. His study is thus comparable to that of Plato or Aristotle or any other of the greatest political thinkers. Agreeing with Reinhardt, Grene, and Stahl that Thucydides evinces a profound humanity, I argue that this humanity is a matter not just of temperament but of thought, of a consistent outlook that remains to be expounded. It follows from his understanding of "the human" (*to anthrōpinon*, 1.22.4), in particular from his articulation of the problem of justice and compulsion.

I will not encumber this introduction with a lengthy discussion of interpretive method. Suffice it to say that I have taken seriously Thucydides' claim to have written for the benefit of all future ages and have tried not to insult him by applying any less stringent standard. In a beautiful passage of Plato's *Republic* that expresses the spirit of classical thought as a whole, Socrates reveals that his "city in speech" is Greek only incidentally, that it equally beckons those who dwell in "some barbaric place beyond the reach of our vision."[25] In our present confusion, it is appropriate to receive such a claim to universality skeptically but not to reject it dogmatically: "Our awareness of human nature defies all historicism; our experience of history defies all anti-historicism."[26] Like Robert Alter's studies of the Bible, my reading "presupposes a deep continuity of human experience that makes the concerns of the ancient text directly accessible."[27]

---

autres choses, du contexte *politique* dans lequel se situe le jeu de la nature humaine. . . . Il n'y a pas la nature humaine, point final. Il y a la nature humaine dans son couplage avec un cadre politique. C'est ici que Thucydide retrouve, prolonge et précise une grande intuition d'Hérodote: le cadre politique est un élément important de l'explication, au moins aussi important que la nature humaine. Sur ce plan, Thucydide est un penseur original par rapport à la sophistique." ("Human nature is what it is, but it does not produce everywhere and always the same effects. What it produces is a function of, among other things, the political context within which the play of human nature takes place. . . . There is no human nature, plain and simple. There is human nature in its linkage with a political framework. It is here that Thucydides recovers, extends, and sharpens a major intuition of Herodotus: the political framework is an important element of explanation, at least as important as human nature. On this plane, Thucydides is an original thinker in relation to the Sophists.")

[25] Plato *Republic* 499c–d. Cf. Thucydides 1.1–6, 2.29.3 (the former barbarism of the present Greeks); 2.100.2 (the amazing progress of Macedonia on the road to Greekness), 8.46, 87, 109.1 (Tissaphernes as pupil and alumnus of Alcibiades and as worshiper of a Greek deity). Cf. Euben *Tragedy* 172 on the community with the reader at which Thucydides aims: "To this community of unlimited, anonymous, necessarily individual partners, located in an unnamable place, in some undefined future and uncertain . . . context, the historian offers himself as tutor and friend, providing an experience . . . that can be repeated . . . in any place and time."

[26] Manent *Débat* 72 (1992) 177–78. ("Nous avons une connaissance de la nature humaine invincible à tout historicisme; nous avons une expérience de l'histoire invincible à tout antihistoricisme.")

[27] Alter *Biblical literature* 205. For a parallel argument regarding Thucydides himself, see Aron *History and Theory* 1 (1960–61) 108–9: "L'homme d'aujourd'hui, qui reconstitue avec

I approached Thucydides with my own questions, without which it would not have made sense to approach him at all. At first these questions reflected my youthful experience of the sixties and behind that my unresolved preoccupation with the horrors of the decades preceding. In those days Thucydides attracted me partly because I mistook his reticence for gloom. I was fortunate enough finally to learn that the first answer to which a reader must remain alert is that he or she did not yet know to ask the right questions. Throughout I have preferred a plausible interpretation that made sense of Thucydides to an otherwise plausible one that did not. While there remains much that I do not understand, it seems safer to ascribe this to my shortcomings than to his. I should add that I have come to see much in Thucydides that I had not wished to find there.

Obviously I do not regard an attempt at a dialogue with a great mind of the past as hopeless. There are, of course, great obstacles to interpreting a thinker of Thucydides' stature, writing against a backdrop so different from our own, and in a language that we know only imperfectly. Yet even these are not the greatest barriers to understanding him. His is one of those books that disclose themselves only to a kind of reading contrary to every inclination fostered by the "information society"; he requires (to borrow a phrase from Nietzsche) readers like cows, readers who know how to ruminate. There is no way to appropriate Thucydides' thought except by thinking it, by reconsidering, with his guidance, the substantive political issues the articulation of which defines his project. In reading his work his contemporaries enjoyed advantages of many kinds. The greatest of these was not, to my mind, that they knew Greek better than we do or even that his particular world was their own while it is so remote from us, but that unlike us they lived and breathed politics while remaining innocent of "political science." So used are we to discussing political life in terms that are not its own that nothing is harder for us than to re-learn to think about it politically, that is, in terms arising directly from political experience.

The form of this book has posed difficulties. Several recent works have vindicated anew the value of presenting one's interpretation of Thucydides in the form of a commentary running from the beginning of the work to its

---

peine l'organisation des Grecs au combat, qui ne partage pas avec les personnages de Thucydide les évidences (intellectuelles et morales) qui constituent la structure de chaque existence, n'en est pas moins capable, pour l'essentiel, de comprendre directement, sans passer par des lois ou des propositions générales, les discours des ambassadeurs et les décisions des stratèges." ("The person of today, who has trouble reconstructing Greek combat formations, who does not share with Thucydides' characters those moral and intellectual givens that structure every human life, is despite this fully capable, in the essential respects, of understanding directly, without the assistance of laws or general propositions, the speeches of ambassadors and the decisions of generals.") Cf. ibid. 125–27.

end.[28] To do so is especially useful for charting the unfolding action of the whole as it is for encouraging attention to the context of each particular episode and its relation to adjacent episodes. Indeed no other approach can do justice to the narrative richness of the work. Unfortunately a sequential treatment proved inappropriate to my project. True, many of the problems that will concern us find their first articulation in Book One; I have therefore been able to devote a long first chapter to Book One—which, however, I have preceded with a prologue that treats a speech from Book Two. Ultimately the very fact that Thucydides binds himself to a strictly chronological presentation of the war according to the natural progression of summers and winters (2.1, 5.26.1) precludes my attempting to imitate him. The episode that best captures a particular aspect of our problem may occur anywhere in the work: a later one may be more conveniently treated before an earlier one, and some may best be adduced as a series despite occurring widely apart. Much of the matter most relevant to us is to be found in the speeches, each delivered on a particular occasion that happened when it happened. The wisest speakers are not necessarily those who spoke latest in the war. In Thucydides, as in all great works of art, each episode whether early or late must be reconsidered in light of the others. For the sake of achieving the most effective presentation of my argument, I have therefore chosen to treat the material in an order other than that of the work itself. Within the limits thus imposed, I have tried in interpreting each episode to pay due attention to its context insofar as this is relevant to my theme.[29]

The reader should be forewarned of what I have not done. I have not tried to criticize Thucydides from the standpoint of "what really happened," as allegedly disclosed by other literary and nonliterary sources; I have not attempted to pass on his accuracy as a historian in the usual sense. That I must leave to the experts, our contemporary historians of antiquity. Neither have I set about unearthing "influences" on Thucydides. Such efforts almost invariably founder on the fragmentary character of the remains of those pre-Socratic thinkers (the "sophists") on whom he is alleged to depend. They make of him, moreover, too literary and "academic" a figure, rather than one whose school was his experience of political life.[30] Without addressing the

---

[28] See for example Kagan's four volumes on the Peloponnesian War; Pouncey *Necessities*; Cogan *Human thing*; Connor *Thucydides*.

[29] Any writer on Thucydides must state a position on the role of the speeches in the work. Those of us whose arguments depend so heavily on our interpretations of these are under a special obligation to do so. Having expressed myself at length in an earlier article (Orwin *RevPol* 51 [1989] 345–64), I have done so more briefly in appendix 1.

[30] Hunter (*Hermes* 114 [1986] 428), for instance, contends that Thucydides owes to none other than Gorgias "a thoroughly recognizable Presocratic view of the world, . . . a basic tenet [of which] is that men's minds reflect the circumstances around them." More particularly,

question of influence, I have noted, usually in the footnotes, various parallels with other ancient writers, including some whom Thucydides may have read and some who certainly read him. These I include for such light as they may cast on the substantive issues.

Lastly, I have kept philological discussion to a minimum, not only because I am not a philologist by training, but so that this book will be accessible to others who are not. I have therefore left it at arguing for my interpretations of key passages and at noting places where my reading of the Greek text differs from that of some other commentators. Translations in the text and notes are mine unless otherwise noted.

As already indicated, I have learned from many and diverse scholars. The excellence of the critical literature on Thucydides is one of the satisfactions of studying him. Would that I had learned still more from this literature; my errors are my own.

"men's minds" tend to become confused in highly stressful situations. Did Thucydides, veteran of battles and popular assemblies, really need to learn this from Gorgias? In any case, as Romilly (*Imperialism* 303) notes after a survey of various hypotheses concerning the Melian dialogue, "it is . . . difficult to believe that the ideas [there expressed] were intended to refer to doctrines actually preached elsewhere . . . [rather] they are directly suggested by the political reality that Thucydides is here analysing." She goes on to "wonder whether it was not this very political reality which gave birth to these ideas, not only for Thucydides himself but also in a more general fashion." Hornblower, having announced (*Thucydides* viii) that the distinction of his book is "to put [Thucydides] in his fifth-century intellectual context as a whole," concludes after much consideration that Thucydides was a "lonely man" "who ultimately went his own way" (135).

Chapter 1

PROLOGUE: THE ATHENIAN EMPIRE AS FREELY
CHOSEN PROJECT: PERICLES' FUNERAL ORATION

THE FUNERAL oration spoken by Pericles at the end of the first year of the Peloponnesian War (2.35–46) is the best known passage in Thucydides. It is widely held to express the author's views as well as the speaker's; at the very least Thucydides is believed to have remained entirely sympathetic to the goals and program of Pericles.[1] A second reason for beginning with it is that it defines one pole of the interpretation of Athenian imperialism. This famous brief for the empire agrees in one thing with its angriest detractors: it presents the empire as unextenuated by necessity.

Pericles depicts imperial Athens as the noblest of human projects, freely undertaken by the citizens of Athens in full awareness of all that it entails. The crown of the Athenian community is the empire, in and through which alone Athens becomes fully choiceworthy. To appreciate the empire we must grasp the shining goal that elicits it.

[1] Regenbogen *Kleine Schriften* 219–47; J. H. Finley *Thucydides*; Romilly *Imperialism*; Grene *Greek political theory*; Kagan *Outbreak* and *Archidamian war*; Parry *YCS* 22 (1975) 51–60; Farrar *Origins*; Yunis *AJP* 112 (1991) 179–200; the list could be extended indefinitely. For dissenting views, see Strasburger *Hermes* 86 (1958) 17–40; Strauss *City and man*; Stahl *Thukydides*; Flashar *Epitaphios*; Lloyd-Jones *Justice of Zeus* 138–44; Bruell *St. John's Review* 32, 1 (1981) 24–29; Palmer *APSR* 76 (1982) 825–36 and *Love of glory*; Connor *Thucydides* 50–51, 62–63. Cf. also Reinhardt *Vermächtnis* 202. Edmunds *Chance and intelligence* is remarkable for the care of its articulation of the Periclean position as well as the balance of its overall treatment of the issue stated in its title. A sophisticated pro-Periclean reading of Thucydides is Euben *Tragedy* 160–201 (esp. 191–99), which follows Edmunds in arguing that ultimately Periclean principles find their proper home not in the political realm (where they are problematic) but in the thought and practice of Thucydides.

For a useful comparison of Pericles' speech with other extant funeral orations (all of which from the classical period are Athenian), see Ziolkowski *Tradition*, which argues persuasively that the similarities between the speech that Thucydides ascribes to Pericles and those actually delivered by others suggests that it is at least grounded in a speech actually delivered by him. This noted, it must be said that Ziolkowski rather minimizes the significance of the differences that he himself unearths between this speech and the others, and so underestimates its boldness. This boldness appears especially in light of the fact that the other extant speeches are all *later* than this one (and some may copy it in some respects) and yet are more traditionalist than it. Edmunds *Chance and intelligence* 7–88 (on this speech, 44–70) rightly emphasizes the newness of Pericles' presentation of human life and of the centrality to it of citizenship in a city now conceived as primary, over and against both the family and piety. For an ambitious treatment emphasizing the role of the genre of the funeral oration in forming Athenian civic consciousness, see Loraux *Invention*.

If we compare this speech of Pericles with other extant Athenian funeral speeches, most striking is the deprecation of the ancestors. The oration, like the ceremony that precedes it, is traditional; the ceremony, at least, enshrines practices of some antiquity (2.34).[2] The empire, on the other hand, is recent; of an ancestral ritual Pericles makes an occasion of celebrating the virtue of the past two generations and the present one most of all. Although he declares the appropriateness of beginning (as was traditional) with the ancestors, the first place proves not to be the place of honor. The generations proceed in ascending order; the greatest progress is the most recent (36.1–3). The speech succeeds, at no great remove, Thucydides' account of how Pericles uprooted the last vestiges of the pre-urban, pre-imperial way of life of the ancestors (2.13–17). The supreme nobility that Pericles praises in this speech is frankly novel.[3]

The nobility of the Athenians is inseparable from their regime and way of life (*epitēdeuseōs . . . politeias kai tropōn*, 2.36.4). Pericles sketches a society in which the fullest development of the citizen is compatible with the greatest devotion to the city. To elucidate the whole of this claim would be to recount the entire speech. While Sparta obtains civic virtue only through painful discipline, Athens sacrifices neither citizen to city nor vice versa. She fosters, in freedom rather than through compulsion, an extraordinary blossoming of both public and private life (37–41). Public life predominates, however (38, 40.1–2). When Pericles praises the Athenians (40.1) for their love of beauty or nobility (*philokaloumen*) and their love of wisdom

---

[2] There is in fact some question as to how old the ceremony was. Cf. Ziolkowski *Tradition* 13–21, Loraux *Invention* 28–30. Saxonhouse *Polity* 10 (1978) 467 suggests that Thucydides might have exaggerated the antiquity of the ceremony in order to underscore the contrasting boldness of Pericles' oration.

[3] There is irony in Pericles' statement that it is appropriate to begin with the ancestors, for this statement occurs only in the third paragraph of the speech. Returning to the actual beginning, however, we note that Pericles had indeed started with the ancestors: to blame that one of them who had instituted the practice of this speech! Pericles thus presents himself as wiser than this ancestor and the law that perpetuates the latter's error; so in the third paragraph (while mentioning the ancestors first) he presents the current generation of Athenians as superior to all preceding ones.

One may contrast the lofty praise of the ancestors and the presentation of them as the still-unsurpassed standard of virtue for the present generation in the funeral speeches of Lysias (3–19 [on the remote ancestors], 20–66 [on the more recent ones], 69); Demosthenes (3–11, 27, 28, 30, 31); and Plato *Menexenus* 237b3–c5, 239a. An exception is Hypereides, who praises Leosthenes, the commander of those fallen in the Lamian War (322 B.C.), as superior in virtue even to the illustrious men of old (35–38). On the other hand, even Hypereides praises the virtue of the ancestors (6–7) more highly than does Pericles. There is reason to believe that Gorgias, the earliest of the speakers whose efforts are extant (although only a fragment remains) also included a section praising the ancestors (Ziolkowski *Traditions* 94 n.18).

Loraux (*Invention* 121–22) acknowledges this "eclipse of the ancestors by the descendants" but fails to note that it undercuts her assertion (145) that this funeral oration, like others, "assimilates the city to an unchanging temporality."

(*philosophoumen*—the only occurrence of this term in Thucydides), the context is public: by "philosophizing without softness" he means combining public deliberation with daring (40.3). It is as a citizen that the Athenian comes into his own, displaying his unequaled sufficiency as an "individual" (*autarkes sōma*, 41.1). For confirmation of these virtues we need only look to the greatness of the empire (41.2–4).

Pericles' emphasis on the spontaneity of the empire appears from his account of its origins. These lie in the Athenians' unique liberality.

> In virtue too we are contrary to most. For not by receiving benefits, but by conferring them do we acquire our friends. Now the one who has acted is the firmer [friend] of the two, so that through goodwill to him to whom he has done the favor he may perpetuate the indebtedness. The one thus indebted is less keen, seeing that such virtuous action as he may offer in return will not oblige the other but merely clear his own indebtedness. We alone confer benefits fearlessly, not from calculations of advantage, but with confident liberality. (2.40.4–5)[4]

Athens was not compelled to undertake the empire, nor has she done so with an eye to gain. For all Pericles' praise of Athenian rationality, he suggests that calculation would have been out of place here, for the province of nice reckoning is advantage, not that liberality (*eleutheria*) appropriate to free men (*eleutheroi*). What chafes the allies of Athens, then, is the burden of their gratitude: being indebted to Athens, they cannot benefit her as freely

---

[4] Most critics agree that this is a reference to the empire. Rusten (*Thucydides Book two* 156) demurs; Connor (*Thucydides* 69 n.45) finds it equivocal. Rusten suggests that Pericles here describes the private relations of the Athenians among themselves. He argues that chapter 40 as a whole treats the virtue of the Athenians as individuals, and he notes that Pericles, ever the political realist, elsewhere (2.63.2) calls the empire a tyranny, and so would not paint it here in terms too rosy to be plausible. Since it is crucial to my interpretation, I will consider Rusten's objection at length.

I cannot agree that chapter 40 describes the private lives of the Athenians. That Pericles has done in 2.37. I interpret all claims in chapter 40 (including φιλοκαλοῦμεν and φιλοσοφοῦμεν) as concerning the activities of the Athenians collectively; cf. Gundert *Die Antike* 16 (1940) 106–7. The immediately preceding passage explicitly concerns the Athenians' unique capacity for public deliberation. Lastly, Romilly *Imperialism* 136 and Diller *Gymnasium* 69 (1962) 201 cite the close parallels with Euripides *Heracleidae* 198, 245, 305–6, and 329–32, where the subject is clearly the foreign policy of Athens.

Nor is it hard to grasp why in a holiday atmosphere Pericles the eulogist of the nobility of Athens should put a better face on the empire than he did later in a very different rhetorical situation. Furthermore, his psychology here is sound, as is his claim that Athens conferred a great favor on her allies by liberating them from the Persians. Far less plausible would be the claim that only (μόνοι, 2.40.5) the Athenians as individuals make friends through liberality: surely some do so in every city. And would Pericles mar a magnificent encomium by the gratuitous assertion that in every friendship *within* Athens one of the friends is an ingrate? The restiveness of the subjects, by contrast, would be on the mind of everybody, and his elegant dismissal of it would doubtless evoke murmurs of approval. Cf. also Loraux *Invention* 79–83.

as she has benefited them. Pericles thus acknowledges the discontent of the allies gracefully and without rancor, while rebuffing any suggestion of Athenian impropriety.[5]

Not that Pericles presents the empire as the vehicle of some transcendent cause (e.g., Panhellenism).[6] Its ends are noble, but they are those of the Athenians, no one else's. The empire is a crucial extension of the city. It affords the citizens the vastest of stages on which to display their virtue and thereby to perpetuate a resplendent memory of themselves. Pericles' presentation of the world is in the highest degree "agonistic."[7] It is competition among cities which forges community among citizens, at least at Athens: a community of equal and exalted glory earned at the expense of other societies. (Whatever his account of the origins, Pericles does not pretend that other cities have reaped only benefits from the empire [2.39, 41.4].)

The power of the Athenians attests above all to their virtue; on this Pericles insists again and again.[8] They not only rule but, unlike most rulers, are worthy to do so (2.41.3). This virtue culminates in dedication to the city and to its power (cf. 1.70, 7.28), as manifest above all in wartime. In war Athenians, like other soldiers, must decide between hanging back and surging forward, between husbanding a fortunate life in a city whose citizens have so much to live for and resolving to risk that life for that city. It is the latter choice on which Pericles congratulates the fallen Athenians (2.42.4, 43), to which he exhorts their survivors, and to justify which is apparently his overarching goal. Pericles may have succeeded in harmonizing (at least in speech) the happiness of the individual with the good of the society, by showing how the citizen comes fully into his own only in this most demanding and fulfilling of cities. To celebrate life in Athens, however, will not by itself suffice to justify dying for her. Tradition had exhorted men to risk their lives for parents, wives, children, and ancestral gods.[9] The city stood vindicated in effect as the protector of these. Pericles' praise of it is much grander. Rather than merely promising glory to those who lose what is most their own (their lives) in defense of their own, Pericles presents glory itself as that

---

[5] Romilly *Imperialism* 138–39 praises Pericles' candor in lauding the empire for its liberality rather than its justice. But liberality is incompatible with injustice (see Aristotle *Nicomachean ethics* 1119b–1122a; cf. Machiavelli *Prince* ch. 16, and Orwin *APSR* 72.4 [1978] 20–30). And in the empire as Pericles here presents it there is no blemish of injustice: it arose from Athens' helping other cities, not harming them.

[6] Romilly *Imperialism* 100–101.

[7] Cf. Nietzsche *Thus spoke Zarathustra* 1.15 ("Of the thousand goals and one"): "'You shall always be the first and excel all others: your jealous soul shall love no one, unless it be the 'friend'—that made the soul of the Greek quiver: thus he walked the path of his greatness." (tr. Walter Kaufmann) On the agonistic character of Pericles' speech see also Loraux *Invention* 95–97, 202–20, 241–43.

[8] Cf. Flashar *Epitaphios* 454–57 and throughout; Loraux *Invention* 85–86.

[9] Cf. 7.69.2; Aeschylus *Persians* 402–5; Plato *Laws* 699cd.

which is most one's own—and the imperial city as the primary human community, because it provides the means of achieving apotheosis through glory.

Pericles' vision thus implies a drastic derogation of the private (the body, family, and property) in favor of a new vision of the public as that realm in which each, rising above the private, achieves that which is most his own, an undying glorious reputation (2.43.2). This explains the abstraction from the body and the pangs of death which pervades the speech, as well as the harshness of his remarks on property and family. The word death occurs but once and is qualified as "unfelt" (43.6). Wealth figures as the rival of glory and the public sphere (42.4, 44.4); Pericles wishes to treat the family as a subunit of the city, a means to its ends. Parents and wives, no less than citizens in their prime, must live for glory. The parents of the fallen are to console themselves in their reflected glory, and, where still possible, to raise up new citizens to replace them—sons whom Pericles does not fail to remind them they must risk losing in turn (44.1–3). As for the youths, they must be consoled not for the loss of fathers and brothers but for the difficulty of outstripping these in fame now that they enjoy the exaggerated reputation conceded to the dead (45.1).

Pericles' address to the widows (2.45.2) conveys the intransigence of his understanding of the city. They too are to live as will gain them renown— which strangely proves to mean as will least attract notice of any sort. This curt injunction jars with the very ceremony preceding the speech (34), which features the public wailing of widows. Each has sought to exhibit her implacable grief for the loss of her husband and thereby her feminine virtue, a virtue the public display of which thus calls attention to its stubbornly private character. Does this explain Pericles' appeal to the women (of whom he speaks at all only under duress: *ei de me dei* . . .) to become invisible within the city? Does he see them as too steeped in the primacy of the private ever to play a helpful public role within his community of civic glory?[10]

Striking also is Pericles' lone reference to the place of the divine in Athenian life. Burial was a rite of the utmost solemnity among the Greeks, as the ceremony of which the speech is a part confirms. At the same time, however, piety itself forbade mention of the Olympian gods on the occasion of a burial: the gods of burial were the chthonic or underworldly gods, who were not gods of the city.[11] It is not surprising, then, that the gods play only a small role in the speech. All the same, this role is typically Periclean not just

[10] Cf. the discussion in Rusten *Thucydides Book Two* 175–76. Lacey (*PCPS* 10 [1964] 47–49) plausibly suggests that a Greek widow was most likely to be conspicuous for her lamentation; otherwise, however, his interpretation of Pericles' injunction as limited to wailing is both too restrictive and too benign.

[11] Loraux *Invention* 277; she cites the funeral oration of Demosthenes (30–31) and Plato *Menexenus* 238b.

in its smallness. At 2.38.1 he mentions the sacred sacrificial rites (*thysiai*) among other instances of recreation (literally, of relaxation from *gnōmē*, i.e., from public deliberation). He thus considers these sacrifices frankly from the standpoint of human utility and pronounces them secondary, just as, in the only explicit reference to a deity to occur in his speeches, he considers the cult image of Athena Parthenos as a resource of gold for expenditures of war (2.13.5).[12] Indeed derogation of gods is implicit in Pericles' derogation of Homer (41.4).[13] In his final speech, confronted by the plague, which the mass of Athenians interprets as heaven-sent to chastise them for the war that Pericles has encouraged them to undertake (2.53–54), he describes it as divine or "daemonic" (*daimonion*, 64.3) but insists that they abide it as a necessity (*anankaiōs*), that is, that they reject the divine admonition it allegedly conveys. Lastly and most conspicuously, given the standard *topoi* of the Attic funeral oration, he fails to ascribe *hybris* to the enemies of Athens and to present her triumphs over them in this light.[14]

This rationalistic approach to the gods is too consistent to be inadvertent. We sometimes hear that Pericles expounded the first "secular" vision of society.[15] To leave it at that, however, is both to understate the case and to overstate it. Pericles presents Athens as the first "atheistic" society and hardly less resplendent than that which Marx envisaged for the end of history. Perfectly self-sufficient at the highest level of human happiness, Athens can dispense with the gods because there is no longer any role for them to play. The empire renders them superfluous, by satisfying, without reference to the divine, the deepest human longings of the citizens. Stretching as far as the mind can see, the empire confers ageless life on each whose radiant virtue shines through it (2.41.4, [42.4?],[16] 43.1–3).

Such also is the final and highest note of Pericles' final speech (2.60–64), in which he defends his war policy amidst the hardships of plague and siege. While the first year of war has brought inconvenience and exasperation, there have been no significant losses, so the funeral speech need not come to grips with these; in this respect the final speech, addressed to an audience sunk in its private miseries, comprises Pericles' true funeral oration. It begins far more soberly, with an argument the inverse of that of the funeral oration: the citizens must stand by the city as the only guarantor of their private

---

[12] Cf. Reinhardt *Vermächtnis* 197–98; Edmunds *Chance and intelligence* 37–39 (which notes that in fact the Athenians never acted on this advice, not even in their most desperate moments).

[13] Compare the emphasis in the other extant funeral speeches on events of the distant past known only from the poets: Lysias 4–16; Plato *Menexenus* 239a–c; Demosthenes 8; Hypereides 35. Cf. Aristotle *Rhetoric* 1396a.

[14] Cf. Lysias 9 and 14; Demosthenes 8 and 28; Hypereides 20–36; Isocrates *Panathenaicus* 80.

[15] Most recently from Kagan *Pericles* 10, 22–23, 169–71. Cf. Flashar *Epitaphios* 459–61.

[16] On this possible interpretation of 2.42.4, see below, note 28.

welfare. The safety and property of each depend upon the survival of the community and so upon success in the present war. What justifies the war is its necessity, and only that. The empire similarly cannot be relinquished without jeopardy to both public and private interests. The Periclean policy and its hardships are to be borne from necessity. This view, so somber and commonsensical, seems far removed from a call to supreme glory. As the speech proceeds, however, Pericles, while continuing to maintain the war's necessity, progressively expands and elevates that notion, until he has once again raised his listeners to view the empire *sub specie aeternitatis*.

At 2.61, then, Pericles stresses the necessity of the war not only to preserve the freedom of Athens, but to avoid the infamy of her failing to live up to her reputation. He thus reintroduces the theme of renown—but renown for doing what safety requires, undeterred by temporary reverses. He makes no suggestion that the Athenians should prefer glory to safety: instead he insists that in their present plight both concerns dictate that they stand fast. At 62, having restored their confidence in his strategy by extolling their dominion over the sea, he reminds them not only that their losses have been small relative to their imperial resources, but that persistence is the way to recover these losses. Again, the honorable course is the safe and advantageous one. At 63 he invokes their pride in the empire in order to shame them into accepting its burdens. Again he insists that the requirements of glory are the same as those of freedom and safety.

> It is no longer possible to step down [from the empire], if anyone, frightened by the present situation, wants to play the virtuous man in idleness; you hold it, so to speak, like a tyranny, which it may have been unjust (*adikon*) to acquire, but which it is dangerous to let go. (2.63.2)

Pericles blunts the force of this statement with the qualifying "so to speak" (*hōs*) and "may have been" (*dokei einai*); still, "the high moral tone of the Funeral Oration has not prepared us for a tentative admission that the empire may be founded on injustice."[17] If the empire is indeed a quasi-tyranny (an argument meant to underline the danger of letting it go), what glory could attach to it? Pericles addresses this problem as follows:

> Reflect, too, that if your city has the greatest name in all the world, it is because she has not bowed to misfortune, and has expended the most lives and toil in war, and has acquired the greatest power yet known. Even if in our own time we should come to grief (for all things that come into being decay), still the memory of it will remain for ever-lasting posterity: how we ruled over more Greeks than any other Greeks, and sustained the greatest wars against them united or separately, and dwelled in the greatest and best provided of cities. The unambitious may blame such things, but the man of action will emulate them.

---

[17] Pouncey *Necessities* 100.

He who fails to acquire them will envy them. To be hated and resented in their own time has befallen all who have resolved to rule others, but he is well advised who incurs spite for the sake of the greatest things. For hatred does not abide for long, but the splendor of the present and the glory of the future remain for everlasting memory. (2.64.3–5)[18]

The resentment that Athens inevitably incurs is due to the envy of those whom she has bested; in time this resentment will pass away and the glory of the city will shine forth undimmed by human pettiness. The sacrifices of the war will secure Athens' immortal renown. Yet if envy is to pass away, so, obviously, must the empire itself. Like all things that come into being, the empire will pass out of it; its glory (defying nature?) will endure forever. The burdens of the Athenians are the transient price of an immortal glory. More, it is precisely the greatest expenditure of both life and treasure on which the greatest glory devolves. The virtue to which the Athenian power attests is above all this acquiescence in private sacrifice for the sake of eternal renown.

Neither here nor in the funeral speech, however, does the power of Athens attest to her justice; that would be too much to ask of any power. As if to balance his concession that the empire might not be just, Pericles now implies that the resentment it evokes is hypocritical: not righteous indignation but envy inspires it. If every people (or every worthy people) aspires to acquire the greatest power, Athens appears not tyrannical or unjust but the glorious victor in a fair competition. There is thus a connection between the Periclean outlook and that of those Athenian apologists whose claims shock ordinary decency (cf. 1.73–78, 4.98, 5.85–113, 6.82–87).[19]

The universal Athenian city/empire thus solves at the highest level the problem of "the individual and society" by reconciling the most exacting demands of the city and the fullest good of the citizen: the "supreme sacrifice" is but the threshold of a most resplendent common good. To return to the funeral oration, for a contribution (*eranos*) of their bodies "in common," (*koinōi*) the fallen will receive "privately" or as "individuals" (*idiōi*) a meed of glory that will never grow old (2.43.2).[20] Among the contributions denoted by *eranos* is an investment in any joint enterprise to which one contributes along with others in the hopes of profiting oneself. That overtone is present here.[21] What the fallen lose, their bodies or their lives, is less (and less their own) than what they gain. They live on in memory; Pericles

---

[18] Crawley translation, revised.

[19] Cf. Strasburger *Hermes* 86 (1958) 29 n.5; Stahl *Thukydides* 50–52; Flashar *Epitaphios*; Pouncey *Necessities* 36–38, 100–101.

[20] Strauss *City and man* 195 n.1; Flashar *Epitaphios* 458.

[21] Rusten *Book Two* 169.

reinterprets the memory of each as his true life: by losing himself in and for Athens, each finds himself, resplendent in the ageless beauty of his fame.

The speech culminates in the astonishing injunction that the Athenians become lovers (*erastai*) of their city. While it is one thing to speak of affection (*philia*) for one's city, it is another to speak of erotic longing for it.[22] Pericles, who denigrates the private bonds springing from *erōs* in its usual sense, would transpose to the public sphere that which is most intensely private. He presents the city as satisfying the deepest yearnings of the citizen. Most striking is that it is not the beauty but the power (*dynamis*) of the city which is supposed to arouse such passion. Presumably Pericles has in mind that only through the empire does the city achieve such a peak of splendor that the citizens yearn from the heart of their being for apotheosis in and through it. It is to the supreme power of the city that they owe the deathless fame that it confers.

Pericles' very deprecation of the gods thus supports Strauss's verdict that "there is something reminding of religion in Athenian imperialism."[23] Regenbogen suggests that Thucydides himself, so skeptical toward the gods of Olympus, has not overcome his religiosity but has invested it in Pericles and Athens.[24] Yet to follow him and others in interpreting the work as the tragedy of Periclean sublimity may be to oversimplify it; we surely must avoid too simple a reading of the funeral oration.

For one thing, we must consider the possible irony of the speech. Pericles begins by stressing, predictably, the difficulty of finding words adequate to the deeds of the fallen. His elucidation of that difficulty, however, is so candid as to cast doubt on the candor of his subsequent praise of these deeds.

> It is hard to speak appropriately on a subject in which even your credibility is established only with difficulty. On the one hand, the hearer who is familiar with and partial toward [the fallen] may think that some point has been developed less fully than he wishes and knows it to deserve; on the other, he who is without experience [of the fallen] may even be led by envy to suspect exaggeration if he hears anything above his own nature. For praise spoken of others is endurable only for so long as each listener can suppose that he too is capable of the deeds of which he is hearing, but because men are jealous of surpassing praise, as a result they actually become incredulous. (2.35.2)

[22] See Lycurgus *Against Leocrates* 100 (ca. 322 B.C.) for a later example of this usage presumably inspired by this passage of Thucydides. J. H. Finley *Three essays* 21 cites two Euripidean parallels of uncertain date, *Phoenissae* 359 and *Erechtheus* fragment 360.54. See also Hornblower *Commentary* 311.

[23] Strauss *City and man* 229; cf. also the beautiful observations of Grene on 2.64 (*Greek political theory* 90).

[24] Regenbogen *Kleine Schriften* 243–47; cf. Grene *Greek political theory* 83–92.

Pericles obligingly sketches *the* problem facing him on this occasion, the solving of which must be his primary rhetorical concern. The difficulty of praising adequately the deeds of the fallen proves to be that of satisfying the expectations of two kinds of listeners, those who crave flattery of the fallen and those who bristle at it (as unflattering to themselves).[25] But how to satisfy two constituencies so much at odds with each other?

On this occasion the second of Pericles' problems overshadows the first, for so few Athenians have died in this first year of war that almost all in the audience are candidates for incredulity and envy.[26] It is these then whom Pericles must please if he is to achieve a popular success. He claims only that listeners bristle at hearing *others* praised beyond their own deserts; does he imply that they are amenable to being overpraised themselves? He surely devotes most of his speech to extolling the city as a whole, thus "praising Athens to Athenians" or the Athenians to themselves.[27] His eulogy of the dead largely proceeds by means of an encomium of the living (2.42.1–2). He not only avoids but openly deplores so praising the dead as to denigrate (and thus spark envy in) the living (45.1). Only of the deceased does he suggest that some of their lives may have fallen short of the Athenian standard (42.2–3); this far does he go to mollify those listeners who care less that he praise the fallen highly than that he not praise them more highly than themselves. Exalted and exalting, the speech is also an elegant piece of flattery. It quenches two opposing thirsts for praise by lavishing glory enough for all.

There is a striking parallel between Pericles' response to this difficulty and his approach to that deeper one that looms over every funeral oration. Death in battle presents the limit case of the problem of "the individual and society," of the tension between the private and the public good. The greatest praise is due those who have made the "supreme sacrifice." But how to reconcile the survivors to that sacrifice and to the necessity of their risking it in turn? Pericles' speech is an attempt at this, perhaps the most ambitious ever undertaken (all the more so in invoking no divine assurances). Here too he offers glory enough for all. Remembrance as an individual (*idiōi*, 43.2–3) for all time and in all places: such is the promised prize for those who die for Athens. Where fame is boundless, it is equal, and Pericles offers the loyal citizens of democratic Athens equality on precisely that extraordinary height and level.

[25] Cf. Pindar *First Pythian* 81–85; Sallust *Conspiracy of Catiline* 3. Pindar does not anticipate, however, Pericles' manner of resolving this difficulty, nor does Sallust the imitator of Thucydides adopt it (which would betray his duty as a historian, ibid.). The other extant funeral orators stress the difficulty of praising the dead adequately but do not ascribe it to envy. Cf. Lysias 1 and 54; Plato *Menexenus* 246b; Demosthenes 1 and 6; Hypereides 4 and 23.

[26] See 2.22 for the only mention of casualties to this point (a few men lost in a cavalry skirmish). Cf. Dionysius of Halicarnassus *On Thucydides* 18 with Hobbes *EW* 9:xxviii.

[27] Cf. Plato *Menexenus* 238c.

It is questionable whether such glory as Pericles offers all Athenians is attainable by anyone. It can hardly be attainable for every last citizen of even so remarkable a city as Athens. We call Athens in her heyday "Periclean," and Thucydides' praise of Pericles is even at the expense of Athens (2.65). Pericles himself elsewhere reminds the Athenians that he knows better than they and that their success depends completely on his policies (1.140; 2.60). Here, however, after Pericles' initial sally at the expense of the ancestors (which, however, manages also to be self-deprecating), his superiority recedes from view. Is his rhetoric also designed to avert envy *from himself*, by eschewing all self-praise in favor of extolling his audience?

For all that is admirable in Pericles' speech, we must not ignore its difficulties. He himself concedes that there is something not quite satisfying in the exchange of earthly happiness for perpetual remembrance; while the citizen is to trust the issue to his virtue and to chance, he may pray for a happy outcome (i.e., a safe one) (2.43.1; cf. 42.4). Indeed it was not only the sacrifice of their bodies that the fallen had shared in common, but the common hope of avoiding it (*koinēs elpidos*, 43.6). If further consolation is wanted, and further reason to share the resolve of those fallen, we must recall the instability of human happiness: the hopes of the fallen, extinguished by death, may yet have been rebuffed by life (43.4–5). Pericles presents the glory gained by the fallen as an eternal life freed from the vicissitudes of life, at the same time sublime and secure. In particular he argues that those whose lives have been fortunate so far (and who thus must anticipate reverses) lose least in death. Still, he thus admits that death involves loss, and for some, at least (those whose fortune might otherwise have continued good or improved), a very great loss indeed.[28]

---

[28] I differ from Edmunds (*Chance and intelligence*) not in denying his claim that Pericles presents a world in which intelligence, manifesting itself as active citizenship, overcomes chance, but rather in my interpretation of the means of this overcoming. For Edmunds (82–88) it is in the perpetuation of the city and its "civic values" that the citizen finds security against the vicissitudes of fortune, regardless of his personal fate. Yet in fact Pericles concedes in his final speech that the city will not last forever; only its glorious memory will (2.64). And Edmunds underestimates, in my view, the significance of 2.43.2, where Pericles specifically states that the compensation that the soldier receives for the contribution (or investment) of his body is undying fame as an individual. The "primacy" of the city of which Edmunds speaks must thus be qualified to this extent: ultimately the city is not the end for the citizen but a means to the perpetuation of his boundless and endless fame. It is with an eye to this exigency that one sees (a point on which Edmunds is silent) that the city must be imperial. Hence its power becomes the focus of the citizens' eros. I may add that if we were to read 2.42.4 as Edmunds suggests—as yet another promise of renown (*doxa*) to the citizen in exchange for his life—that would only strengthen the interpretation offered here.

This response to Edmunds also applies *mutatis mutandis* to Loraux, who, underestimating the rationalism of the speech, presents it (as allegedly demanded by the genre) as a glorification of the *polis* as abstract and transcendent (rather than, as I would maintain, a means to the self-fulfillment of the citizen). Loraux *Invention* 328–30 and throughout.

Similarly, Pericles stresses the deliberateness with which the citizens collectively confront great dangers (2.40.2–3) and presents each of the fallen as having similarly chosen, if not his fate, then at least to risk it. His approving reference, however, to their determination to wreak vengeance (*timōria*) on their city's enemies as primary for them (*tōn enantiōn timōrian potheinoteran autōn labontes . . . ; . . . tous men timōreisthai*, reiterated for emphasis, 42.4) cuts against conceiving of this fatal choice as well calculated. Spirited men (cf. *phronēma echonti*, 43.6) minded on vengeance seem not so much to confront the risk of death as to ignore it; their death takes them very much by surprise. If these fallen have truly met an unfelt death (*anaisthētos thanatos*, 43.6), is it not because hope and anger had joined to anesthetize them to it?[29]

Still, Pericles does present the choice to risk one's life for the city as rational. Those who survive live to risk another day, while continuing to enjoy the fruits of life in the greatest of societies; those who die gain a reward more than proportionate to the loss. In a final disarming stroke of candor, Pericles notes in the very last words of his speech (in commending a policy of public subsidies to the orphans of the fallen) that "where the rewards for virtue are greatest, there one will find the best citizens." Civic virtue flourishes where its blandishments are most alluring. Candor requires us to consider whether Pericles, whose understanding of the world seems so clear-eyed and sober, has conceived his hyperbolic presentation of the immortality conferred by the empire as the grandest reward for civic virtue ever proffered by anyone.

Like any great tour de force, the speech may be taxed with a certain levity. Courting anachronism for the sake of making a broad point, we may compare it with the Gettysburg Address. Lincoln for his part does not minimize the sacrifice of those who have died that popular government might survive. That they "have given the last full measure of their devotion" means precisely that they have relinquished all that was good for themselves for the sake of the Union and of all the peoples of the earth. The immortality they have gained thereby is not offered as compensation either to them or to the bereaved, for to suggest that compensation was possible would detract from the sacrifice and the loss. Instead Lincoln asserts only that the cause is worthy of the sacrifice. Because speech can do justice to neither, he limits himself to saying as much as necessary and as little as possible.[30] His famous

---

[29] Cf. 2.8.1; Plato *Republic* 375a–b, 439e–440d; Tolstoy *War and peace* bk. 10 ch. 30.

[30] See his letter to Edward Everett of November 20, 1863 (*Speeches and writings, 1859–1865* 537). Cf. his letter of November 21, 1864 to Mrs. Lydia Bixby, who had lost five sons on the battlefield: "I feel how weak and fruitless must be any words of mine which should attempt to beguile you from the grief of a loss so overwhelming. . . . I pray that our Heavenly Father may assuage the anguish of your bereavement, and leave you only the cherished memory of the loved and lost, and the solemn pride that must be yours to have laid so costly a sacrifice upon the altar of Freedom." (Ibid. 644)

deprecation of the adequacy of speech to deed thus rings truer than that of the expansively eloquent Pericles.

In presenting the empire as a project freely chosen by the Athenians for the sake of endless glory, Pericles raises many questions. So conceived, the empire owes nothing whether to necessity or to advantage (2.40.4); nothing has compelled the Athenians to wield the empire, and the reasons for their choice are only the loftiest. But is so great a superiority to necessity and advantage possible for any polity? Must not the Athenian empire, like others known to us, owe at least something to these factors? Elsewhere Pericles himself not only concedes but stresses this debt, especially (as we have seen) in his final speech: safety joins nobility in demanding that Athens make the greatest sacrifices in order to maintain the empire. The greater riskiness (and perhaps the greater justice) of letting the empire go, however, does not sort very well with the superior nobility of clinging to it. Firmness in such circumstances may be prudent, but can it aspire to the cachet of immortality?[31]

We must pursue, moreover, the question of the origins of the empire. When Pericles in the Funeral Oration traces the empire to benefits spontaneously conferred, he must mean Athens' liberation of her future subjects from the Persian yoke. In his final speech he is silent as to the empire's origins, except for his remark that these were perhaps unjust. The implication is that while Athens is unfree to abdicate her burden, she might once have been free to decline it. If, however, necessity weighs so heavily on her in her present situation, is it plausible that it played no role in the earlier one? This question bears on that of the justice of the empire. If Pericles in presenting the empire as spontaneous must also present it as just (2.40), it does not follow that its justice depends on its spontaneity: what is done under duress is just, in the sense that we cannot be blamed for it. Had Athens expanded only under compulsion, that might vindicate the empire more convincingly if not more loftily than Pericles' vision of it as freely undertaken.

There are still more reasons for entertaining a more prosaic interpretation of the empire. In the funeral oration Pericles insists that the imperial project is not only noble but reasonable, that is, good. Admittedly, it does not serve advantage in its usual guise of safety or profit; these figure only in the final speech. Rather the Athenians pursue through the empire that greatest of goods available to only the noblest men, those willing to part with every lesser good including life itself. In claiming, however, that civic virtue is worth choosing for its consequences, does Pericles not detract somewhat from the nobility of that virtue? Once we recast it as a shrewd bargain (43.2) virtue loses its noble luster—even if the promised reward is, as here, a

---

[31] Cf. Romilly *AnSoc* 4 (1973) 55 n.47: at 2.63.1 Pericles urges the Athenians to choose the path of fortitude, while at 2.63.2 he insists that they have no choice but to follow it.

crescendo of noble luster. If the benefits of noble sacrifice outweigh the
costs, if we may speak of "the [fallen] soldiers' ultimate success (since their
loss has been richly compensated by glory),"[32] where is the sacrifice, and
where the nobility?

If, however, we conclude from the funeral speech that in order to be
defensible the empire must prove not only noble but reasonable, the question arises whether the noble is, as Pericles implies, truly best for us. The
speech combines the rationalism characteristic of him with a fervent praise
of glory as the ultimate object of human striving. Even eros figures in
Pericles' speech as something freely (i.e., rationally) bestowed on the
city/empire as the only fully worthy object available to it. This union of
glory and rationality seems uneasy. If it were possible for a city to slip the
yoke of necessity, would it then be well advised to pursue empire? Are great
risks worth running for the sake of the glory to be gained or only where to
shirk them would be to incur greater risks still? The dependence of the
ubiquitous renown of the citizens on the ubiquitous power of the empire
points in the direction of a policy of constant expansion: is such a policy
compatible either with interest or justice? In principle or in speech, the
empire is universal (2.41.4, 43.1–3); in practice Pericles promotes a strategy of temporary restraint (1.144.1; 2.65.6–7). Yet in urging the Athenians
to stick by this strategy, he does not refrain from reminding them that their
dominion is potentially as boundless as the sea (2.62). His poetic vision is at
some odds with his prosaic policy.

It is usual to understand Thucydides' account of Athens as one of tragic
descent from a Periclean peak. There is obviously something to this: Athens
lost the war, and Thucydides speaks explicitly of her decline in certain
crucial respects (2.65). In contemplating this decline, however, we must
make all necessary distinctions. According to Thucydides' explicit judgment, what declined was the quality of the city's leadership. He praises
Pericles above all for the skill with which he managed the people (65.8–9).
What happened after Pericles' death was predictable of any "great and imperial city" (65.11) that lacked extraordinary leadership. Rather than focus on
the alleged "decline of Athens," it is probably more sensible to emphasize
the exceptionality of Pericles.

While Athens indeed declines, in the precise sense already indicated, and
while her fate is in some sense tragic, neither "the decline of Athens" nor her
"tragedy" adequately captures Thucydides' concerns or accurately describes
a highly complex and ambivalent process. Decline may foster self-awareness
or the appreciation of certain truths.[33] The funeral oration articulates, with

---

[32] Rusten *Thucydides Book Two* 162. Cf. Connor *Thucydides* 69 and Kagan *Pericles* 136–50.

[33] Romilly *AnSoc* 4 (1973) 58 speaks of the war as fostering "la mort de ce qu'on pourrait
appeller la τιμή naïve." ("The death of what we may call naive τιμή [concern with honor or
reputation].") A decline in naïveté comprises a progress in understanding.

the highest artfulness, a portrait of the Athenian empire in its Sunday best. Far from offering an unproblematic view of the empire, to be subscribed to by Thucydides himself and all readers of sense, it raises questions worthy of the efforts of a Thucydides to resolve. In the pages that follow we will explore these efforts. Having begun by removing the speech from its broad context, we will seek to restore it to that context. Above all we will consider the question to which the funeral oration offers one answer—and an extreme one—at odds even with Pericles' other speeches. To what extent is the empire to be understood as a project freely undertaken and sustained, and to what extent as a burden that Athens has had no choice but to shoulder and to continue to bear? And what are the implications of the answer to this question for our understanding of two crucial aspects of the human situation, the perpetual tension between the demands of justice and those of necessity, and the possibility of a noble politics?

Chapter 2

THE OUTBREAK OF THE WAR AND THE
PROBLEM OF BLAME

THE STATE OF THE PROBLEM

In Thucydides' so-called "Archaeology," his account of times prior to his own (1.1–23.4), he is silent as to the rights and wrongs of the wars ascribed to those times. In expounding these wars he confines himself to conclusions supported by the extant evidence (*tekmērion*, 1.1.2; cf. 20.1, 21.1); these conclusions apparently do not extend to justice or injustice. Justice comes to light only in the claims and counterclaims of the combatants: we cannot sift or even ascertain such claims amidst the sparse detritus of the past.[1] As for the poets and local tradition which have preserved the memory of these events, they are neither impartial nor accurate; old wars likely owe their reputed justice to poetic or popular "beautification" (1.21.1, 22.4; cf. 2.29.3, 3.104).[2]

The Archaeology, however, not only omits to comment on the rights and wrongs of specific past wars (including the Trojan and Persian wars), but depicts the remote past as innocent of considerations of right.[3] The progress Thucydides depicts in the Archaeology is progress in, among other things, justice—within cities if not clearly among them.

In the beginning, humanity was wholly subject to its necessities. All lived from hand to mouth and hardly saw beyond the needs of each day (1.2.1–2). The ascendancy of the stronger was openly the rule of life. Piracy was an honorable profession (1.5). Only a certain rough magnanimity mitigated the hardships of the weak: pirates supported not only themselves but the needy.

Eventually cities began to appear: necessity and interest laid their foundations (1.8.3–4). Stronger individuals and factions coerced or cajoled the cooperation of weaker ones much as stronger states have subsequently

---

[1] Cf. Ostwald on the absence of judgments of ἀνάγκη (necessity or compulsion) from the Archaeology (*Ananke* 34, 65).

[2] Cf. Cicero *De finibus* 5.19. On the Archaeology, see Romilly *Histoire et raison* 240–98; Parry *YCS* 22 (1975) 51–59; M. I. Finley *Use and abuse* 17–33; Détienne *L'Invention* 105–12; Erbse *RhM* 113 (1970) 52–53; Pouncey *Necessities* 45–53; Connor *Thucydides* 21–32; Funke *QS* 23 (1986) 78–84; Orwin *RevPol* 51 (1989) 345–64.

[3] Cf. Pouncey *Necessities* 48–52.

done. The first powerful kings were successful pirates; "law and order" was initially only the consolidation of conquest (1.4, 7–8). The first cities, then—such as ancient Athens—represented progress in wealth and security: people no longer lived on the edge (1.6.1–2). This was a condition of all further progress. The ways of the earliest cities, however, were not political ways (1.6.3). In Athens as elsewhere, the rich flaunted their wealth and indolence and apparently gave no thought to the common.

At this point enter Sparta, to which Thucydides accords the extraordinary credit of having discovered the common. There the rich ceased to display their wealth and to lord it over the other townsfolk: they ordained a new civic garb common to rich and poor alike (1.6.4). One was a Spartan first, rich or poor only secondarily. The Spartans went further still; Thucydides continues to represent their progress in sartorial terms. Having discarded their lavish robes for sober ones, they proceeded to disrobe entirely on specified public occasions (1.6.5). Thucydides notes that this practice of competing in the nude distinguishes Greeks from barbarians (and thus reminds us that the Greeks too were once barbarians). The Greeks alone display themselves not just as Greeks but as men, as they have proceeded from the hands of nature. Each discloses fully his nature the better to compete to establish his natural superiority; they have overcome their shame at nakedness in the service of their love of victory.

"Greekness" is from the beginning a distinctive blend of community and competitiveness, concealment and disclosure. It combines the assumption of a conventional common identity with the practice of revealing one's nature without false shame. Each represents a triumph of moderation and reason. The link between justice and the discovery of the common is clear; is there one between justice and disclosure? The justice of Athens at least will feature a noble candor and a corresponding hatred of sham.

The Archaeology exhibits an apparent tension between its belittling of the old in favor of the new and its resounding praise of Sparta, long the most conservative of Greek cities (1.18.1). It offers no corresponding praise of Athens, lately the boldest and most vital of them. The praise of Sparta, however, is not at odds with that of progress. The latest innovations need not be the greatest; the greatest has been Greekness itself.[4] The Spartans, moreover, have been not only the most successful practitioners of Greekness—for "though after the settlement of the current Dorian inhabitants they suffered from *stasis* for the longest time of any city known to us, yet even so from the earliest times enjoyed good laws and were free of tyrants throughout" (1.18.1)[5]—but the greatest contributors to its consolidation.

---

[4] Cf. Levi *Parola del Passato* 7 (1952) 99–104.
[5] Cf. Aristotle *Politics* 2.8.1.

Taking it upon themselves to depose tyrannies wherever they have found them, they have thus removed the final barriers to a dynamic and political way of life (1.17–18).

As for the nemesis of Sparta—progressive, maritime, democratic Athens —she has succeeded an older, pious, landlubberly one. This older Athens was governed quietly by tyrants (2.14–16, 6.54–59), whose expulsion was the precondition of her subsequent dynamism and power. For this act the Athenians claim the credit—but in fact they owe it to Sparta (cf. 1.18.1 with 1.20.2).

Some degree of justice within the city, then—a political regime founded on a common civic identity, good laws, and freedom from tyrants—emerges from the Archaeology as crucial to the ascent from barbarism to Greekness. Progress in war has also depended decisively on this progress in regimes— Sparta's power is due to her regime, as more recently is that of democratic Athens and, to a lesser extent, of all cities that have achieved the transition from tyranny to a stable democracy or oligarchy.[6] Thucydides is silent as to whether justice among cities has kept pace with the progress of justice within them and with the consequent growth of their power.

Still, we have no sooner left the Archaeology than Thucydides presents at length the claims and counterclaims of the two sides as to where justice lies between them, that is, as to who bears the blame for the war (1.23.5–146).

> All [of these evils] befell them with the war, which the Athenians and Peloponnesians began when they broke the thirty years' truce made after the conquest of Euboea. As to why they broke the treaty, I have first recorded the *grievances* (*aitiai*) and points at issue, so that no one ever need seek whence so great a war arose among the Greeks. For *the truest allegation, although least conspicuous in speech* (*tēn alēthestatēn prophasin, aphanestatēn de logōi*), I hold to be that the Athenians by becoming great and provoking fear in the Lacedaemonians *compelled them to resort to war* (*anankasai es to polemein*).[7] As for *the grievances openly spoken* (*hai . . . es to phaneron legomenai aitiai*) on either side, from which resulted the breaking of the treaty and the outbreak of the war, they were as follows. (1.23.3–6)

The principal issue that this passage has been taken to present is whether Thucydides' treatment of his topic is "scientific." The "grievances and points at issue" among the parties include of course charges of injustice and, since the wrongs alleged are urged as *casus belli*, accusations of blame for the war. (The word *aitia*, which I have translated as "grievance," means in the first

---

[6] Cf. Herodotus 1.65–66, 5.78, 7.101–4; Farrar *Origins* 139–40, 145, 180–81.

[7] I cannot on balance accept the reading of the clause offered by Ostwald *Ananke* 1–5 and captured by Crawley's rendering ("that the growth of the power of Athens, and the alarm which this inspired in Lacedaemon, made war inevitable"). Such a reading, however, would only strengthen the case for the interpretation of the passage that I will propose.

instance an imputation of blame, then by extension the blame thus imputed.)[8] Thucydides clearly assumes that his reader will take such questions
seriously; that he explores them so fully suggests that he takes them seriously himself. Still, his intention is hotly disputed. Does he seek to convey
to posterity an account of the *blame* for the war? Or does he leave such
concerns behind and set out rather to expound its *causes*?

The question is whether Thucydides shares the concerns of his characters
(and of political actors generally)—at most taking issue with one side (or
both) over how to apportion the war guilt—or whether he is up to something new and academically respectable. Political actors quarrel about
blame; historians (if they are scientific) search for causes. To those scholars
to whom Thucydides is the father of scientific history, his great achievement
in treating the origins of the war is precisely to have abandoned the question
of blame for that of cause. Many of them praise him for applying to the
study of politics the spirit, method, and terms of Hippocratic medicine, the
most advanced natural science of his day.[9]

An opposing view insists that the notion of Thucydides as a scientific
historian rests on a misinterpretation of the terms of his discussion. He is
not concerned with "causes" at all; for him, as earlier for Herodotus, to
explain the origins of a war is merely to relate the grievances alleged by the
participants. He has looked no further into the "causes" of the war; his
understanding is on a par with that of his characters—and not what we
would expect of a scientific historian. To demand more of him, however,
would be anachronistic.[10]

One school holds, then, that right and wrong are of concern to
Thucydides only as the appearance he must penetrate in order to reach the
reality; the other that this question occupies him in just the same way as it
does his characters. The one contends that Thucydides rejects the question
of blame for the war as superficial; the other, that he treats it superficially.
There are intermediate positions (including my own), but for the sake of
clarity it is useful to begin by stating the extremes.

Most of the dispute about this passage turns on the meaning of *tēn
alēthestatēn prophasin*, translated above as "the truest allegation." The partisans of the scientific Thucydides take this phrase to mean "real cause." The
point of the passage, they think, is the opposition between the "real cause"

[8] Pearson *TAPA* 83 (1952) 205–6, 221–22; Kirkwood *AJP* 73 (1952) 55–61; Lynn S.
Wilson *Aitia and prophasis* 48–53.

[9] Cochrane *Thucydides* 17; Schwartz *Thukydides* 250 (*Ursache* vs. *Rechtsgrunde* [αἰτία]);
J. H. Finley *Thucydides* 68; Jaeger *Paideia* 1:389–94; Grene *Greek political theory* 56–61;
Rawlings *Prophasis*, which argues that Thucydides uses two distinct senses of πρόφασις based
on two different Greek roots, but that the usage at 1.23 is the "medical" one.

[10] Cornford *Thucydides mythistoricus* 52–76; Sealey *CQ* NS 7 (1957) 10–12 (which holds,
however, that this is but one of two contradictory strands in Thucydides' use of the term).

of the war and the grounds (of justice and injustice) actually alleged by the belligerents. Their opponents insist, however, that *prophasis* means, in Thucydides as before him, merely an ascription of subjective grievance or pretext, with no connotation of a deeper or truer stratum of explanation. We cannot therefore understand *prophasis* as opposed to the *aitiai* as the true cause to the alleged ones; *prophasis* itself never means more than an alleged cause.

Those critics who contest the interpretation of *prophasis* as "scientific" or "objective" rely on the everyday usage of the term. A prophasis was in the first instance an account offered for an action, one's own or another's. Such is the basis for asserting that in using it Thucydides means to convey no more than a subjective motive or even merely a party's claim as to its subjective motive. This position, however, is too narrow. While centered on "reason given," the term *prophasis* embraced a range of meaning, from a reason given that was untrue (so frequently "pretext") to the true reason, even if not given. (This whole range is present in Thucydides.) Sometimes "motive" will render *prophasis* in English; sometimes even "occasion," insofar as the occasion figures as an explanation of the action. The reasons that one gives for one's own actions are commonly justificatory; "justification" is therefore often a good translation for *prophasis*.[11]

Prophasis was, moreover, a frequent term in the forensic oratory of Thucydides' day. There it commonly denoted an allegation in the service of fixing aitia or blame, whether that allegation tended to inculpate your opponent or to refute his inculpation of you. Very often, of course, an orator would accomplish the latter by means of the former: he would invoke his adversary's misdeeds to vindicate his conduct toward him. For this reason *prophasis* often meant grounds of indictment or accusation.[12] What the successful orator required was an *epieikēs prophasis* (3.9.2; cf. 3.40.6), a "sufficient justification" of his course of action or of his rejection of that of his opponent; otherwise put, he required adequate *aitiai kai prophaseis* (the plurals) (3.13.1). The recurrence of the two terms in tandem in this later

[11] Pearson *TAPA* 83 (1952) 205–23 and 103 (1972) 381–94; Kirkwood *AJP* 73 (1952) 37–61; Schuller *RBPhil* 34 (1956) 976–84; Sealey *CQ* NS 7 (1957) 1–8; Andrewes *CQ* NS 9 (1959) 224–25; Schäublin *MH* 28 (1971) 133–44; Lynn S. Wilson *Aitia and prophasis*; Heubeck *Glotta* 58 (1980) 222–36; Richardson in *Owls* 155–61. For a brief elaboration of the case against the "scientific" interpretation of πρόφασις in this passage, see appendix 2.

[12] On πρόφασις as the ground of indictment or justification for a charge laid, see Theognis 364; Antiphon 5.59, 60; Lysias 6.19; 9.7 (τῆς αἰτίας τὴν πρόφασιν "the ground of the accusation"); 12.28; 14.1; Lycurgus *Against Leocrates* 6; Plato *Menexenus* 240a. As the ground of justification or exoneration of oneself, see Ps.-Xenophon *Constitution of Athens* 2.17; Aristophanes *Wasps* 339, 468; Euripides *Hecuba* 340, *Iphigenia at Aulis* 1434; Antiphon 5.21, 22, 26, 65; 6.14, 26; Lysias 6.19; 8.3, 14; 9.7, 13, 15; 12.6, 28; 16.12. Cf. Schuller *RBPhil* 34 (1956) 976–84; Lynn S. Wilson *Aitia and prophasis* 48–53.

passage recalls their juxtaposition in 1.23.6 and suggests the proper interpretation of it.[13]

Given the context of recrimination and the prominence of *aitia* at 1.23.6,
Thucydides' contemporaries might well have read *alēthestatē prophasis* in this
"forensic" sense.[14] They would have taken it to mean the "truest reason
given," in the sense of the "truest allegation made" or "truest justification"
offered by any of the parties in their attempts to fix or avert aitia or blame.[15]
This interpretation would help explain why Thucydides, far from slighting
the "grievances and grounds of dispute" of the belligerents, proceeds to
develop them in detail.

Such a reading of *prophasis* at 1.23.6 finds confirmation in Thucydides'
uses of the term later in Book One, once in tandem with *aitia*.

> Not many years later [sc. than the last of the events recounted in the "Fifty
> Years"] there occurred the matters already recounted, the affairs of Corcyra and
> Poteidaea and other such *prophasis* of war (*tou polemou*). (118.1)

> Such were the grievances (*aitiai*) and points of issue on both sides, arising
> immediately from the events at Epidamnus and Corcyra. Nonetheless there was
> communication between them and they still frequented one another without
> heralds, although not without suspicion. For the events underway were a dis-
> turbance of the treaty, and *prophasis* of war (*tou polemein*). (146) (final words of
> Book One)

In these passages the term is usually rendered "occasion" of war; Kirkwood has suggested "motive for war."[16] Yet a more plausible rendition is
casus belli, that is, that issue or issues alleged as sufficient justification for
resorting to war. For such is the clear meaning of *prophasis tou polemou* in its
only other occurrence in Book One and in the work as a whole.

> In the meantime [the Spartans] kept sending embassies to expostulate with
> the Athenians, so as to have the greatest possible grounds for war (*hoti megistē
> prophasis . . . tou polemou*) should [the Athenians] not comply. (1.126.1)

The Spartans wanted the greatest possible justification of their decision to
go to war; that is, the greatest possible grounds for accusing Athens. Sim-

[13] Cf. a similar juxtaposition in Ps.-Xenophon *Constitution of Athens* 2.17.

[14] Pearson *TAPA* 83 (1952) 219–23; Andrewes *CQ* NS 9 (1959) 226; De Ste-Croix
Origins 54–58. Heubeck *Glotta* 58 (1980) 232–35 and Richardson in *Owls* 157–61, although
not stressing the forensic aspect of the word, note that the phrase "truest πρόφασις" suggests a
choice among the competing προφάσεις actually advanced by the antagonists.

[15] So, too, at 6.6.1 the same phrase refers ambiguously to the truest motive of the Athenians
in invading Sicily (in contrast to the pretexts they stated) and the truest allegation of their
enemies in imputing to them the blame for the invasion (in dismissal of these same pretexts): cf.
6.33.2 and 76–80.

[16] Kirkwood *AJP* 73 (1952) 54–55.

ilarly at 1.118.1 the *aitiai* comprise the *prophasis tou polemou* in the sense that all the grievances taken together, each exacerbating and exacerbated by the others, afforded the combatants their *casus belli*. So too at 146 the "events underway" that comprised a "disturbance of the treaty" may be taken as synonymous with the *aitiai*.

If Thucydides thus uses *prophasis* much as any political speaker of his day would use it, we would expect his "truest prophasis" to enable us to fix aitia or blame for the war. In fact he is silent on this point so crucial to his characters. Explicitly his "truest allegation" clarifies why both parties broke the treaty (1.23.3–4) rather than which did so first; he leaves it to us to decide its implications for aitia.

Lionel Pearson has proposed one answer to this question.[17] A prophasis being an allegation offered in the course of either fixing aitia on another or averting it from oneself, the "truest allegation" looks to be an instance of the latter kind. It could serve a Spartan effort to avert blame from Sparta, on the grounds that she acted as she did only under Athenian duress. It would thus imply an admission that Sparta was, legally speaking, the culprit, the aggressor in the war. True, the Spartans never actually offer this argument; nor do they admit to having been the first to break the treaty. The "truest prophasis" states, however, the excuse that *they would have offered* had they admitted their guilt for the war. It is in this sense that it is "the truest allegation, but the least manifest in speech." Thucydides' use of *prophasis* implies that he views Sparta, not Athens, as bearing aitia for the war.

All of this rests, however, on the presumption that if Sparta has initiated the hostilities, she thereby bears aitia for the war. In fact the Spartans claim to resort to force only because Athens has already broken the treaty and has thereby incurred aitia for the war. In truth it is most unclear who first broke the treaty. After the Theban attempt on Plataea all saw that it had been broken (2.7.1), but since this action followed years of charges and counter-charges, this first clear violation was not the clearly first violation (1.35, 40, 52.3, 53, 55.2, 66, 67, 87, 118.1, 146). The attempt on Plataea, moreover, occurs before the first Spartan invasion of Attica but after the Spartan declaration of war. Neither was this declaration, however, the clearly first violation of the treaty, being neither clearly first (for many alleged infractions had preceded it) nor clearly a violation: treaties must be broken in deed, not in word. By the time Sparta invaded, however, the treaty was a dead letter, the Theban action having intervened. In context, then, while we must interpret 1.23.4–6 as raising the question of *aitia*, it does not suffice to resolve it.

The Pearson school holds, moreover, both that Thucydides here uses

---

[17] Pearson *TAPA* 83 (1952) 219–23. This answer is accepted also by the other authorities listed in note 10 above.

prophasis in its forensic sense, and that we must imagine this "truest allegation" in the mouths of the Spartans. As we have seen, however, and as Pearson concedes, the allegation that Sparta broke the treaty under duress neither fixes aitia on Athens nor clears Sparta of it—it neither alleges that Athens first broke the treaty nor denies that Sparta did. In Pearson's language, it presumes that Sparta was "technically" the aggressor. Yet what may seem a technicality to modern scholars is anything but that to Sparta. For her the question of infraction is decisive for that of aitia, of guilt before gods and mortals. No wonder all of her actual arguments aim to impute the infraction(s) elsewhere: these, and not the "truest *prophasis*," comprise Sparta's prophaseis in the forensic sense.

It follows that if the allegation that Sparta was the first to break the treaty (albeit out of her fear of Athens) is a prophasis in the forensic sense, it is a prophasis against Sparta. And it is in fact so offered by the only speakers in Thucydides who raise it. These are the Corcyreans, in responding to the objection that the alliance they seek with Athens against Corinth would be dangerous to Athens because likely to provoke a wider war. "And if there be any among you [Athenians] who think that the [wider] war is avoidable, know that Sparta is already conspiring against you out of fear (*phoboi*) of your growing power, and that war is as good as upon you" (1.33.3).[18]

We may now grasp why Thucydides does not commit himself on the question of aitia. The question of who bears blame is inseparable from that of what constitutes it and therefore from that of what extenuates it. According to the Corcyreans, evidently, either fear is not (or is not always) strictly compulsory or compulsion does not extenuate blame (at least not sufficiently to cancel it); the Spartans will be no less responsible for the war for having undertaken it from fear. In this view the Spartans concur. They do not assert in Book One that their fear excuses their violation of the treaty; rather they obstinately deny having violated it. And as we learn much later (7.18.2–3; cf. 4.20.3), they come to attribute their lack of success in the war to the fact that they bear aitia for it; that is, that they were the first to break the treaty, no matter what their grounds for so doing.

The modern reader may well respond that the "truest allegation" renders the question of aitia moot. For if that term imputes legal or moral responsibility, does not the "truest allegation" distance us from it? Does it not adduce dynamics of power, rather than legality, as primary in the world?[19]

Such a reaction is not modern only; it expresses an "Athenian" perspective on these issues. It figures in Thucydides as one side—but only one—of a complicated story. By introducing the issue of compulsion in the context

---

[18] Cf. Hornblower *Commentary* 64, 78.
[19] See Fliess *Traditio* 16 (1960) 9–13 and *Bipolarity*.

of that of blame or of right, he confirms that the issues are related. He does not mean to discourage us from sorting them out.

"It Is Right . . ." "It Is Necessary . . ."

The first of the "grievances openly avowed" arose from the imbroglio between Athens and Corinth over the latter's attempts to chastise Corcyra (1.24–55).[20] This episode contains the first speeches in the work (31–43), the importance of which to us emerges from their very first words. The Corcyreans begin "[it is] right [or just])" (*dikaion*, 32.1), the Corinthians, "[it is] necessary" (*anankaion*, 37.1). "These two opening words indicate the point of view from which Thucydides looks at the Peloponnesian war."[21] Yet it is not immediately clear how the speeches advance the theme of this contrast. It does not seem either that the Corcyreans take their stand on the priority of right or the Corinthians on that of necessity. Rather each city insists on the justice both of its cause against the other and of the course that it enjoins upon Athens. Nor does either concede any tension between right and necessity: each insists that both concerns unite in support of its argument. Perhaps the utility of the speeches consists in just this, that while they join in denying such a tension they also join in disclosing it.[22]

The Corcyreans, whose keynote is justice, certainly profess to take it seriously. It is just, they begin, that petitioners such as they, who can invoke neither past services nor a current alliance, should prove that aid to them would be advantageous to the party petitioned. It is just, in other words, that those who cannot invoke justice be required to invoke expediency. This implies that justice is decisive: only those unable to invoke it must satisfy other criteria. Such is the respectable view: the expedient is attractive, but the just is obligatory, and expediency affords no excuse for injustice. The Corcyreans continue to respect this view in explaining why it is a fine stroke

---

[20] For a provocative treatment of this episode, see John Wilson *Athens and Corcyra* 25–34, 119–25.

[21] Strauss *City and man* 174. Cf. Huart *Réseaux* 18 (1972) 17.

[22] Cohen *QUCC* 45 (1984) 37–39 argues that the Corcyreans appeal to interest and the Corinthians to justice (although he notes that the former present justice as in the interest of Athens). Stahl *Thukydides* 38–39 and Cogan *Human thing* 8–20 contend that the question of justice is irrelevant to the debate; Heath *Historia* 39 (1990) 389–90 stresses that both parties invoke it. Crane *CA* 11 (1992) 1–27 rightly emphasizes the "traditionalism" of both presentations in stressing elements of an archaic prestige. White *Words* 60–70, besides offering a perceptive analysis of the speeches, suggests (plausibly enough) that Thucydides here offers some ordinary Greek discourse about justice and interest as a foil to the bold approach of the Athenians at Sparta (1.72–78). White's ascription to Thucydides of a primary concern with the role of specific terms of discourse in constituting a "culture of argument—of which it is Thucydides' object to tell the history" (67)—has persuaded a number of critics, including Euben (*Tragedy*). One must beware, however, of a post-Heideggerian Thucydides—at least to the extent of doubting that Thucydides himself was post-Heideggerian. Cf. chapter 8, note 9.

of luck that they have appeared on the doorstep of Athens. They insist that in aiding them Athens will be helping those sinned against, not sinning (1.33.1).[23] They expound the justice of Corcyra's quarrel with Corinth (34), and the injustice of an Athenian policy that favored Corinth (35.3–4). Nor in receiving Corcyra into her alliance will Athens violate the thirty years' treaty (35.1–2). Whatever the advantages of acquiring Corcyra and her large navy (36), the envoys emphatically deny that Athens need sacrifice justice to these.

While the keynote of the Corinthian speech is necessity, the first necessity that the speakers proclaim is that of defending their reputation for justice against the imputations of Corcyra. This they do at length (1.37–40.1). To listen to them, there has never been a city so unjust as Corcyra or one so blameless as Corinth. Nor can Athens receive Corcyra without infringing the treaty (40.2–3). While Corcyra, moreover, is legally speaking nothing to Athens, Corinth is in a sense an ally (as Athens' partner in the treaty), so justice bids Athens rest neutral or even assist Corinth (40.4). The speakers insist not only on the rights of Corinth (*dikaiōmata*, 41.1) but on her claims on Athenian gratitude (41.1–3). They advise Athens that even or precisely with an eye to advantage one should place justice first: "he who offends least for the most part succeeds best" (42.2). Abstention from injustice against one's equals confers a power more solid than any fleet (42.4). The two embassies seem to agree, if on nothing else, that there is no substitute for justice. Is this how to take the opposition dikaion/anankaion—as implying that justice is the thing most necessary?

Not necessarily. The opening statements of both embassies refer to their respective situations as speakers. Justice requires that the Corcyreans invoke advantage (and ultimately necessity); necessity demands that the Corinthians treat of justice. Both beginnings allude to the *rhetorical* necessity that every speaker in such a situation invoke justice. While both embassies respect this necessity, their arguments on the relationship of justice and necessity in the wider world are finally ambiguous.

The Corcyreans, as we have seen, begin by implying the decisiveness of justice. They go on, however, to preach that of necessity (1.32.5); does necessity excuse deviations from justice? And while they continue to invoke justice throughout their speech, there are hints that it is only bunting on the masts of their powerful fleet. While denying that Athens must choose between justice (the treaty) and alliance with them, they enjoin any Athenians who persist in seeing such a conflict to opt nonetheless for alliance. "And should any . . . think our proposal useful, but fear lest persuaded by it you will break the treaty, consider that whatever your fears your strength will strike fear into your adversaries, while whatever confidence you may feel

---

[23] Literally, "those who are victims of injustice and not those who are harming others."

from having rejected us, you will be weak and less fearsome to a strong enemy" (36.1). Justice is no tower of strength: the imminence of war (33.3–4, 36.1) both compels and excuses whatever is necessary for war. The Corcyreans cannot even help suggesting that the policy most advantageous to Athens is the least just available to her: allying herself with Corcyra in the hope that Corcyra and Corinth will wear each other out, thereby clearing the seas for Athens (35.5). So, too, in assuring Athens of Corcyra's fidelity as an ally, the speakers adduce not the justice of which they have boasted but the necessity of that fidelity given that Corcyra is too weak to face Corinth alone (ibid.). It is not surprising that in their peroration, in which they claim to sum up their argument "in general and in particular," the Corcyreans do not invoke justice but only the balance of power (36.3).

What of the Corinthians, who are even more insistent than their foes both that justice is with them and that it defines the best policy for Athens? In fact this last argument is subtly qualified. Only "for the most part" (*malista*) is one who transgresses the least the most successful; this itself suggests that statesmanship requires knowledge of the crooked path and when to take it. (The Corinthians' own experience confirms this, even as they themselves present it, for who could have been more just than they claim to have been in their dealings with Corcyra, from which they have reaped only frustration?) Similarly ambiguous is their application of this maxim to the present case, namely, that Athens will draw more strength from avoiding injustice toward an equal than from the accession of the Corcyrean navy. This suggests, however inadvertently, that the crucial thing is not justice but skill in gauging relative power, that is, in distinguishing equals from inferiors. (We note how grievously Corinth underestimated the actual and—given the availability of an alliance with Athens—the potential power of Corcyra.) Not justice but superiority is to be pursued, for justice fetters only equals. Yet what Corcyra offers Athens here is precisely such superiority. Corinth, even now no better than a distant second to Athens among the naval powers of Greece, would be still less her equal should Athens enroll the third (or second? cf. 1.33.1, 35.5) such power, Corcyra. If it is her influence with Sparta that emboldens Corinth to pose as the equal of Athens, the question is whether the policy offensive to Corinth here does not offer Athens the means of slipping the tiresome yoke of equality with the Spartan confederacy as a whole.

Both Corcyra and Corinth offer apparent arguments for justice. These are equivocal, however, as to the reasons for choosing justice. They suggest now that justice is to be preferred to expediency, now that it is to be preferred because of its expediency. They thus leave open the possibility that the very reasons upholding justice might sometimes support its opposite, or that justice is clearly preferable only when successful injustice is clearly impossible. If justice is to be valued primarily for its utility in obtaining certain results, then its choiceworthiness is contingent on its necessity for obtaining these results.

To return to the terms of the antithesis that begins the speeches, either justice is necessary or necessity threatens to eclipse it. The issue of justice aside, the claim of the Corcyreans that Athens must receive them in order to secure their powerful fleet is more powerful than that of the Corinthians to the contrary. While the latter can threaten that alliance with Corcyra will lead to a wider war, they cannot guarantee that such a war will not come in any case. If war with Sparta is near enough at hand so that the Corinthian threat to instigate it is credible, then Corcyra is right that Athens must in self-defense secure her fleet. A sensible country has no choice but to become and remain stronger than its likely enemies. This means however that *considerations of justice included*, the case of the Corcyreans is stronger. Once we grasp that the questions of justice and necessity converge (because necessity justifies), the Corcyrean arguments for the necessity of the alliance that they propose, if convincing, also vindicate its justice.

The Athenian deliberations that follow these speeches issue in two decisions, the second of which reverses the first. Thucydides reports with some thoroughness the grounds of the ultimate decision in favor of Corcyra; he is silent as to those of the provisional one in favor of Corinth. The Athenians may incline initially to Corinth for any or all of the following reasons: because she seems less unjust than Corcyra, because they themselves fear to commit injustice by breaking the treaty, or because they hope that it is still not too late to avoid a general war. That justice plays no role in Thucydides' account of the people's second decision does not preclude its having figured in the first one: a people's first inclination may usually be to act as seems just to it (cf. 3.36–49).

While noting that the Athenians have come to regard the wider war as inevitable, Thucydides also mentions that in deciding to conclude a merely defensive alliance with Corcyra, they mean to remain within the terms of the thirty years' treaty. The Athenians may hope, but do not expect, that by avoiding a breach of the treaty they will also avoid or postpone the war: their concern to avoid aitia for the war accompanies their anticipation of its imminence. They thus dodge the question raised by Corcyra of whether the presumed inevitability of the war might justify them in breaking the treaty. Like both Corcyra and Corinth, Athens here seeks to avoid or deny any tension between the respective demands of justice and necessity.

To the First Spartan Congress and the Speech of the Corinthian Envoys

Predictably, the Athenians fail in their efforts to combine support of Corcyra with avoidance of hostilities with Corinth. The blow that Corinth suffers on this front (1.50–52) leads to conflict on another one, where she faces a further setback (56–67). Her whole sphere of influence is at risk, and only Spartan intervention can save it. To this point Athens has arguably avoided breaking the treaty (cf. 51–52). We cannot say as much for Corinth, which has incited the revolt of Poteidaea, an Athenian ally.

Even so, the Spartans vote in the end that Athens has broken the treaty and war must be waged against her (1.87–88). In so posing the question they honor the primacy of legality or right over expediency; Sparta's interests (let alone her necessities) are not even on the table. That Sparta takes her stand on justice is stressed by the fiery Sthenelaidas, who refers to Athenian injustice six times in the course of a very brief speech (86). The official issue is that of justice only, and justice in its primary and narrowest sense of law-abidingness (the law among nations being defined by treaties). This would not seem to bode well for the Corinthian envoys. While thundering against the injustice of Athens, they adduce no specific infraction of the treaty. (It is, however, likely that earlier speakers at the congress have done so: cf. *enklēmata* ["accusations, indictments"] at 67.4, echoed by the Corinthians at 68.2, by Thucydides at 72, and by the Athenian envoys at 73.1). In any case "the Spartans voted as they did not so much because of the speeches of the allies, as because they feared the growing power of the Athenians, seeing that most of Greece was subject to them already" (88.1). Thucydides thus recalls us to what the Spartans' framing of the question before them obscures: the "truest allegation" of 1.23.6. Indeed, we might conclude that precisely this "truest allegation" supplies the theme for the whole of this conference (or even the whole of Book One): throughout, the crux is not justice but the necessity posed by Athenian imperialism.[24]

This, however, would be to go too far. Again Thucydides' statement does not supersede but supplements those of his speakers. He does not depict the Spartans as indifferent to justice. (Nor even here does he assert that they were wholly unswayed by the speeches of their allies.) Like Corinth and Corcyra before her, or Athens pressed by Corinth and Corcyra, Sparta congratulates herself on not having to choose between the demands of necessity and those of justice.[25]

More ambiguous is the speech of the Corinthians, to which we have already referred (1.68–71). It too stresses the harmony of the requirements of justice and necessity, there being no city more unjust than Athens nor any more menacing. At the same time the speech insists that Sparta cannot hope to thwart Athens unless she becomes more like her. Indeed it expounds the inefficacy of justice (i.e., of the peaceful course of avoiding injustice) for securing a city's safety: that city is safest which is most terrible to its adver-

---

[24] Romilly *Imperialism* 17–36; Rhodes *Hermes* 115 (1987) 154–65.
[25] Cf. Heath *LCM* 11 (1986) 104–5.

saries, and Athens is far more so than Sparta. The daunting power of Athens comes to light as inseparable from her constant and unquenchable activity or motion, her restless spirit of domination and progress and therefore her rampant injustice. In affairs among nations, it seems, necessity must prevail over justice. Still, the envoys manage to suppress this difficulty: it is in the just cause of opposing Athens and of restoring the status quo that Sparta must come to resemble Athens; that is, must cease to be a status quo power.

The speech of the Corinthians concludes with a threat to bolt from the Spartan confederacy (1.71.4–7). Although few scholars take this threat seriously, the envoys must expect Sparta to do so, as otherwise it would be very foolish to utter it. As we shall see, there is every reason to believe that the Spartans do take it seriously, that it is just the prospect of this desertion on the eve of a possible war with Athens which drives Sparta to resolve that Athens has broken the treaty. For Corinth and her dependents—wealthy and seafaring cities—represent the allies against Athens that Sparta can least afford to lose. Nor can we say how many others (including strategic Megara) might have followed Corinth in bailing out of the weakened confederacy, whether to throw in their lot with Sparta's old rival Argos or to seek the best available terms from Athens.[26] The dilemma that Sparta confronts resembles the earlier one of Athens. The defection of the fleets of Corinth and her clients (and their possible acquisition by Athens or Argos) and denial of access to the invasion route to Attica through the Megarid—these can be no less worrisome to Sparta than Corinth's acquisition of the fleet of Corcyra would have been to Athens.

Thucydides offers his lengthy account of the "grievances and points at issue" neither to demonstrate their emptiness nor merely to fill out the historical record. The "truest prophasis" does not stand in relation to these aitiai as the true (but subterranean) reason for the war stands to the proclaimed (but specious) ones. The episodes of Corcyra and Poteidaea are not trifling and the rise of Athenian power consequential; rather they represent the critical stages of that rise.[27] When Athenian policy towards these cities threatens to strip Corinth of her sphere of influence, she in turn forces Sparta to choose between confronting Athens with the Spartan confederacy intact and avoiding war at the risk of losing her most valuable allies. Sparta can no longer dither: Athens has "laid hold of [Sparta's] alliance" (118.2). Oppressed by perceived necessities,[28] the cities balance on the brink of war while disclaiming all aitia for its outbreak.

---

[26] Cf. De Ste-Croix *Origins* 59–60.

[27] Adcock *JHS* 71 (1951) 10; Kirkwood *AJP* 73 (1952) 60; Walker *CQ* NS 7 (1957) 27–38; Westlake *CQ* NS 8 (1958) 103–4; Andrewes *CQ* NS 9 (1959) 224–25; Strauss *City and man* 174–75.

[28] Cf. Ostwald *Ananke* 21–32.

NATURE, NECESSITY, AND JUSTICE: THE SPEECH OF THE ATHENIAN ENVOYS AT SPARTA

The most thorough exploration in Book One of the tension between necessity and justice is the speech of the Athenians at Sparta (1.72–78). This is the debut of Athenian speakers in the work, and Thucydides has reserved it for a moment of high drama. These anonymous envoys, in town on other business, step forward at their own request to reply to the complaints of Corinth.

The Corinthians have offered contrasting portraits of Athens and Sparta. Athens is a city in constant motion; Sparta wishes only to remain at rest. In stressing the restlessness of Athenian injustice, however, the Corinthians as much as imply that the Athenians simply cannot help it.

> And so they pass all the days of their lives in toils and perils of every description, enjoying far less than others what is already theirs, so busy are they adding to it; the only holiday they observe is to do whatever requires to be done, and they think unremitting toil a lesser misfortune than the tranquility of a quiet life. In short, they were born (*or* it is their nature)[29] neither to enjoy any rest nor to leave any to others. (1.70.8–9)

Owls hoot, olives ripen, Athenians harry their neighbors. This almost suggests that the Athenians too are victims of their empire, their thirst for which deprives them of all repose (cf. 2.49.5–6).

Which, however, suggests a defense against the very charge of injustice that it is meant to support. This defense would plead an overwhelming internal compulsion, which, because overwhelming, exonerates the actor of all responsibility for what would otherwise be imputed as an injustice. So, in fact, these Athenian speakers do plead—with a remarkable twist. Not just as Athenians but as human beings are they congenitally unable to leave their neighbors in peace.[30] Such a defense of the empire diverges from that of the funeral oration with its celebration of Athenian exceptionalism. Obviously it departs from it also in presenting imperialism as weighing upon the Athenians rather than as freely chosen by them. (In this, however, the envoys anticipate Pericles' final speech.)

The Athenian reply is that speech in Thucydides which the most critics find the least credible. They deem it too bold to have been publicly uttered—least of all before a powerful enemy in order to incline that enemy to peace (72.1).[31]

---

[29] Πεφυκέναι is a cognate of φύσις, "nature."

[30] Cf. Cogan *Human thing* 24–26, which, however, fails to see that φύσις (nature) supplies the theme of the Athenian speech no less than that of the Corinthian one.

[31] Schwartz *Geschichtswerk* 105; Jaeger *Paideia* 1:396; Romilly *Imperialism* 242–72; Stahl *Thukydides* 43; De Ste-Croix *Origins* 12–13. For able defenses of the plausibility of the speech

The speech is indeed candid. It is so, however, for the reason that most speeches are not: because candor serves the turn of the speakers. Lest we miss this, Thucydides briefs us beforehand as to the envoys' intentions (72). This may seem superfluous, since the speakers themselves will begin by doing the same. The accounts differ, however, suggesting that the envoys are less than candid about the reason for their candor.

According to Thucydides, the speakers do not at all intend to defend Athens against the charges of her detractors but to show the Spartans that the question before them ought not to be decided hastily, and at the same time to demonstrate the power of Athens (1.72.1). According to the speakers' own account (73.1), they have not come forward to refute the charges of the other cities, as they neither have a mandate from home to do so nor recognize the authority of the tribunal. They do hope to prevent the Spartans from yielding too easily to the persuasion of their allies. They aim also to show that, all things considered, Athens holds her empire "not unfairly" (*oute apeikotōs*) and that their city is "one to be reckoned with" (*axia logou*).

Thucydides substitutes an unstated intention, that of displaying the power of Athens, for the stated one of vindicating her use of it. This is crucial for grasping the speech. Informing their defense of Athens is an aim the speakers omit to state; that of expressing her power through the very boldness of that defense.[32]

The envoys begin their apology for the empire by recalling its birth in the great deeds of Athens in the Persian Wars (1.73–74). Clearly they also recount the power of the antagonist that Athens was and is. They contrast her resolve, her zeal, her sagacity and her seamanship with her rivals' want of all these—a contrast as invidious to Sparta as to Persia.

To this point, then, vindication doubles as a reminder of power. And since the speakers admit that the vindication is a tired one (1.73.2), to remind of power is very likely their chief intention.[33] Having finished with the Persian Wars, they proceed to a discussion of their imperialism that manages to be "both fastidious and frank."[34] This frankness is without precedent or sequel. Unlike Communist imperialists of our day, Thucydides' Athenians do not deny that an empire is what they possess. Unlike imperialists of the nineteenth century, they do not claim that their subjects are incapable of ruling themselves. Nor do they pretend, as earlier Eastern dynasts had done,

---

and of its boldness, see Busolt *Griechische Geschichte* 3.2.833; Pohlenz *Thukydidesstudien* 1:95–138; Adcock *Thucydides* 31–32; Grant *CQ* NS 15 (1965) 265; Kagan *Outbreak* 293–300; Cogan *Human thing* 28 n.17 (259–60).

[32] Strauss *City and man* 170–71; Pouncey *Necessities* 62; Heath *Historia* 39 (1990) 386.

[33] Strauss *City and man* 170–72; Stahl *Thukydides* 44–47; Kagan *Outbreak* 295.

[34] Strauss *City and man* 172; cf. Aron *History and Theory* 1 (1960–61) 104.

to wield empire by the will and hand of a god.[35] They admit to ruling, without divine warrant and for their own purposes, while conceding that to be ruled even by them is an evil.

The envoys do not, however, claim that "might makes right." They concede that Athenian rule rests on superior strength (which they ascribe in part to superior virtue: 1.74, 75.1; cf. 1.145; 2.35–46, 64), and they contend that the stronger will invariably rule. They do not present such a state of affairs as just. They do insist, however, that Athens holds her empire, if not justly, then at least "not unfairly" (*oute apeikotōs*). In support of this assertion they claim both that no people has ever been so just as to resist the temptation to rule (76.1–2) and that Athens has at least resisted it more successfully than others (76.3–4, 77).

"Not by force" did Athens acquire an empire (1.75.2) but through prosecuting the Persian Wars to their conclusion. For this task Sparta had lacked both aptitude and zeal and so had driven the island and coastal cities into the arms of Athens. The envoys contend here not that the empire itself is as noble as the victory over the Mede but merely that it was from acting nobly that Athens found herself subject to the compulsions that she offers as extenuating the empire. "And [it followed] from this very action [i.e., our acceptance of the allied command] [that] we were compelled in the first place to advance our empire to its present state, [swayed] first of all by fear, although later by honor too and lastly also by profit" (75.3). The great issue of the speech is the status of these alleged compulsions.

Chief among these was fear, often a respectable extenuation even of crimes among individuals. Fear, the envoys claim, not only called the empire into being but has continued to preside over it. For some time now, admittedly, Athens has most feared not the Mede but her own allies, viewed as prospective defectors to Sparta. "And it no longer seemed safe to risk letting the allies go, now that we were hated by most of them, and some having already revolted had been reduced to subjection, and you were no longer friendly as before, but were suspected by us and at odds with us. And our deserters would have gone over to you. No one can be blamed, in matters of the greatest risk, for seeing to his interests as best he can" (1.75.4).

At this point the envoys turn to glance at Sparta. She too has arranged the affairs of Peloponnese as suits her. Had she, moreover, persisted at the head of the Panhellenic alliance, she would soon have found herself compelled (*anankasthentas*, 1.76.1) to the same harsh measures as Athens. The prob-

---

[35] Cf. Grene *Greek political theory* 4–6; Chatelet *La naissance* 132, 136. Some commentators (e.g., Romilly *Imperialism* 78–80; Galpin *CJ* 79 [1983–84] 100–109; Connor *Thucydides* 123) assert that Athenian justifications of imperialism here and elsewhere rest at least implicitly on "the Greek idea that ruling others is an expression of true freedom" (Connor). If there was such a Greek idea, Thucydides' Athenians do not invoke it. They present their empire as in need of extenuation, and the one they offer is not that it is "an expression of freedom" but something to which they are compelled.

lem with this claim is that Sparta has not proceeded even inside Peloponnese from hegemony to empire, nor, outside it, had she persisted in her hegemony. That the very Spartans to whom the Athenians proclaim the necessity of empire appear to live free of it does not augur well for the success of this argument.

Undaunted, the envoys continue to expound the compulsions to acquire an empire. "So we have done nothing to be wondered at, or off the beaten track for human beings, in accepting an empire that was offered us and in not relinquishing it, overcome by the greatest things, honor and fear and profit" (1.76.2). Varying now the original order of their mention of these alleged "compulsions," they force us to reflect on the consequences of regarding all of them as equally that. They imply that it does not matter on which of these compulsions their empire rests, for all rank among the "greatest things," honor and profit no less than fear, equally irresistible and so equally extenuating.[36] They thus erase the distinction between necessity and mere expediency. They imply that every usual *motive* of empire qualifies as an *extenuation* of it; that empire is an offense for which it is a sufficient alibi to have committed it.[37]

What is the evidence for this astonishing position? The envoys' case is as simple as it is audacious. We must grant that all inclinations to empire are compulsory and irresistible very simply because no society has been known to resist them. "Nor have we innovated in this: it has ever been the case that the weaker have been subjected by the stronger.[38] We held ourselves, moreover, worthy of this role, as indeed did you, until now for reasons of interest you raise the argument from justice—which none has ever adduced to his loss when he stood to gain something by force" (1.76.2). The justice that cities invoke is specious: each demands it only of others. None prefers justice to the three compulsions; each cultivates it only insofar as these dictate.

---

[36] So stunning is this transposition of the order of the alleged compulsions (cf. 75.3) that the translator Crawley refuses to render it, thereby concealing it from his readers. Cf. Bluhm *Political Studies* 10 (1962) 19–20.

[37] "The Athenians would thus appear to fulfill, by the offer of an inadmissible defense, their promise not to defend themselves: for what under certain circumstances might be allowed to fear, could not without the gravest consequences be granted to the desire for honor and profit." Bruell *APSR* 68 (1974) 13. Romilly argues that in substituting honor for fear as the foremost compulsion, the envoys put their best foot forward, honor being the most impressive and "désintéressé" of the three motives (*Imperialism* 251 n.1; *AnSoc* 4 [1973] 55–56). Yet even or precisely honor is hardly honorable as an excuse for injustice. That the envoys present τιμή as a *compulsion* further deprives it of its allure; inasmuch as they have been vanquished by it (νικηθέντες, just as by fear and profit: 1.76.2), they enter it as an extenuation rather than as a claim of virtue. On the fate of τιμή in the work, see Romilly *AnSoc* 4 (1973) 52–58; Pouncey *Necessities* 21 and n.20; Forde *Ambition to rule*.

[38] Cf. Democritus fr. 267: Φύσει τὸ ἄρχειν οἰκήιον τῷ κρέσσονι ("By nature it is innate in the stronger to rule").

The Athenians admit, then, that they rule because they are strong enough to get away with it and because they no more than anyone else can resist the temptations to rule. In their weakness before these temptations, they are no better than other cities. Their first excuse is that neither are they any worse.

Their second excuse is that in their manner of ruling their superiority reasserts itself. "And praise is due to all who, while so far subject to human nature as to rule over others, yet are juster than they need be considering their power" (1.76.3). Justice is praiseworthy, and the impeccably just city would abjure ruling other cities.[39] Here the envoys think as others do. They differ in seeking to narrow the realm of a city's accountability for justice. To be praised is the city that rules as justly as possible; to refrain from ruling is not possible.

Unlike other imperial powers, which take what they like when it pleases them to take it, Athens practices rule by law. In her disputes with her subjects, she submits to litigation, at Athens or even in the subject town (1.77.1).[40] She thus continues to preserve the appearance of equality, and indeed the envoys argue that this is more than merely an appearance: their subjects are used to consorting with them as equals. On the other hand the speakers do not conceal that this equality is imperfect. The subjects remain subjects (*hypēkooi*, "those who hearken and obey"); the envoys use no euphemism. Their claim is rather that Athens treats her subjects with restraint (*metriazomen*), taking but little from them, and this judicially (*dikazesthai*) rather than by force (*biazesthai*)—although they later qualify even this (77.3). It is understandable, even to the envoys, that the subjects mistake this justice for litigiousness.

> [Our subjects,] however, are used to associating with us as equals, so that if they are crossed in any way in something, whether by a legal verdict or by the power that empire confers on us, and their own opinion as to what is called for does not prevail, they give us no thanks for leaving them with most of their possessions, but resent their losses more bitterly than if we had from the first cast law aside and openly gratified our rapacity. In that case even they would not have disputed that the weaker must make way for the stronger. As is only likely, people get angrier at an unjust verdict than at being constrained by force, for the former seems like being cheated by an equal, the latter like being compelled by a superior. (77.3–4)

If Athens observes restraint, it is not for reasons of honor, safety, or profit. Were she not to do so, her subjects would resent her no more, perhaps less.

---

[39] Romilly *Phoenix* 28 (1974) 95.

[40] There is disagreement over the syntax, substance, and basis in imperial practice of the envoys' claim here. See De Ste-Croix *CQ* NS 11 (1961) 94–112; Meiggs *Athenian empire* 228–33; Winton *MH* 37 (1980) 89–97; Hornblower *Commentary* 122–23. Ps.-Xenophon *Constitution of Athens* 1.16–18 speaks only of trials at Athens and suggests a variety of ways in which the Athenian *demos* benefited from them.

Athens' restraint is just costly enough, in the coin of the three compulsions, to qualify as genuine justice. At the same time it defers to these enough—indulging even their appetite for empire—that though genuine it is feasible.

The end of the speech (1.78) confirms that Athenians can speak conventionally when they want to. The envoys invoke the unforeseeable fortunes of war, a theme well suited to appeal to Spartans (cf. 1.80, 2.11.4, 4.17–18). They finally invoke the thirty years' treaty, which they stand accused of breaking. It contains a clause prescribing arbitration of grievances: while Athens' violations of the treaty are doubtful, Sparta's, if she ignores this clause, will be flagrant. Precisely the most literal "Spartan" notion of justice (as scrupulous performance of sworn obligations) happens here to favor Athens. Not only is nature with Athens (75–76) but so are the gods (78.4). That the envoys save these traditional appeals for the last suggests that they expect them to prove the most effective (all the more so for following upon a reminder of Athenian power). These diverse appeals have in common that they speak to Spartan timidity.

Although the envoys speak of justice, their strategy as speakers relies on fear—of chance, of the gods, and of themselves. They succeed on some or all these counts with the peace-loving king Archidamus (1.80–85). Most of the Spartans, however, vote with the ephor Sthenelaidas for war, "not so much because they were persuaded by the speeches of the allies as because they feared the rising power of the Athenians, seeing that most of Greece was already subject to them" (1.88). The envoys have mistaken the direction in which fear of Athens would incline Sparta. They would have acted as consistently with their insight into the primacy of fear for Sparta had they sought to *allay* her fear of Athens. Perhaps as Athenians they cannot conceive of being deterred from war by lack of fear of the adversary. In any case both the Athenian speech and the Spartan ones that follow largely confirm the characterizations of the Corinthians. Here as elsewhere the two vastly different societies, each addressing the other as if it were a rival resembling itself, succeed only in talking past each other.[41]

The speech of the envoys is not puzzling if read in the light of its thesis. As they assert that not justice but the "compulsions" are the passions to be reckoned on, so their strategy is to reckon on them, particularly fear. The speech is not simply conciliatory; neither, however, is it intentionally provocative. Hoping to defer the war but eschewing appeasement, the envoys opt for deterrence. They aim both to convey the power of Athens and to confront the Spartans with truths about justice that every first-rate power should know.[42] As sensible men, however, they place their hopes for deter-

[41] Cf. 4.17–21; De Ste-Croix *Origins* 13; Cogan *Human thing* 28, n.17 (259–60).

[42] Grant *CQ* NS 15 (1965) 265; Kagan *Outbreak* 295–300. Cf. Immerwahr, in Stadter ed. *Speeches* 24: "The first speech of the Corinthians and the Athenian speech at Sparta have in common the purpose of frightening the Spartans; the Corinthians hope to frighten them into war, the Athenians into refraining from war." For opposing views, see Cogan *Human thing*

rence chiefly in power rather than justice, and so in arguments from justice the boldness of which itself conveys an impression of power.

THE "FIFTY YEARS" AS A COMMENTARY ON THE ATHENIAN SPEECH

Before analyzing schematically the contribution of the envoys' speech to the theme of necessity and justice, it is worth testing their account alike of their empire and of Sparta against that provided by Thucydides himself in the chapters almost immediately following (1.89–117), known traditionally as the Pentecontaëtia ("account of the fifty years"). Thucydides himself divides the passage into two parts: 89–96, on "the manner in which the Athenians came to be placed in the circumstances under which they increased in power" (89.1); and 97–117, "an account of the manner in which the empire of the Athenians was established" (97.2). The first passage thus relates how Athens came into the hegemony, and the second how she came to acquire an empire of increasing power. This last account is sometimes said to manifest the "truest prophasis" of the war, by those who take that term as "real cause" in opposition to the "grievances openly alleged." In that case these chapters might seem to form the crucial section of Book One.

Precisely this last passage, however, Thucydides describes as a digression (*ekbolē*, 1.97.2), and the reason for it that we have quoted is not even the primary one that he offers. Indeed he presents the quoted reason almost as an afterthought (*hama de kai*, "at the same time," "also"). (As for the primary reason offered, it is merely the correction of the chronology of Hellanicus' *Attic Chronicle*, now lost.) What are we to make of this? Not that these events are unimportant, for in that case Thucydides would not have provided such an account of them. Still, the clashes of the Fifty Years, while necessary for the outbreak of the war, were not sufficient for it. As of their conclusion, the power of Athens had not yet risen to the point where Sparta felt herself compelled to make a determined effort to destroy it. Indeed, after decades of sporadic conflict, the two cities and their alliances were joined by treaty (115.1) and enjoyed a seemingly stable peace, reenforced by the failure of the Peloponnesians to support the Samian revolt (115–17; cf. 40.5, 41.1). The aim of 118.2 (Thucydides' restatement, within the broader perspective afforded by 89–117, of Sparta's motive in going to war) is not to divert our attention from the "grievances openly avowed" to the Athenian ascent of the decades preceding, but rather to direct us to interpret these grievances as further (and for Sparta decisive) episodes of this ascent.[43]

Be that as it may, the Pentecontaëtia also permits us to assess the Athenian

---

23–27; and Coby *CJPS* 24 (1991) 70–75, which underestimate the boldness of the tone of the speech and of its overall presentation of the question of justice and empire. But cf. Cogan 28.
[43] Cf. Connor *Thucydides* 33.

speech. The standing naval power of Athens had originated in the mind of Themistocles, who had led Greece to victory over the Mede (1.14.3, 73.4–74.1). In conceiving it, he might seem to have committed the common error of planning for the last war rather than the next one (93.7). In this case, however, hindsight doubled as foresight and indeed foresight had predated hindsight, for even prior to the Persian Wars Themistocles had conceived of a new Athens centered not within the walls of its ancient acropolis (cf. 2.15) but in a new walled harbor in Peiraeus (1.93.3). Only after the defeat of the Mede, however, was there time to act on this project.

The Athenians, having abandoned their city and taken to their still-untried ships, had achieved their astonishing victory and thus regained the homeland that the Mede had sacked in their absence. Themistocles appears to have concluded that the success of the city-fleet implied the conversion of the city itself into something resembling a fleet. He reasoned that Athens could best prepare against the return of the Mede or a similarly formidable enemy by walling both itself and its harbor, so that ships and city would be impregnable from land and the ships would make the city impregnable from the sea (1.93.6–7). "He straightway went about making a beginning [sc. of the work of fortification]" or "he straightway went about laying the foundations of the empire." (The Greek [*kai tēn archēn euthys xynkateskeuaze*, 93.4] is ambiguous.)

The subsequent power of Athens thus rested on a decision inspired by fear, that is, an essentially defensive one. The fleet thus sheltered, however, was obviously as potent an offensive weapon as a defensive one, and the walls that shielded Athens from an unprovoked attack by land shielded her equally from retaliation. It was not surprising that Sparta and her allies balked at this project (1.90.1). Sparta's traditional hegemony had rested on her supremacy in land warfare, the usual means of coercion among the Greeks, and she had within living memory intervened militarily at Athens (1.18.1, 6.53.3, 59.4). The new arrangement was thus bound to alter the balance of power in Greece. This, too, Themistocles presumably foresaw (1.138.3).[44]

Athens would also enjoy a louder voice in Greek affairs as a result of thus assuring her parity with Sparta (1.91.4–6). Themistocles had experienced firsthand the deficiencies of Spartan strategy[45] and had every reason to conclude that Greece as well as Athens would benefit from greater Athenian influence in the common deliberations. His policy was then at the same time a crucial step toward empire and entirely reasonable with an eye to the security of Athens.

Similarly ambiguous was Athens' simultaneous acceptance of the command of the Panhellenic coalition, soon to be the Delian League. It made

[44] On the great subtlety of Themistocles' policy as Thucydides presents it, see Cox *Politikos* 2 (1992) 89–107.

[45] Herodotus 7.139; 8.40, 57–64, 108. Cf. Thucydides 1.69.

sense to consolidate the hard-won victories that had driven the Mede from the Greek heartland—where even so he maintained an enclave at Thebes (1.90.2)—and to sweep him from the sea, thus freeing the eastern Greeks. Athens herself, principal target of the wrath of the Mede even prior to the war in which she had taken the lead in humiliating him,[46] could hardly choose to leave him a foothold anywhere nearby. The victory had been a near thing (1.69.5, 73.4–74.1, 14.3) and had clearly shown that the unity of the Greek cities was not to be presumed (2.71–74, 3.34, 3.54–67).[47] Sparta having abjured the command, there was no one to assume it but Athens, to whom in any case the allies had spontaneously appealed (1.95–96, 130).

But what of the transition from hegemony to empire (between which Thucydides clearly distinguishes at 1.97–99)? Here too he defends Athenian policy, or at least refrains from blaming it. Athens, an exacting leader which, however, demanded no more of her allies than of herself, met with resentment and eventually revolts—revolts that found the rebels unprepared. Slackers in defending their new independence, the allies had opted for tribute in lieu of military service, thus funding the concentration of power in the hands of Athens. Thucydides accordingly blames the *subjects* for their subjection (99.2).

But was Athens justified in "applying duress" (*prosagontes tas anankas*, 1.99.1) to her allies? The first revolt, at least, that of Naxos, occurred before the great victory of Cimon at the river Eurymedon (100.1) had driven the Persians from even the easternmost shores of the Aegean. In subduing Naxos and thereby enforcing the unity of the alliance, Athens merely acted as her safety required. After Cimon's triumph, the Persian threat was much diminished. Just then, however, when Thasos revolted and was besieged by Athens, the Thasians extracted a secret promise from Sparta to invade Attica (100.2, 101.1–2). Nothing came of this promise—Sparta was distracted by problems at home—and we are not told whether it became known at Athens. Here is evidence, however, that while the transition from hegemony to empire was gradual, that from the friendship of Sparta to her enmity was rapid. It was soon to become as open as it was unmerited (102). Thucydides' account thus supports the implication of the envoys that Athens had repelled the Persian menace only to incur the hostility of Sparta and was therefore never free of compulsions to maintain the empire—not even if we interpret compulsion rather more narrowly than the envoys themselves.[48]

---

[46] Herodotus 5.96–102, 105; 6.94; 7.8, 138; 9.7–11.

[47] Cf. Herodotus 7.138–72 and the citations in note 45 above.

[48] Chatelet *La naissance* 136–37; Bruell *St. John's Review* 32.1 (1981) 26–27. As Pouncey notes (*Necessities* 66–67), Thucydides' account also confirms the legitimacy of the Athenian claim that she had to fear the defection of her revolted allies to the Spartans.

That one could thus justify the Athenian empire in terms of a legitimate concern with security would not of course imply that this was her only or even her primary reason for maintaining and expanding it. The envoys themselves have invoked two other alleged compulsions, and the deportment of the Athenians in the Pentecontaëtia is not that of a careful empire. Instead they present a spectacle of action on every front, of vast risks and stunning losses, of indomitable resolve and resourcefulness—a spectacle of the whirlwind of activity described in the speech of the Corinthians. The Athenian love of danger and of exploits, her willingness to risk what she has in order to add to it (cf. 1.70), precludes ascribing her empire only to her fear of the effects of losing it. It is also in honor (*timē*) and even in the aspiration to something beyond it that we must seek the motive of Athenian imperialism.[49] But are we to follow the envoys in interpreting timē as a form of compulsion? Or are we to follow Pericles in interpreting it as freely and nobly chosen?

If the Pentecontaëtia largely confirms the envoys' characterization of their own empire (while not resolving its ambiguities), it also supports their portrayal of Sparta. It surely confirms that Sparta had treated her allies more high-handedly than Athens (1.95, 130), and thus that her persistence in the hegemony might indeed have subjected her to the same hatred as Athens. The account also confirms, however, that Sparta had not persisted in the hegemony, but had acquiesced in its transfer to Athens (95.7). This she had done in no evident thralldom to any of the three compulsions and so in apparent defiance of them. Neither safety, honor, nor profit compelled Sparta to step aside to make way for Athens. Although Thucydides does ascribe Sparta's decision to a fear, it is not one that experience confirms as compulsory: she feared lest her citizens "become worse" through the exercise of hegemonial authority (95.7). Sparta preferred the virtue of her citizens to the blandishments of empire. She left the honor, profit, and trouble to Athens, trusting her (perhaps foolishly) to see to Sparta's safety (ibid.). If this is not quite the same as preferring justice for its own sake, it does challenge the contention that honor and profit are compulsory.

UNRESOLVED TENSIONS IN THE SPEECH OF THE ATHENIANS AT SPARTA

Athens as the envoys present her enjoys the best of both worlds, combining the empire that other cities envy with the justice that they only feign. Finally, however, the envoys do not resolve the tension between empire and justice but only begin to articulate it.

---

[49] On the astonishing, even erotic, daring of Athens as Thucydides presents it in the Fifty Years, see Forde *APSR* 80 (1986) 433–38 and *Ambition to rule* 20–26.

In stressing the justice of the empire, the envoys remind us of the funeral oration. Yet the benefits that Athens confers on the subjects, and her own sacrifices to this end, they present as distinctly secondary. While they claim, moreover, that Athens practices justice freely, they reject the implication of the funeral oration that she had freely undertaken the imperial project as a whole. On this primary and overriding question, the envoys invoke the three compulsions. Even if we accept both their thesis of the necessity of empire and the genuineness of their attachment to justice, their practice of the latter is as unsatisfying as half measures always are.

We need not deny the gentleness of Athenian policy in comparison with Persian (1.77.5) or that the subjects have mostly flourished under Athenian rule. Still, either she truly treats those allies as equals (which the envoys proclaim impossible) or her efforts to do so are bound to seem hypocritical. According to the envoys, only Athens truly honors justice, because she alone makes real sacrifices for its sake. Abstaining from rule by main force, the Athenians establish tribunals that place them on a nominally equal footing with their allies. In fact, however, they thus set themselves up as judges in their own cause. Although blaming their allies for branding all adverse outcomes as unjust, they readily admit that they sometimes take advantage of their superior position (77.3). Athens, eschewing naked force in favor of the forms of justice, finds herself with her slip always showing, and with allies more aggrieved at the pretense of right (even if it is partly genuine) than they would have been at its abandonment. As Machiavelli was to proclaim, "there is no proportion between him who is armed and him who is not";[50] surely legal forms cannot establish such proportion, which must remain illusory without equal subjection to enforcement of impartial decisions (cf. 5.89).

We might even wonder whether justice strictly speaking is applicable to affairs among cities. Again according to the envoys, justice implies association *apo tou isou*, "on fair or equal terms" (1.77.3), or equal subjection to laws that guarantee to each his own. However appropriate to citizens, such justice seems out of place among cities. For these, as the envoys claim, comprise no community constituted by a common good, such as all political justice presumes.[51] Cities know only struggle, in which nature impels each to serve itself and fear compels the weaker to serve the stronger.

The point here is not that the argument of the envoys implies that the victor treat the vanquished harshly; it does not (1.77). The question is whether mildness in such cases is properly conceived as justice. By the just we normally mean the obligatory or lawful, done because owed by the doer

---

[50] Machiavelli *Prince* chap. 12.

[51] 3.82.8; 4.60–61, 85–88; 5.90–91; 6.89.1; Aristotle *Nicomachean ethics* 5.6.4; cf. Bruell *St. John's Review* 32.1 (1981) 27.

to those to whom it is done. It is hard to grasp from the envoys' presentation what one city might owe another. The restraint practiced by the stronger looks less like something owed than something granted, the extension of some of the benefits of justice to a terrain where it no longer applies.[52]

The envoys present their argument, moreover, as resting on an insight into not merely the dynamics of the "international system," but human nature itself. As such it implies grave questions about life *within* the city.[53] If nature drives communities to contend for scarce resources rather than aspire to a common good, must we not conceive it as acting similarly on individuals? Must not the common good among citizens prove as hollow as the envoys make it out to be among cities? The stance of the envoys is doubly problematic. They refrain from applying to justice at home the implications of their critique of its weakness abroad. At the same time domestic justice continues to supply them with the principle—equality—to which they claim to adhere (as much as possible) abroad. Their standard of justice thus remains both ungrounded and untested.

Lastly the speech raises the problem of the link between justice and piety. At 1.78 the envoys admonish the Spartans to abjure impiety lest they drive the gods into the arms of Athens. What, however, of their own standing with the gods? Is piety compatible with their drastically lowered standards of justice? Greek as well as Biblical piety implies a certain righteousness: the old-fashioned Melians will describe themselves as "blameless (i.e., pious, *hosioi*) men defending themselves against [the Athenians] who are unjust" (5.104; cf. 7.77). The envoys might seek to save their piety by stressing their justice, which, if less than the tradition requires, is (so they claim) the most that can be reasonably expected. But do the gods take as indulgent a view as the envoys of the human capacity for justice?

The Athenian empire emerges from this speech as an effort to square the political circle. Although the envoys are proud of it, they do not present empire as such as something to be altogether proud of. While the compulsory may be excusable and in that sense just, it is not praiseworthy; one may avoid blame for it, but one cannot claim credit. The Athenians, however, are determined that their empire be a credit to them. It excels other empires inasmuch as it grew from earlier virtuous achievements (1.73.2–75.2) and inasmuch as Athens concerns herself with more than just the honor, safety, and profit that empire brings.

As emerges still more clearly from the funeral oration, Athens is not what

---

[52] Romilly *Phoenix* 28 (1974) 96 notes that having praised themselves and their fellow Athenians at 1.76.3 for being more just than their situation requires, the envoys immediately proceed to characterize their behavior not as just but as ἐπιεικής ("reasonable, equitable, not extreme"). This goes with μετριάζομεν ("we behave in a measured way"); cf. the cognate οὔτε ἀπεικότως ("not inequitably"), at 73.1, applied to their holding of empire.

[53] Cf. Saxonhouse *Polity* 10 (1978) 477 and Galpin *CJ* 79 (1983–84) 100–109.

we moderns mean by a "state," nor does its empire serve the limited goals that we ascribe to the state. In and through city and empire the citizens achieve happiness in the fullest human sense. To this crown of human ends honor, safety, and profit emerge from our speech as necessary but somehow insufficient. There is more to human life and more, the envoys claim, to their empire. Their *worthiness* to rule is the crucial point (1.76.2), and this depends on their virtue: they are proudest of the empire itself only as it attests to their virtue. Virtue includes justice, however—the envoys are far from denying that true justice is a virtue—and of all the virtues justice is the one most obviously in tension with empire. They do their best to resolve this tension: they assert that while the empire is not strictly speaking just, still they are worthy of it and hold it "not unfairly"; without being fully just, it is sufficiently justified. Unable to pull up short of the brink of empire, the envoys pride themselves on having checked their plunge just a step or two beyond it. To understand the speech is to grasp how justice (Athenian deficiencies in which the envoys are so amazingly frank about) returns through the back door—not because might makes right, but because necessity extenuates in the presence of the intention of acting as justly as possible.

Still, it cannot be denied that justice itself (and so the just intention) emerges from the speech as problematic. If nature drives human beings to prefer honor, safety, and profit to justice, might we not conclude that these are by nature better for us than justice? That they are good by nature and justice is good only by convention? If so, does it even make sense to practice justice "more than one's circumstances require"?

If, on the other hand, as the envoys also seem to suggest, justice remains the ultimate object of aspiration for human beings, can we rest satisfied with the envoys' solution to their dilemma? Can they be right to pride themselves on a justice seemingly so vestigial? Perhaps on further reflection the pursuit of safety, honor, and interest beyond the limits of justice will not seem compulsory in any strict sense—in which case we cannot invoke them as alibis in a strict sense. If the first of two alternatives is not quite impossible, then the second is not quite necessary. Precisely if the Athenians pride themselves more on their justice than on their honor, safety, or profit, ought they not bring themselves to make greater sacrifices of these for its sake?

THROUGH SPARTAN EYES

The Athenian speech treats explicitly that problem of the relationship between the just and the necessary which is implicit throughout Book One. It does so, moreover (as, given its occasion, it must), in the context of the question of who will bear aitia for the war. The "truest prophasis" was an instance of constraint; it was unclear precisely how that constraint bore on the question of aitia. The envoys acknowledge no link between the two.

They present the question of aitia as entirely that of the first violation of the letter of the treaty (1.78). Guilt will devolve on Sparta, which refuses arbitration, not on Athens, which offers it. As a rhetorical strategy this makes good sense: the envoys are appealing to a Spartan audience, and it is precisely this aspect of their appeal that seems most likely to succeed with one.

In a broader sense, however, the speech of the envoys tends to exonerate Sparta's decision to go to war, even in spite of the treaty. For it is not adherence to treaties or even avoiding offense to the gods which the envoys have presented as the ultimate human necessity. Can we possibly assign blame (aitia) to a Sparta that, acting out of fear, "is making the best provisions for [her] interests in matters of the greatest risk," thus behaving in just that manner the envoys have described as blameless (*anepiphthonos*)?

Sparta does not conceal that she goes to war only under duress: Sthenelaidas prevails over Archidamus not by denying that war is to be deferred where possible, but by denying that this war may be deferred. But it is hardly to impugn Sparta's concern for justice to note that she goes to war only when necessary. Even the Corinthians, in blaming Spartan quiescence, concede that the Spartans themselves view quiescence as the avoidance of injustice (1.71.1). Despite the threat posed to her hegemony by the growing power of Athens, Sparta holds fast to the principle that what expediency demands is to be done only if justice permits. She thus denies that any action is strictly speaking necessary unless it is also just—and affirms that abstention from injustice is itself a necessity for the prudent.

Just this view is implicit in the speech of the decent king Archidamus, whom Thucydides introduces as the oracle of respectable Spartan opinion (1.79.2). His plea to defer the war is at the same time a defense of the Spartan regime against the strictures of Corinth (80–85). He defends Sparta's famous education as one in the "most necessary things" (1.84.4), the only occurrence of *ananke* or a cognate in his speech.[54] Archidamus discusses the strategic situation at length, the justice of declaring war only briefly. Critics therefore assume that strategic concerns are primary for him. Consider, however, that he saves his discussion of justice for the end (85), arguably the point of maximum impact. Consider also that a Spartan never uses more words than necessary (4.17.1) and that while it may take many arguments to etablish the imprudence of war at the present juncture, Archidamus may consider that one suffices to establish its injustice. He certainly presents the issue as simple. Noting that the treaty in force enjoins arbitration of all disputes (which clause the Athenian envoys have just invoked), he states merely that "it is not lawful (*ou nomimon*) to proceed against someone offering arbitration [as one would] against a wrongdoer (*adikounta*)."

---

[54] The Spartan regime educates the citizen "to recognize to which ἀνάγκαι he is to assign the highest priority" (Ostwald *Ananke*, 30; cf. 17). For an argument for a narrower interpretation, see Edmunds *Chance and intelligence* 96 and n.10.

Law in this case means more than positive law. Like all treaties, this one rested on the most solemn oaths: the very word for treaty (*spondai*) refers to these oaths. Honoring treaties was thus a requirement of divine law. As an old-fashioned Spartan Archidamus may be supposed to take this fact seriously. (Subsequently he is the only Thucydidean character to address a speech not to a human audience but to gods, to persuade them of the rectitude of an action that he is about to undertake [2.74.2].) He presents the issue of the treaty as clear and unequivocal—to proceed without arbitration would be *ou nomimon*, and Sparta simply must not do it. Were the military balance favorable to her, this prohibition would still apply. Justice and necessity (in Archidamus' view, the exigencies of Sparta's unpreparedness) unite in demanding that war be deferred until arbitration has failed. True, even Archidamus indicates that an otherwise odious expedient is licit when required for self-preservation (1.82.1). Still, he does not suggest that to violate the treaty would be permissible under any circumstances.

Justice and necessity similarly converge in the speech of Sthenelaidas, although both tend in favor of war. His speech is so brief and his denunciations of Athenian injustice so loud that in heeding it the Spartans might seem to be swayed primarily by considerations of justice. On scrutiny, however, the speech yields also the suggestion that Sparta's security depends on her allies, whom she will lose unless she now succors them. "For others have much wealth and ships and horses, but we have good [or brave] allies, who must not be handed over to the Athenians . . ." (1.86.3). The rise of Athenian power strikes at the heart of the power of Sparta, by threatening to strip her of her allies whether by defeat or defection (cf. 71.5–7). This conveys Sthenelaidas' refutation of Archidamus' strategic analysis. Sparta's position may be weaker than that of Athens, but the crucial question is whether deferring war is likely to widen or shrink the gap between them. Whatever allies may remain to be found elsewhere, the defeat or defection of Corinth and her dependents (who alone of Sparta's current allies possess the ships and money that Archidamus himself has identified as crucial [81–83]), is not likely to be made up elsewhere.[55]

While disagreeing on so much else, Archidamus and Sthenelaidas agree in invoking both right and compulsion on behalf of their respective positions. "The Lacedaemonians voted that the treaty had been broken and that they must go to war not so much because they had been persuaded by the speeches of their allies as because they feared lest the Athenians grow still

---

[55] Of recent commentators, Bloedow *Historia* 23 (1981) 135–37 and *Hermes* 115 (1987) 60–66; Cohen *QUCC* 45 (1984) 41–42; and Connor *Thucydides* 38–39 pronounce Archidamus wise and Sthenelaidas simplistic; they miss the latter's point about the allies. Romilly *Imperialism* 133 does not miss it. J. H. Finley *Thucydides* 135 and Stahl *Thukydides* 56 also praise the speech. The best discussion is Allison *Hermes* 112 (1984) 10–16. For a treatment alleging the primacy of justice in the speech, see Heath *LCM* 11 (1986) 104–5.

more powerful, since they saw most of Greece already subject to them" (1.88). Still, what they voted was that the treaty had been broken. However they may be swayed by considerations of necessity, the Spartans pose the crucial question as one of right. Thucydides refrains from stating his opinion on the question of right. He does stress, however, the inadequacy of Sparta's response to the rapid rise of Athenian power.

> The Lacedaemonians, while aware [of the growth of Athenian power,] opposed it only fitfully, remaining inactive most of the time, being of old slow to go to war unless compelled to do so, and hindered in the present case by wars at home, until the power of the Athenians became obtrusive, and undertook to lay hands upon their own alliance. (1.118.2)

Thucydides indicates again that what decided Sparta to war against Athens was the threat to her own confederacy; in the absence of such a clear and overwhelming threat, Sparta would have delayed or flurried and subsided, as she had done so often in the past. (This passage again makes clear the relationship between the "accusations and points at issue" and the "truest prophasis": Corcyra and Poteidaea marked that point at which the growth of Athenian power threatened the cohesion of the Spartan alliance.) Still, while Sparta does not go to war primarily because Athens had broken the treaty, she does treat her having done so as a necessary condition of going to war (1.118.3).[56]

Not relying, moreover, solely on their own decision that Athens has broken the treaty, the Spartans consult the god at Delphi (1.118.3). Although they do not pose the question of the treaty directly, they must take the god's encouragement as confirming Athenian culpability (cf. 123.2). By appealing to the god, the Spartans continue to imply that their decision is a matter of choice rather than necessity, as well as that divine concerns must prevail over merely human ones.

Once their allies too have voted for war, Sparta sets about preparing for it and sending embassies to Athens, "so as to have the greatest possible grounds for war (*hoti megistē prophasis . . . tou polemein*), should [the Athenians] not heed [Sparta's complaints]" (1.126.1). While some would translate the cited Greek phrase as "the greatest pretext for war," there is good reason not to take *prophasis* as pretext here. As we have seen, in the two other places in Book One where the identical or a similar phrase occurs (118.1, 146), it means not pretext for war but something like *casus belli*. Nor need we doubt that the Spartans take these new accusations seriously.

---

[56] Cf. Heath *LCM* 11 (1986) 105: "Even if it is true that Sparta would not have gone to war over the αἰτίαι ἐς τὸ φανερὸν λεγόμεναι had they not felt threatened, they would nevertheless hardly have gone to war had they not been able to persuade themselves that it was the Athenians who were in breach of the treaty. So the αἰτίαι have genuine explanatory force."

Thucydides, for his part, relates them at length: of the 146 chapters of Book
One, 21 concern these charges and the Athenian responses to them.

Sparta begins by remonstrating with Athens to expunge a violation of
sacred law, which (at the time of the Spartans' invocation of it already some
180 years old) Thucydides obliges them by relating in detail.

> Such was the curse that the Lacedaemonians commanded the Athenians to
> expel, thus (or so they claimed [dēthen]) first of all avenging the honor of the
> gods, but also knowing that Pericles . . . was linked with the curse on his
> mother's side, and holding that were he to be banished it would be easier for
> them to obtain what they hoped for from the Athenians. Not that they expected
> that he would actually be banished, but that he would be subject to murmurs in
> the city that the war was partly due to his ill fortune. (1.127.1–2)

The gods might well ask why Sparta has taken so long to redress the
alleged insult to their honor, and Thucydides makes it clear that only after
resolving on war for other reasons does she see fit to urge this one. She sees
to the gods' business only in the course of minding her own.[57] Still, to mind
one's own business is a common definition of justice.[58] That Sparta's piety is
genuine, moreover, appears from her very expectation that Pericles' prestige
will suffer from his connection with an ancient curse. At Athens this charge
sinks without a ripple,[59] but we must infer that at Sparta people would have
muttered about a leader in poor standing with the gods (cf. 5.16–17).[60]

The sequel suggests similar reflections. Here too Sparta at first appears
ridiculous. Athens counters her accusation with not one but two alleged
instances of flagrant Spartan impiety (1.128). While Athens, however, has
been lax in driving out the curse that she incurred,[61] Sparta has scrupulously

---

[57] Cf. the Spartans' decision a century earlier to expel the Athenian tyrants, which decision
Athenian exiles had obtained by inducing the Delphic oracle so to admonish the Spartans
whenever they consulted it. According to Herodotus 5.63, the Spartans finally acted despite
the fact that "they were bound to [the tyrants] by the closest ties of friendship," because "they
esteemed the daemonic [or heavenly] things more highly than the things of man." Aristotle
Athenian constitution 19, acknowledges the role of the oracle, but ascribes the decision "at least
equally [to] the friendship between the [tyrants] and [Sparta's archrival] Argos." In his brief
accounts of the incident (1.18.1, 6.59.4), Thucydides is silent as to the role of the oracle.

[58] Cf. 1.71.1 with 2.40.2, 63.2, and 64.4; cf. 6.87.2 (πολλὰ . . . πράσσειν) and 6.87.3
(πολυπραγμοσύνης) with Plato *Republic* 433ab.

[59] According to Plutarch *Pericles* 33.1 these accusations actually increased Pericles' "honor
among the citizens as a man who was most hated and feared by the enemy."

[60] Thucydides delays until this moment his introduction of Pericles as the prime mover of
Athenian policy. To this end he may even have suppressed Pericles' decisive role in the decision
over Corcyra (Plutarch *Pericles* 29.1). He thus contrives Pericles' entrance as a figure tainted by
an ancient impiety. Keeping in mind the doubtfulness of Pericles' own piety, this may suggest
Thucydides' sympathy with the characteristically "Spartan" concern with sacred law.

[61] The fragmentary first chapter of Aristotle's *Athenian constitution* apparently describes the
initial attempt to expel the curse a generation or so after the offense. The descendants of those

honored the gods' requirements (as conveyed by the Delphic Oracle) for expunging one of her two curses (134.4). As for the other, it too she has taken far more seriously than the Athenians have taken theirs. She believes that the gods have punished her severely for it, and upon the recurrence of similar circumstances she has carefully avoided repeating it (128.1; cf. 103.1–2).

Book One concludes with other, strictly political, demands by Sparta (1.139), which Athens can hardly accept (but which we are also to understand as aiming at *hoti megistē prophasis . . . tou polemein*),[62] and with Pericles' speech confirming the resolve of Athens not to capitulate (140–44).[63] It leaves us poised on the brink of war (145–46) and in a position to reflect on the very different outlooks of Sparta and Athens.

The Spartans, while long accustomed to warring only under duress, refuse to acknowledge that necessity impinges on them to the extent of impairing their freedom to act with justice and piety. There is then a clear opposition between the Athenian way and the Spartan one. Sparta eschews Athenian "enlightenment," that is, sophistication in alibis: she neither offers nor accepts such alibis. While slow to act even under duress, she rejects duress as an excuse for injustice. Instead she persists in maintaining that her actions require no such excuse. She thus implicitly denies that human beings ever find themselves with their backs to the wall; denies that they are ever so deserted by the gods as to be compelled to ignore their obligations to them.

Book One proves then not to resolve but only to pose the question of who bears the blame for the war—while deepening our understanding of that question. What is surprising is that, on reflection, the case for Sparta depends on the Athenian position on the relationship between right and necessity, and the Spartan position on that issue implies the vindication of Athens. For if the traditional notion of aitia is adequate—if cities are re-

---

tainted must have remained or returned, however, for when, the Athenian tyrants having been deposed, the Spartan king Cleomenes intervened for a second time in Athenian affairs on behalf of the party of Isagoras against that of Cleisthenes, he demanded that "the accursed" (who included Cleisthenes) be driven from the city. Upon Cleomenes' withdrawal, the Athenians, treating the matter as one of faction rather than of piety, recalled Cleisthenes and the others thus expelled. Cf. Herodotus 5.70–73; Aristotle *Athenian constitution* 20.

[62] On these demands and Thucydides' reasons for minimizing their significance, see appendix 3.

[63] This speech is worth noting for the very reason that it is tangential to our theme: the cautiousness of Pericles' treatment of the issue of justice. In exhorting the Athenians to war, Pericles wholly abstracts from the necessities bearing on Sparta and indeed from the existence of the Athenian empire. (He mentions the empire only in enumerating the resources that promise a happy issue to the war.) He can thus present the Spartans as aggressors bent on stripping Athens of what is rightfully hers; he goes so far as to draw a parallel between the present situation of Athens and that at the time of the Persian Wars, thus likening Sparta to the Mede. Cf. Levi *Parola del Passato* 7 (1952) 93 and Heath *Historia* 39 (1990) 388.

sponsible for acting justly with no ifs or buts—then Sparta, as Archidamus sufficiently indicates, transgresses in refusing to pursue arbitration.

In fact, as Thucydides informs us much later, the Spartans come to attribute their setbacks in the first ten years of the war to their having been the first to infringe the treaty (7.18.2–3; cf. 4.20.3). They thus imply that justice enjoys cosmic support and that it weighs heavily upon human beings not as a necessity in the strictest sense (in which case they would be unable to flout it and could not claim merit for observing it) but as a supreme law. Yet precisely if that law is to remain supreme, one cannot plead necessity as grounds for flouting it. The Spartans, accordingly, eschew extenuations of their infractions: they either admit or deny them (cf. 1.128.1 with 1.103.1). Their natural all-too-human tendency is surely to deny them; but the experience of consequences that they have learned to regard as divine punishments suffices to persuade them entirely of a guilt (aitia) they have suspected all along. The Spartan substitute for necessity, *nomos* as sanctioned by the divine, is compatible with choice: one is not constrained in one's choice between justice and injustice; instead (as is appropriate only where a choice is free) one is held to account for it and punished or rewarded accordingly.

If, on the other hand, as the envoys insist, much more permissive standards of justice apply—precisely because the gods or nature are much less permissive than the Spartan view implies, allowing far less leeway to mortals—then Sparta is vindicated in resorting to war even against the letter of the treaty. This is not to say that Athens is thereby arraigned: it was in response to her own alleged necessities that she has driven Sparta to the brink of war. The traditional or Spartan understanding exculpates Athens; the novel or Athenian one exonerates both parties.

It would be misleading to leave Book One, however, without noting a crucial tract of ground common to the Spartan and Athenian positions. Despite the Athenian stress on, and the implicit Spartan denial of, the encroachment of necessity on the realm of justice, the Athenians we have heard at Sparta were no less determined than the Spartans themselves to subject necessity to limits. The human world as they present it remains humanly tolerable in that there is still room in it for choice and hence virtue. The claim of the envoys, again, is not that justice does not bind Athens but that Athens respects justice more than others do. While insisting that justice inevitably defers to other goods that much abridge its scope, they do not dismiss it as a sham to be practiced only as a means to these same goods. They claim that Athens at least practices justice more than these other goods require and to some small (but crucial) extent in spite of them. Hers is genuine justice, practiced for its own sake. If nature compels Athenians like others to pursue honor, safety, and profit, that on which they most pride themselves—their virtue, including their justice—distinguishes them from others. The envoys stress the long reach and strong arm of natural necessity.

Yet they are not wholly ungrateful to nature. If Athens wields empire under nature's duress, she practices justice of her own free will. For all its power natural necessity stops well short of crushing human freedom. To the strongest at least nature permits the possibility of genuine justice, which gains in nobility even as it does in difficulty and rarity. Such justice as is to be found among nations is the grace of the strong toward the weak, rooted in the grace of nature toward those who aspire to virtue. The war will provide a harsh test of this understanding.

Chapter 3

JUSTICE AS USUAL

As WE HAVE seen, the Athenian envoys at Sparta argue on their city's behalf neither that might makes right nor that there is no such thing as right, but rather that right, which is distinct from compulsion, prevails only within the limits established by it. Every city is constrained to pursue its own safety, honor, and profit to the detriment of those of other cities: only when its appetite for these is glutted to the point of empire can it reasonably (and thus justly) be expected to study justice. The evidence that the envoys adduce is concrete: the known and invariable behavior of cities. Is such the view of Thucydides himself? Does his narrative as a whole confirm it?

The present chapter considers four instances in Thucydides of alleged justice as practiced by cities other than Athens. A cynic might suggest that the grander a city's pretensions, the hollower; still, we stand to learn the most from cities that defend their justice as exemplary. We will look at three such cities—Mytilene, defending at Olympia the decision to revolt from her protector Athens (3.9–14), and Plataea and Thebes, reviewing their respective records vis-à-vis Sparta, Athens, Greece as a whole, and each other (3.53–67). In each of these cases, the city in question is defending herself before Sparta, the presumed champion and exemplar of justice as traditionally understood. Our final example, then, will be Sparta herself, the most obvious candidate for the honor of counterexample to the Athenian thesis.

JUSTICE, VIRTUE, AND THE DUTIES OF ALLIANCE: THE SPEECH OF THE MYTILENIANS AT OLYMPIA (3.9–14)

Our first instance of a foreign policy presumptively shaped by justice involves a revolted Athenian ally seeking admission to the Spartan alliance (3.9–14). The issue, as Mytilene's envoys state it, is not whether Sparta and her allies will receive her, but only whether they will respect her (9.1). Still the Spartans' confidence in the reliability of Mytilene and hence their zeal to assist her may depend in part on their respect for her. So her spokesmen, like those of Plataea and Thebes later in Book Three, find themselves compelled to justify her policy before the Spartans and their allies. They proclaim that their first topic must be justice and virtue (10.1); theirs is the only speech in all of Thucydides that proclaims these as its topic. In defending the justice of their defection they must raise the question of the role of justice in alliances generally. Theirs is the preeminent treatment in Thucydides of "alliance politics."[1]

Mytilene both urgently needs assistance and has a lot to explain. She must account not only for her recent betrayal of Athens, but also for her past loyalty; not only for "having betrayed [Athens] in danger, having been honored by her in peace," but for having remained in her good graces throughout the Fifty Years. No Athenian ally has faired better than Mytilene.[2] Though most others have revolted and been reduced to subjection, she has remained an independent ally, free of tribute and retaining her own walls and ships and even her oligarchic regime. Nor, to all appearances, has any ally of Athens acquitted itself more loyally.

Because the Mytilenian envoys find Sparta and her allies assembled at Olympia for the games, they address them in the temple there (3.14); theirs is the only speech in the work spoken in a temple. Zeus, whose greatest temple and festival this was (1.126), was the scourge of perjurors, the guarantor of oaths, including of course oaths of alliance.[3] It is therefore highly appropriate for the envoys to praise justice and virtue.

The speakers begin by addressing the issue of treason.

> Nor is [the usual contempt for defectors] unjust, provided that the rebels and those from whom they secede are alike (*isoi*) in outlook and mutual goodwill, as well as a match for each other (*antipaloi*) in preparedness and power, and where there exists no reasonable excuse (*prophasis . . . epieikēs*) for revolt. It was otherwise with ourselves and the Athenians. (3.9.2)

Granted that where there is no ground for friction in an alliance there is none for treason. In the real world, however, ought not a loyal ally honor its obligations *in spite of* the frictions that inevitably trouble any alliance? What is a loyal ally if not one that places justice before advantage, the good of the alliance before its own?

The envoys themselves proceed to stress the role of "justice and virtue." These, they say, must supply their theme, because they "seek alliance, and there can be neither firm friendship among individuals nor partnership (or community, *koinōnia*) among cities unless each takes the other to be virtuous

---

[1] The best discussion of the speech and its contradictions is Macleod *JHS* 98 (1978) 64–68, which, however, too quickly dismisses (64–65) the seriousness of the issue of justification. Romilly *ClMed* 17 (1956) 124–26 stresses the realism of the speech. Cohen *QUCC* 45 (1984) 44–45 sees a contradiction between the envoys' initial appeal to justice and a later one to interest. Heath *Historia* 39 (1990) 389 denies that the later appeal contradicts the earlier one. Gomme *HCT* 2:259–70 is useful; see also Cagnetta *RFIC* 111 (1983) 422–31 (which stresses the parallels between this speech and that of Cleon at 3.37–40) and Cogan *Human thing* 44–49.

[2] Cf. Aristotle *Athenian constitution* 24. Kagan *Archidamian war* 138 rejects the rebellion as "completely unjustified."

[3] Hesiod *Works and days* 279–85; Aristophanes *Clouds* 395–402.

and their ways are compatible otherwise" (3.10.1). All human association, private as well as public, depends on trust, and trust is above all trust in virtue. (This is the most sweeping statement in Thucydides on the role of virtue in human life.) Interpreting this formulation in the context of the speakers' earlier one, we might conclude that virtue's role in an alliance is to ground the "mutual goodwill" there mentioned.

What, then, had justice and virtue required of Mytilene? At the outset, loyalty, and Mytilene had complied. But she had subscribed to the Delian League as "the all[y] of the Greeks against the Mede, not of Athens against the Greeks." Athens soon revealed her true colors, and "from difference in outlook springs difference in conduct" (3.10.1). For nearly fifty years, however, Mytilene kept her scruples to herself. Why has she acted on them only now?

If Mytilene had reason to fear that docility would eventually lead to subjection, she had even better reason to fear that such would be her fate if she revolted. The envoys concede that Athens has treated them as equals but stress how it must have galled her to do so and so how unlikely it was that this would have continued much longer. They declare that the only sure basis of alliance is equal fear; but they then suggest that it was not fear which deterred Athens from subjecting them, but rather the convenience of possessing an ally who was nominally free while actually compliant. They admit that Mytilene had acquiesced in helping Athens reduce the other cities, until finally only a handful of free allies remained. If Athens had begun with them, the envoys claim, she would have had a harder time of it. Instead, she had feared Mytilene's navy, and Mytilene had flattered her *dēmos*, and an uneasy stalemate had prevailed. Still, Mytilene could not expect to preserve her independence very much longer, and so has revolted. For how could she trust Athens? The only basis of the alliance was mutual fear. The envoys conclude their apologia, however, by denying that Athens had feared Mytilene as much as Mytilene feared her—this by way of justifying their own decision to strike the first (allegedly preemptive) blow—thus undermining the claim that what had restrained Athens was fear.

Although the envoys proceed to congratulate themselves on the *prophaseis kai aitias*[4] they have assembled in support of their case (3.13.1), that case is confusing. Its most obvious contradiction concerns the proper role of fear in an alliance. Having presented mutual fear as the only solid basis of alliance (one wanting between them and Athens), they go on to justify their defection by claiming the alliance had rested only on mutual fear (cf. 11.1 with 12.1). Earlier, we recall, they had presented virtue and compatibility as the only solid bases of alliance; they seem to renege on that by propounding mutual fear as the basis, and then to return to it by rejecting such fear as

---

[4] Cf. our discussion of these terms in chapter 1.

insufficient or even detrimental. Here, as so often in Thucydides, to be able to account for these contradictions is to understand the speech.

When the envoys affirm that mutual fear is the key to a stable alliance, this is in the context of denying that such fear had prevailed between them and Athens (3.11.1–3). When they later deny that such fear fosters stability, that is in the context of affirming that it had prevailed between them and Athens (11.4–6, 12.1–2). Their denial that a balance of fear had prevailed between them and Athens supports the claim that they had reason to expect that Athens would move to subject them; their affirmation that such a balance had prevailed allegedly explains why she has not done so. There are problems with both these claims. The second one, that mutual deterrence had sufficed for fifty years to dissuade Athens, would suggest that such deterrence was reliable and so that the revolt had been gratuitous. Hence the envoys must finish by denying once again that the fear between the cities had been mutual (12.3–4). If, however, the imbalance had been such that Mytilene lived in constant dread of Athens, then the argument fails to account for Athenian quiescence. The envoys must both affirm and subvert their premise that five decades of Athenian good faith have rested only on mutual deterrence. They must both insist and deny that Athens has respected the independence of Mytilene no more than was absolutely necessary.

What then has restrained Athens? As seems likely, precisely Mytilene's compliance as an ally (reformulated for an oligarchic crowd at 3.11.5 as "flattery of the commons and its leaders"). Or, to state it less invidiously, Mytilene's loyalty as an ally, which loyalty Athens has repaid (as she has that of Chios and Methymna). Granted that Athens might have thought twice about attempting to subject Mytilene, given the power of the latter's fleet, there is no evidence (certainly the envoys adduce none) for thinking that Athens has thought even once about it. Loyalty aside, there was advantage for Athens in respecting Mytilene's independence (as the envoys have admitted at 11.2–3).

We know, moreover, from the speech of the envoys at Sparta, that Athens prides herself on the gentleness of her treatment of her allies (1.77). In fact, so far as Thucydides shows us, she has reduced no ally to subjecthood that has not first revolted from her (1.98–101, 114, 115–17). Mytilene, Methymna, and Chios have remained free allies. They have made no move to revolt, because Athens has made none to subject them, and she has made no move to subject them, because they have made none to revolt (or at least none of which she is aware). This sounds like a more solid and durable basis of alliance than the envoys of Mytilene are prepared to admit; there is no obvious reason why these terms should not have persisted indefinitely. Surely Athens would have made no attempt to subject Mytilene during the war, and presuming loyal service during it, there is no reason to suppose that

Athens would have done so thereafter. The envoys grasp at straws and come up empty-handed. Although they claim to have revolted in order to defend the freedom that they concede that Athens has so far respected, it very much looks as though only by revolting have they jeopardized it.

The envoys raise, in the context of alliance politics, the question addressed by the Athenian thesis of the relative weights of right and compulsion in human affairs. They begin by suggesting that the soundest alliance would rest on elements of both inclination and constraint. (Justice will figure in their speech as one aspect of the requisite inclination.) "Agreement and goodwill" would unite the partners, who would, however, be equally matched in powers and resources (3.9.2). (The opposition is striking in the Greek: allies must be "alike (*isoi*) in policy and in mutual goodwill" but also *antipaloi*, "counterparts" or "opposites.") A sound alliance would feature spontaneous concord but would not rest on it exclusively. It would rely as well on the mutual capacity of the partners to enforce the alliance and on the mutual respect so inspired. Good defenses make for good allies only where the allies are already good (i.e., compatible)—but no allies are so good as to dispense with the need for good defenses. In their second formulation (10.1) the envoys stress the necessity of a mutual perception of virtue— another aspect of the requisite inclination toward maintaining the alliance—while stopping short of presenting it as sufficient. In their third formulation (11.1) they urge again the need to tap the power of compulsion, that is, mutual deterrence; in their fourth (12.1), they note the instability of deterrence in the absence of trust based on other things.

Yet for all that the envoys stress sympathy and inclination as well as compulsion, the latter looms larger for their conception of alliance than they make clear, and perhaps than is clear to them. The function of both mutual virtue (conceived as self-restraint) and mutual preparedness (through which each party restrains the other) is to keep the parties true to each other when they are not otherwise so inclined. Virtue schools each ally to prefer the interests of the alliance to its own; fear (of some harm to itself) links its own interests to that of the alliance negatively if not positively. Surely, however, the key to the success of an alliance is that the parties are usually inclined to honor it, so that constraint to do so is superfluous.

Why conclude, however, that this affirmation of the primacy of inclination vindicates that of compulsion? Because if we search in the speech for the ground of this inclination, we will find it in subjection to constraint of yet another kind, that imposed by fear of a common enemy. For so long as Athens and Mytilene addressed themselves to the Mede, their alliance was unproblematic (3.10.2–4). And it is just this guarantee on which the envoys count to resolve the most pressing question before them, that of why Sparta can count on their loyalty whereas Athens could not. Having betrayed Athens in the moment of her greatest peril and in collusion with her worst enemy, there is no turning back for Mytilene (3.14).[5] Ironically it is the very flagrancy of her treason to Athens which insures her loyalty to Sparta. Necessity makes firm bedfellows. Fear reemerges as the only reliable basis of alliance, but it is common fear of a third party rather than a mutual fear of each other.

The Mytilenian envoys to the Spartans lack the boldness of their Athenian counterparts. They may also lack their sophistication, although this we cannot conclude with certainty. (While their speech is both more conventional and more contradictory than that of the Athenians, it is also better suited to its purpose and its audience.) The two speeches have in common that they cast a similar light on the relationship between justice and those concerns the Athenians have described as compulsory. The Mytilenians deny that they have preferred interest to justice and so marked themselves as unworthy allies. But their justification of their conduct clearly betrays that it has revolved around the fixed star of their interests. First fear of Persia and then fear of Athens had held them true to their allegiance. As the alliance was founded in nothing but these, it would be not only foolish but unjust to expect Mytilene to adhere to it once these no longer prevailed or no longer tended in favor of the alliance. Where interest is (as we would say) vital, it is, for all practical purposes, compulsory, and being compulsory it justifies.

The Mytilenians claim credit for their fidelity to Athens in the early years of the alliance, whereas their subsequent loyalty they want their listeners to ascribe to necessity. Like the Plataeans a little later in Book Three, they claim to have acted well whenever they possibly could, that is, whenever necessity left them free to do so. And in their case, just as in that of the Plataeans, the line between freedom and duress is blurred, for Mytilene was compelled to cooperate with Athens for the same reason after the Persian threat had receded as when it still remained to be repulsed. In both cases she could obtain or maintain her freedom (such as it was) only by bowing to the constraints of her situation. If freedom is compulsory for a city (in the specific sense of excusing whatever is undertaken for its sake), Mytilene has acted under duress throughout.

The Mytilenians do not raise the question of necessity in a more extended sense; they speak only of safety and freedom and blame Athens for her imperial ambitions. In this they hardly falsify the Athenian thesis, according to which the rhetoric of justice is to be expected in the mouth of the relatively weak. And in their deeds they strive not only for freedom but for as

---

[5] The sequence of oppositions in 3.14 (ἴδιον μὲν τὸν κίνδυνον τῶν σωμάτων . . . κοινὴν τὴν ὠφελίαν ἅπασι . . . κοινοτέραν τὴν βλάβην) points to the firm congruence between the particular interest of Mytilene and the presumed common one of the Greeks (or the particular one of Sparta). "Do not sacrifice us, who, having incurred *a mortal risk particular to ourselves*, by succeeding will confer *upon all a general benefit*, or, should we fail (through your not agreeing to help us), a *yet more general harm.*" Cf. 2.43.2.

much empire as is feasible for a third-rate power.[6] In fact, this thirst for empire at the expense of fellow subjects of Athens, and the necessary and proper Athenian effort to repress it are their real reasons for revolting when they do. We note this not to blame them but merely to confirm that they do not afford a counterexample to the Athenian thesis—the truth of which thesis would preclude blaming them.

PLATAEA AND THEBES

The speech of the Plataeans at the travesty of a trial to which Sparta subjects them upon their surrender to her is often regarded as the most moving in Thucydides, and the Theban rebuttal of it as the most hateful.[7] Thebes and Plataea have in common, however, that by their mutual recriminations each drives the other to present herself as a shining beacon of devotion to the common good of Greece. Thebes may not be alone in falling short of such lofty self-praise. To scrutinize the claims of the Plataeans is not to vindicate the procedure of the Spartans. It is merely to advance our question of what may reasonably be demanded of a city in the way of justice.

Devotion to the common good of Greece is not, be it noted, the standard imposed on the Plataeans by their Spartan "judges." They demand that the prisoners come forward individually to state their recent benefactions to Sparta and her allies (3.52.4). The Spartans may take it for granted that what is good for Sparta is good for all Greece, given their stated war aim of the liberation of Greece. The captured Plataeans, in any case, having acted as loyal allies of Athens, cannot possibly answer the appointed question, so, in their desperation, they beg leave to speak. Unable to plead recent services to Sparta, they plead older ones that at the same time benefited all Greece.

Readers of this heartrending speech (3.53–59) may conclude that Thucydides means it to convey an invidious or nostalgic contrast between the glory of the Persian Wars and the sordidness of the Peloponnesian.[8] The Plataeans themselves, however, while stressing their own devotion to repulsing the Mede, remind us that many other Greeks had fought on his

---

[6] Cf. their purposed union (ξυνοίκησις) of all the cities on Lesbos under their control (3.2.3), an action which Athens, with an eye to the interests of these other allies of hers as well as to her own, cannot possibly permit. See Kagan *Archidamian war* 137–38; John Wilson *Historia* 30 (1981) 158–59.

[7] Dionysius of Halicarnassus *On Thucydides* 42 (which praises the plea of the Plataeans as the finest speech in Thucydides); Huart *Réseaux* 18 (1972) 23–25 (cf. 31–34). On the speeches, see also Gomme *HCT* 2:336–55; Hogan *Phoenix* 26 (1972) 241–57; Macleod *GRBS* 18 (1977) 227–46; Cagnetta *QS* 19 (1984) 203–12; Erbse *Agora* 333–39. Macleod applies to the speeches his vast knowledge of ancient rhetoric and is particularly sensitive to the role of the issue of compulsion.

[8] Pouncey *Necessities of war* 17 (but cf. 43–53); Cagnetta *QS* 19 (1984) 206–7; Connor *Thucydides* 93–94. Cf. Cogan *Human thing* 67–68; Euben *Tragedy* 183–86.

side.[9] And even Plataea's motives may not have been quite as her spokesmen present them. Her valor was undeniable. Did she, however, display such zeal for justice as to confute the Athenian thesis?

The Plataean speakers have no choice but to stress ancient history, while only too conscious of it as such. They therefore must argue that their own conduct has not been unworthy of their fathers (3.56.4–7). They insist that they have acted toward Sparta as well as circumstances have permitted, the crucial circumstance being an alliance with Athens thrust on them by the enmity of Thebes and the refusal of Sparta to receive them: faroff Sparta had herself directed them to nearby Athens (55.1). Now long-allied with Athens and rich in benefits from her, Plataea has stuck with her through all, as befits a worthy ally. Thus is the course for which the Spartans would now extirpate Plataea of a piece with that for which they had formerly honored her above all other cities.

> It is just, then, to weigh our error [or transgression, *hamartia*] now (if error there has been) against our zeal then, and you will find that the latter excedes the former, and at a time when scarce were those Greeks who would oppose their virtue to the power of Xerxes, and when more highly praised were those who did not respond to the invasion by looking to their own interests in safety, but who freely dared the best things [i.e., those things that were best for all the Greeks?] amid dangers. To these we belonged, and none were more highly honored for it, but now we fear to be destroyed for the very same conduct, having cleaved justly to Athens rather than gainfully to you. (3.56.5–6)

Like Sparta in posing the question of war in terms of Athenian injustice, Plataea presents herself as having chosen freely to act as she has. Such constraints as she pleads are largely those of virtue itself. She has never put her safety or interests first, but always her duty; if she seems not to have done her duty to Greece or to Sparta in the present war, that is only because her duty to Athens supervened. And if Athens went astray and the Plataeans with her, the fault is hers not theirs (3.55.4). Plataea acts well on her own, badly only at the instigation of Athens—and even then only so as to do her duty or act well.

The Thebans, predictably, deny this of Plataea—while asserting it of Thebes. The aim of their speech, as they make clear (3.61.1), is to assault Plataea's good reputation and to defend their own bad one. It is Thebes, not Plataea, which has always acted nobly when free to do so. For she was not herself when she medized (being the captive of a narrow oligarchy, as opposed to the broader one that has ruled her since), and ever since has

---

[9] Besides the numerous cities in Boeotia and Thessaly that medized, the Corcyreans and the Cretans remained aloof, as did Argos, the greatest land power after Sparta, and Gelon the powerful tyrant of Syracuse. Cf. Herodotus 7.147–72.

demonstrated her devotion to the common good of Greece by her zeal against those who have "atticized," Plataea foremost among them.

> Our differences with them first arose when we had settled Plataea. . . . These fellows not deigning to be guided by us, as had been first set down, but seceding from the rest of the Boeotians and renouncing the ancestral ways, we applied compulsion, and they betook themselves to the Athenians, with whom they did us much harm, for which we retaliated.
>
> Next, when the barbarian invaded Greece, they say that they were the only Boeotians who did not medize. . . . We say that if they did not medize, it was because the Athenians did not do so either, just as afterwards by the same token when the Athenians attacked the Greeks, [the Plataeans] were again the only Boeotians who atticized. . . . (3.61.2–62.1)
>
> . . . Thus did you [Plataeans] plainly show that not even then was it for the sake of the Greeks [as a whole] that you alone did not medize, but because the Athenians did not do so either, and you wished to act as they did and contrarily to the rest [of us]. And you now presume (of all things!) to claim credit for having been brave men at the behest of others. Not likely! You chose the Athenians, and you must stand or fall (*xynagōnizesthe*) with them (64.1– 2). . . . Of our unwilling medism and your willing atticism this then is our explanation (64.5).[10]

The Thebans deny Plataea's claim to special virtue even for its obstinacy in opposing the Mede. They link what the Plataeans have kept separate, its alliance with Athens and its subsequent refusal to medize. The Plataeans, understandably enough, began by stressing the latter before proceeding to extenuate the former; readers lacking a firm grasp of the sequence of events may conclude that the Athenian connection postdates the Persian Wars. The Thebans remind us that it does not. They concede that the Plataean decision not to medize was freely taken—but freely taken to please Athens. Plataea's devotion to Greece was spurious, her enmity to the Mede incidental. And she had been or should have been free at that time not to please Athens, for she need never have strayed from the loving care of Thebes. As for her fidelity to Athens in the decades since, and consequent complicity in her empire, that too has been gratuitous. Even granting her some right to defend herself from Thebes, she cannot plead this as her excuse, for she could have looked elsewhere than to Athens: namely, to Sparta, relying on

---

[10] Cogan *Human thing* 69–73, followed by Euben *Tragedy* 184–85, interprets the Theban coinage of "atticism" as a counterpart of medism as signaling a new "ideological" stage of the war. I would take it as no more than an ad hoc rhetorical expedient. By stressing their zeal in opposing "atticism," the Thebans seek to mitigate the ignominy of their flagrant medism, while reminding Sparta of their usefulness in the present war. It is mainly with an eye to this usefulness that the Spartans render their decision (3.68.4); even in their deliberations as to the justice or injustice of Plataea, no considerations of "atticism" figure (68.1).

the Spartan oath of 479—following the battle at Plataea in which she had so distinguished herself against the Mede and his Theban ally—which guaranteed her autonomy (3.63.2). And of course she could and should have accepted the Spartan offer of neutrality (64.3).

The Thebans agree, then, that Plataea has acted freely, not under constraint. Indeed they go further in asserting this than the Plataeans themselves have done. To the claim that Plataea has acted freely and well, the Thebans retort that she has acted freely (i.e., gratuitously) and badly. As Plataea does not wish to diminish her reputation for glorious deeds freely undertaken against the Mede but to assimilate to it her subsequent loyalty to Athens, so the Thebans wish to tar the former with the latter. Each party has its reasons for minimizing the role of compulsion in Plataean affairs.

No one would mistake the Theban position for the Athenian thesis. Accepting (with the Plataeans) the conventional view that cities are free to act well and that those who do are to be praised while those who do not must be punished, they insist that Thebes has acted well and Plataea badly. They acknowledge (again with the Plataeans) that cities are sometimes subject to compulsion: this the Thebans invoke wherever handy as an alibi for themselves while denying it to their enemies. So they argue that Plataea has always acted to please Athens (or, by extension, to spite Thebes) without ever having been compelled to do either. They deny both the claim of the Plataeans to have acted justly and that these had ever been subject to a compulsion to act otherwise. Indeed they argue (it might seem, bizarrely) that there had never been any advantage to Plataea in acting unjustly (except, presumably, the pleasure of spiting Thebes). They concede Plataea a reasonable motive neither for seceding from Thebes nor for maintaining her alliance with Athens nor (in the end) even for repelling the recent Theban attempt to seize her in the dead of night (for in this too Thebes had acted only for the good of Plataea and as it were at her invitation [3.65–66.1]).

It is possible, and for our purposes necessary, to conceive of a sort of debunking of Plataea different from that propounded by Thebes. Yes, Plataea fought zealously against the Mede, defending the liberties of Greece, and yes, she has acquiesced in the Athenian empire, thus offending these same liberties. But what unites the two cases is neither, as the Plataeans claim, that both display her exemplary justice nor, as the Thebans claim, that both exhibit her malice. Plataea's consistency was of a different sort. She aimed throughout at certain goods to herself: independence from Thebes at the outset, protection from Theban retaliation thereafter. In order to keep Thebes at bay, Plataea had no choice but to stand by Athens; why doubt that her zeal in 480 B.C. was partly or even mostly directed against Thebes? While Plataea speaks as if self-interest had dictated submission at that time (3.56.5), what more could she have expected from that than servitude to the King's Theban creatures? So, too, she had little choice thereafter but to honor the terms of her alliance with Athens: Athens was not about to release her from them, and she still needed protection from Thebes. The suggestion of the Theban speakers that Plataea should have refused to fulfill her obligations to Athens—in effect, should have revolted—and turned to Sparta for protection is ludicrous. While Sparta remained on good terms with Athens she would hardly have intervened against her far from home, on behalf of a revolted ally, and with nothing to gain but her enmity; indeed the thirty years' treaty had bound each great power not to support revolts from the other (1.66). Once on bad terms with Athens and hungry for the support of Thebes, Sparta would hardly have intervened to prevent Thebes from reclaiming an errant client. Under such circumstances, a Plataean revolt from Athens would indeed have displayed devotion to the liberties of Greece. It would also have been quite mad. Most recently the men of Plataea have found themselves unfree to accept the Spartan proposal of evacuation for the duration of the war and return of their city to them at its conclusion (2.72–73); their wives and children were at Athens.[11]

Tiny Plataea has struggled for a century to achieve and maintain as much independence and security as is compatible with her location on the border between Boeotia and Attica. She has had no choice, having repudiated the protection of one power, but to accept such terms as she could obtain from the other. To this extent the Thebans are right: the fixed star of Plataea's policy has been her refusal to submit to the "ancestral ways of the Boeotians," as the Thebans grandly style their hegemony (3.61.2; cf. 65.2). Like all cities known to the Athenian speakers at Sparta, Plataea appears to have acted primarily to secure her own good. This is not to say that she has not run risks, or otherwise demonstrated virtue, but only that the risks that she has run have been for her own sake, no one else's. It is to question her claim to have served as a beacon of disinterested justice, where this is conceived as devotion to the common good of Greece.

Yet the Theban claim to serve the cause of Greece is equally hollow. Whereas tiny Plataea has hoped for no more than to avoid being ruled, Thebes has aspired to rule. In fact, one concern seems to have animated Theban policy under whatever regime: enmity toward Plataea and her protector Athens. (Might Thebes have medized for just this reason?) Not that we could blame her is she had. If the Athenians speak truly, it is as natural for Thebes to covet Plataea as for Plataea to cherish her freedom from Thebes.

We confront here a typical example of political justice as debunked by the Athenian thesis, in that all parties act so as to confirm the thesis and the strong punish the weak for doing so. The parties are not black and white but more or less equally gray. Still, the Plataeans, abandoned by Athens and delivered by Sparta to the hatred of Thebes, enjoy "the innocence of all

---

[11] Nor would they have been wise to accept this offer: given the Spartans' abject zeal to gratify Thebes, it is not credible that Plataea, once in Spartan hands, would ever have reverted to the Plataeans. Cf. Huart *Réseaux* 18 (1972) 33.

victims."[12] That they cannot prove themselves much more just than the Thebans leaves the latter no less odious in their hypocrisy.

THE JUSTICE OF SPARTA AND THE ATHENIAN THESIS

Of the possible counterexamples to the Athenian thesis, the most imposing is Sparta—a city so indifferent to empire that she had readily abandoned to the Athenians her place at the head of the Panhellenic alliance against the Mede (1.95.6–7); a city whose most conspicuous vice is not an itch for expansion but an excessive craving for tranquility (1.68–71); a city whose stated war aim is the liberation of Greece (1.139.3; 2.8.4–5; cf. 4.85–87, 121.1); a city that holds, in other words, to the notion of a common good of Greece consisting of the equal autonomy of each Hellenic city.[13] Oppressed or menaced by the rampant imperialism of Athens, it is to Sparta that the other cities turn. They chide her not for imperialism but for what we would call her "isolationism": a reluctance to assert herself in foreign affairs even when her own vital interests demand it.

The Corinthian envoys at Sparta concede that Spartan habits are superior to Athenian ones for domestic purposes: "for cities at rest, unchanged ways are best" (1.71.3). They remark on the trust or confidence which is the hallmark of Spartan life (1.68.1); this emerges from the speech of Archidamus as trust in the regime itself and in that education to civic virtue on which it rests (1.84; 2.87; 4.126.2; 5.72.2–4). Sparta generally discloses herself as more concerned than Athens to habituate her citizens to virtue: Pericles claims in the Funeral Oration that such drudgery would be superfluous at Athens, where the surpassing virtue of the citizens is the spontaneous fruit of noble emulation (2.39). Even the "isolationism" of the Spartans reflects their concern for civic virtue: we recall that they decided not to press their claim to co-hegemony over the Panhellenic alliance for fear that "those whom they sent out might become worse as Pausanias had" (1.95.7). Sparta wisely places domestic concerns ahead of foreign ones; Spartans resemble the only Athenians whom Thucydides ever calls "moderate," those who preferred a defeat that would undo the demagogue Cleon to a victory that would assure his continued predominance (4.28.5).

Nor is Sparta's concern with the virtue of her citizens in vain: as even Athenians must admit, the Spartans "practice virtue in the highest degree among themselves and where the laws of their country are concerned" (5.105.4). Their self-discipline is remarkable (4.39; 5.70) as are their obedience to law (5.60.2; cf. with 5.60.5–6) and their sense of martial honor (2.92.3; 4.40.2; 5.34). At the climax of the battle of Mantineia, where poor leadership has led Sparta to the brink of disaster, the courage of her ordinary

---

[12] Pouncey *Necessities of war* 18.

[13] Strasburger *Hermes* 86 (1958) 17–40 goes so far as to argue that Thucydides' work is decidedly pro-Spartan.

soldiers salvages victory where any other army would have broken and fled (5.72; cf. 5.75.3).

Related to the civic virtue of Sparta is a deep sense of civic solidarity. In marked contrast to Athens, which prides herself on a willingness to expend rivers of Athenian blood (2.64.3), Sparta seeks always to minimize her losses. In order to rescue three hundred of her citizens threatened with capture by Athens, she is apparently willing to end the war on very unfavorable terms (4.15–22). When the offer is rejected, she prefers the safety of these men to the maintenance of her proud reputation, permitting them to surrender rather than requiring them to fight to the death (4.38, 40). Thereafter the hope of retrieving them continues to animate her entire war effort (4.41, 108.5, 117.2; 5.15.1). There is no Spartan parallel to the orgy of distrust and persecution that erupts at Athens after the affair of the Herms and that culminates in the execution of many of the best citizens (6.27–29, 53–61).[14] Nor is there a Spartan parallel to the *stasis* (civil strife) into which Athens eventually plunges (8.47–98).

Outside Peloponnese, Sparta not only lacks aspirations to hegemony, but, once stirred to action, captains the struggle for freedom against Athenian imperialism. Her ultimatum to Athens on the eve of the war is that she leave the Greek cities free, and this becomes Sparta's battle cry (1.139.3; 2.8.4). Accordingly, almost all of the Greeks incline to her cause. Her greatest effort in this direction is the daring expedition of Brasidas to the Athenian subjects in the Thraceward regions. This evokes the warmest enthusiasm among those to whom it is sent. Only in the name of the liberty of Greece do the Spartans feel justified in exerting compulsion on the unwilling (4.85–87). During the later Ionian campaign, Lichas, although not averse to reasonable accommodation to Sparta's Persian allies (8.84.5), balks at conceding the King a right to rule Greek cities (8.43.3–4, 52).

Even so, some readers may hesitate at recognizing the justice of Sparta. There is no denying that she perceives herself as just and finds imperialism uncongenial or that many cities hope that she will live up to her great reputation. The question is whether Sparta is indifferent to empire out of justice or for another reason more compatible with the Athenian thesis. For that thesis states, again, not that no society has ever abstained from empire but only that none has done so out of justice when honor, safety, and profit beckoned.

There seems no greater blot on Spartan justice than her butchery of the defeated Plataeans. We recall that these last, besieged and facing starvation, surrender their city "voluntarily"—a bizarre legal fiction concocted by the

---

[14] Contrast also the Spartan treatment of Pausanias with the Athenian treatment of Themistocles (1.128–38). Athens moves with disgraceful haste against her greatest benefactor, condemning him in absentia at the mere imputation of his Spartan enemies. The Spartans accord Pausanias, of whose treason they possess manifest evidence, a degree of due process so scrupulous as to be comical.

Spartans lest an eventual settlement require the return of cities taken by force (3.52.2; cf. 5.17.2). In return the Spartans promise them a trial before Spartan judges—that is, they apparently undertake not to hand them over to the vengeance of the Thebans. These "judges," as we have seen, propose to question each captive as follows: "What have you done to help Sparta or her allies in the current war?" As the Plataeans, having acted as loyal allies of Athens, cannot possibly hope to answer this question successfully,[15] they ask leave to deliver the speech we have already discussed. As we have seen, the Thebans present, fearing that this speech might have moved the Spartans to abandon their original procedure, ask to deliver their own in reply. Either this reply is highly effective, or the fears that evoked it were misplaced. The "judges" have no trouble deciding that the proposed question is fair, which means that asking it must prove a mere formality.

Sparta has promised the captives a trial, which implies a determination of justice. In a capital case one would expect the judges to sift all relevant evidence. These "judges" evidently take a narrow view of what evidence is relevant. They simply ignore the matters at issue between Plataea and Thebes, as between Plataea and the rest of Greece. As they do not absolve Plataea because the enmity of Thebes has compelled her to remain loyal to Athens, so they do not condemn her for her alleged injustice to Thebes or even for her alleged "atticism" or treason to the liberty of Greece. They consider only her relations with Sparta herself (as well as with Sparta's allies considered only as allies) and these relations only since the outbreak of the war. Not presuming to pass judgment on Plataea's obligations to Greece as a whole, to Athens, or even to Thebes, these "judges" scrupulously limit themselves to deciding in their own case.

The judges can find no excuse for Plataea's failure to renege on her alliance with Athens. They reason that having from the very beginning invited the Plataeans to defect (and having even offered them neutrality), they are discharged of the obligation to respect their autonomy dating from the long-ago oath of Pausanias (3.68.1; cf. 2.71–74).[16] The question put to the captives is therefore reasonable. Such is the extent of the Spartans' deliberations. They acknowledge the obligatoriness of their sworn oaths; in this they are men of honor. Like so many legalists, however, they apply the law loosely to themselves and strictly to others. While they raise the possibility that Plataea has acted from constraint in remaining true to Athens, they overlook that such has in fact been the case.

---

[15] They cannot unless, of course, they were to point out that they have willingly and without duress abandoned Athens for Sparta, the very fiction that the Spartans have foisted on them. But Sparta will have it both ways: the "voluntary" adhesion of Plataea is to be alleged later, when it will suit the advantage of Sparta, as it here suits her advantage to ignore it.

[16] The Spartan decision here thus presupposes the handwashing of the pious Archidamus at 2.74. Cf. Cagnetta *QS* 19 (1984) 208–9.

Most instructive for us, however, is that not one of the "judges" questions the justice of the demand put to the Plataeans. They deliberate only as to whether the Plataeans had enjoyed sufficient opportunity to comply with this demand. "What have you done for Sparta lately?" is an appropriate question for mother Sparta to put to her own children, but not to outsiders who are not even allies of hers. To ask it is to treat foreigners as if they were citizens of Sparta,[17] which is not to say that it is to treat them well.

Upon the failure of their captives to answer the question, the Spartans butcher them and wipe their city from the face of the earth. In the words of the same Athenians who praise the Spartans for their virtue among themselves, "of their conduct toward others much might be said, but one could not summarize it more clearly than this: that more than any others whom we know they treat the agreeable as noble and the advantageous as just" (5.105.4). We can now see that this contrast between their conduct among themselves and toward others is only apparent: the standard is the same in both cases. Sparta erects her own good as the universal principle of justice, binding on all alike, on non-Spartans no less than on Spartans.

From the ruins of Plataea the Spartans build a temple to Hera (3.68.3), an example of their piety. Having earlier related the reasoning of the Spartan "judges" we have just discussed, Thucydides now discloses their chief motivation in this affair and in all their dealings with Plataea, namely, a desire to gratify the Thebans, whose support was deemed useful in the war then raging (68.4). "Chief," however, is not "only," and we need not doubt the sincerity of the "judges'" conclusion that the question put to the Plataeans was just. These "judges" are judges at least in this: they have not discussed whether extinguishing Plataea would be useful, but only whether it would be just.[18] Yet, as we have seen, the implicit charge against the Plataeans is neglect of the interests of Sparta. It is not then surprising that the Spartans pander to Theban vindictiveness without recognizing that they are preferring the expedient to the just. Long habituated to act as their interests seem to require, they do so as smugly as if meting out impeccable justice.[19]

The fact remains that Sparta abjured the hegemony from which grew the subsequent Athenian empire and habitually exerts herself (as the Corinthians at Sparta suggest) only defensively, tardily, and fitfully. Far from expanding to the limits of her considerable power, she devotes herself (again as the

---

[17] I am indebted for this point to Harvey C. Mansfield, Jr.

[18] Strauss *City and man* 215. Heath *Historia* 39 (1990) 390–91 complains that Thucydides describes the Spartans as having rendered their verdict on "a judgment of self-interest," "mak(ing) no effort to reconcile this assessment . . . with his report of their deliberations."

[19] Euben *Tragedy* 184–85 correctly notes that despite her claims Sparta here acts according to expediency and hence, in a sense, after the manner of Athens. To describe this as "corruption," however, is to imply that Sparta has previously acted otherwise. This nostalgia finds no support in Thucydides; the Athenians, at 5.105.3–4, in enlightening the Melians about the principles of Spartan conduct, are not describing a recent lapse from impeccability.

Corinthians observe) to preserving what she already enjoys. She thus continues to pose a challenge to the Athenian thesis.

Like all facts, that of Spartan abstinence from empire requires interpretation. Just as wary investors are not as such more just than bold ones, so Sparta might not prove more just than Athens. Let us examine what appears the most just and most daring of Sparta's ventures, Brasidas' Thracian campaign.

Of all of Thucydides' Spartans, Brasidas is the most resplendent. In the first years of the war, he alone has distinguished himself, acting usually on his own initiative (2.25.1–2; 3.79.3; 4.11–12, 70–73); he has never been entrusted with an important command. In the eighth year, there finally beckons a project worthy of his capacities: to strike at what he rightly perceives as the Achilles' heel of the Athenian empire. This is the cluster of allied cities in the Thraceward regions, which are coastal (and hence within the Athenian sphere) but also accessible by a daring march overland (4.78). He is the first Spartan commander to act on the slogan of the liberation of Greece, to the point of treating Athenian allies (even loyal ones, and even, at Amphipolis, Athenian citizens) as unwilling subjects to be liberated rather than as enemies to be butchered (4.105.2, 114, 120.3–4; cf. 2.67.4, 3.32.1). He alone succeeds in fostering in these subjects a firm trust not only in himself, but in Sparta. Thucydides praises him not once but three times. "[By] showing himself just and measured toward the cities, he induced most of them to revolt . . ." (4.81.1). (No other character is explicitly praised for his justice.) "The virtue and intelligence of Brasidas . . . was what mainly inspired in the allies of Athens a longing for the Spartans. . . . For he, being the first to go out and gain repute as a man virtuous [*agathos*] in all respects, left behind a confident hope that the others were so as well" (81.2). Finally, at 4.108.2, Thucydides alludes, as he has at 4.81, to the "measuredness" of Brasidas' conduct toward the cities whose revolt he induced as well as to his gentleness (*praotēs*) toward them.

This is high praise. Is it qualified by the emphasis in each case on the impression that Brasidas left and its usefulness to Sparta? Does Thucydides entirely share the perspective of these allies? Might he lean toward the view of the Spartan peace party that Brasidas was zealous for war not for love of justice but for love of honor (5.16.1)? This question of justice proves complicated. Brasidas appears just above all in his assurances that Sparta intends no subjection of the cities that defect to him, as well as no imposition of oligarchic regimes (4.86.2–4; cf. 1.19),[20] and in his mildness toward even those Athenian subjects who have demonstrated a decided loyalty to

---

[20] Cf., however, the fate of Megara (a city previously rescued by Brasidas from the clutches of Athens), which is no sooner within the sphere of Sparta than it undergoes a bloody purge and the installation of a narrow oligarchy, "which lasted for a very long time although arising from the στάσις of a very few men." Cf. Connor *Thucydides* 132–33.

Athens. At 4.108, where Thucydides notes Brasidas' "measuredness," thus recalling 4.81, he does not now speak of his justice, mentioning instead his gentleness. He also notes for the first time that Brasidas' assurances that his forces were sufficient to protect these cities were "seductive but untrue." There follows a strong indictment of the folly of those cities seduced by him.

The question for us is not Brasidas' intentions but those of Sparta, to which his must remain subordinate, perhaps despite his hopes to the contrary. He himself admits, in the course of his masterful speech at Acanthus, that ultimately the Acanthians must look for their safety not to his personal assurances nor even to the "strongest oaths" by which he has bound the Spartan magistrates, but to the exigencies incumbent on the Spartan regime (4.87.1). His statement of these exigencies, while perhaps persuasive to his audience (who must also mull his threat to ravage their lands just before the harvest), is open to an obvious objection. The chief incentive for Sparta to treat Acanthus well if she revolts from Athens is the prospect of inducing other such allies to revolt as well. Sparta's hopes of turning the tide of the war depend heavily on this strategy. This implies, however, that should Sparta emerge victorious, she will thereby have outgrown the only dependable constraint on her treatment of these cities. In any case, Sparta (perhaps unlike Brasidas) does not aspire to total victory but is war weary and longs for nothing more than recovering the prisoners held by Athens. Revolted allies are to her so many bargaining chips to be returned to Athens to obtain a settlement (4.81.1, 117).[21]

The guarantees that Brasidas offers are therefore misleading. It is true neither that the forces at his disposal suffice to protect the revolted cities from Athenian recapture and reprisal (4.122–23, 129–31; 5.2–3, 6 [Galepsus]) nor that Sparta intends to shield them for long. Brasidas' ambitions may excede those of Sparta. He may well intend a vast extension of her influence, through a new confederacy of former Athenian allies, as much Brasidean as Spartan. Undeterred by the armistice obtained through his dazzling successes, he presses onward, hindering peace now rather than furthering it (4.122–23, 135). He and Sparta are on a collision course (4.108.5), and at the peak of his triumphs she resorts to unprecedented means to curb his authority in the towns he has liberated (132.3).[22] His glorious death is promptly succeeded by a settlement (5.12–20). It specifies the return of all the towns not yet retaken, albeit with face-saving conditions that Sparta lacks the power to enforce (5.18.5; cf. 18.8). She instructs Clearidas, her commander at Amphipolis, to return the city to Athens

---

[21] Cf. Brunt *Phoenix* 19 (1965) 275–77.

[22] For a balanced treatment of the ambiguities of Thucydides' presentation of Brasidas, see Connor *Thucydides* 130–40, 236.

(5.21). He declines, and despite the withdrawal of his Spartan force Amphipolis manages to hold out. Thereafter, the Spartans (having in fact disengaged from the region) plead their inability to fulfill the terms of the treaty by compelling the revolted cities to surrender (5.35). These cities thus fare better than might have been expected, not because Sparta is firm in defending them but because she stumbles in betraying them. As for most of the rest of her allies, they are so unhappy with the treaty that they promptly begin to intrigue against both it and Sparta (5.17, 22, 25, 27 ff.).

The discrepancy between the interests of Sparta and the liberties of Greece is even clearer in an earlier instance in which Sparta seeks a settlement of her conflict with Athens. In a vain effort to forestall the capture at Pylos of the three hundred men whose retrieval will dominate her concerns thereafter, she sends envoys to Athens (4.15–16). This lone Spartan speech at Athens (17–20) offers a counterpart to the lone Athenian one at Sparta. It too aims at peace, it too is a failure, and it too reveals a great deal about the character of both speakers and audience.

The speakers declare that they must reconcile the interests of Athens with the honor (*kosmon*, "credit" or "face") of Sparta (4.17.1). Their reference to the unaccustomed necessity (for Spartans) of speaking at length suggests that this will not be easy. (Is a long speech necessary primarily to save Spartan face?) They at first suggest that the recent successes of Athens are due to fortune: cities experienced in war should know to trust their prosperity least, and so to quit while they are ahead. They appeal, as did the Athenians at Sparta, to what the two cities have in common: in this case, experience of vicissitudes. To be convinced, they say, just look at us (18.1). Who stood higher than us? Yet now we have been brought low, by errors of judgment to which all are equally liable.

> And so it would not be reasonable (*ouk eikos*) for you to conclude from the present strength of your city and its recent successes that fortune will always be with you. They are moderate men who act so as to secure their advantages in the face of a doubtful future—just as they would also deal more clear-headedly (*euxunetōteron an prospheroionto*) with adversity—and as to war are aware that it will not remain within the limits to which one would confine it, but that it drags on and on, and follows where its chances lead it. And so such men . . . will soonest make peace while luck is with them. (4.18.4)

It follows from this argument that Athens would be wise to accept Sparta's surrender. But is Sparta wise to offer it? The Spartan speech is exposed to this powerful objection: if the prosperity of Athens is so precarious, Sparta ought not surrender so abjectly to adversity. Compared to the Athenians in 480 B.C., fighting on after having already lost their city, or to the British or Free French in 1940, Sparta appears pusillanimous indeed. At

4.18.5, the envoys grudgingly concede that the success of Athens owes something to virtue—but from this, too, they conclude that Athens ought not brave the fickleness of fortune.

The Spartans offer Athens not only a treaty but an alliance (4.19). The only condition is the return of the men on the island. Sparta prefers not to hold out to the end, that is, until the actual capture of their men at Pylos, but if they are willing to make a peace so favorable to Athens now, what might they not offer once the men have in fact been captured?

At 4.20, the envoys allude to the broader Greek context. They claim that by ending the war the two cities would gratify both themselves and the other Greeks, who do not know whom to blame for the war but who would have Athens to thank for the peace. But will the cities thank Athens for this peace resulting from Sparta's capitulation? And just how thankful will those Greeks be who went to war looking to Sparta to bring down the Athenian empire? At 20.4, the envoys suggest that the two great powers once reconciled will easily keep the rest in line; that is, Sparta looks to Athens to help keep down Sparta's soon to be disgruntled allies.[23]

Sparta, her strength otherwise unimpaired, offers to betray both her allies and her own best interests simply in order to avoid the possibility of the loss of three hundred citizens. Without having lost a major battle she is willing to concede the war. Fortunately for herself, however, Sparta has misjudged the Athenians. She imagines them war-weary like herself. Instead she finds them regarding her (as her speech has unwittingly encouraged them to do) with the eye of a hawk that can pounce on its prey whenever it pleases. The envoys succumb to Cleon who, anxious to prevent an agreement, demands terms so onerous that they cannot possibly accept them outright and on the spot (4.21). Not only must Sparta surrender, pending a final agreement, the very men besieged at Pylos whom she has come to Athens to save, but she must agree to revise the old thirty years' peace to give Athens a commanding position around Peloponnese. Sparta is thus asked to concede everything that she has been fighting to prevent, including strategic encirclement. The envoys do not reject even this (22.1). They merely ask to discuss it in private. Cleon then offers his Woodrow Wilson impersonation: if the Spartans were honest, they would submit to open covenants openly arrived at. This sabotages the settlement. Sparta might have betrayed her allies, but cannot offer publicly to do so in negotiations that might miscarry (22.3).[24]

[23] Cf. Connor *Thucydides* 112 n.10.

[24] Kagan *Archidamian war* 231–37 defends the Athenians' rejection of the Spartan proposals and their demand for territorial concessions rather than a mere return to the insecure status quo ante. With his usual firmness, he even defends the Athenian refusal to explore the Spartan willingness to negotiate concessions, insisting that such negotiations could not have succeeded. My differences with Kagan depend on my analysis of the Spartan speech as abject in tone, as well as on Thucydides' suggestion that the envoys were willing to contemplate serious

The liberation of Greece is effectively a slogan for advancing the interests of Sparta. Her understanding of those interests, however, is "conservative" rather than expansive. Spartan "justice" seems to be most accurately praised as an almost singular moderation in prosperity (8.24.4). She does not risk the good that she enjoys for the sake of possibly illusory ones (1.70). Above all she keeps to the regime and the laws on which her success has so long depended—a reasonable policy for a city that has enjoyed such long success (1.18.1, 83–84; cf. 5.66.2–4, 69.2, 70).[25]

If not Spartan justice, can we say that Spartan moderation subsists in defiance of the Athenian envoys' alleged compulsions? This too seems questionable. Thucydides discloses the iron anchor of Spartan caution in explaining the most striking departure from it: the decision to send Brasidas to Thrace (4.79–80). Brasidas is eager; Sparta, however, submits to his scheme only under the utmost duress. Beleaguered and reeling after defeats at Pylos, Cythera, and elsewhere, Sparta strikes back at Athens however she can. Above all she seeks an excuse to send out an army of Helots as far from Sparta as possible, for fear that in the present crisis these will revolt, as they have done in past ones. While Thucydides ascribes the grandest of Athenian projects to eros (6.24), this most ambitious of Spartan ones is rather a case of excretion.

In this context Thucydides relates a Spartan atrocity (4.80). It proves to be a bizarre parody of the Plataean affair. At some unspecified time, the Spartans invited those Helots "who ha[d] most distinguished themselves in the city's wars" to step forward to claim their emancipation. "As many as two thousand were selected accordingly, who crowned themselves and went round the temples, rejoicing in their new freedom." The Spartans soon afterwards secretly slew them, "so that no one ever knew how each of them perished." This deed at first appears as senseless as it is shocking. Rather than kill foreigners for failing to meet the standard rightly expected of citizens, the Spartans here kill their Helots for having succeeded in meeting it. Helots are and are not outsiders; peculiar to Sparta and essential to it, the regime looks to them even for soldiers while otherwise utterly excluding them. "Fear of their numbers and obstinacy" informed Spartan policy here,

---

concessions. I agree with Cawkwell *YCS* 24 (1975) 58–59, 65 that the peace mission represented a complete betrayal of Sparta's allies, and so precisely the outcome of the war that Pericles had originally intended. The question is whether that outcome would have sufficed; Kagan argues not. Connor *Thucydides* 112 n.10 is similarly skeptical. Gomme *HCT* ad loc. (3:460) and Strauss *City and man* 220–21 go still further by denying that Thucydides regards Cleon's position as mistaken. Fortunately the issue here is merely the character of Sparta.

[25] J. H. Finley *Thucydides* 132 is thus wrong to condemn Archidamus' speech at 1.80–85 for "its scorn of reason"; Archidamus' point is that for Sparta to stick to its old ways is reasonable (as is the education that teaches those ways). Cf. Thucydides' "reasonable" explanation, at 5.70, of a Spartan practice the reader might otherwise ascribe to piety.

"as it was thought that the first to claim their freedom would be the most spirited and the most likely to rebel." The Spartans both need and must fear "the numbers and obstinacy" of their Helots; Spartan and Helot are locked in a deadly embrace.[26]

In relating this incident Thucydides remarks that "the greater part of the Spartans' institutions have always been with an eye to precautions against [the Helots]." Sparta tosses on stormy seas; her lifeboat is her disciplined and stable regime. Spartans are not introspective; all the more striking, then, is a certain remark of Brasidas. Finding himself in as tight a spot as any in the war, deserted by his Macedonian allies and charged by a host of screaming barbarians, he exhorts his men that superior numbers should not daunt "those who come from regimes in which the many do not rule the few, but the few the many, having acquired dominion in no other way than by prevailing in battle" (4.126.2). (Amazingly, Brasidas delivers this speech to an army composed in good part of Helots.)[27] Sparta's school for her wars without is the war that simmers within. The creation of the common, that masterpiece of Spartan policy (1.6.4–6), appears in a new light if considered as a response to a common [internal] enemy, as does her contrivance of "good laws" to control faction and suppress tyranny (1.18.1).

It is not surprising that the justice of Spartans consists in a single-minded devotion to what is advantageous to Sparta. Just as they strive never to fall short of this standard, so they can hardly ever see beyond it. Thucydides' narrative confirms the assertion of the Athenian envoys on Melos: the Spartans interpret what is advantageous to them as just (5.105.4). To this, however, it must be added that they hold injustice to be disadvantageous to them. This second aspect of their outlook clearly implies some standard of justice other then the path of momentary least resistance. That standard appears to be now the common good of Greece and now (and much more seriously) those obligations Sparta has undertaken under oath. Sparta is reluctant to break the Thirty Years' Treaty or violate Pausanias' fifty-year-old guarantee of the autonomy of Plataea. (The decent Archidamus is particularly reluctant in both these cases.) More broadly (for there is reason to conclude that for the Spartans, as for their colonists the Melians, injustice is shunned as a type of impiety; cf. 5.104), Sparta hesitates to act in any matter contrary to the will of the gods. In case after case, for example, the Spartans refuse to stir militarily when the omens are against them, even when every

---

[26] On the Spartan dependency on the Helots, note the assertion of Herodotus 9.28–29 that *seven times as many* Helots as Spartiates (citizens) were deployed against the Mede at Plataea and that although light troops, they were all well armed.

[27] I am assuming that "the Peloponnesians whom [Brasidas] still had with him" (4.124.1) included the seven hundred Helots who had first departed with him from Sparta (4.78.1; 80.5).

strategic or political consideration cries out for them to proceed (5.54.2, 55.3, 82.3, 116.1; 6.95.1).[28]

How then is Sparta able to reconcile a tendency to identify the just as what is agreeable to Sparta with a clear perception of the just as distinct from, and a constraint upon, the agreeable? Only through an artful or artless hypocrisy. When Sparta must act (i.e., when even she can see that she must act) she acts as she must—yet without asserting that necessity justifies injustice or impiety. She claims to resort to the necessary only where the deed would have been just even had it not been necessary. Having been stirred to act, she is only too ready, as at Plataea, to regard as just whatever conduces to the success of her action. She is also only too ready, however, to interpret any setback as divine chastisement for injustice or impiety (1.128.1; 7.18.3; above, pp. 56–62). She is chronically slow to act even where action is required, apparently hampered by vague forebodings or premonitions of such chastisement. Dwelling as a garrison in their own city, the Spartans know better than anyone that the gods exact a price even for successful expansion.

Sparta stands as a counterexample to the Athenian thesis only for so long as we overlook her "internal" empire. While praising her for her unequaled moderation in prosperity, Thucydides implicitly relates this moderation to the problem of the Helots (cf. 8.24.4 with 40.2), that is, to the worm that gnaws her amidst her prosperity. Spartan aversion to expansion (like her cultivation of civic virtue) cannot be understood apart from that concern with security that the envoys posit as more powerful than justice. If she eschews new conquests it is because she senses, clearly or dimly, that she is only strong enough to maintain old ones.[29]

This is not to deny Sparta her peculiar dignity, which is that among themselves and in their devotion to their city her citizens are capable of nobility of a high order. Nor is it to deny the genuineness of Spartan piety. It

[28] Cf. Herodotus 6.106, 7.206, 9.7 and 11; Xenophon *Agesilaus* 2.17 and *Hellenica* 4.5.11; Pausanias 3.10.1, 4.19.4.

[29] Cf. Strauss *City and man* 191. Thucydides' presentation seems then to support the judgment of M. I. Finley: "[In Sparta after the Second Messenian War] the *fonction guerrière* became a police function rather than a proper military function. It was aimed against an enemy within rather than at enemies real or potential without. To preserve the difficult position of a ruling class in those special circumstances, the whole society was structured to fulfill the police function. Even the efforts expended to found and maintain the Peloponnesian League, though they required repeated warfare, may be accurately described as part of the police function." Finley also stresses the Spartan ἀγωγή or upbringing as the capstone of the whole structure. What undid Sparta, according to him (her "tragedy"), was her being drawn ineluctably into wars more extensive than this structure could support. Finley in Vernant ed. *Problèmes de la guerre* 157–60; cf. Farrar *Origins* 180–83. Cf. Critias fr. 37 (Diehls/Kranz); Aristotle *Politics* 2.6.2–4. For a valuable modern discussion of Sparta which collects the leading ancient evidence, see Rahe *Republics*.

ought not even evoke blame of Spartan injustice, for precisely by confirming the Athenian thesis, Sparta does her part to undermine blame of empire as unjust. More generally, Sparta, confronting the dilemma that she does, does what she must to maintain herself, and "no one can be blamed, in matters of the greatest risk, for seeing to their interests as best they can" (1.75.4). Sparta's extreme predicament dictates extreme measures. Her success in adapting to that predicament is as impressive as it is repulsive.

All roads lead back to the Athenian thesis. Thucydides "did not know of a strong city which failed to rule a weak city when it was to the former's interest to do so, merely for reasons of moderation, i.e., independently of calculation."[30] Nor did he know of any that had renounced empire for the sake of justice. The argument of the Athenian envoys at Sparta concerning the primacy for all cities of considerations other than those of justice finds only confirmation in the evidence that Thucydides places at our disposal. Where does that leave us? With the problems of that argument. It does not follow from the accuracy of this empirical observation that we must accept all that the envoys conclude from it. The "Athenian thesis" is not identical with this observation but comprises a particular *interpretation* of it *as disclosing a natural necessity.* Yet something can be true in every case known to us without thereby attesting a necessity; the reasons for its prevalence would still require scrutiny. The envoys offer one interpretation of these reasons, the power of which cannot be denied. Still, as I have tried to suggest, this interpretation is, in function as well as placement, the first word in Thucydides on these matters, not the last. Many further questions follow, on which Thucydides' speakers differ considerably. The first to which we must turn concerns piety.

[30] Strauss *City and man* 192.

Chapter 4

PIETY AND NECESSITY

THE SPEECH of the Athenian envoys to Sparta raised among other questions that of the status of piety (above pp. 55, 62). In invoking the gods and urging piety on their auditors (1.78.4), the envoys implied, sincerely or not, that they would practice it themselves, that prudence enjoined piety. The speech was primarily noteworthy, however, for its bold attempt to specify the compulsions to which human nature is subject, and in this connection the envoys were silent about piety.

There is nothing shocking in the omission of piety from the roster of strict compulsions. The pious must balk at the suggestion that sacred law weighs on their actions with irresistible force, depriving them of all choice between it and its opposite. Subversive of piety in the envoys' speech was rather the implication that human beings were subject to true necessities, of which piety was not one and to which, therefore, piety too must yield. The envoys, moreover, stated explicitly that the three compulsions compromised justice, which implied that they constricted piety as well. Is any sort of piety compatible with the laxity of the new Athenian standards of justice? Every pious man or woman understands the gods as requiring righteousness or justice. Indeed, is it not from these that piety draws much of its power? The happy accident of the arbitration clause, in permitting the envoys to strike their pose of piety, also invited them to obscure the problem posed for piety by their invocation of necessity.

It also appeared, however, that the Athenians had this much in common with the Spartans, that they sought to limit the sway of necessity (see ch. 1, "Unresolved Tensions in the Speech of the Athenians at Sparta"). Despite, or because of, the boldness of their teaching, they stepped back from its boldest implications; they, too, presented themselves as somehow sheltered from necessity.

The notion of piety as faith in a shelter from necessity appears clearly from 2.17, one of two places where Thucydides vindicates an oracle. There he notes an ominous fragment of a Delphic oracle to the Athenians: "Better the Pelasgian ground left unworked." This parcel of land, lying just below the Acropolis, the name of which recalled the pre-Greek occupants whom the Athenians had supplanted, was held to be accursed. In deference to the curse and the oracle, it had been left vacant even as Athens arose all around it. Wartime crowding, however, a consequence of Pericles' strategy, now compelled the Athenians to occupy it. In commenting on the forebodings thus aroused, Thucydides vindicates the truth of the oracle, but not as we might expect. Other Athenians have seen in it a warning that evils would *result* from the occupation of the ground.

> In my opinion the oracle came to pass in the sense opposite to the received one. For the misfortunes of the city did not arise from the illegal occupation, but the necessity of the occupation from the war, and the oracle, although without specifying this, foresaw that no good would attend the day when this lot came to be occupied. (2.17.2)

The transgression was ominous with a view not to its consequences but to that of which it was a consequence, not for any evil it entailed but as a symptom of the evil that entailed it.[1] In a brilliant gloss on this passage, Seth Benardete has suggested that piety implies the promise of the gods never to subject human beings to utmost necessity.[2] In demanding abstention from some action of possible utility, piety presumes protection from such duress as would compel resort to that utility. A cursed lot can remain vacant as long as there is space enough elsewhere. In viewing such arrangements as perpetual, a society presumes that the gods will spare it extreme adversity.

The presumption of the pious is, thus, that it is always possible to hold fast to the way of piety: mortals incur evils only by forsaking that way. The Athenians have assumed that if evil befell them in connection with the oracle, it would result from their disregard of it; they interpret their subsequent trials accordingly. They resist considering that the gods might be either less just or less powerful than they would wish them.

Thucydides vindicates the oracle but at the cost of failing to vindicate the power and even the justice of the gods. He claims that the oracle foresaw that it would be an evil day when the Athenians flouted the prohibition, that is, that they would do so only under the greatest duress. In denying that the calamities that followed the transgression comprised a punishment for it, he clears the gods of the imputation of punishing the Athenians for unwilling offenses. Yet he also implicitly denies the gods the will or power to shelter the blameless from disaster. His account acknowledges only "natural causation." If the calamity in this case preceded rather than followed the offense, obviously abstention from offense is no protection against calamity; the gods, in ceasing to scourge human beings, cease by the same token to shield them. The god of the oracle as Thucydides presents him grasps the dependence of piety on good fortune or the primacy of necessity over piety; he grasps the limits of his power as a god. Thucydides is silent as to whether the god had foreseen the particular events that necessitated the transgression. What vouches for the god's divinity (as manifest in his oracle) is his knowl-

---

[1] Strauss *City and man* 178; cf. Gomme *HCT* 2.65–66.
[2] Benardete *PolSciRev* 8 (1978) 18.

edge of the general relationship between piety and necessity, a knowledge which he shares with Thucydides. Thucydides does not credit the god as the source of his own wisdom; the god appears no wiser than the author and the vindication of his wisdom is due to Thucydides' wisdom.[3]

In holding themselves to have been punished by the gods for their occupation of the forbidden ground, the Athenians blame themselves unfairly, while at the same time apparently exaggerating divine power. Still, they would not have drawn much comfort from Thucydides' interpretation. The chastisement that follows most directly the profanation is (in Crawley's translation) "that most calamitous and awfully fatal visitation, the plague." The phrase so rendered is Thucydides' very first reference to the plague (1.23.3); the context raises the possibility that the plague is a token of divine wrath. So does the phrase *loimōdēs nosos* (Crawley's "awfully fatal visitation"), literally "plagueish illness." Although not unique to Thucydides, this phrase is notable in that *loimos* ("plague") is first found in Homer, and only at Iliad 1.61. The term thus recalls the most famous of all Greek plagues, that sent by Apollo to chastise the Danaans for disdaining the sacred person of his priest. Indeed many Athenians ascribed their own plague to the gods and to Apollo in particular (2.54; cf. 64.2, where Pericles addresses this belief). Thucydides' own account implicitly discourages this interpretation: the outbreak was not confined to Athens (even if it largely spared the Spartans) but arrived there only after having afflicted many other places (47–48). The Athenians, however, prove strongly wedded to this hope that the plague is a divine visitation—for a hope it is.

> As was only likely, among the other things that [the Athenians] remembered in their distress was the following verse, which the old men said had been uttered long ago: "A Dorian war shall come and with it a plague" (*loimos*, the Homeric term again). So a dispute arose over whether famine (*limos*) and not plague had been the word in the verse; but at the present juncture it was of course (*eikotōs*) decided in favor of the latter, for the people adapted their recollection to their sufferings. I suppose, however, that if another Dorian war should ever come upon us, and a famine should happen to accompany it, the verse will probably be read in that way. The oracle also that had been given to the Lacedaemonians was now remembered by those who knew of it [cf. 1.118.3]. . . . With this oracle, events were supposed to tally. For the plague broke out as soon as the Peloponnesians invaded Attica [and afflicted primarily Athens, largely sparing Sparta]. (2.54.2–5)

[3] Cf. 5.26.3–4. On the interpretation of divine prophecies as revealing merely foreknowledge, cf. Calvin *Institutes of the Christian religion* 1.16.4 with Locke *First treatise of government* sec. 118. So ambiguous is Thucydides' presentation that whereas Gomperz (*Greek thinkers* 1:510) thinks it clearly a "destructive satire," Marinatos *JHS* 101 (1981) 138–40, Veyne *Grecs* 84, and Ostwald *Ananke* 59–60 deny that Thucydides rejects the basic veracity of the oracle.

The people freely choose the reading of the verse that makes of the plague an event foretold, just as they seize on any evidence that supports the theory of a divine visitation. This might seem the more hopeful theory, for what the gods have sent they can rescind, and they may after all be amenable to human petition. So relentless is the plague that the Athenians have abandoned attempts to propitiate the gods (53.4). Even so, they balk at ascribing their ordeal to chance or necessity; they demand that their suffering be "meaningful."[4]

The Athenians insist in imputing a will to the force affronting their own will. They would rather concede the implacable hostility than the weakness or indifference of the gods; they insist on believing they have somehow brought the plague on themselves. Thucydides' comment on this is conveyed by his *eikotōs*. But why are people to be expected to interpret their sufferings in this manner? To conceive their present situation as the Athenians do is to aggravate its hopelessness: they are victims of a divine enmity they no longer hope to mollify. Still, by relinquishing hope in this case they preserve their right to it in others. The horror that has befallen them does not contradict but confirms the existence of just and powerful gods; evils such as the plague remain within human power to avert. The status of justice in the world remains secure vis-à-vis necessity.

In this respect, ordinary Athenians remain pious even amidst the despair of the plague. Yet not all Athenians are ordinary; enough adhere to a novel outlook for us to have called it the "Athenian thesis." We have seen that this thesis implies hard questions about piety. The notorious confrontation of the two outlooks is the Melian Dialogue. Their first test, however, occurs somewhat sooner.

PIETY, NECESSITY, AND THE ATHENIAN THESIS: THE DELIAN DEBATE

In the eighth year of the war, the Athenians invade neighboring Boeotia (4.76–77). Having occupied, fortified, and otherwise desecrated the shrine of Apollo at Delium, they suffer a decisive defeat in battle, without, however, being as yet dislodged from the sanctuary (89–96). Seeking to recover under truce the bodies of their fallen, a supplication of the utmost solemnity which is rebuffed nowhere else in Thucydides,[5] they are advised by the Boeotians that they need not seek the bodies until they have evacuated the temple. After exchanging vituperations, the two sides part with neither having gained its object (97–99). The Boeotians then besiege the Athenian garrison and succeed in driving it from the temple. They now acquiesce in

---

[4] Cf. Nietzsche *Genealogy of morals* 3.28.

[5] It is rebuffed only once elsewhere in our accounts of the classical period; cf. Xenophon *Hellenica* 3.5.21–24 (where the villains are again the Boeotians), and Pritchett *Greek state* 4.211–12.

the recovery of the bodies, seventeen days after the original battle (100–101).[6]

The parties to this dispute address fundamental Thucydidean questions: the relation of justice to piety and of both to force or compulsion. The occasion, moreover, is one of only three (with the speech of the envoys at Sparta and the Melian Dialogue) in which Thucydides identifies the speakers for Athens simply as "the Athenians."[7] These features identify this passage as a major exposition of the "Athenian thesis" and (given its location in the work) perhaps a bridge between the two more-celebrated ones.

The complaint of the Boeotians runs as follows; as with all the speeches on this occasion, Thucydides reports it in indirect discourse.

[T]hat the Athenians had not acted rightly in transgressing the usages of the Greeks, for it was established practice for them all, when invading each other's territories, to refrain from the sanctuaries therein. The Athenians, however, had fortified Delium and were now making themselves at home there, acting in every respect as men do on unconsecrated ground, even drawing for ordinary use the water that they themselves never touched except for use in the sacred rites. Wherefore the Boeotians, on behalf of the god and themselves, invoking the local divinities and Apollo, served them notice to take up their [dead] upon evacuating the temple. (4.97.2–4)

To which the Athenians reply as follows:

(1) . . . [T]hat they had not wronged the temple, nor would they willingly harm it. That was not why they had entered it, but rather that from it they might defend themselves against those who were wronging them. (2) As for the law of the Greeks, it was that to whoever wielded power over a country, be it more or

---

[6] Seventeen days is a long time in the summer sun, and most critics who have remarked on the passage have followed the Athenians and Grote *History of Greece* 6.394–95 (part 2 chapter 53) in blaming the Boeotians for flouting sacred law in the hopes of extorting an unearned victory. See, for example, Gomme (*HCT* 3.571), for whom "Thucydides' insertion of this long dispute, his insistence on this argument of words, was due to his feeling that the Boeotian refusal to allow the Athenians to collect their dead was another evil resulting from the war . . . , an abandonment of one of the recognized, and humane, usages of Greece." What Thucydides' characters dispute, however, is not the "inhumanity" of the refusal, but whether it and the behavior of the Athenians that provoked it are offenses against the law of man that forbids dishonoring the gods. Can indignation at the Boeotians' "inhumanity" really explain so detailed an account of this wrangling over points of sacred law? In the end even Gomme seems to doubt it; he mutters that "Thucydides is curiously interested in this sophistical stuff" (ibid., p. 569; cf. Strauss *City and man* 208 n.70). For brief mentions of the incident, see Strasburger *Hermes* 86 (1958) 39 n.2; Schneider *Information und Absicht* 106 n.213; Lateiner *CW* (1977) 101–2; Pouncey *Necessities of war* 94–95; Proctor *Experience* 82–83; Rawlings *Structure* 51 n.46; Cicciò in Sordo ed. *Santuari* 138–39; Mikalson *Studies S. Dow* 224; Pritchett *Greek state* 4:191–92. Strauss *City and man* 208 n.70, while not discussing the incident at length, indicates why one might do so; cf. Palmer *CJPS* 15 (1982) 111 n.19.

[7] Proctor *Experience* 82–83.

less extensive, to them the temples also always belonged, to be tended, to the best of their ability, in the ways already customary.[8] (3) After all, the Boeotians, along with most others who had taken over a country by force and expelled the original inhabitants, had begun by attacking as belonging to others temples they now possessed as their own. (4) And as for themselves, had they succeeded in establishing their power over more of the country of the Boeotians, so matters would have stood for them. Even as it was, moreover, they held that part of it in which they stood as their own and would not of their own will depart from it. (5) As for the water, finally, they had disturbed it under duress (*anankē*), which they had not wantonly incurred, having been compelled to use the water in defending themselves against those who had first invaded their land. (6) Besides which, anything done under stress of war and danger might reasonably claim some indulgence even in the eyes of the god. For the altars were a refuge from the consequences of involuntary[9] offenses, and transgression was a term reserved for those under no compulsion to be bad, not for those whom misfortune drove to dare. (7) More impious by far were those who demanded that temples be exchanged for bodies than they who refused to relinquish temples in return for what was properly theirs already. (8) What they demanded to hear from [the Boeotians], loud and clear, was not "to depart from Boeotian territory"—for where they stood was [the Boeotians'] no longer, themselves having acquired it by the spear—but to take up their bodies under truce in accordance with ancestral ways. (4.98)

The Athenians do not deny that their actions were prima facie impieties.[10] From the outset their appeal is to the extenuating circumstances. They begin conventionally enough by discriminating between wronging and harming, invoking the respectable distinction between just and unjust

---

[8] Reading, with J. M. Stahl, πρὸ τοῦ εἰωθόσι ("in the ways already customary") for the πρὸς τὰς εἰωθόσι ("in ways additional to those customary") of the codices.

[9] Reading ἀκουσίαν ("involuntary") with codd. C, E, and F2 rather than ἐκουσίων ("voluntary") with A, F, and M.

[10] Barton and Chavasse (*Thucydides book four* 122–23) decry "the wanton outrage of which [the Athenians] were guilty in seizing and fortifying a holy place and damaging its condition, and the impudent paradoxes by which their act was justified," further noting that in refusing to withdraw from the temple in order to recover the bodies of their fallen, the Athenians "prefer the retention of a political prize to the performance of a pious duty." (In the only other such case on record [see note 2 above] the Spartans would prefer the pious duty.) Lonis *Usages* 73; Garlan *Guerre* 37; Parker *Miasma* 190; and Ducrey *Guerre et guerriers* 282, agree that the offenses were serious ones, Parker noting in defense of the Boeotians that temple robbers were commonly punished by refusal of burial. In Athens itself the violation of a temple was punishable by death (cf. Demosthenes 24.120), as was, nominally at least, the uprooting of sacred olive trees (Aristotle *Athenian constitution* 60.2, cf. Lysias 7). On the cutting of sacred vines specifically, cf. 3.70.4–5 and Parker *Miasma* 165 n.21. For an overview of the whole question of sacrilege, see Parker ibid. 144–90, and of the violation of temples in wartime, see Sordi in Sordi ed. *Santuari*. Jordan *TAPA* 116 (1986) 130 joins Eatough *AJP* 92 (1971) 244–46 in decrying the Athenian speech as among the most sophistical in Thucydides.

wars (98.1). They suggest that nothing undertaken in a just cause could rightly be blamed as impious. They proceed, however, to a much bolder defense of their seizure of the temple (98.2–4). In expounding a right allegedly conferred by conquest, they no longer bother to distinguish between just and unjust conquest. Now their point is that conquest as such (i.e., conquest insofar as it succeeds) confers on the conqueror legitimate possession of both lands and shrines—or how did the Boeotians come to be rightful possessors of Boeotia, to which they enjoy no claim save that of having driven out their predecessors? That the Boeotians are in fact rightful possessors the Athenians can afford to concede, even as they try to dislodge them, precisely because (on their theory) possession is ten points of the law. Since whoever possesses does so by right, one need only dispossess him in order to possess by right oneself—pending the appearance of the next dispossessor. The tiny sliver of Boeotia that Athens still holds after her defeat in the battle, however recently snatched and however soon to be retaken, she possesses by the very title—force which conveys right—of the Boeotians to the rest of the region. Right thus utterly collapses as a limit on conquest.

As for the gods, they too acquiesce in a fait accompli. Such, at least, is implied by Greek custom itself. The conquest once effected, life goes on, in sacred matters as in others. The subjection, expulsion, or extirpation of a people—what are these to the gods? The sacrificial fire is rekindled, and the cult of the god resumes; the honors once offered by the vanquished are now the obligation of the victors. The Athenians here develop an unwitting suggestion of the Boeotians themselves. These presented impiety as unjust but not the rest of injustice as impious: the invasion of Boeotia they no doubt regarded as unjust, but it was only the seizure of the temple that they presented as impious.[11] The Athenians then need only point out that temples, like oaks and rocks, come with the (conquered) territory. If it is not impiety to occupy the land then neither can it be to occupy the temples, and if a shrine happens to be the first acreage seized, offense to the gods is neither intended nor taken.

So far the Athenians have addressed the seizure of the temple but not its desecration. They therefore go on to allege that the gods might reasonably take not only conquest but even impiety in stride, accepting here the plea of

[11] Thucydides' Melians, who have led a life far more sheltered than either the Athenians or the Boeotians, imply at 5.104 that piety includes justice (and so that all injustice is impious). Mikalson *Athenian popular religion* 27–30 argues that it was a respectable and perhaps even the predominant view at Athens by this time that only certain injustices were of concern to the gods, namely those (such as homicide and temple robbery) that were also impieties or specific affronts to the gods. Such, however, is clearly not the view of Thucydides' Nicias and the rank and file of the Sicilian expedition, surveying the ruin of their unjust hopes (7.76–77). Connor *AnSoc* 19 (1988) 161–88 argues that this older outlook was in fact still the accepted one in Athens at this time.

necessity (98.5–6). And they again adduce a fundamental practice of Greek piety, this time that of providing asylum to involuntary offenders who could make their way to an altar. (The typical case was that of accidental homicide.) The Athenians, however, are stretching the usage in claiming immunity for their actions. The annals of Greek piety record no case of asylum at an altar for one whose offense was to have defiled that altar.

The Athenians insist then that the gods might and should accept the defense of involuntariness in cases of impiety as in those of injustice. The standards of extenuation that they ascribe to them are, moreover, amazingly easygoing. By involuntary offenses worthy of indulgence, the Athenians do not mean just those that are unintentional in the usual sense. Nothing could have been more intentional than their seizure of Delium, as part of a master plan for taking over Boeotia (4.76). By involuntary the Athenians merely mean committed under duress, and duress in a highly diluted sense. Anything done under pressure of war qualifies as done under duress; if, as in the present case, desecration is just good strategy or (as in the case of the use of the lustral water) a necessary consequence of good strategy,[12] there is your plea of necessity. The gods apparently grant that danger imposes necessities of its own: they do not expect even unjust warriors to lie down and die.

"Is nothing sacred?" bellow the Boeotians confronted with the Athenian desecration of their sanctuary. No, nothing, the Athenians reply, not even the sacred. For it too admits of numerous exceptions. Do the Athenians innovate in thus diluting the demands of piety? They claim not. Rather they profess to act on the same time-honored principles as every other city. Their innovation is confined to the clarity of their grasp of these principles and the candor of their presentation of them. They defend their piety as impeccable, not because they put piety first but because nobody does, and because they can argue (however inconsequently) that in the present case the impiety of the Boeotians is worse than their own.

These arguments of course recall the speech of the envoys at Sparta. They too, while adopting a novel candor in speech, denied that in practicing empire they thereby innovated in deed. They too, without rejecting the authority of justice, insisted on the propriety of a much broader range of exceptions to it than generally admitted in speech. They too, arguing from universal experience, alleged necessity as the ground of these exceptions, and they too adduced it as extenuating even conquest and empire.

All of this our Athenians apply to the case of piety. The transition from

---

[12] Pritchett *Topography* 3.295–97 suggests that seizing Delium was in fact a strategic necessity for the invaders; as he has written to me, "it was this or nothing." The availability of the lustral water must itself have been a crucial strategic asset of the place. The author is indebted to Professor Pritchett and to Malcolm B. Wallace for their patient advice on points of Greek sacred law and military practice.

justice is by way of the practice of asylum for involuntary offenders. If the gods indulge involuntary injustice, why not also involuntary impiety? The Athenian thesis naturally proceeds from justice to piety because the indicated excuse for neglecting them is the same: necessity drove me to it.

This Athenian position is self-contradictory. If they may invoke the necessities of war to justify profaning the temple, why should not the Boeotians do so to justify their refusal to yield the bodies? The assertion that the impiety of the Boeotians is graver than their own is insufficient, for the relevant question is not whose offense would be graver in the absence of extenuation, but who can offer the more persuasive extenuation. Here the cases are equal, it being as necessary to the Boeotians to dislodge the Athenians as it is to the latter to retain their foothold. To haggle over comparative necessity portends the disappearance of sacred restraint, as belligerents pitch ever lower the threshold for flouting it without impiety.

The crux of the Athenian argument is that even respect for the sacred must yield to the necessities of human life. Obviously this implies that such respect does not itself rank among these necessities. It is worth contrasting this perspective on piety with the traditional one (while keeping in mind the Athenians' claim to have found it in the traditional one). According to the respectable view, the blessings of human life are the gods' to dispense and are therefore contingent on our piety; piety persuades the gods to spare us the rigors of (what we might otherwise mistake for) necessity.[13] In the absence of natural necessity, piety is the only necessity.

Without having thought the matter quite through, these Athenians imply the emancipation of necessity from the gods, or the emergence of necessity strictly speaking. In so doing, it must be admitted, they do not so much break with ancestral Greek piety as develop its minor strain. Such piety was ambiguous from the outset concerning the relation of the gods and necessity, simply because it did not revere the gods as omnipotent creators. Unlike the Bible, Homer and Hesiod do not present the world into which we were born as perfect (i.e., as having become imperfect only through our rebellion). They do not depict the world (which is not the work of the Olympian gods but is itself divine and an older god than they) as simply good even for the Olympians themselves, but as marred by evils beyond their power to mend. The subjection of the gods to fate thus coexists uneasily with the subjection of human beings to the gods. It also precludes that the Olympian gods, dogged as they are by their own necessities, should achieve the status of holy gods. The God of Israel will be what He will be; those of Greece are subject to fits of being what they cannot but be. For this

---

[13] Hesiod *Works and days* 232–34; Homer *Odyssey* 19.109–14; among the biblical parallels, Deuteronomy 11:13–21 and Psalm 92. On the complex teaching of the *Odyssey* as a whole, see Clay *Wrath of Athena*.

reason, to say nothing of others, even the god of justice is not reliably just or even attentive.[14]

These Athenians articulate certain tensions that, if especially pronounced among the Greeks, are observable in practice everywhere. Traditional piety is contradictory, for in recognizing in practice certain exceptions to itself, it concedes, if only despite itself, that some things are more fundamental for us than piety. Not that the Athenians go so far as to deny that the gods chastise impiety, wherever it is willful, that is, wherever it is in fact impiety. They do deny, however, that the gods can reasonably expect us to put the sacred first, ahead of the compulsions to which we are subject as human beings. Unwilling or unable to address our subjection to necessity, the gods acquiesce in it. Only thus do our needs become true necessities, necessities in the fullest and harshest sense, from which not even a god can save us—and against which piety could avail us nothing.[15]

Clearly such an argument subverts divine authority. If the gods are powerless before our necessities, what can we hope for from them? The minor strain in Greek piety that subordinates the gods to fate thus threatens to emancipate human beings from their tutelage—while however enslaving them to necessity (cf. 2.17 and above, pp. 88–90). This outcome is highly problematic. In fact, it appears that, contrary to the logic of their argument, piety has not yet lost all authority with these Athenians. Here too their position is self-contradictory. They remain concerned to recover their corpses, a matter of sacred law; "from the point of view of the Athenian ambassadors to Melos—or of Socrates—the fate of the corpses would be a matter of utter indifference."[16] This contradiction points to the residual piety of the Athenians. Without caring to observe sacred law except where convenient, neither have they purged their souls of the hopes and fears that piety nurtures.

This neglected passage, in which the Athenians first extend their characteristic outlook to relations between god and man, is crucial for grasping their unfolding political theology of imperialism—which achieves its zenith in the Melian Dialogue.

---

[14] Hesiod *Works and days* 35–36, 225–85; cf. Homer *Iliad* 14.153–360; Aristophanes *Clouds* 398–402, 902–6, 1080–82; *Birds* 1494–1693; *Peace* 382–425; *Wealth* 87–92. Cf. Lloyd-Jones *Justice of Zeus* 176: "to put it in a nutshell, . . . in one sense Zeus was but in another sense he was not just."

[15] Cf. Clay *Wrath of Athena* esp. 230–31.

[16] Strauss *City and man* 208 n.70. Cf. Heraclitus fr. 96; Epicharmus fr. 64.

Chapter 5

THE MELIAN DIALOGUE AND THE FATE OF MELOS

IN THE SIXTEENTH year of the war, while nominally at peace with Sparta, the Athenians assail tiny Melos. A colony of Sparta, but an island and thus vulnerable to Athens, Melos has sought to avoid offense by siding with neither. Athens, however, having earlier taken a stab at reducing Melos (3.91), now sets about it in earnest, landing a powerful force on the island (5.84). Before ravaging the countryside, however, the generals send some unnamed envoys to the Melians. There ensues the most dramatic passage in Thucydides—indeed, the only one that is dramatic strictly speaking. This parley alone he presents both in direct discourse and in dialogue form, with each party responding to the previous contribution of the other. He thereby achieves not only the sharpest confrontation but the most ample clarification of opposing outlooks—of the Athenian manner and the Melian manner, the latter proving to be a purified or pristine version of the "Spartan" one. In reading the dialogue, we must ask above all what *happens* in it.[1]

WHY A DIALOGUE: SPEECH AND CONTEXT (5.84–89)

It is when the Athenian envoys find themselves led before "those in office and the few" rather than the multitude that they propose a format of frank give-and-take (5.85). Grasping that they have been kept from the people lest these "be deceived by enticing arguments that went unchallenged, having been exposed to them all at once," the envoys suggest a "safer" course still: that the magistrates too respond point by point to the Athenians "wherever what is said does not seem satisfactory." "But first say whether it suits you that we continue speaking."

The conference must then begin with a choice of format and so with a discussion of discussing. The Melians, for their part, acclaim the envoys' proposal as a model of fairness (*epieikeia*, 5.86). The envoys, however, have stated their motive in renouncing rhetoric not as fairness but as the safety of the Melians. By this they mean first of all security from their own presumed forensic wiles. They will also shortly proclaim, however, the "rescue" or

---

[1] Cf. Stahl *Thukydides* 161: "Our question is rather what *happens in* the Melian dialogue, *within* the movement of the conversation." ("Unsere Frage ist vielmehr was *im* Melier-Dialog, *innerhalb* der Bewegung des Gesprächs, *geschieht*" [emphasis in original].)

salvation (*sōtēria*, 5.87)[2] of Melos as the sole end of the conversation, which rescue depends on their success at persuading the Melians. For if the dialogue form affords the Melians protection from specious arguments, it also offers the envoys their best hope of refuting specious objections. Strong cases need not fear close scrutiny.[3] In their choice of format the envoys reveal sovereign confidence in the power of their arguments.

It is presumably the equity of the envoys' proposal (5.86) which inspires in the Melians the hopeful or ironic request that follows. Challenged to a fair debate, they jump to the conclusion that the subject of the debate will be fairness. They complain that the Athenians' martial preparations bespeak men who come as judges in their own case rather than to abide an impartial determination of justice. (They thus imply that they themselves would bow to such a determination, come what may.) The Athenians, to establish their bona fides, must withdraw their forces pending a verdict on the justice of landing them.

It is no accident that the issue of justice thus first arises in the context of a discussion about discussing. The two issues are related. The world as the Melians would have it is lawful, subject to an "international moral order." The Athenian presence on Melos is presumed to be contingent on its justice; so Athens must withdraw pending the verdict of justice. Just speeches (cf. *dikaiōn logōn*, 5.98) order all things, overriding disparities of power.

To the Melian insistence on the primacy of right the Athenians oppose that of compulsion (5.87). Their superior power defines the context of the conversation, a fact which discussion cannot undo and from which it therefore must begin. The Melians have complained that the Athenian preparations were present or at hand (*paronta*) rather than merely prospective (*mellonta*), as if there could be no fair discussion of a fait accompli. The envoys now summon them to eschew conjectures about the future (*hyponoias tōn mellontōn*) and to consult about the safety of their city in the light of things present and visible (*ek tōn parontōn kai hōn horate*)(87). To the request that they alter the situation to suit the conversation, the envoys reply that a conversation must suit its situation. The Athenian threat to Melos does not unfairly crimp discussion. It is what the parties have to discuss.[4]

[2] Accepting against Cagnazzi *Spedizione ateniese*, the traditional allocation of the parts to Athenians and Melians and, against Cagnazzi and her mentor Canfora (*Belfagor* 1971 409–26), that the dialogue is the work of Thucydides, not a later insertion by Xenophon. On this, see Macleod *Historia* 23 (1974) 396–97.

[3] Compare also the Melians' formulation of the procedure suggested by the envoys as "instructing one another at leisure" (5.86) with 3.42.1–2 and 3.48.2; 5.26.5. The Melian Dialogue parallels, on the level of practical discourse, Thucydides' own efforts to elucidate what is, has been, and must be (1.22.4; 3.82.2; cf. 5.105.2). Levi *Parola del Passato* 8 (1953) 6–8 rightly stresses the "Socratic" (as opposed to "sophistic") character of the conversation. Cf. also Cagnetta *QS* 32 (1990) 159–62.

[4] Macleod *Historia* 23 (1974) 387 concedes that the dialogue is conceived not as a sophistic *elenchus* but "rather as an ideal mode of common deliberation about a practical matter; so in

Chastened, the Melians agree (5.88): the subject of these talks will be their own deliverance. They apologize for their failed gambit, pleading that it is "normal and excusable" (*eikos . . . kai xyngnōmē*) that men in their situation should turn this way and that. They concede that their argument from justice was thrust on them by their weakness.

The Athenians pardon the Melians, provided they not invoke justice again (5.89). Eschewing "fine words" (*onōmatōn kalōn*), the Athenians will not assert that either their empire or the present expedition is just, in return for which the Melians must refrain from protesting the justice of their own position. The arguments from justice that the envoys pledge to forgo are unpersuasive (*apiston*); not so those they forbid the Melians. They insist, however, that as the Melians very well know, "claims of justice (*dikaia*) are adjudicated (*krinetai*) in human speech only where the parties are subject to equal compulsion (*apo tēs isēs anankēs*), while those who have the upper hand (*hoi prouchontes*) do as they are able, and the weak make way for them."

For all their notoriety, the envoys claim here not that there is no such thing as right nor that "might makes right."[5] They respect the tension between the two. They insist for now, at least, not that Athens and Melos are equally just but that their superior power must silence the Melians' superior justice. Justice prevails only among equals in power—among such equals, not justice but equality in power prevails. Where right reigns, just as where it does not, it defers to compulsion.

The envoys speak undiplomatically but not thereby implausibly.[6] For

---

5.101 the Athenians pointedly contrast the Βουλή they have undertaken with the ἀγών they have rejected." At 389: "Thus far the . . . dialogue is an ideal form of deliberation. It combines the practicality of public speech with the precision of dialectic. It clearly defines its subject, it is based on the facts of the case, not on idle speculation, and it aims to do no more than what those facts allow of, to discover what is possible or expedient." Even so, Macleod proceeds to criticize the envoys bitterly for dictating the substance of the discussion: "the words . . . create the illusion of equality in the face of brute facts; but this cannot mask that what is possible for Melos is surrender and that the Athenians are the real agents, whereas the Melians must simply endure" (390). But why should the Athenians "mask" a truth crucial for both parties?

[5] Nor do they assert, I think, that justice arises only out of equality of power. Such was Nietzsche's interpretation of the passage: see *Human all too human*, aphorism 92 (trans. W. Kaufmann in Nietzsche *Genealogy of morals*). The question is how to take κρίνεται (judge, determine, decide, adjudicate, declare, pronounce): as implying the creation of the rights of a particular matter or merely their discernment? The latter interpretation appears the more plausible of the two. Cf. Romilly *Imperialism* 299–300: "The Athenians in this passage do not deny that the idea of justice can have a certain validity: they only point out that the cases to which it can apply are very limited." At 300 n.1 she considers Nietzsche's interpretation.

[6] Critics of its plausibility include Grote *History of Greece* 7:109–112 (but cf. his own citation at 110 n.1 of the similar bluntness of the British ambassador to Copenhagen in 1807, when Britain, with no warrant but its own necessities, attacked the fleet of neutral Denmark lest it fall into the hands of Napoleon); Hudson-Williams *AJP* 71 (1950) 167–69 (but cf. 164–67); and Romilly *Imperialism* 297. Grant *CQ* NS 15 (1965) 261–66 and Kagan *Peace of Nicias* 149–51 argue persuasively that (as Kagan puts it) "we need not doubt the authenticity of the dialogue in its essentials."

them, as earlier for the envoys to Sparta, candor is to their purpose. They can avoid the trouble of a siege only by persuading the Melians that this time they mean business (cf. 3.91). They need not dissemble because they have nothing to hide; like their predecessors at Sparta, they can conceive of no argument more persuasive than their overwhelming power. They can well afford to converse on equal terms with the Melians: their superiority to them is irrefutable. It is irrefutable because it is impervious to speech.[7] For this reason, speech cannot be impervious to it. The dialogue must begin from an awareness of the limits of dialogue.

Ought the Athenians Attack? (5.90–99)

The Melians profess to accept these limitations. In the exchanges that follow, while professing to hew to the useful, they struggle to bridle it as a stalking horse for the just.

> We, however, think it useful (for thus are we compelled to speak, since you have laid it down that we are to consider the advantageous rather than the just) that you should not destroy the common good (*to koinon agathon*), but that there should be claims of equity and justice for whomever is at any time in danger and that he benefit somewhat from them, even if he has not entirely proved his case. And this concerns you as much as any, in that your fall would occasion the greatest vengeance and serve as an example to others. (5.90)

It is useful for Melos to be able to appeal to justice; it is useful to Athens to grant this appeal so as to be granted it in time to come. The Melians seek to teach Athens the long view. They do not go so far as to assert that Athens would fall for having wronged Melos. But they do suggest that when she fell this wrong would be visited upon her. There is to this extent a power supporting justice, which thus becomes a common interest; the badness of doing wrong follows from that of suffering it.

The Athenians rebuff this suggestion (5.91). They are used to considering that their empire must end (cf. 2.64). That prospect does not unsettle them. The empire must fall either to another imperial city or beneath the blows of its own enraged subjects. Imperial cities are not so very terrible to those they vanquish. The envoys do not elaborate, but they probably doubt that one empire would much blame another for the "crime" of imperialism. In any case, it would have other concerns than settling other cities' old scores for them. The envoys concede that revolted subjects are to be dreaded. To the extent that vengeance is justice, justice is indeed a force in the world. But would Athens' other subjects resent her less if she refrained from subjecting

---

[7] Cf. Plato *Republic* 327c; Cogan *Human thing* 247 n.8. On Thucydides' expression of the plight of the Melians through verbal images of physicality, see Bahr-Volk *CB* 52 (1976) 59–60.

Melos? Athens must beware of enemies with their own scores to settle; she would be foolish to tremble over posthumous avengers of Melos.[8]

The Melians have failed to show that justice defines a common good between the two cities. They must therefore confront the rejoinder that the interests of both converge in the prompt surrender of Melos. The envoys do not speak of a common good. They do praise submission, however, as mutually beneficial: "wishing as we do to rule you without trouble, and that you should be saved to the advantage of us both" (5.91.2). The Melians demur (92): "And how could it prove as advantageous for us to serve, as for you to rule?" "Because it would be to your advantage to submit before suffering the most terrible things, and we would gain by not destroying you" (93). Like one who offers us our life in return for merely our money, Athens has made Melos an offer that she cannot refuse.

The Melians are effectively silenced, subsiding (5.94) into a lame plea for their continued neutrality. The envoys patiently explain (95) why the hostility of Melos is more congenial than her neutrality: the former cannot hurt Athens, whereas their subjects will take the latter for a sign of Athenian weakness.

This reply spurs the Melians to another indirect argument from justice (5.96). Do these allies not distinguish on grounds of equity between themselves, most of whom are Athenian colonists and conquered rebels to boot, and Melos, which has nothing to do with Athens? The subjects, they imply, deserve their vexation; surely they can see that Melos does not, and they will interpret Athenian forbearance accordingly.

Their subjects, reply the Athenians (5.97), are not so naive as that. They know that not right but force prevails in these matters. Their own subjection they assuredly do not ascribe to justice; and as for the freedom of Melos, they can only ascribe it to Athenian weakness. Thus do the Athenians bristle at the notion that their empire might owe something to justice.

The Athenians have promised at 5.91 to show that they come against Melos for the benefit of their empire; at 95, they have asserted the importance of their subjects' assessment of their power.[9] This last consideration,

---

[8] Liebeschuetz *JHS* 88 (1968) 74–75 argues that the sequel vindicates this prophecy of the Melians. No evidence in Thucydides supports this assertion. Neither at 7.18 nor anywhere else during the Sicilian campaign or after does he mention the Melian affair as a source of indignation toward Athens. Xenophon *Hellenica* 2.2.5–20 cannot sustain conclusions as to how Thucydides would have presented the debate following the defeat of Athens. The text as we have it affords no clear basis for the conjectures of Regenbogen *Kleine Schriften* 227 n.13, Scharf *Gymnasium* 61 (1954) 507, and Rawlings *Structure* 243–49 that Thucydides intended an eventual treatment of the fall of Athens dominated by recollections of Melos.

[9] Cogan *Human thing* 87–93 argues that what is new in the Melian Dialogue, and what justifies Thucydides' presentation of it, is the expressed Athenian fear of revolts by their subjects. Cf. also Macleod *Historia* 23 (1974) 392. In fact the Athenians have betrayed this concern at much earlier stages of the war, as witness the statement of the envoys to Sparta, the

they now reveal (97), has spurred them on their present mission (and explains why they cannot abandon it): by defeating Melos they will dash the hopes of their restive subjects, thereby safeguarding their existing dominions. It is out of self-defense that Athens must engulf Melos.

This assertion evokes the Melians' longest contribution to the parley (5.98). It is as if they only now see their way to the argument that will persuade the envoys—perhaps because, compelled to address Athenian interests, only now have they learned the interest on which Athens claims to act. They begin, in any event, by invoking her announced concern with security. They remind the envoys that this appeal conforms exactly to the logic of the argument that the envoys have imposed on them.

> But do you not hold that there is security in the other course? For here, too, it is a requirement of our situation (*dei*) that, just as you, having forced us to forsake just speeches (or arguments from justice, *tōn dikaiōn logōn*), would persuade us to harken to what is in your interest, so also must we, expounding (or teaching, *didaskontas*) what is useful to us, try to persuade you, if it so happens that it is also such to you.

The Melians' repetition of "teaching" (cf. 5.86) suggests their conviction that they have finally found their voice.[10] After so many rebuffs, they now wield a winning argument. By attacking Melos Athens will alarm other neutrals, thus multiplying her enemies and impairing her security rather than enhancing it. No, reply the envoys: most neutrals, being landsmen, hold no terror for Athens, because she holds none for them; they deem her power to be confined to the sea (5.99; cf. 2.62, 6.90). Again the Melians have relied on a "juridical" distinction, and the Athenians have instructed them that the relevant considerations are those of power.[11]

Athenian panic and subsequent fury over the revolt of Mytilene, and their response to the successes of Brasidas. Romilly *Imperialism* 287–89 correctly notes that there is nothing new about the fear of their subjects that the Athenians express here, any more than there is about their argument for the necessity of maintaining the empire: the two go hand in hand.

[10] The use of this term in a deliberative context bears overtones of both Pericles and Diodotus; cf. 2.40.2 and 60.5–6; 3.42.2 (διδασκάλους). Cf. Yunis *AJP* 112 (1991) 184–85.

[11] Liebeschuetz *JHS* 88 (1968) 74–75, following Romilly *Imperialism* 275, cites 8.2 as fulfillment of the prophecy at 5.98, but Thucydides there cites not the Melian affair but the much more ambitious Sicilian expedition as having put neutrals on notice that there was no safe haven from Athens—and the failure of that expedition as having persuaded these fair-weather warriors that Athens was now an easy prey. Bartoletti *RFIC* 67 (1939) 301–18 argues that the Melians in their stubbornness express the "spiritual forces" that will bring down the empire in the end, abetted by a Spartan resurgence which the Melians correctly foresee. To this attempt at a posthumous vindication of the Melian position, one should compare Thucydides' own statement as to the reason for the Athenian defeat (2.65.11). Nor is the mood of Athens' enemies after the Sicilian disaster either stubborn or spiritual: it is merely overconfident (8.2).

Ought the Melians Resist? (5.100–113)

So far the drama of the dialogue has consisted in the efforts of the Melians to evade the terms of discourse imposed on them by the envoys.[12] Commanded to discuss advantage, not justice, they have struggled to vindicate justice in terms of advantage. In failing, they have likewise emptied their quiver of arguments from Athenian interest. They have devised no objection to the expedition that does not begin from the fact of its injustice. At 5.100 they shift their ground. The issue is no longer whether Athens can reasonably attack. It is whether Melos can reasonably resist.[13]

The Athenians have presented themselves as willing to face danger for the sake of empire (5.91). They have described their subjects as "exasperated by the necessity of empire" and prone to reckless risks for the sake of freedom (99). The Melians pick up on this (100): "then surely it would be great baseness and cravenness in ourselves who are still free not to try everything before submitting to servitude." "No, not if you deliberate with moderation. For this is not, for you, a contest on equal terms where manly virtue is at stake, and not incurring disgrace; the discussion concerns your safety, and not resisting those who are much stronger than you" (101).

The envoys let pass the suggestion that submission would be disgraceful. They deny, however, that the Melians should concern themselves with honor. They anticipate Aristotle's distinction between the noble and the necessary, virtue and its "equipment."[14] Manly virtue, they assert, together with the reputation for it—their use of the term *andragathia* blurs this distinction—is a prize to be sought when the odds are even and no vital interests are at stake; it is not itself a vital interest. It is a worthy pastime for those blessed with safety and leisure. It is not for the Melians, whose struggle is unequal and concerned with the strictly necessary. If they persist in pursuing it, they will not have deliberated "with moderation." The envoys do not call on the Melians to renounce virtue as such. They imply that moderation is the benchmark, the standard for the pertinence of all other virtues. Moderation is the virtue of knowing to bow to necessity.

This argument, too, leaves its mark on the Melians. Rather than insist that they must resist even against overwhelming odds, they venture that perhaps the odds are less than overwhelming (5.102). The vagaries of fortune give them hope; success is not always proportionate to numbers. The issue is now not the nobility but the plausibility of Melian resistance; the Melians have tacitly conceded that the former depends on the latter.[15] The Athenians decry the folly of entrusting one's ventures to hope (103; cf. 3.45.5–6,

---

[12] Cf. Ferrara *Parola del Passato* 11 (1956) 345.
[13] Cf. Romilly *Imperialism* 286–87.
[14] Aristotle *Nicomachean ethics* 1.8.15–17.
[15] Strauss *City and man* 186–87.

4.62, 4.108.3). Like honor, hope is only for those rich in other resources, whom it "may harm, but does not undo." In their great weakness, the Melians would risk all.

The Athenians sniff more in the air than fortune.

> Nor must you behave just like the many, who while human means of deliverance are yet at hand, when they are in distress and manifest grounds of hope are lacking to them, turn to immanifest ones, divination and oracles and that sort of thing, which crush [the unwary] with hopes. (5.103)

The envoys, not the Melians, are the first to evoke the divine. It is the Melians, however, whose stubborn hopes appear to the envoys to force the question. The envoys are not mistaken. The Melians concede how hard it would be to contend against both fortune and the power of Athens (5.104). They trust, however, (*pisteuomen*) that "as blameless men standing against unjust ones" (*hoti hosioi pros ou dikaious*) they will "not be at a disadvantage in the fortune that is from the divine" (*tēi . . . tychēi ek tou theiou*). As they rely on the divine to equalize their fortunes, so they depend on the Spartans—who are "under a necessity, even if for no other reasons than from kinship and out of shame"—to come to their aid and thus equalize their power. "And so it is not entirely unreasonably (*alogōs*) that we are confident."

The question, as the Melians here remind us, remains that of whether their confidence is reasonable. They name power along with fortune as a deficiency that must be supplied if they are to withstand Athens. The gods, it seems, can save the Melians only if the Spartans venture to do so. And while the Melians present the Spartans as under a compulsion to aid them, they make no such claim about the divine. The most obtrusive of their errors is not their misjudgment of the divine.

The Athenians consider the divine and the Spartans in turn.

> Well now, as far as the divine is concerned, neither do we suppose that we shall fall short of you in its regard. For there is nothing that we claim (*dikaioumen*) or do that departs from what human beings believe of the gods or from how they regard one another. From what is reputed (*doxēi*) of the divine and what is manifest (*saphōs*) of human beings, we conclude that always, by a necessity of nature, they rule to the limits of their power. And it was not we who made this law, nor were we the first who finding it in force have submitted to it, but having found it in being, will leave it in being for all time to come. And so we do submit to it, knowing that you and anyone else, coming into the same power as we have, would do the very same thing. As regards the divine, then, the likelihood is that we need not fear being at a disadvantage. (5.105.1–3)

As Walzer tersely puts it, "it is not only the Melians here who bear the burdens of necessity."[16] The envoys do not proclaim a right of the stronger, if that means one enjoyed by the stronger to the exclusion of the weaker.

---

[16] Walzer *Just and unjust wars* 5.

Relative strength confers no right; the right of Athens does not exceed that of Melos (nor does that of the gods exceed that of human beings). How could it, when the rights of both derive from the very compulsion which bears equally on both parties? Each power can claim the right to act to the limits of its strength; neither can complain at enjoying no more than its strength (or fortune) obtains for it.

The Melians take the respectable view that the gods favor those who are blameless toward them against those who are unjust; that is, injustice toward human beings, by which they mean aggression, incurs blame also with the gods.[17] This the Athenians reject, all the while denying that they innovate in the approach to the divine. Though they do not claim accurate knowledge of the gods as they do of human beings, their notions of them stem from received opinion. From it they have concluded that the gods, too, are in the habit of ruling wherever they can. This conclusion is surely plausible. The received accounts of the gods, offered by poets and endorsed by cities, paint them as perpetually quarrelsome. Olympians versus Titans, Ouranos dethroned by his son Kronos and he in turn by his son Zeus, the differences among the Olympians themselves—inciting and incited by those of human beings—all sustain the Athenian position.[18] Zeus himself, god of justice and scourge of perjurors, is but the most successful tyrant and so perhaps a patron of tyrants.[19]

However venerable these stories, however, the envoys' conclusions from them are not. There was also a well-established tradition as to what the gods required of human beings, and here the Melians would appear to stand on the firmer ground. Piety, after all, has always acknowledged the impossibility of one law for gods and men: the divine, as the source of law, cannot be held to account before law. Imitation of the gods is *hybris*, the ultimate outrage against the divine.[20]

---

[17] On ὅσιος ("of blameless piety") as including δίκαιος ("just"), see van der Valk *Mnemosyne* 3d ser. 10 (1942) 118–23; Eatough *AJP* 112 (1971) 238–51. See also Connor *AnSoc* 19 (1988) 161–88. Cf. the parallel position of Nicias, 7.77.

[18] Hesiod *Theogony* 147–210, 454–506, 617–735, 819–85 (see Clay *CPh* 88 [1993] 27–38); Aeschylus *Seven against Thebes* 501–20 and *Prometheus bound* 350–74; Pindar *Sixth paean* 50–95. Cf. Xenophanes fr. 1, 11, and 12; Heraclitus fr. 53; Plato *Euthyphro* 5c–6c; *Republic* 377b–378e.

[19] Cf. 1.126, where Thucydides reports with equanimity a suggestion of the Delphic oracle that the greatest festival of Zeus was an appropriate day for a tyrannical coup—and himself suggests that the attempt might have failed only because the aspirant had mistaken which of the festivals of Zeus was greatest. Cf. also 1.13.6 (the first mention of a god in the work—as the beneficiary of a tyrant) and 6.54–55, 59 (the remarkable piety of the old Athenian tyrants). Cf. Aristophanes *Clouds* 900–905; that the rule of Zeus among the gods depends upon his superior power rather than his superior justice, Homer *Iliad* 1.565–69; 8.5–32; Aeschylus *Prometheus bound* 201–44.

[20] Homer *Iliad* 24.602–12; *Odyssey* 5.116–28 and 11.576–600; Sophocles *Philoctetes* 678–80 and *Antigone* 825–31; Pindar *Second Pythian* 21–48 and *First Olympian* 52–64; Acusilaus fr. 16 and 40a; Athenaeus 281b.

It is the Athenians' implicit defense against the charge of hybris which displays their true innovation concerning the sacred. This innovation originates in their understanding of the human—in what they claim to know manifestly rather than just by hearsay. If they reject the subjection of human beings to the divine law, it is not because they arrogantly impute to them a godlike freedom. Indeed they deprive them of such freedom as tradition had held them to possess, that of transgressing or not, of choosing "blamelessness" over "injustice." "There is no pride in [their] statement; for they claim to be doing only the inevitable. . . ."[21] In a word, they invoke the Athenian thesis: man is compelled to assert himself by a necessity of his nature.

Gods, then, who enforced the divine law as the Melians expect them to do, would punish men not only for acting as the gods too act, but for acting as they cannot but act being men. By siding with Melos, they would chastise Athens for doing just what Melos would have done in her place. This, I believe, is the key to the Athenian position. Surely the gods must recognize that mortals no more than gods can contain themselves, and just as surely they would not be so inconsequent as to punish them for it.

Nor, of course, would the gods likely reward them. When the Melians say they do not fear to suffer from the fortune that comes from the divine, they mean they expect it to favor them. The Athenians, in saying the same, likely mean only that they expect no worse luck than the Melians, their equals in the eyes of the divine. In the two most relevant respects, the envoys can afford to accept what they have been told about the divine. In both of these respects, however—the reputed justice of the gods toward human beings and their reputed belligerence among themselves—they reinterpret the accounts of the divine in light of their novel understanding of the human. We cannot stress too much that the "anthropology" of the envoys colors their "theology." What they have heard about the anthropomorphic gods happens to jibe with what they know about men.

The priority of the envoys' understanding of the human explains their most daring innovation in presenting the divine: their subjection of it to the natural. In nothing else do they so foreshadow Plato, while radicalizing what we have described as the minor strain in traditional piety. The gods are not the first beings on which all else depends; they depend, like the others, on nature. In this respect, the theology of the envoys is "philosophical"; it is so by extension from their anthropology.

The envoys preach a reformed theology. The old gods were unjust and hypocritical, holding us to a standard harsher than nature, divine or human, can bear. The envoys, while denying strict perfection to the divine, do expect it to make due allowance for the natural imperfection of human beings. Oddly, they agree with the poets that the gods are needy (for need is

---

[21] Macleod *Historia* 23 (1974) 395.

ubiquitous in nature), while implicitly rejecting the possibility that they are capricious in their treatment of mortals.

Not that we can sound the envoys' deepest thoughts on the divine. Their speech reflects their practical intention: they raise these questions only because the Melians have, and they must treat them in terms the Melians can understand. Their rejection of the likelihood of divine sanctions against their empire is compatible also with other hypotheses not presuming the justice of the gods.

If the envoys question the Melians' hopes in the gods, they deal more sternly still with their trust in the Spartans, which confirms the Melians' naïveté (*apeirokakon*, literally "inexperience of evils") and their witless folly (*aphron*). This greater vehemence concerning the Spartans accords with the greater certainty the envoys profess about human things. We have discussed above (pp. 75–86) their characterization of the Spartans and the resolution of its apparent paradox. As citizens and as a city, the Spartans observe a single standard: the good of Sparta. To it they submit all other interests, whether their own as individuals or those of other cities as cities. The Melians do not challenge this view of Sparta: they even present it as confirming their hopes (106). The very advantage of the Spartans must impel them to rescue Melos: for how could they betray their friends, thereby helping their enemies?

No, reply the envoys (5.107), for advantage consorts with safety; only the noble and the just brook danger. The Spartans are the least daring of men. This, too, the Melians accept; it, too, seems only to boost their confidence (108). They minimize the dangers involved and so the Spartan unwillingness to face them. The envoys dispute this assessment in all of its aspects (109). They especially deprecate the notion of the Spartans' mounting an expedition by sea when they hesitate to do so on their own element of dry land, with many forces and against near neighbors.

The Melians show one sign of having been impressed by the envoys' argument: hereafter, they speak of Spartan intervention only in the optative mood.[22] Yet their visions of such intervention become ever more inspired, imaginative, and improbable. If not an expedition by sea (by Sparta or by her allies), why not one by land? They mention an invasion of Attica and a reprise of the bold Brasidean scheme of marching against those Athenian subjects accessible by land (cf. 4.78 ff.). They speak then of a full-scale resumption of hostilities. They must not grasp what it takes to drive Sparta to war (cf. 1.118, 7.18) or the rare constellation of events required to launch the campaign of Brasidas (4.79–80). Mention of Brasidas—the only individual named in the dialogue—recalls Thucydides' judgment on those cities seduced by Brasidas to revolt from Athens (4.108.3). Their folly was no less

---

22 Strauss *City and man* 188.

because he was on hand and the Athenians seemed far away. Here the Athenians are on hand and the Spartans far away. Still the Melians persist, and their intransigence grows even as the envoys strip them of one hope after another.

Finally, the envoys weary of this and reprove the Melians with great earnestness (5.111). They are concerned (*enthymoumetha*) that although the Melians have agreed to take counsel about the rescue (*sōtēria*) of their city, they have so far mentioned nothing through which any human being would confidently expect to be saved. Again invoking present realities against future hopes, they warn that the Melians will show great unreason (*alogismos*) if, when the envoys depart, they do not "judge matters somewhat more moderately than at present." And again the envoys smell a rat.

> For surely you will not resort to that notion of disgrace which in those dangers that while disgraceful are plain to see, so often destroys human beings. For many, even as they foresee the sort of things toward which they are being borne, are so led on by the thing called disgrace and the seductive power of a name, that, worsted by a word, they quite gratuitously (*hekontas*) sink into incurable disasters in deed, thus incurring a disgrace the more disgraceful because due to folly rather than bad fortune. This, if you deliberate properly, you will guard against and not deem it unbecoming to be worsted by the greatest of cities, when it offers you mild (*metria*) terms: to become its allies, retaining the country that is yours while paying tribute—nor, having been offered the choice between war and security, will you hold out for the worse of the two. It is those who do not yield to equals, who bear themselves with dignity (or nobly or honorably, *kalōs*) toward superiors, and who are mild (*metrioi*) toward inferiors, who most often prosper. (5.111.3–4)

The Melians seem determined to push on while lacking any visible resources. Despite or because of this intransigence, the envoys retract their dismissal of honor. They now contend not that disgrace is irrelevant to a city beset with dangers, but that to fail to avert those dangers is disgraceful, hence their distinction between "the thing called disgrace" and "disgrace the more disgraceful because due to folly rather than bad fortune." They do not quite claim that the former is false and only the latter is true disgrace; perhaps disgrace cannot be entirely separated from the reputation for it. Vast, nonetheless, is the discrepancy between the degree of disgrace that the vulgar fix on as definitive and the depths into which that fixation may plunge them. The Melians must choose between being "worsted by a word" and being "worsted by the greatest of cities." Only a fool would incur destruction so as to bow (disgracefully) to a phantom rather than to superior power.

Here the envoys do not reprove the Melian aversion to disgrace but seek to educate it. The plight of Melos does not present an intractable conflict between the demands of nobility and those of good sense. In preserving their city as intact as circumstances permit, the Melians will do the same for their honor.

Having conceded, however, the relevance of honor to the case of Melos, the envoys must anticipate an objection. Are there not fates so shameful as to be resisted against all odds and at all costs? If so, it is not to such a fate that Athens summons Melos. Although the "greatest of cities," the terms that she offers one of the weakest are mild (*metria*).[23] The envoys urge on the Melians the very course they would adopt themselves: deferring somewhat to superiors belongs to the same grand policy as firmness with equals and demanding of inferiors only that they defer to you somewhat. Although the envoys praise these policies as prudent, they also cast them as honorable—their word for the indicated bearing of inferiors toward superiors is *kalōs*. The dignity of the weak, like their safety, begins with their admission of their weakness. That of the strong includes respecting the dignity of the weak.

The Melians, having conferred apart (5.112), reaffirm their intention of resisting, trusting, as they announce, in the fortune that is from the gods and, from human beings, in aid from the Spartans. The envoys reply (113), with evident exasperation, that the Melians alone appear to hold what is yet to happen as more certain than what they see before them. They have sealed their doom by trusting in "the Spartans, fortune, and hopes"; fortune, with no suggestion that it is from the divine.

The drama of this half of the dialogue lies in the contrast between the obstinacy of the impotent Melians and the impotence of their erstwhile educators. The envoys' strategy of dialogue has miscarried, with disastrous consequences—for Melos.

SPARTAN NEGLECT, ATHENIAN CRUELTY, DISASTER IN SICILY

The narrative that follows is unsurpassed even in Thucydides for eloquent reticence.[24] It moves matter-of-factly between the Athenians and Melians, on the one hand, and the Spartans, on the other. Neither are the gods neglected.

The Athenians begin their siege of Melos: meanwhile, in Peloponnese, among other matters briefly noted, Sparta fails to declare war on Athens despite repeated violations of Spartan territory. The Melians take a part of the Athenian siegeworks and then withdraw, teaching the Athenians to keep a better watch thereafter. That winter, the Spartans set out to invade the Argolid, but, the sacrificial omens being against them, they return home.

---

[23] Gillis *RendIstLomb* 112 (1978) 198–200; Cogan *Human thing* 89.
[24] Méautis *REG* 48 (1935) 275–78.

Meanwhile, the Melians repeat their earlier success. Reinforcements from Athens arrive in consequence and press the siege with vigor—there being also some treason among the Melians—so Melos surrenders on condition that its fate be referred to the Athenian assembly *(hōst' ekeinous peri autōn bouleusai*, 5.116.3). The decision is to kill the adult male Melians while enslaving the rest, after which Athens colonizes the place herself.

The drama of the narrative is twofold. In the first place, the Melians' successes arouse false hopes. If the gods manifest themselves as fortune (cf. 5.103–5, 112–13) and if one can credit fortune with the negligence of one's enemies, then the gods have indeed granted Melos more than equal fortune with her besiegers. In the end this avails her nothing given the disparity of forces (to which it is clear that Melos owes her luck, the fruit of Athenian complacency). But then not even the Melians expected divine favor to redress this disparity: for that they counted on Sparta (104).

The second thread of the narrative, then, is just the indifference of Sparta, which not only fails to intervene but never considers it. Reluctant to stir against Athens, despite manifest cause, or even against Argos—a neighbor, a land power, and a foe of proven weakness—the Spartans fully vindicate the envoys' assessment of them.[25]

If conversation aims at agreement, this one has proved a failure. That need not mean, however, that it proved inconclusive, that is, that no satisfactory ground for agreement emerged. One side can be right without the other's being persuaded. The Athenian arguments, while repellent, are convincing, at least as regards the reasonableness of the hopes of the Melians. That they fail to persuade the Melians suggests that the envoys' project of "enlightenment" itself rested on unreasonable hopes.

The Melians announce at 5.112 that their trust in the divine remains whole. This is their belated reply to 105: their silence at that point had not signified assent. It must, then, have conveyed their shock and their conviction that further argument was hopeless—that is, that the envoys were hopelessly impious. This conviction can only have quickened alike their anger and their hopes, both from the gods and from the Spartans. The greater the impiety and injustice of Athens (and both are on display at 5.105), the deeper the disgrace of yielding to it, the keener the presumed concern of the gods, and the graver the fancied compulsion on Sparta to save its blameless colonists. Only after 5.105 do the Melians dig in their heels: it is only their least reasonable hopes that they absolutely refuse to abandon.[26]

So much for the pathos of the episode insofar as the Melians are its subjects. We must also consider, however, its place within the work as a

[25] Reinhardt *Vermächtnis* 197.

[26] Cf. Stahl *Thukydides* 166–71. "The basic psychological disposition of man, *as established by Diodotus,* . . . *remains valid . . . even in the most extreme situation.*" ("*Die von Diodotos festgestellte psychologische Ausgangsdisposition* des Menschen . . . *bleibt sogar für die äusserste Situation*" [emphasis in original, 167].)

whole, of which not Melos but Athens is the quasitragic protagonist. We must consider, then, the great "tragic" sequence Melian Dialogue/Sicilian disaster. The drama of Melos finds its completion only in this still greater drama. Yet what does it signify? How does the Melian episode incur or foretell the disaster that follows?

An obvious suggestion is that Athens falls victim to divine nemesis, which, if it did not preserve Melos, vindicates her hopes to the extent of punishing Athenian hybris.[27] Thucydides, however, not only offers human reasons for the Sicilian debacle, but stresses their decisiveness (7.4, 42, 48–49, 50; 8.96).[28] Is it then mere chance that the "chastisement" of Athens on Sicily follows her "transgression" on Melos? The sequence Melos/Sicily is poetic, that is, more beautiful than true (cf. 1.21.1). Because Thucydides is more than a poet, however, we may presume that it points to some important truth.

Does the Athenian disaster in Sicily, which is to say their fatal errors in Sicily, somehow follow from the understanding espoused by the envoys? Or may we describe these errors as Melian, that is, as repeating those of the Melians? In either event, Melos would be avenged; in the second case, only ironically so. This last outcome would confirm the superior wisdom of the envoys—unless, of course, their understanding was itself somehow "Melian." In addressing these questions we must begin by elaborating that understanding.

THE ENVOYS TO MELOS AS EXPONENTS OF THE ATHENIAN THESIS

We often read that the butchery of the Melians reflects the decline of Athens under the impact of war.[29] Since we also read that the statements of the envoys reflect this decline, clarity demands the recognition that the relation between the two is ambiguous. On the fundamental point, moreover, in denying the primacy of justice over interest, these envoys merely restate the argument of the Athenian envoys at Sparta and (as we have argued) the implicit view of Pericles himself.[30] The question of "decline" thus proves elusive.

[27] See Cornford *Thucydides mythistoricus* 174–87; De Sanctis *RendLinc* ser. 6, vol. 6 (1930) 299–308. Grote *History of Greece* 7:117–18; Regenbogen *Kleine Schriften* 227; Scharf *Gymnasium* 61 (1954) 510 and n.17; and Liebeschuetz *JHS* 88 (1968) 76–77 all note the ὕβρις of the Athenian speech and/or action at Melos, by means of which Thucydides establishes the expectation of divine retribution.

[28] Cf. Reinhardt *Vermächtnis* 214–16. Herter *RhM* 97 (1954) 330 observes that "Nemesis avenges not the injustice [of the Athenians], but the[ir] imprudence."

[29] The classic statement is J. H. Finley *Thucydides* 208–12. Most recently, it is Euben *Tragedy* 167, 178, 197–98.

[30] Cf. Kagan *Peace of Nicias* 151. Cajani *Prometheus* 6 (1980) 21–28 contends that the irony of the debate lies in the Melians' exposition of the "Periclean values" once cherished by Athens; he overlooks that the "values" of Pericles were imperialistic.

The destruction of Melos is indeed shocking.[31] Cruelty is of course the norm for cities other than Athens, nor is this even her only example of it (cf. 2.67, 4.57, 5.32.1).[32] The reader of Thucydides to this point, however, will have encountered the Mytilenian debate (3.36–49),[33] in which the Athenians prove themselves more open than any other people in Thucydides to arguments for mildness toward vanquished foes. The argument that prevails on that occasion, moreover, that of Diodotus, is notorious for its hard-headed realism and its neglect of issues of justice in favor of those of expediency. His opponent Cleon, on the other hand, who advocates harshness toward Mytilene, loudly invokes justice as well as expediency. As the clemency of Athens toward Mytilene is not, then, the result of any preference for arguments from justice over those from expediency, so her harshness toward Melos cannot follow simply from a deprecation of the former in favor of the latter.

Indeed the very arguments of Diodotus would seem to point to clemency in this case as well. With Melos as with Mytilene, an orator might have found ample grounds of interest, precisely on the basis of the Athenian thesis, for "holding as few as possible responsible" (3.46.6). Diodotus' case against massacring the Mytilenians invokes, among other things, the utility of graduated punishments for affecting the outcome of future revolts. To punish harshly a city that surrenders when it could have held out longer is to drive future rebels to hold out for as long as they can (3.46); to punish the many along with the few who actually instigated the revolt is to drive the many in other cities into the arms of the few (3.47). Diodotus asserts, on dubious grounds, both that Mytilene could have held out longer and that the many had seized the first opportunity to hand over the city to Athens (cf. 3.27). Such an argument appears at least equally feasible in the case of Melos. We know that the people were excluded from the decision whether or not to resist (5.84.3); and we know that some piece of treason—by the people?—had helped compel the city's surrender (116.3).

In the case of Mytilene the Athenians had not decided for a massacre, but rather had reversed such a decision on the basis of the arguments common to Diodotus and our envoys.[34] We must keep in mind that it is not the envoys we hear who decide the fate of Melos, nor the generals who sent them, nor the one who succeeds these. The decision is taken in Athens by the citizenry assembled.[35] Euben assimilates the manner of the people to

[31] Most eloquent is Grote *History of Greece* 7.114–15.

[32] Kagan *Peace of Nicias* 153: "the Athenian treatment of Melos was only an extension of the policy that destroyed Scione." Cf. Gillis *RendIstLomb* 112 (1978) 187–94; Cogan *Human thing* 89 and n.6.

[33] We will consider this debate in detail in chapter 7.

[34] Cf. Liebeschuetz *JHS* 88 (1968) 73–74; for a parallel argument with reference to Pericles, see Wassermann *TAPA* 78 (1947) 23–24.

[35] This is implied by the formula of the capitulation at 5.116.3 and confirmed by Plutarch *Alcibiades* 16.6.

that of the envoys in declaring that the Athenians act from "cold calculation" in destroying Melos.[36] In fact, Thucydides offers no account of their deliberations. They might have acted in a towering rage, as when they passed the initial Mytilenian decree.

As for the "cold calculation" of the envoys themselves, we must not assume that it vindicates the massacre. They specifically commend avoiding excess in treating one's inferiors (5.111.4)—a maxim which Athens may have honored in the terms that she had offered Melos, but not in annihilating her for refusing to accept these. The envoys offer this maxim, moreover, as following from the "realistic" policy in which they try to instruct the Melians. While prudence as they present it does not defer to justice, neither does it incline toward cruelty, for prudence and excess are inimical. Simply stated, the Athenian destruction of Melos seems punitive. Yet there is no basis for a punitive attitude in the arguments expounded by the envoys. They themselves tax the Melians not with wickedness but with folly (5.105.3, 111.2). And folly ought to evoke not anger but pity.[37]

Indeed it is less the envoys' view of Melos that would justify harsh vengeance than the Melian view of Athens; whereas they regard Melos as ill advised, she regards Athens as unjust and worthy of punishment both human and divine. To conclude, then: the envoys' adherence to the Athenian thesis, i.e. to the primacy of advantage over justice, does not in itself brand them as symptoms of decline, let alone as abettors of butchery.

How then do the envoys compare with previous exponents of the thesis? If they express themselves more bluntly than their predecessors, that may be due as much to the specifics of the case as to their finding themselves in it after so many years of the stress of war. Like all Thucydidean speakers, they address their particular situation.

While the envoys to Sparta spoke as if to equals and men of the world like themselves, the envoys to Melos address men not only far weaker than themselves (on whom that fact must be impressed) but far less practiced as well. There is also the important fact that Athens has attacked Melos before but only half-heartedly (3.91). The envoys must convince the Melians that this time Athens will not be denied, that nothing will deter her from taking Melos, surely not talk about justice. And given the resistance of the Melians to seeing the world as Athens sees it, the envoys must state their position starkly and unrelentingly.

Does this position differ at bottom from that of the envoys to Sparta? Both embassies insist that the stronger must prevail over the weaker, as far as to rule over them, but that they ought to rule them not harshly but mildly. Our envoys differ in presenting this mildness not as justice (which they

---

[36] Euben *Tragedy* 178.

[37] Cf. Stahl *Thukydides* 165–66. Fliess *Bipolarity* 156–57; Amit *Athenaeum* 46 (1968) 217; De Ste-Croix *Origins* 14; and Cogan *Human thing* 89–90 also deny that the envoys' arguments anticipate the annihilation of Melos.

declare, at 5.89, to apply only between equal powers) but as policy: those stronger powers "fare best" who adopt it (*pleist' an orthointo*, 111.4). It might seem that these envoys, seized by a new and more rational or hard-headed spirit, differ from those to Sparta by referring all to considerations of advantage, where advantage is more akin to safety and profit than to honor and has finally banished thoughts of justice or nobility.

Even this stress on advantage, however, owes something to rhetorical considerations. Having eschewed all claims to justice, the envoys can hardly ascribe to justice the mildness of the terms they bear. If the only issue on the table is advantage, they must present their policy accordingly. And yet even so, as we have noted, they stress at 5.111.4 that the policy that is advantageous for Melos is at the same time dignified or honorable for her.

In adopting this tack the envoys may not be disclosing their own concern with the noble so much as conceding that they have been unable to dissuade the Melians from this concern. There is, however, further evidence that the envoys have failed to wash their own souls of the just and noble. It follows their assertion that the Spartans equate the noble with the pleasant and the advantageous with the just (5.105.4), and the reply of the Melians that they rely on just such motives (*pisteuōn tōi xympheronti*) to bring Sparta to their side. To this the envoys rejoin as follows: "so you do not suppose that advantage consorts with safety (*to xympheron men meta asphaleias einai*), while the just and the noble can only be attempted with danger, which the Spartans brave the least of anyone" (5.107).

This retort is strangely ambivalent. Obviously, the envoys press on the Melians the folly of presuming on the aid of so cautious a power as Sparta. They might also hope that as loyal colonists of Sparta the Melians will take her for their model and act with like circumspection themselves, looking to their advantage within the horizon of the tangible and manifest. Be this as it may, the envoys cannot resist an implied comparison of Athens and Sparta which is invidious to the latter. Like the envoys to Sparta, they plead necessity but would deny that their subjection to it is abject.

Even more emphatically than their predecessors, these Athenians present Athens as the prisoner of the compulsion to empire. Necessity presses her relentlessly; the realm of her freedom is ever more tenuous. Even so, the envoys still long to pride themselves on their Athenian virtue. The implicit contrast with Sparta implies that Athens does not equate the pleasant with the noble or the advantageous with the just; nor does she lack the daring, which is the condition of just and noble deeds. She rises above merely cautious expediency—above, that is, the very policy which the envoys claim that she has followed in the present case and which moreover, they urge on Melos. Are the Melians to take this advice? Or are they to emulate the noble firmness of the adviser, a city that by its own proud admission has never abandoned a venture "for fear of any one" (5.111.1; cf. 112.2)? Although the envoys will proceed to reinterpret honor even as they rehabilitate it (assimilating it as much as possible to expediency [111.3 ff.]), their residual pride in Athenian daring and contempt for Spartan pusillanimity cannot but undercut this strategy.

Have the envoys, in glancing at the conduct of Sparta, recollected something about themselves, and is this recollection reflected in their subsequent rehabilitation of the noble? For at 5.111, as we have seen, while reproving for a second time the Melians' erroneous notions of disgrace, they recant their earlier dismissal of this issue. Instead they distinguish levels of disgrace, of which the lowest is heedless folly; rather than reject a concern with the noble as incompatible with reason, they attempt to reconcile the two. This proves to be subject to problems of its own.

Even in 5.111 the Athenians stop short of identifying disgrace with folly or implying that what is sensible can never be disgraceful. Such, however, is what their argument seems to imply. They assert that to submit to the so-called disgraceful is, where less foolish, the less disgraceful of the available options: to act sensibly is to act as honorably as the case permits. Is less foolish always less disgraceful? If the standard for action is safety, is the safest course then always the most honorable—even if it is by any usual standard disgraceful? The envoys thus unwittingly recall Archidamus, who concludes a general's harangue the theme of which is caution by declaring that "the noblest as well as the safest thing [is] the sight of many [troops] subject to a single discipline" (2.11.9). Noblest and safest: that these notions should converge in the mind of the most respectable spokesman for Sparta confirms the assertion of the envoys at 5.105. Yet a powerful undercurrent of their own argument tends in just this direction—even as they appear in their slighting reference to Sparta to reject it.

The envoys want to have it both ways, to congratulate themselves alike on their sensible caution and on their noble daring. On the one hand, they imply that the sole defensible standard for political conduct is rational advantage, with its inherent emphasis on safety. They claim to have come against Melos (an enterprise in no way risky) precisely out of their aversion to risk: they could not let Melos be without imperiling the security of their empire. On the other hand, they suggest in glancing at the Spartans, that daring (a link to the noble and just) is a matter of pride. Might they pride themselves on a fancied freedom from the very concern for advantage on which they act in the present case, and which they commend to Melos even while contemning it in Sparta? In the end they seem to split the difference between the two positions by commending caution itself to the Melians as the least ignoble option open to them.

We recall that Pericles praised Athens as the home of both unsurpassed daring and unequaled rationality. He did not deny that these are in tension; he claimed that of all cities only Athens had succeeded in uniting them (cf.

2.40.3). Yet if (as Pericles claimed) all the risks Athens runs are fully weighed by reason, must their daring not be subordinate to some rational principle of advantage? Reason can hardly stop at enumerating the risks to be run, without considering whether it makes sense to run them. If Athens never ventures except as her interests direct, we may praise her for her prudence and firmness[38] but hardly for her nobility. For can the noble be subordinated to safety and interest and still remain the noble?

It is not surprising, then, that the Melians rebuff the tenuous or "enlightened" view of the noble that the envoys press at 5.111. The envoys have underestimated the depth of the Melians' resistance to reason, the likelihood of which a more reasonable strategy would have taken into account.[39] The Melians themselves have agreed that the issue on the table is whether resistance is reasonable: they concede that a hopeless stand would be foolish and so of doubtful nobility. Despite all the arguments of the envoys, however, the Melians will not grant that their situation is in fact hopeless. By a strange but all-too-human turn of thought, they must suppose that some god (or Sparta) will save them precisely because they have preferred the noble to the safe, because they have taken a stand as the blameless party against the unjust one. Nobility, which demands indifference to success or happiness, appears to inflame the Melians' hopes for these beyond all reason.

Nor, as we have seen, are such hopes peculiar to the Melians. Without quite describing Athens as just and noble, the envoys balk at severing her lifeline to these. Though subject to universal necessity, Athens is not just another city: in her clarity, candor, and daring, she remains a uniquely deserving one. If the Athenians persist in regarding their policy as somehow noble, do they resist presuming on the success they hold themselves to deserve thereby? Can we credit their claim to rely on the manifest alone?

The tension between the rational/manifest and the noble/immanifest is not the only one in the envoys' speech. There is also that between both of these pairs and the strictly compulsory. These envoys go beyond those at Sparta in subjecting Athens to the yoke of necessity. It is not now merely certain motives on which the powerful (like everyone else) are compelled to act: the mere fact of possessing power compels one to rule to its limits (5.105). This does not depend on the decision of the powerful but precludes it. We can infer all kinds of reasons for the present expedition;[40] still, according to 5.105, specific motives are beside the point. Athens must conquer Melos because it is there.

But is subjection to so ironclad a compulsion consistent with a cool, deliberate policy any more than with a noble, disinterested one?[41] Three

---

[38] Cf. Plato *Laches*, esp. 192cd.
[39] Cf. Stahl *Thukydides* 158–71, esp. 167–68.
[40] Kagan *Peace of Nicias* 148–49; Sealey *History of city-states* 350–51.
[41] Romilly *Imperialism* 288–89.

versions of Athens vie in the envoys' remarks: Athens as freely and therefore nobly choosing to practice daring; Athens as avoiding all excess (including daring) as she freely and masterfully chooses the wisest policy for advancing her safety and interests; and Athens as prey to a brute, intractable expansiveness hostile to choice of either of these kinds.

This lack of clarity in the speakers poses a final problem for interpreting the dialogue. By the end of the discussion, the envoys, disappointed in their hopes of persuading the Melians, speak as if offended by their self-destructive obtuseness. Folly as such, as we have noted, merits not anger but pity (cf. 5.105.3). The envoys, however, having gone to such trouble to enlighten the Melians, complain that their folly is not innocent (and thus excusable) but willful and perverse (*hekontas*, 111.3). Especially in issuing their final warning, in which they wash their hands of the Melians for their allegedly unique refusal to come to terms with reality (5.113), they sound very much as if they believe their foes deserve to suffer. In this sense, whatever their part (if any) in the subsequent decision as to the fate of Melos, their reaction does foreshadow it, and here the reader may feel that the argument has come full circle.

The envoys have claimed to banish all concern for justice from the conversation, but they have not banished it from their hearts. In their anger they display a peculiar kind of retributiveness, that of the debunker of justice (and thus of retribution) angry because his debunking has been rejected. If this interpretation is correct, then they are as deficient in self-understanding as they are in their understanding of the Melians.

Again, it must be stressed that the issue is not the Athenian thesis but the failure of even these "sophisticated" Athenians fully to face up to its implications. (We must, of course, consider this failure in our overall appraisal of the thesis.) These envoys have in common with the other principal anonymous (or "representative") spokesmen for Athens—those at Sparta and at Delium—that their boldness exceeds their clarity and thus falls short of the greatest boldness. For this last, we will look in chapter 7 to other speakers—Diodotus and Hermocrates.

Chapter 6

MELOS AND SYRACUSE

THE WISDOM AND FOLLY OF NICIAS

We return to the sequence Melian Dialogue/Sicilian disaster. That sequence first strikes the eye as one of crime and punishment. Continuing on their career of injustice, the Athenians overreach themselves, with terrible consequences.[1]

The Sicilian project may indeed remind us of the doctrine of the envoys to Melos; surely Athens is determined to rule to the limits of her power. Overreaching oneself, on the other hand, that is, acting on hopes beyond one's power, is what those envoys had vainly warned the Melians against. In the debate over the expedition, Nicias echoes the wisdom of the envoys by discouraging his compatriots from infatuation with the immanifest and from risking their all on it (6.9–14; cf. 6.1.1, 24).[2] On this view of the Sicilian disaster, the "punishment" of the Athenians would result from their repeating the error of the Melians.[3] This might seem gratifying: irony is appropriate to tragedy. We must bear in mind, however, that such an interpretation would appear to leave the position of the envoys to Melos unrefuted.[4] For it is no refutation of a position that those who abandon it for its opposite fail.

Any interpretation, moreover, of the Sicilian expedition as "Melian" is open to the following objection. However ignorant or credulous most of the Athenians were who voted to undertake it, Thucydides indicates that the project itself did not exceed the power of Athens. The expedition actually dispatched was "remarkable for its overwhelming strength as compared with the peoples against whom it was directed" (6.31.6). Indeed a smaller one (such as that originally proposed; cf. 6.8.1 with 25.2 and 31) might have sufficed; it would surely have been better suited to the strategy in-

---

[1] Cornford *Thucydides mythistoricus* 185; De Sanctis *RendLinc* ser. 6, vol. 6 (1930) 305–8; Liebeschuetz *JHS* 88 (1968) 76–77; Lloyd-Jones *Justice of Zeus* 143.

[2] His use at 6.13.1 of ἀναρριπτούσης ("casting the die") echoes the warning of the envoys to the Melians at 5.103. His περὶ τῶν ἀφανῶν καὶ τῶν μελλόντων κινδυνεύειν ("To run risks over immanifest and future things," 6.9.3) echoes the envoys' use of ἀφανής at 5.103.2 and at 5.113, and of μέλλοντα at 5.87. For this general view of Nicias, see Stahl in Stadter ed. *Speeches* 71–72.

[3] Cornford *Thucydides mythistoricus* 185; Topitsch *WS* 61–62 (1943–47) 58; Herter *RhM* 97 (1954) 330–31.

[4] Cf. Liebeschuetz *JHS* 88 (1968) 75.

tended by Alcibiades and actually adopted upon arrival: that of "divide and conquer." (It would also have been much less risky.) In the event the project founders "not so much because of a miscalculation of the power of those against whom it was sent as through a fault of the senders in making disadvantageous decisions in assisting those who had gone out, choosing rather to occupy themselves with private cabals for the leadership of the people" (2.65.11).[5] We learn that the crucial failure of support was the direct result of the partisan cabals: it was the removal of Alcibiades from joint command of the expedition (6.15). Thucydides' endorsement of Alcibiades' conduct of the war may or may not express the point of view of the Athenians rather than his own; be this as it may, the sequel confirms that Alcibiades would have brought that expedition to a victorious conclusion. His strategy of winning over key Sicilian cities might yet have succeeded, especially if backed by further Athenian victories (cf. 6.74.1, 88, 103). In any case, had it failed, he would still have had plenty of time to devise another. For even the desultory efforts of Nicias failed only because help finally arrived in Sicily from Peloponnese. And this help arrived in time only because Athens had sought to recall Alcibiades to put him to death on trumped up charges (6.61.4), thus provoking his defection to Sparta.[6]

In the end Nicias actually bolsters the Athenians' resolve to undertake the Sicilian project. Having failed to dissuade them from the expedition, he must decide whether to resign his joint command of it. In grasping his

[5] On the meaning of οὐ τὰ πρόσφορα ("disadvantageous decisions"), see Hornblower *Commentary* 348.

[6] Cf. Gundert *Die Antike* 16 (1940) 102. Kagan suggests that Alcibiades' strategy was too clever by half, and all the less promising given the size of the expedition as launched, which unmistakably signaled its true intention of the conquest of all of Sicily (Kagan *Peace* 213–14, 248, 255–56). Yet key cities and tribes did remain neutral, and several sided with Athens. Alcibiades himself identifies Messane as the key to his strategy (6.48): that city seems on the verge of coming over, following the initial Athenian victory, before Alcibiades' recall leads him to betray the plot he himself had instigated (6.74.1). The attitude of Camarina, which finally decided to lean toward Syracuse only because of her greater fear of her (6.88.1), suggests that a more vigorous prosecution of the Alcibiadean strategy than Nicias undertook might have enjoyed more success (cf. 6.103). In any case, if not for the urging of Alcibiades, Sparta would never have intervened in time to save Syracuse, nor would that intervention have availed if not for Nicias' failure to press adequate offensive and defensive measures. Cf. Romilly *REG* 103 (1990) 376–78 and *Construction* 98; Herter *RhM* 93 (1949) 137–38; Lateiner *CP* 80 (1985) 212.

It remains an unanswerable question whether Alcibiades might earlier have supported the bolder strategy proposed by Lamachus (6.46.5–50). He must have suspected that the demagogues were contriving against him in his absence (6.29), in which case he needed not only good results in Sicily but quick ones. A strategy of diplomacy promised no such quick results. He might, of course, have regarded Lamachus' plan as unfeasible. One thing is certain: Nicias would never have acquiesced in the proposal of Lamachus, whereas that of Alcibiades was deliberate enough to obtain his consent; this might explain why Alcibiades shunned Lamachus' plan and why the latter immediately threw his support to the former.

choice not to do so, we must recall his earlier fiasco over Pylos. Faced with a similarly risky commission, he had resigned it to Cleon, whose astonishing success in it had sealed the latter's political ascendancy (4.27–28, 39). Is Nicias to hand a like opportunity to the callow Alcibiades? Instead, he resolves to speak again to urge the necessity of an expedition much greater and more costly than planned, so as to disgust the Athenians or, if they acquiesce in his estimates, thus to assure the expedition's safety (and his own).

While Nicias would prefer the former outcome, he quite predictably obtains the latter (6.24). Nicias, who in his first speech has called on his fellow elders to join him in quenching the mad longing for the absent (i.e., for conquests) (*dyserotes apontōn*) of their younger compatriots succeeds only in fanning the eros of all, young and old alike. Persuading them that the augmented project is perfectly safe, he renders it perfectly irresistible. He thus makes of reliance on the manifest not a deterrent but an inducement to the expedition.

Besides reassuring the citizens, Nicias' staggering estimates appeal to their love of the showy and extravagant. At its mustering, the fleet affords a spectacle not of sober preparedness but of more-than-Periclean splendor, the acme of conspicuously competitive public-spiritedness (6.31; cf. 1.71). Such a profusion of resources cannot but comfort the people in their last-minute apprehensions (6.30.2–31.1).

In thus ineptly inducing the people to undertake so gigantic an expedition, Nicias also commits himself to the goals of the project as they conceive it. He cannot employ such an armada for nothing more than beating a safe retreat (6.47–48)—or for anything less than the conquest of all Sicily.

While Syracuse is there to be conquered and Nicias still boasts ample resources, he fails to press his advantage. Victorious in the initial battle, he departs to winter elsewhere (6.63–71). Having returned and won several more engagements, the Athenians are about to complete a circumvallation of Syracuse, thus depriving her of all hope of relief (94–102). The Syracusans sink into defeatism and dissension (103.3–4). At this crucial juncture, however, it appears as if Nicias reposes only too much confidence in his manifest material superiority. Despising the initial reenforcements from Peloponnese, "because of [the report that he receives of their] scanty numbers," he mounts no effective guard whether by sea or land to prevent their arrival in the city (6.104.3, 7.2, 7.7.1). Nor, even after the advent of these forces with their Spartan commander Gylippus, does Nicias hasten the progress of the circumvallation. The scantiness of the reenforcements notwithstanding, the situation fast deteriorates. With Nicias lying low rather than offering vigorous opposition, on the second try Gylippus defeats the Athenians, and the Syracusans carry a counterwall past the unfinished siege wall of their enemies (7.3–6). On the brink of certain victory, the besiegers have become the besieged.[7]

Nicias makes no offensive use of the navy, the military arm in which Athenian superiority is most overwhelming; he appears merely to hold it in reserve so as to assure a safe retreat. Indeed, in order to assure the safety of the fleet, he immures both his crews and his naval stores on land just when Athens has lost her superiority there: so confined, "even thus did the deterioration of the crews first occur" (7.4.6). The site and its forts are soon taken and many men and stores and much money lost, along with command of the resupply route. "And [this] most of all caused the expedition to deteriorate" (24.3). The fleet has lost the initiative without having tried to exploit it.

Though solely responsible for the gigantism of the expedition, Nicias never turns it to strategic advantage: without pressing for great gains, he exposes Athens to terrible losses. Unfortunately, safety is to be had only through victory or retreat, each of which entails risks and demands a decisiveness that he lacks. Instead he repeats an earlier error. While the force still at his disposal is perfectly sufficient for retreating (and while the Syracusans would still be glad to permit it to depart), and now that even a larger force can no longer assure victory, Nicias offers the Athenians at home a choice between recalling the expedition and committing to it most of their remaining resources. By now he really ought to know which of these options they will adopt (7.10–16).

A relief expedition eventually arrives, one larger than the initial expedition as originally planned (cf. 7.16.2, 20.2, and 42.1 with 6.8.1). Its commander, Demosthenes, sizes up the situation as one of wasted opportunities (7.42.3): the moment has passed when even the now-augmented force could reasonably hope to prevail. He sees one possibility: to outflank the Syracusan defenses by means of a nocturnal dash up the heights overlooking the city. Either the Athenians will thus reestablish themselves as the besiegers, or the entire force should withdraw immediately (42.4–5). In a vivid and dramatic episode "[in] which ignorant armies clash by night," his daring plan narrowly fails (43–45). Accordingly Demosthenes counsels immediate departure (47.3–4).

Now, however, that victory has slipped away from Nicias, and his chances of success are as illusory as he originally proclaimed them, he succumbs to false hopes (7.48). Ironic in many ways (not least in supposing in the Syracusans a "fiscal conservatism" as great as his own), these hopes salve Nicias' self-respect and undo the expedition. They permit him to blur what would otherwise loom as a stark choice between the good of Athens and his

---

[7] For reckonings of Nicias' errors of both omission and commission, see Kagan *Peace* 267–76 and Pouncey *Necessities* 117–30.

personal wish to die with dignity, "privately" at the hands of the enemy in Sicily rather than "publicly" on an unjust charge at Athens (49.3–4); they blind him to the fact that he is committing an act tantamount to treason.[8] Demosthenes sees clearly that only retreat can save the expedition and the power of Athens; he thinks only of saving them. He proposes, however, a compromise to allay Nicias' personal misgivings: to withdraw not to Athens but to a safer location in Sicily (49.2–3). Nicias still objecting, however, his obstinacy immobilizes Demosthenes. Precisely because Nicias' stated case against retreating is so weak, Demosthenes concludes that he must have a stronger one he is concealing (49.4). Thus Demosthenes too permits himself to hope. Thucydides' crucial lesson to the Demostheneses of the world is not to trust the Niciases, that is, not to underestimate their surprising propensity to rely on the immanifest.

The folly of Nicias' position soon becomes evident even to himself: on the predictable arrival of enemy reenforcements to counter the recent Athenian ones, he too agrees that the invaders must depart posthaste (7.50.1–3). Despite all Nicias' other errors, the force would still have escaped largely intact had it not now resolved to delay its urgent retreat "thrice nine days" (7.50.4; cf. 5.26.3–4) because of a lunar eclipse. At the crucial moment an Athenian army prefers reliance on the immanifest to what it sees clearly with its own eyes, that it must decamp immediately; the result is its utter destruction. For this Thucydides blames Nicias, as "somewhat too given to divination."[9] More than anything else, it is Nicias' faith in divine concern with human affairs that undoes his hopes of that deliverance for which he looks to the divine (7.77.2).

However dubious the expedition, it would probably have succeeded if conducted according to the principles of the envoys to Melos; it would certainly have avoided disaster. Thucydides does not blame the Athenian rank and file for interpreting the eclipse as god-sent: he agrees with the envoys on Melos that "the many" are always "Melian" (5.103). At 8.1, in reporting the Athenian reaction to the catastrophe of the expedition, he discloses what he has earlier suppressed: that divination and oracles had "caused [the Athenians] to hope (*epelpisan*)" in the success of the expedition (cf. 6.31.6).[10] Nor must we overlook their frenzied obsession with omens adverse to that success (6.27–29, 53–61). Most Athenians have never been as "Athenian" as their envoys to Melos, never as self-reliant or as conscious

---

[8] Cf. Pouncey *Necessities* 125–26. The harm done Athens by the decent and pious Nicias while in command of her own forces dwarfs any done her by the exiled Alcibiades while guiding the forces of her enemies.

[9] Cf. Plutarch *Nicias* 23–24.1 with Plutarch *Pericles* 35.2 and Tacitus *Annals* 1.28–30.

[10] On the meaning of the word, see Powell *Historia* 28 (1979) 15–16; the rest of this article is also quite useful.

of the folly of relying on the divine.[11] Weather that the troops at first accept as seasonal (i.e., natural) later dejects them as ominous or god-sent (cf. 6.70.1 with 7.79.3; cf. 7.71.3).[12] The Syracusans, for their part, are the most "Athenian" foes of Athens (6.33.5, 7.55, 8.96.5).

Athens fails in Sicily not because the project is doomed from the start, but because Nicias and the rank and file doom it by their Melianism.[13] It is in this sense that the "punishment" of Athens fits the "crime." The cautionary tale Thucydides tells does not simply vindicate piety. The necessary condition of the debacle is that having once launched the expedition, the Athenians reject the impious Alcibiades for Nicias, whom they trust because of his piety. To grasp the political or rational significance of the sequence Melos/Sicily is to grasp the relationship between the Melian affair and the Athenian turn from Alcibiades to Nicias.

Alcibiades almost incarnates Athens: he models his conduct on hers. The first speaker openly to introduce the Athenian thesis into domestic affairs, he addresses his fellow Athenians as Athens addresses other cities. Accused by Nicias in the Sicilian debate of harboring private ambitions ruinous to the city, he denies neither his ambitions nor that these are private. Instead he has the cheek or candor to insist that his attempt to cast the widest shadow of any individual among the Greeks benefits incidentally the city as well: from his opulent splendor foreigners infer that of the city. Alcibiades is the sun, Athens the moon (6.16.1–4). Whereas Pericles had insisted that each Athenian derived his eternal remembrance and so his true being from the city, Alcibiades reverses this dependency: Athens will be remembered for him. What Pericles had suggested of the present generation of Athenians—that it lent luster to its ancestors rather than borrowing it from them (2.36)—Alcibiades applies to himself as an individual (6.16.1). (His ancestors include Pericles.) As Pericles had asserted that posterity would acknowledge Athens as the peak (2.41, 64.2–6), so Alcibiades insists that future Athenians will claim descent from him, even falsely (6.16.5). He thus assures his audience that their grandchildren will delight to cast them as cuckolds: Thucydides not only notes (6.15.4) but portrays the private offense that Alcibiades gave to each of his fellows. While Pericles had extolled

---

[11] Cf. Plutarch *Nicias* 13 and Aristophanes *Knights* 974–1052: the imperialism of Demos depends on oracles.

[12] Cf. Tacitus *Histories* 4.26.

[13] Jebb *Essays and addresses* 403; Schwartz *Geschichtswerk* 139; Lavagnini *Saggio* 50; Luschnat *Feldherrnreden* 91; Méautis *REG* 48 (1935) 278; Wassermann *TAPA* 78 (1947) 30–31; Strauss *City and man* 192–209. Stahl in Stadter ed. *Speeches* 64–69 claims that the outcome vindicates Nicias' counsels against the expedition; he fails to acknowledge that it does so only as a consequence of Nicias' own subsequent errors. Cf. Romilly *REG* 101 (1990) 376–78 on the ambiguous failure of Alcibiades' prophecies of victory.

an equality of glory among citizens predicated on the preeminence of Athens among cities, Alcibiades enjoins his fellow citizens to confront their common inferiority to him.

Athens can afford to offend other cities, because she does not depend on their sufferance. Alcibiades by contrast remains dependent on his fellow citizens. Faced with the imputations of Nicias, which threaten to scuttle the expedition on which his vast ambitions depend, he must secure the support of the people. Yet how can he expect them to back someone who so clearly despises them? Evidently by resorting to an even-more-than-Athenian candor. Promising to feast them richly with crumbs of wealth and glory from his table, he calls on them to overcome their resentment of him for the sake of realizing ends of their own that just happen to be congruent with his.

Summoning the citizens to a tacit pact for the advancement of their respective interests, Alcibiades reinterprets the city as merely the arena of such interests. Human beings are ultimately individuals, whose own interests or goods are frankly prior to their duties to the city. Alcibiades can easily seem the most "modern" or "liberal" character in Thucydides. In fact, he is the most "Periclean" one. Accepting Pericles' principle that glory is the crown of human life, he states the conclusion that Pericles had failed to state: glory can no more furnish the basis for a true common good within cities than among them. He dispels the Periclean illusion of an equality on the level of a civic glory. Glory, among individuals as among cities, is by its very nature both scarce and relative, "because . . . if all men have it no man hath it, for [it] consist[s] in comparison and precellence."[14] The city that defines its good as an ever-larger share of glory amassed at the expense of other cities sets a bad example for those of its citizens who think that example through (as the Athenian thesis bids them to do). For why not imitate the city by pursuing the greatest renown for oneself at the expense of one's fellow citizens? The common good "unjustly understood" proves vulnerable to its inherent contradictions.[15]

Alcibiades is aware that for him in his relations with his fellow citizens, just as for Athens in her relations with other cities, the burden of envy cannot be dispelled in his lifetime (6.16.5; cf. 2.64.4–6). Full reconciliation

---

[14] Hobbes *De Cive* 1.2.

[15] Gundert *Die Antike* 16 (1940) 112: "Alkibiades diese stärkste Durchbrechung des periklischen Kriegsplane mit einer Weiterführung periklischen Gedanken begründet." ("Alcibiades justifies this complete departure from the Periclean strategy with a radicalization of Periclean thought.") Cf. Burckhardt *Force and freedom* 218 and 336; Reinhardt *Vermächtnis* 205; Grene *Greek political theory* 30–32; Strauss *City and man* 193–94; Macleod *Collected essays* 68–87 (an identical discussion appears in *QS* 2 [1975] 39–65); Pouncey *Necessities* 111–12; Barel *La quête du sens* 227–30; Forde *Ambition to rule*, and Palmer *Love of glory* for valuable discussions of Alcibiades as the incarnation of the problem of the "individual and society" in its peculiarly Athenian manifestation, a problem already fully implicit in the Funeral Oration.

with his fellow citizens can occur only posthumously. Still, he requests the forbearance of his fellows. He appeals not only to their interests, but also to their justice. It would be unjust to begrudge him the lion's share of the glory: he is, after all, the lion. It would be unjust to demand of him that he treat them, his inferiors, with greater deference than they display toward theirs, unjust to insist that he adhere more firmly to the principle of equality than they do (6.16.4). Their resentment of him springs from envy; he calls on them to be just enough to swallow that envy. In this too he imitates Athens, which asks other cities to be honest with themselves by admitting that she treats them no differently than they would treat her were the roles reversed. Like other exponents of the Athenian thesis, Alcibiades is candid about himself and demands equal candor from his hearers. His masterpiece in this vein is his slightly later speech in Sparta, after his defection from Athens (6.89–92), in which he defends his having acted as a "patriot (*philopolis*, 92.4–5) for himself."[16]

The Athenians cannot admit, however, that with citizens as with cities, it is ultimately every one for himself. These possessors of a quasityrannical empire cannot stomach the prospect of tyranny or even oligarchy at home (cf. 8.68.4). They cannot admit that the community that treats other communities merely as means to its ends is composed of citizens who are merely that to each other. They cannot admit that the common good is an illusion, that no more secure basis for trust exists among citizens than among cities.

The problem of Alcibiades affords Thucydides the context for reopening the question of Athenian democracy. That democracy proves to rest on two cherished falsehoods: the harshness of the old Athenian tyrants and the patriotism of their erstwhile deposers (6.53–59).[17] The people regard themselves as heir to this patriotism; they suspect Alcibiades of selfish designs on their liberty. They turn to demagogues who, while professing common concerns, wish only to supplant Alcibiades (6.28.2, 29; cf. 2.65.11, 3.82.6, 6.35–40). As Alcibiades has reenacted Hipparchus' error

[16] The phrase is Pouncey's, *Necessities* 105. The only speaker in Thucydides who speaks outside his own city not as its official representative but as a traitor to it, Alcibiades is accordingly the only one who justifies to his foreign listeners not his city's conduct but his own, vis-à-vis both his own city and that of the audience. Indeed, he addresses the Spartans as their [collective] equal, who, although but one man and nominally a citizen of Athens, has dealt with both her and them as both have dealt with him, that is, on equal terms, for all the world as if he by himself constituted a city. He admits that he places his own good ahead of that of his city: his "patriotism" consists of a loyalty to it that is wholly contingent on its treatment of him, of the rightness of which he of course appoints himself the judge. On this speech also see Forde *Ambition to rule* 96–115; here, as elsewhere, Forde's treatment of the role of Alcibiades in Thucydides supersedes all previous ones.

[17] On this so-called "digression" and its actual relevance, see Schadewaldt *Geschichtsschreibung* 91–95; Rawlings *Structure* 100–117; Farrar *Origins* 147–48; Forde *Ambition to rule* 33–37; Palmer *Love of glory* 80–89.

of giving private offense to Harmodius and Aristogeiton (cf. 6.15 with 56.1), so the demagogues, in gaining his condemnation, reenact the tyrannicide, with motives as selfish and results as dire. Seizing on his presumed impiety as proof that he aims at tyranny, they initiate a wave of persecution which engulfs many of the best citizens (6.53, 60). Alcibiades, recalled from Sicily with the intention of putting him to death, escapes with some companions to Sparta (6.61.6–7).

Nicias' accusation of Alcibiades (6.12.2) thus proves both effective and prophetic. As the harshness of the Athenian tyranny was the effect rather than the cause of the attempted "tyrannicides," so Alcibiades' alleged plotting against Athens comes to pass only as a result of his banishment on charges of such plotting. Sparta accepts his tutelage in foreign affairs, while retaining its accustomed regime. Athens, by contrast, confides its crucial undertaking abroad to the quasi-Spartan Nicias, while all-too-Athenian demagogues impose on the people at home. These strange juxtapositions entail the best of both worlds for Sparta; the worst of both for Athens. In their distrust, the Athenians have left their Sicilian venture in the hands of the one man whose unquestioned justice and piety repel distrust and who, acting on Melian hopes, incurs for himself and the whole armada a Melian fate.

The Dialogue on Melos and the Mendacity of Euphemus

The speech of Euphemus at Camarina (6.82–87) is, apart from that of the envoys at Sparta, the only systematic defense in Thucydides of the justice of the Athenian empire. Although Euphemus borrows freely from earlier speakers, his defence of Athenian policy breaks new ground (for an Athenian) precisely because it is so old-fashioned. He defends the empire as just without invoking a relaxed interpretation of justice. His speech is not celebratory, however, as is the Funeral Oration; that would be unsuitable to the occasion. Indeed it exudes the "realism" of the envoys to Sparta and Melos. Still, Euphemus defers completely to traditional notions of justice.[18]

Like the speech at Sparta, that of Euphemus rebuts an attack on the empire. Athens having defeated Syracuse in their initial encounter (6.69–

---

[18] Strasburger *Hermes* 86 (1958) 33 regards this speech as the definitive unmasking of Athenian policy. Stahl *Thukydides* 120 n.51 describes it as the climax of the degradation of justice in the work ("den Höhepunkt in der Entwertung des Dikaion"). Heath *Historia* 39 (1990) 386–87 holds it devoid of considerations of justice and so an ineffective reply to Hermocrates' attack on the empire. Proctor *Experience* 98–101 rejects it as a "feeble utterance" while noting in it surprising recollections of the grand (even Periclean) tradition of Athenian speechifying. For brief comparisons of this speech and that of the envoys to Sparta, see Romilly *Imperialism* 243–44; Schneider *Information und Absicht* 102–4; Rawlings *Structure* 117–22. For a brilliant discussion, see Forde (*Ambition to rule* 61–67), with whom I am not entirely in agreement but to whom my debt is profound.

71), the parties have come to Camarina, nominally the ally of both, each hoping to persuade her to join it. The Athenians claim to be in Sicily at the behest of local allies who are Ionian Greeks like themselves, while both Syracuse and Camarina are Dorian; these facts color the debate.

Hermocrates, the Syracusan spokesman, insists that Camarina must side with Syracuse for the good of both (6.76–80). Athens is not, as she claims to be, an enemy to Syracuse alone and thus a godsend to all Sicilian cities, Ionian or Dorian, that (like Camarina) fear their powerful neighbor. Her concern for the Ionian Leontines is bogus: she aims not to protect Ionians from Dorians but to contrive the subjection of both, just as closer to home she has subjected the Ionian cities that she "liberated" from the Mede. Even so, Hermocrates can depict the struggle as one of Dorians versus Ionians, of Dorian freedom versus Ionian tyranny and slavishness (77.1). Indeed he goes so far as to describe the Ionians as eternal enemies of the Dorians (80.3).[19]

These claims, replies Euphemus, mask the imperial designs of Syracuse herself, designs checked only by Athens' presence in Sicily. He derides fears of any such designs on the part of Athens. To this end he declares himself "compelled to speak of the empire, how we hold it legitimately (*eikotōs*)" (6.82.1; cf. 1.73.1: *oute apeikotōs* ["not illegitimately"]). To hear him tell it, Athens rules her subjects only out of fear. What a free city fears for is first of all its freedom, and it was to maintain her freedom that Athens acquired and retains her empire. (Euphemus thus introduces, however implicitly, a note of honor: it is a worthy not a slavish fear which sustains the empire.) Beginning from Hermocrates' assertion of the enmity between Ionians and Dorians, Euphemus ascribes the empire itself to Athenian resolve to throw off the yoke of subjecthood to Sparta. This she could do after the Persian Wars, having acquired a fleet; and having emerged as the chosen leader of the Greeks liberated from Persia, she has maintained her hegemony, thinking herself thereby less likely to fall under Peloponnesian sway (6.82.1–3).

Lest someone object to Athens' sacrificing other cities' freedom to her own, Euphemus also endorses Hermocrates' assertion of the slavishness of Ionians, at least of those now subject to Athens. These had neither risked all to defend their own freedom nor had they refrained from marching with Persia against that of Athens their mother city. "Strictly speaking," then (*to akribes eipein*, 6.82.3), "not unjustly" has Athens subjected them. Her empire is impeccable alike in its policy and in its justice.

Euphemus now summarizes the grounds for the claim that Athens is worthy of her empire: that she had contributed the largest fleet and the most unstinting zeal to the cause of the Greeks (cf. 1.74.1), that her subjects-to-

<hr/>

[19] For good treatments of the relationship between Euphemus' speech and that of Hermocrates, see Romilly *Histoire et raison* 186–94 and Bayer *Festschrift F. Egermann* 57–65.

be had so readily accompanied the Mede against her, and that she sought to strengthen herself against the Peloponnesians. Fearing, however, lest he has overdone it, he abruptly shifts his ground and disclaims all fine words (6.83.2; cf. 5.89). He congratulates himself on not having founded Athens' claim to empire on her having overthrown the Mede single-handed, or on her having exerted herself for the freedom of her present subjects any more than for that of all [the Greeks] or for her own. The implication in the first case is that she had help, and in the second that in helping all the others her first concern was to help herself. "But no one is to be begrudged seeing to what pertains to his safety" (6.83.2).

As for subsequent ventures of Athens, including her present one in Sicily, these have aimed merely at maintaining her empire, and hence her security, in the face of the enmity of Sparta. She has sought subjects only to avoid having masters, and in far-off Sicily this end is best served by bolstering the foes of Syracuse, not subduing them. Only thus can she keep Syracuse at bay, too occupied near home to send aid to Sparta. The Camarinians can sleep easy in the sultry Sicilian night, knowing they have a friend in Athens—a friend all the faster in that her amity depends on a calculated community of interests.

To bolster this last argument, Euphemus undertakes his most remarkable rhetorical sally. Hermocrates has noted that it would be utterly unreasonable (*ou . . . eulogon*, 6.76.2; cf. *alogōs* 79.2) for the Athenians to be bent on liberating in Sicily the very Chalcidian/Ionian "kin" they have subjected closer to home. Euphemus retorts that "for a man who is a tyrant and for a city holding empire nothing is unreasonable (*alogon*) that is advantageous nor anything kindred that cannot be relied on, but case by case who is friend and who foe must depend on the time and situation" (6.85.1). In context, this aims to reassure Camarina: since Athens is too weak to conquer Sicily, reason dictates that she bolster the freedom of all who can be trusted to oppose Syracuse, be they Ionians, such as she has elsewhere subjected, or even Dorians, objects of an erstwhile eternal enmity. It remains remarkable, however, that Euphemus should bracket with tyranny the empire that, almost alone among Athenian apologists, he has defended as thoroughly just—as it is remarkable that he should identify the only principle of this impeccable venture as expediency.[20]

If the frankness of Euphemus' stress on interest recalls the approach of earlier Athenian apologists, his oily insistence on the justice and timidity of the empire repudiates that approach. In context his pretended frankness serves only to exaggerate Athens' (alleged) timidity. The Athenians at Sparta

[20] Euphemus' statement is less bold than those of Pericles (2.63.2) and Cleon (3.37.2): while they have likened the empire to a tyranny in its possible or actual injustice or in the disaffection of its subjects, he merely likens it to a tyrant in its concern for expediency, while denying that it has in fact committed quasityrannous injustice.

had aimed at deterrence, at impressing the Spartans with the power of Athens. Euphemus, by contrast, would persuade the Camarinians of her relative weakness. His pretended candor is mendacious: the empire has not aimed merely at safety, nor has Athens come to Sicily because she felt her safety threatened.

Might not Euphemus here play into the hands of Hermocrates? Camarina is small, and an Athens incapable of winning without her help is a poor bet to win even with it. Hermocrates, for his part, does not just beseech Camarina: he threatens to punish her defection. He warns that Syracuse could well win without her and affects confidence that united the two would prevail easily (6.79.3, 80; in which assessment Euphemus perhaps imprudently concurs, 84.3, 85.3, 86.3).[21] Should Camarina act on the promises of a weaker Athens or on the threats of a stronger Syracuse? Weak as she is, she has the most to hope from a permanent stalemate and, if that cannot be, from avoiding offense to both parties and backing the winner as soon as she can pick one. It is still too early to pick one here, and Athens has won the initial engagement. Even so, the Camarinians tentatively opt for complicity with hated Syracuse, wholly on the basis of their assessment of the relative strength of the antagonists (88.1). While there is no sign that Euphemus has convinced his audience of the justice of Athens (cf. 88.1), his smarminess might have helped to persuade it of her weakness.

It seems likely that Euphemus' diffidence is the key to understanding his speech. Consider the shiniest of his red herrings, his presentation of the empire as arising from the enmity between Ionians and Dorians.[22] Of Athenian apologists for the empire, only he presents the ethnic factor as figuring at all, yet he seems to insist that it is *the* issue. True, he addresses Dorians, who can be presumed both to despise Ionians and to assume some enmity between the groups (2.87.3–4; 5.9.1; 5.108; 8.25). By exploiting this presumption, moreover, Euphemus turns the rhetorical tables on Hermocrates. We recall that the latter, who began by ridiculing any such approach to the Athenian presence in Sicily, ended up invoking it himself, evidently as too useful a resource for any Dorian speaker to neglect. Euphemus steals Hermocrates' thunder by artfully (if bizarrely) employing the alleged perpetual enmity of Ionians and Dorians to persuade Dorian Cam-

---

[21] Bayer *Festschrift f. Egermann* 65 derides Hermocrates' appeal to Dorianism as old-fashioned ("altväterische") in comparison with the "sophistic" arguments of Euphemus. This is unjust to Hermocrates: he does not wheedle, he threatens.

[22] An aspiration to military and political parity with Sparta had played its part at the inception of the empire (as Themistocles stresses to the Spartans, at 1.91.4–7), just as later on its growth had fed rivalry between the two powers, which in turn had fed its growth. Still, judging from Thucydides' narrative, Athens had neither feared Sparta in the formative years of the empire nor ever been subject to her, nor had ethnic antagonisms played any part in these matters whatever.

arina that she has a firm friend in Ionian Athens. Lastly, Euphemus may see some gain in stressing the seamless continuity of Athenian imperial policy, defensive and anti-Spartan from the first, to the extent that he can present this policy as reassuring to Camarina.

Be this as it may, Euphemus lacks the boldness of earlier Athenian apologists. He differs from the envoys to Sparta most conspicuously in his failure to proclaim the Athenian thesis. He agrees with these envoys that Athens has had empire thrust upon her. His account of this process, however, is more cautious (and less truthful) than theirs. He does not even invoke compulsion (save for the rhetorical one under which he labors: 6.82.1; cf. 89.1). He attempts no expansion of the accepted limits of legitimate self-concern. As we have seen, he garbs the empire in security and freedom alone, those goods fear of the loss of which anyone would recognize as politically decisive.

Euphemus, however, does more than narrow to fear the Athenian excuse for wielding empire. As we have seen, he declares the empire fully justified by standards of distributive and punitive justice. Athens, which risked all for freedom, has rightly snatched it from those who, less daring than she, collaborated under duress with a power that would have deprived her of hers (6.82–83). Athens may justly treat her subjects with utmost punitive rigor—which is to say that she may justly subject them entirely to her interest.[23] But what could be more demeaning to the Athenian decision to risk all for freedom, daring against all odds and beyond all hope, than to treat as culpable all cities that fail to match it?[24]

We return to the crux of the speech, the ambivalence of Euphemus' dual emphasis on justice and interest. He insists on the justice of the empire and, moreover, that the Athenian presence in Sicily serves the cause of what will surely look to Camarina like justice: the independence of each Sicilian city, in particular those menaced by Syracuse. He goes so far as to present Athens, "compelled to act on many fronts because [she] must guard against many dangers" (6.87.2), as the protector of victims of injustice everywhere. Yet he explains Athenian interventionism wholly in terms of interest, without suggesting that Athens has at any time actually concerned herself with justice. "The Athenians . . . turn out to be unjust champions of justice and immoderate enforcers of moderation, men on off-white horses, we might say."[25] In effect, Euphemus claims that they are in justice excused from any such concern, for a merely expedient policy (which in turn merely happens to coincide with the expediency of Camarina) is required for the preserva-

---

[23] Connor (*Thucydides* 182–84) is the only critic to note this "coalescence of arguments from interest and justice."

[24] Cf. Forde *APSR* 80 (1986) 436–37.

[25] Forde *Ambition to rule* 64–65.

tion of their empire, which is required for the preservation of their freedom, and "no one is to be reproached for seeing to his safety."

What, at bottom, is the premise of Euphemus' alleged argument from justice? That there are goods no city can justly be required to sacrifice to anything, not even to justice itself. That security and freedom, in particular, are so precious that a city is entitled to do whatever it deems necessary to preserve them. On reflection, however, this argument proves to imply carte blanche for the imperialism both of every country that, like Athens in 480 lacks empire but could use it in order to defend its own freedom, and of every country that, like Athens now in 415 possesses empire (no matter how acquired) and fears for its freedom and security should it lose it. Into the first of these categories falls, of course, almost every nonimperial power, and, into the second, almost every imperial one.

Which is to say that even Euphemus' self-righteous pronouncements on the justice of the empire, which clash so starkly with his predecessors' promulgation of the Athenian thesis, in fact imply that very thesis. Whatever the rhetorical oddness, there is no tension in principle between his early emphasis on the justice of the empire and his later one on its exclusive devotion to interest. Ultimately Euphemus differs from the envoys at Sparta not (as first appears) in offering the Athenian empire itself as a counterexample to the Athenian thesis, but in presenting that thesis surreptitiously, in a moralized (and thereby sanitized) version.[26]

The timid mendacity of Euphemus' speech is especially striking when we consider the speaker he is replacing. For his is the most anticlimactic performance in Thucydides: the speech that Alcibiades never gave. He speaks in furtherance of the strategy that the expedition has inherited from Alcibiades—winning over the Sicilian cities to a grand alliance against Syracuse—and there can be no doubt that were Alcibiades still on the scene, it is he himself who would speak (cf. 6.50.1, 51.1). We can only conjecture what sort of speech Alcibiades would have given; it spurs such conjectures that scarcely has Euphemus left off than Thucydides wafts us to Sparta and one of Alcibiades' most remarkable performances (89–92). It differs strikingly from Euphemus' in that far from dissembling, it exaggerates the boldness of Athenian intentions in the west (cf. 90.2 with 15.2: Alcibiades ascribes to his compatriots an aim of his own so implausibly ambitious that he has kept it even from them). Might Alcibiades, so much more forceful a speaker than Euphemus, have proved more so than even Hermocrates?

---

[26] The reader may wonder whether Euphemus' name bears overtones of "euphemism." The short answer is that it does: cf. Liddell and Scott *Greek lexicon* s.v. εὐφημέω, εὔφημος. Euphemus is also the only named Athenian speaker prior to Book Eight whose patronymic Thucydides omits to provide. We must consider whether the name does not fit the speech a little too perfectly to be credible as the name of the actual speaker.

Having observed that his strategy of luring the Sicilian cities had succeeded thus far only with Catane, which had acted under perceived compulsion (51), might he have cudgeled as well as coaxed?

As for the speakers on Melos, Euphemus resembles them in explaining the imperatives of empire in terms of safety and profit alone; indeed he goes further in this direction than they. Ironically for someone affirming perpetual enmity between Ionians and Dorians and between Athens and Sparta in particular, he paints a remarkably "Spartan" picture of the Athenian empire. If the envoys to Melos remained suspended between Athenian daring and Spartan caution, Euphemus has resolved this tension in favor of Sparta. As we saw, reliance on the manifest was not friendly to Athenian daring; to dare is to dare beyond one's manifest power. The empire as Euphemus presents it is wholly a matter of the manifest, defensive and calculating; as there is nothing ambitious, so there is nothing magnanimous about it.

In one sense Euphemus is the most "realistic" apologist for the empire yet. For all its "activism" (*polla . . . prassein*; 6.87.2), Euphemus' version of the empire simply looks to the bottom line, where the terms of the ledger are safety and interest. If Alcibiades achieves one pole of Athenianism in individualizing the pursuit of universal glory, Euphemus achieves another in his thoroughly prosaic rationalism.

It might seem unfitting that the final apologist for Athens in the book should embrace that mendacious hypocrisy which all of his predecessors have scorned. Here too, however, Euphemus may merely prove more consistent than the envoys to Melos. Athenian rationalism tends in the end away from daring in favor of safety and interest. Does not such a focus, however, with its implicit contempt for honor and daring, reopen the way to the employment of sham to advance safety and interest? One might shrink from acknowledging Euphemus, that Thucydidean speaker uniquely blessed with the perfect name for a speaker, as the most self-conscious and consistent of the political exponents of the Athenian thesis—and thus as the one who expounds it the most surreptitiously, the most selectively, the most deceptively.

There is a last respect in which Euphemus deserves notice. If Alcibiades symptomizes the Periclean quest for glory liberated from the bonds of citizenship, Euphemus represents the city liberated from the quest for glory. He speaks as if it were an association bent on nothing more than safety and interest. The superiority of the city to its citizens, however—the cement of their loyalty to it—must be something the city stands for and that transcends mere safety and interest. If the city is not higher than ourselves, how can it claim to be prior to ourselves? This question, which has bedeviled liberal thought from its Hobbesian beginning, appears also in Thucydides. Citizens who are freed alike from traditional restraints of piety and from the ennobling novelties of Pericles will have no fixed star by which to guide themselves if not their personal safety and interest. Such citizens have already reared their heads in Athens, and many more will appear in the years following the defeat of the Sicilian expedition.[27] Even more clearly than the envoys to Melos, Euphemus anticipates this problem. He surely reflects, no less than Nicias and Alcibiades, whatever we mean by the "crisis" of Athens. Of his fate we must conjecture that he was one of the many Athenians who never returned home (7.87.6).

ATHENS AND MYCALESSUS

In the midst of the Sicilian campaign, a band of Thracian mercenaries appears at Athens. They were to have accompanied Demosthenes on the relief expedition but are too late to do so: the Athenians, short of funds, decide to return them to Thrace.

Between his account of this decision and that of its consequences, Thucydides explains the necessity for it. He tells us, however, more than we need to know to grasp the city's fiscal crisis: although the occasion of the passage, this crisis by no means supplies its focus. Thucydides stresses the extraordinary hardships the Athenians have incurred and the indomitable spirit with which they meet them.

> But what most oppressed them was that they had two wars at once, and had thus attained such obstinacy (*philon[e]ikia*) as none would have thought credible before the fact: [such obstinacy] that even when besieged by the Peloponnesians entrenched in Attica, they would still, instead of withdrawing from Sicily, stay on there besieging in like manner Syracuse, in itself a city quite as large as Athens, or would so confound the Hellenes with their power and daring that while, at the beginning of the war, some thought they might hold out one year, some two, none more than three, if the Peloponnesians invaded their country; now seventeen years after the first invasion, after having already suffered from all the evils of war, they would go to Sicily and undertake a new war quite as large as that already upon them from Peloponnese. (7.28.3)[28]

This passage recalls 2.65, where Thucydides has stressed the superabundant resources of Athens. *There*, however, Thucydides seemed to mean by resources the sort of tangibles enumerated by Pericles (1.141–43, 2.13), while we now see that the ultimate Athenian resource is their unsurpassed devotion to the cause of their city. They will face any hardship, eschew any

---

[27] Forde *Ambition to rule* 130–39 has charted this difficulty with the help of the figure of Phrynichus.

[28] Crawley's version, revised in the direction of literalness. The passage appears to be corrupt (the last sentence both misdates and mis-situates the Sicilian expedition), but I know of no satisfactory emendation of it. Cf. Schwartz *Geschichtswerk* 199–202; Schadewaldt *Geschichtsschreibung* 78–82; Bartoletti *SIFC* 14 (1937) 230–31.

comfort rather than renounce the war. Read this way, the passage comprises praise of a very high order, perhaps the highest that Thucydides ever bestows on Athenian "patriotism": it is striking that it occurs in the context of the Sicilian expedition.[29]

Two things qualify Thucydides' praise of Athenian persistence. The first is that he does not call it *tolma* ["daring"], the favorite term of Athenian self-description, but *philon[e]ikia*. Etymologically, this is "love of victory," but it is not a word of noble or even positive connotation (cf., above all, 3.82.8). The implication is not of free and noble dedication but of all-consuming frenzy. The second qualification inheres in that event the context of which this passage supplies but which also colors our reading of it: the fate of Mycalessus.

So absorbed are the Athenians in their perils that their only concern with the band of Thracians is to rid themselves of the costs of maintaining it. The resulting expedition thus resembles that of Brasidas, whom the Spartans had sent out less in hopes of what he might accomplish than in order to rid themselves of the Helots who accompanied him (4.80). And, like the Spartans earlier, the beleaguered Athenians wish to strike back at their foes however they can; as they still must pay the Thracians while conveying them, they may as well get some use out of them. So they order one Dieitrephes to harm the enemy as opportunity offers in the course of returning the swordsmen to Thrace.

Dieitrephes, conveying the Thracians by sea, lands undetected on the coast of Boeotia to lead a foray inland.

> The night he passed unobserved near the temple of Hermes [the god of stealth], not quite two miles from Mycalessus, and at daybreak assaulted the town, which is not a large one, the inhabitants being off their guard and not expecting that anyone would ever come up so far from the sea to molest them, the wall too being weak, and in some places having tumbled down, while in others it had not been built to any height, and the gates also being left open through their feeling of security. The Thracians, bursting into Mycalessus, sacked the houses and temples and slaughtered the inhabitants, sparing neither youth nor age, but killing all they fell in with, one after the other, children and women, and even beasts of burden, and whatever other living creatures they saw; for the Thracian race, like most barbarians, is bloodiest when confident [of impunity]. And not only did mayhem reign and destruction in all its forms, but in particular they attacked a boys' school, the largest in the place, which the boys happened just to have entered, and butchered them all. In short, the disaster falling upon the whole town was unsurpassed in magnitude, and unapproached by any in suddenness and horror. (7.29.3–5)[30]

[29] Cf. Bartoletti *SIFC* 14 (1937) 227–35; Pouncey *Necessities* 123–24.
[30] Crawley's translation (revised).

And so Mycalessus suffered evils which relative to her size were as worthy of lamentation as any that occurred during the war. (7.30.4)

The fate of Mycalessus is not tragic—the little town lacks the grandeur for that. It is partly the fault of the victims: why had they not tended their walls? It is as if the Mycalessians, of whom we readers about the war have had yet to hear, have yet to hear of the war. They live at rest amidst the greatest motion (cf. 5.26.5), trusting in fortune and their insignificance to preserve their anomalous prosperity. The savagery that engulfs them is such as has happened and will happen, so long as human nature remains the same. But what is Mycalessus to Thucydides that he should interrupt (as he does for it alone) his continuous narrative of the Sicilian campaign?

For Stahl, Thucydides' attention to Mycalessus discloses his true theme: not what was done in the war, but what was suffered because of it. Mycalessus is noteworthy, like Ambracia earlier, because its calamity was proportionally so terrible; it is thus a microcosm of the war as a whole.[31] Reinhardt, who adduces Mycalessus as his first example of Thucydides' concern with "the human," argues that the point of the passage is the contrast between the trivial cause (penny-pinching) and the horrible consequence: this unintended disproportion (*Missverhältnis*) belongs to the physiognomy of war.[32] Grene suggests that Thucydides responds to the utter gratuitousness of the destruction, which answers no political or military necessity.[33] Only in such cases, Grene thinks, does Thucydides regard "moral comment" as appropriate.

There is something to each of these suggestions. There is also something more at issue here. We recall that Thucydides' longest exercise in "moral comment" responded to the phenomenon of stasis. The calamity of Mycalessus, a small town with a large school (which is not even its only school), likewise discloses the very greatest of the dangers the war holds: the dissolution of Greekness itself. The Thracians act as Thracians will: their bloodthirstiness will surprise only readers unfamiliar with them. What *is* shocking is the complicity of Athens.

At one time the inhabitants of Greece were Thracians or may as well have been: they practiced extreme savagery (2.29). That savagery had receded only in the course of the lengthy ascent to Greekness and its two poles, Athens and Sparta, which issued finally in the war between them. The fate of Mycalessus is especially poignant when we consider the one close analog to the Mycalessian way of life to be found elsewhere in Thucydides: the old way of life at Athens herself, interrupted but not extinguished by the Persian

---

[31] Stahl *Thukydides* 137–38; on Ambracia, see 134–37.

[32] Reinhardt *Vermächtnis* 207–8: "Its meaning is . . . man's fate under the law of war." ("Sein Sinn ist . . . Menschenschicksal unter dem Gesetz des Krieges.")

[33] Grene *Greek political theory* 75; see also Bowersock *AntRev* 35.1 (1965) 135–36.

Wars (2.15–16). That life was peaceful, conservative, pious, and agrarian but deeply civilized. Its last vestiges have now fallen victim to the Spartan occupation of Deceleia. Only the new Athens remains, Fortress Athens, defying the world: Themistocles' vision of an Athens severed from the Attic land has been realized as an impressive nightmare. At the peak of its doggedness, the new Athens inundates with Thracians a hapless image of her former self.

In the Funeral Oration and in his final speech, Pericles had presented Athens as the epitome of Greekness. This was no empty boast. Yet the true political distinction of Athens, the reality underlying his exalted rhetoric of civic devotion, is her indomitable *philon[e]ikia* (cf. esp. 2.64.2–3). And this last, in its very single-mindedness, its indifference to everything but victory, threatens a relapse into barbarism. The fate of Mycalessus is terrible. That of Athens is tragic. Had Thucydides not paused in his account of Athens in Sicily to note this deed of Athens in Boeotia, he would not have acquainted us with every aspect of her tragedy.[34]

THE FOLLY AND WISDOM OF NICIAS

The theme of Nicias' moving final speech (7.77) is hope.[35] Following the defeat in the Great Harbor, the plight of the survivors seems hopeless. Routed on both sea and land and denied even an escape by sea, exhausted and with few provisions, they must now retreat by land through hostile territory. Preparing to leave, they shudder at the sight of the heaps of their dead, toward whom they have failed to perform the most sacred of duties, that of burial (cf. 2.52; 4.42–44, 97–101). The sick and wounded, whom they must abandon, entreat them and tear at them, finally calling down the wrath of the gods on them (75.3–4). The men cannot but reflect on the contrast between their departure for Syracuse and their departure from it, for this was "the greatest reverse ever to befall a Greek army." "And yet even this seemed bearable in comparison with the greatness of the danger that lay ahead" (75.6–7). Nicias, seeing the despondency of his men, contrives to rally them. In so doing he must raise the issues that have concerned us throughout this study.

Nicias begins by noting that some have been saved from circumstances even more dreadful than these, and he tries to comfort the men, who now blame themselves bitterly for the expedition, by asserting that they suffer undeservedly (*para tēn axian*, 7.77.1).

---

[34] Longo *Studi Barigazzi* (1984) 1.366 alludes to "barbarization" at Mycalessus but not to the theme of Greekness.

[35] On the speech, see Luschnat *Feldherrnreden* 101–6; Edmunds *Chance and intelligence* 135–39; Pouncey *Necessities* 128–29; Lateiner *CP* 80 (1985) 207–8.

Why, I myself, who am superior to none of you in strength (for you see how I suffer from my illness [cf. 6.102.2, 7.15.1–2, 16.1]), and who am, I think, second to none in my good fortune, whether in private or public life, now find myself in as much danger as the least of you. And yet I have spent my days performing many prescribed duties (*nomima*) toward the gods, and many just and blameless (*anepiphthona*) actions toward human beings. I therefore maintain all the same a confident hope for the future, and our disasters do not frighten me as much as if I had deserved them (*kat' axian*).[36] (7.77.2–3)

Nicias' hopes for salvation rest on his personal piety and justice. Will this cheer the average soldier, whose conscience may be less spotless? And is Nicias' blamelessness not tarnished by his complicity in the present project? His own plight thus calls in question precisely the hope in divine justice to which he appeals.[37] Alternatively, it suggests that the justice of the gods is terrible. In their arrogant strength, these Athenians had set out to enslave Sicily: they now face death or enslavement themselves. Can Nicias accept the "tragic" framework of divine justice while denying that the suffering of the Athenians is merited? He continues as follows.

Indeed [our misfortunes] may be lightened. The enemy has enjoyed all possible good fortune, and if by our campaign we have incurred blame (*epiphthonoi*, cf. *anepiphthona* just above) before one of the gods, we have already suffered ample punishment. For others there have been who have attacked their fellows, and having done what human beings will do (literally, "having done human things," *anthrōpeia drasantes*), have suffered no more than they could bear. We may then plausibly (or fairly, *eikos*) expect kinder treatment from the divine (for surely by now we are more deserving of pity than resentment [*phthonou*]). (7.77.3–4)

Nicias subscribes to the justice of the gods, not to the Athenian thesis. He surely does not mean to banish the notion of transgression from human life. Yet he presents it as the characteristic human deed (*anthrōpeia*), transgression and punishment as the typical pattern of human life. He implies not its necessity, only that its ubiquity furnishes some grounds for divine indulgence. Like all who are truly pious, Nicias knows that just as no one can escape the divine call to justice, so none can heed it wholeheartedly; perfect justice is an illusion of the impious. (Has not Nicias himself been swept along on this doomed expedition?) To this extent, piety itself endorses the Athenian thesis.[38] Still, it would be hoping for too much (and too little)

---

[36] I interpret κατ' ἀξίαν after Pouncey *Necessities* 128.

[37] Cf. Plutarch *Nicias* 26.3–6.

[38] Of the commentators only Pouncey (*Necessities* 95–96, 128–29) appears to have noted this parallel. In his moving treatment, he characterizes the speech as an "absolution from guilt" of the entire army, one tacitly endorsed by Thucydides himself.

from the gods—it would be hoping for more (and less) than justice—to expect them to overlook offenses entirely. Human beings experience the divine above all as resistance to their plans.[39] In any case, merely indulgent gods would furnish no bulwark against injustice. Just gods, however, would at least take note of human frailty in measuring the fit of punishment to crime; such frailty would evoke their pity. And in assessing present culpability, they would credit past righteousness. Unlike the Athenian envoys to Melos, Nicias makes no attempt to subsume the gods under a universal law of natural compulsion such as allegedly rules human beings; as we have seen, he stops short of subjecting human beings to such a law. Nicias expects the gods to enforce justice reasonably; he does not think that reasonable gods would forgo enforcing justice.

As for human beings, they in principle maintain their freedom to act or to forbear from acting whether justly or unjustly. Being pious Nicias denies himself the alibi of strict necessity. Such a claim would be both humiliating (in denying human beings the dignity of autonomy) and presumptuous (in denying their subjection to divine law). Instead, he expects the gods to spare him subjection to strict necessity (cf. chapter 4): his inability to recognize it when it looms contributes to his (and the expedition's) undoing. Through all his vicissitudes he persuades himself that he can avoid the necessity of choice; he always looks elsewhere for his salvation, even, if need be, to the enemy (7.85.1). It is true that Nicias, conscious of his reliance on the gods, fears to tempt them; he strives to avoid offense (4.42–44) and to keep himself out of harm's way (5.17), to venture only cautiously and when armed with all human means. (Even at this last juncture, he reassures his men that they remain, on their own, a match for the enemy [7.77.4–7].) Yet this much diffidence before the gods, as punishers of injustice and hybris, is obviously not incompatible with hopes in them as vindicators of the just and blameless (*anepiphthona*, 77.2).

The hopes of Nicias are utterly dashed. His persistence in effecting the retreat, greater than that of Demosthenes, only exposes his troops to greater slaughter (7.84).[40] Having surrendered to the Spartan commander, in whose goodwill he trusts, he is soon butchered, disappointed, like the Melians, in his hopes in both the gods and the Spartans. He is in part the victim of his own past hopefulness: the Syracusans whom he had expected to betray the city now want him safely dead, lest he disclose their dealings (86.2–4). As for the rest of the Athenian soldiers, whether slaughtered as they drank the befouled waters of the Assinarus (84), or confined in the stifling quarries of Syracuse (87.1–3), "they were destroyed, as the saying

[39] Cf. Aristophanes *Knights* 30–34 (on the grounds of Nicias' belief in the gods); Tacitus *Histories* 1.3.

[40] Cf. Pouncey *HPTh* 7 (1986) 1–14.

goes, with a total destruction; all of their sufferings were great, and few out of many returned home" (87.6).[41]

MOTIVE AND COMPULSION IN THE SICILIAN CAMPAIGN

If Thucydides questions Nicias' hopes in divine justice, he lends a certain support to Nicias' understanding of "transgression," which permits us to speak of Nicias' wisdom.

Toward the climax of Book Seven, Thucydides offers, for the first and only time in his work, a schematic classification of the deeds of cities according to their compulsoriness. The context is the impending battle in the Great Harbor, on the brink of which Thucydides pauses to offer a catalogue of the combatants on either side (7.57–58). In this, one of his two counterparts to Homer's catalogue of ships (*Iliad* 2; cf. 2.9), he pursues a question that Homer had not: the motives of the various contingents. He offers, moreover, in each case his own verdict as to whether participation is willing or coerced.

In this passage, an element obtrudes that, while frequently in the mouths of Thucydides' characters, is largely absent from his own: the presumed kinship of members of the same ethnic stock.[42] He details the multiple anomalies of the contest if viewed in this light: Aeolian subjects of Athens contending against Aeolian allies of Syracuse, this or that colony contending against its mother city or against another of that city's colonies. So numerous are these anomalies that we quickly grasp that they comprise as much the rule in Greek affairs as the exception. Indeed Thucydides states explicitly that kinship (*xyngeneia*) counted for little in forging the contending alliances (including then, implicitly, those alliances that happened to be between kinsmen). By invoking kinship as a quasinatural standard, however, Thucydides situates himself to pass judgment on the different excuses of those who deviate from it.

The most obvious such excuses are justice and compulsion. Thucydides pronounces "legitimate" or "warranted" (*eikotōs*) the intra-Boeotian grudge of the surviving Plataeans against the Thebans (7.57.5). He also states explicitly, however, that justice (*dikē*) played as little role as kinship in determining the configuration of forces. Most who joined whichever side did so either under compulsion (*kata anankēn*) or for reasons of advantage (*kata to*

---

[41] We must take Thucydides' celebrated eulogy of Nicias (7.86.5) to articulate the expectations of Nicias himself. Cf. Strauss *City and man* 208–9; Pouncey *Necessities* 129–30; Lateiner *CP* 80 (1985) 209–10. I accept the reading of νενομισμένην in the eulogy as "law-bred" or "conventionally presumed," that is, as qualifying the attribution of virtue to Nicias.

[42] Cf. 2.87.3–4; 5.9.1; 5.108; 6.77.1, 80.3, 82–87; 8.25.5. On the present passage, see Romilly *Imperialism* 82–84, Dover *HCT* 4:433, and Romilly *Construction* 36–41.

xympheron) (57.1). Ranged under compulsion, on the Athenian side, are nominally free allies which, being islands, are exposed to Athenian constraint (*kateirgomenoi*, 57.7). So, too, are some political exiles, who, due to their misfortune (*kata xymphoran*), must fight alongside Athens, which has received them (57.8). Also so listed, however, are the Corcyraeans, who, while pleading necessity as a pretext (*anankēi men ek tou euprepous*), are moved by their long-standing hatred of Corinth (57.7), and the Plataeans, fired by that enmity toward Thebes that Thucydides finds *eikotōs* (57.5). His criterion is, thus, not motive but circumstance, for Corcyra and Plataea, which might have campaigned alongside Athens even in the absence of constraint, qualify as compelled because they are in fact constrained.

The list of willing allies of Athens is shorter (7.57.9–11). Their predominant motive is advantage (*to xympheron*)—whether public or (as with mercenaries) private—which Thucydides at 57.1 has distinguished from compulsion. Willing also are the Acarnanians, who, although serving for pay, are actuated primarily by friendship (*philia*) for Demosthenes and Athens.[43] Lastly, Thucydides lists the allies of Athens from Italy and Sicily: all rate as willing save the Thurians and Metapontines, whom the harsh necessities of a time of stasis (*en toiautais anankais tote stasiōtikōn kairōn*) have thrown into the lap of Athens (57.11). On the Syracusan side, only tiny Sicyon is said to campaign under compulsion (*anankastoi strateuontes*, 7.58.3; cf. 5.81.6).

What might seem surprising about Thucydides' principles of classification here is that they appear closer to those of Sparta (and of Nicias) than to those of his subtle Athenians. He certainly eschews the view that safety and profit express a distinction without a difference; he entertains the plea of compulsion from those whose survival or that of whose regime is at the mercy of Athens, but not from the Athenians themselves or any others who seek merely to better their lot. Nor indeed does fear qualify as simply compulsory. No Sicilian cities on either side are mentioned as contending under constraint, although most of them evidently do so for fear of either Athens or Syracuse (or both). Nor can we ascribe this omission to the fact that all of these are Dorians fighting alongside Dorians or Ionians alongside Ionians, as if those who support their kin are always presumed to do so freely. For Thucydides mentions the Sicyonians, Dorians fighting alongside Dorians, as campaigning only under constraint.

Voluntary, according to Thucydides' schema, is the participation of all who, whatever their motive, are under no direct external constraint to act as they do. The Sicilian cities that join Syracuse may have strong motives for so doing; the fact remains that they were free to decide, with Acragas (7.58.1), that the risks of neutrality were to be preferred to those of participation.

Thucydides exculpates as acting under compulsion only those who act in

---

[43] On the Acarnanians, see Engeman *Interpretation* 4.2 (1974) 65–78.

the grip of the motives of *others*. He withholds his authority from the claim that all who seek to conquer act by a necessity of nature (1.76.3, 5.105.2); the least we must say is that he has seized an opportunity to distance himself from the Athenian thesis.

Nor, however, does the passage burn with the anger typical of opponents of the thesis. Thucydides no more displays outrage at those who share in the campaign for money than he does at the Acarnanians, who do so for love. He presents deviations from the supposed norm of kinship as so common as to cast doubt on the motives of even those who appear to uphold it. Like the pious Nicias, he appears to hold that transgressions, if strictly speaking uncompelled, are nonetheless so much to be expected—so typically human (cf. *anthrōpeia drasantes*, 7.77.4)—as hardly to merit indignation.

Chapter 7

THE ATHENIAN THESIS RECONSIDERED: DIODOTUS AND HERMOCRATES

THE ATHENIAN manner and the Spartan manner have proved less opposite than they at first appeared. Sparta succeeds as much because of her hypocrisy as piety; Athens fails as much because of her piety as her impiety. Each displays the virtues and vices characteristic of its distinctive manner of balancing piety and impiety, its claim to justice and its deference to necessity; each commands the reader's respect, but neither can claim Thucydides' endorsement.

To approach the peak of Thucydides' argument, therefore, we must look to those of his characters whose outlooks rise furthest toward his own. We must study two protagonists who resolve their pressing practical dilemmas in a manner that reveals the depth of their reflections on political life.

THE MYTILENIAN DEBATE

In the fourth year of the war, Mytilene revolts unsuccessfully from Athens (see chapter 3). In his presentation of the resulting debate at Athens (3.36–49), Thucydides offers his richest treatment of the question of right and necessity.

Mytilene had surrendered as follows (3.27 ff.): The commander sent from Sparta, despairing of reinforcements, had armed the city's demos. These, on the verge of starvation, had turned on the ruling oligarchs, demanding grain from the public granaries on pain of their surrendering the city. Alarmed at the prospect of an agreement from which they would be excluded, the oligarchs resolved to hand over the city themselves.[1]

The debate at Athens is over whether to punish the demos. Oddly, Thucydides himself nowhere passes judgment on the degree of its complicity in the revolt. Was the demos, which neither sparked the revolt nor was in a position to prevent it, hostile to it? It seems impossible to say. Even had the rulers considered the demos sympathetic to the revolt, they would not have placed themselves at its mercy by providing it with heavy arms. On the other hand, would the Spartan commander have armed the people, even in desperation, without consulting the oligarchs? Once armed, the demos rose,

---

[1] On the Mytilene campaign, see Stahl *Thukydides* 103–12; Kagan *Archidamian war* 124–52; John Wilson *Historia* 30 (1981) 144–63.

but from starvation not partiality to Athens. Thucydides' reticence has spawned a heated debate on "the popularity of the Athenian empire."[2] By depriving us, however, of the information required to form a firm opinion one way or the other, he insures that our response to the ensuing debate will turn on more fundamental issues.

The debate that Thucydides recreates is a reconsideration. The Mytilenians have surrendered on condition that their fate be referred to the Athenian people (3.28). The Athenian commander on the scene has shipped a thousand partisans of oligarchy to Athens as those most responsible for the revolt. The Athenians, in the heat of passion, have resolved to kill not only these, but the whole male citizenry, and to sell the women and children as slaves. They have duly dispatched a ship to Mytilene to enforce this decree (36).

Like most decisions taken in a towering rage, this one registers concerns not of advantage but of justice. We must recall that Mytilene, almost alone among the allies, had never been reduced to subjection and tribute but had retained her walls and fleet, continuing powerful, prosperous, and free. In return she had betrayed Athens in a manner that argued long premeditation, introducing a Spartan fleet into the heart of the Athenian seaborne empire. Retributive justice is the Athenian concern, premeditated treason the verdict (3.36.1–3).

So, too, when the Athenians awaken the next day with a massive moral hangover, what troubles them about their decision is not its expediency. "They began to consider what a great and cruel decree it was, that not the authors only, but the whole city should be destroyed" (3.36.4, Hobbes's translation). The way is open to a reconsideration of the justice of the decree.

This last point is worth stressing in the face of a seeming anomaly. The reconsideration as it unfolds appears to turn less on the justice of the decree than on its expediency. This reflects the strategy of Cleon, "the most violent of the citizens and at that time by far the most persuasive with the demos" (3.36.6). Having carried the motion of the previous day, he is the most violent and persuasive speaker against rescinding it. His speech depends on two main stratagems. To the question of the justice of the decision, he adds that of its expediency. And in addressing the foreign policy issues, he raises the domestic one of loyalty, in particular the loyalty of clever speakers who would dare to defend Mytilene. He seeks to harden hearts not only against the rebels, but against any domestic rival who might seek to discredit him by

[2] De Ste-Croix *Historia* 3 (1954) 1–41; Bradeen *Historia* 9 (1960) 257–69; Andrewes *Phoenix* 16 (1962) 64–85; Legon *Phoenix* 22 (1968) 220–25; Gillis *AJP* 92 (1971) 38–48; Quinn *Historia* 20 (1971) 405–17; Macleod *JHS* 98 (1978) 76–77. I agree (although for different reasons) with Westlake *Historia* 25 (1976) 429–40 that Thucydides' reticence is intentional.

defending them. These two steps are connected, and we must keep both of them in mind in approaching the great speech of Diodotus that follows.

Although we may detest Cleon's speech, we cannot deny its effectiveness. Rambling, vehement, and contradictory, it is a masterpiece of populism. Beginning by invoking the trust that allegedly prevails in Athenian life (cf. Pericles at 2.37), Cleon proceeds to blame his listeners for being too trustful of their allies (cf. 1.68.1–2). Cleon proves equally adept at flattering his followers and at flaying them for their fickleness toward him.[3] He argues forcefully that all who would speak for repeal of the decree are traitors to the people, and he thus seeks to cow them into silence. He plays alike on the people's distrust of "elites" (3.37, 38.1–3) and on their distrust of themselves—for not being distrustful enough of "elites" (38.4–7).

It makes sense for Cleon both to introduce the theme of advantage and to assert its priority over justice. He has to fear that an appeal to justice alone would now fall flat. The public mood on this issue has shifted, and earlier speakers (3.36.6) are sure to have appealed to it. Certainly Cleon must defend the justice of his decree, but he also opts to stress its expediency—and to insist that where the two are in tension, expediency must prevail over justice.

In the other interwoven strand of his speech, in which he expounds his new, improved position on Mytilene, Cleon begins with what seems an unlikely assertion. He claims both that the Athenians live with their subjects as fearlessly and trustfully as with one another and that their empire is an out-and-out tyranny (3.37.2; cf. 1.122.3, 2.63.2, 6.85.1). They are a tyrant without facing up to it and so without acting as a tyrant must: their democratic incapacity for empire consists in this (37.1). Cleon contrives to tax the Athenians with their leniency and the Mytilenians with their ingratitude, to urge his listeners to see to their safety without attention to the niceties of justice, while assuring them that justice too cries out for the extermination of the Mitylenians. If incoherent in theory, this works admirably in practice.[4] It appeals in turn to the two harshest passions: fear and anger.

While professing just retribution, Cleon incites to unrestrained bloodlust. The trick lies in his method for calculating the equivalency of punishment and crime. He protests against delay in chastising the rebels "which is all to the advantage of the guilty. For the victim proceeds against the culprit with his anger blunted, instead of punishing him while the pain is still fresh, and exacting as equivalent a retribution as possible" (3.38.1). He urges the Athenians to regain the frame of mind into which the first news of the revolt had put them (40.7): justice is to be calculated from the perspective of maximum anger.

---

[3] I have analyzed the populism of Cleon's speech at greater length in *The American Scholar* 53 (Summer 1984) 313–25.

[4] Winnington-Ingram *BICS* 12 (1965) 76–77; Cohen *QUCC* 45 (1984) 47–48.

We have seen why Cleon can present Mytilene as "hav(ing) wronged [Athens] more gravely than [had] any other city" (3.39.1). The Mytilenians themselves, speaking to a most receptive audience, had been hard put to justify their actions (3.10–14). Still, Cleon's version of justice is to act on those passions that least conduce to it. Now that the Athenians are ready to listen to reason, he sets out to recreate their original frenzy.

On the specific question of the guilt of the demos, Cleon has little to say. "All alike assaulted us," and "the people rose together with the few, believing this to be the safer risk" (3.39.6). He clearly expects his listeners to reprove so perfidious a calculation of safety. He devotes most of his effort to vilifying the revolt as such, in the hope that the anger of his audience will spill over from the few to the many.[5]

As already noted, Cleon does not limit his appeal to alleged considerations of justice. In addressing those of interest, his case is clear. Unless Athens shows that the penalty for rebellion is death (3.40.7), all her subjects will soon be up in arms, the prize of success being freedom and the price of failure nothing terrible (39.3). To punish all the Mytilenians will, therefore, be both just and advantageous (40.4). If, however, the Athenians let the rebels off, "you will not be gratifying them, rather you will be passing judgment on yourselves. For if they did right to rebel, then you must be doing wrong to rule. If, however, be it ever so unbecoming, ruling is what you see fit to do, then, yes, even if it is unfair, still you must punish these men, or have done with empire and play the virtuous man in safety" (40.5; cf. 2.63.2–3). Thus Cleon would have it both ways: the Athenians are just rulers, who may justly punish desertion, or they are unjust ones, who must punish it regardless.

Cleon's speech does suggest certain gambits available to his opponents. He asks who will be so impudent or corrupt as to maintain "that the crime of the Mytilenians is advantageous to us" (3.38.1), thus suggesting the possible tack that punishment should be rejected as counterproductive, albeit just. He concedes that were the offense involuntary or compelled by an external force (the enemy), it would be worthy of indulgence (39.2, 7). In a somewhat different vein, he comes close to blaming the revolt of the Mytilenians on Athens for having coddled them so. "Why, if we had long ago esteemed them in no way differently than the others, they never would have become so insolent. For it is as natural for human beings to despise servility as to be awed by firmness" (39.5). Similarly, Cleon stresses the puffed-up folly of the rebels, deterred neither by the failures of others nor by their own

[5] Legon *Phoenix* 22 (1968) 208–9 suggests that in insisting that the few and the people were equally responsible for the revolt, Cleon is taking up the plea of the envoys of the few, while Diodotus will take up that of the envoys of the many. This may be, although it is unclear from Thucydides' brief mention of Mytilenian ambassadors present at Athens (3.36.5) whether they represented both factions or, if only one, which one.

prosperity (39.3). While he offers these considerations as aggravating rather than as extenuating, they lend themselves to the very different treatment they will receive at the hands of Diodotus.

The more we consider the speech of Diodotus, the more it will be seen to owe to Cleon.[6] It too begins with an analysis of the place of deliberation within the city, an analysis as outspoken in its criticism of the audience as it is of the opposing speaker. But while Cleon has attacked deliberation, Diodotus reproves him for doing so and the Athenians for failing to maintain the proper conditions for public debate. Indeed, he maintains that things have come to such a pass that no adviser can even hope to succeed by speaking his mind, however wise his advice or impeccable his motives. "The city and only the city is such that it is impossible to benefit it without deceiving it" (3.43.3). We will reconsider the context of this remarkable statement later.[7] For now, we note only that Diodotus thus summons us to consider what deception lurks within his treatment of the Mytilene question.

If there is one thing on which the commentators agree, it is that Diodotus' plea for clemency for the Mytilenians rests on expediency rather than justice.[8] He begins by insisting that his issue is not the deserts of Mytilene but the interests of Athens (3.44), and he ends by stressing the impossibility of a policy that respects both (47.5). Still, justice is by no means absent from his speech. Rather Cleon has forced it into hiding.

Diodotus begins his discussion of Mytilene by talking even tougher than Cleon. He comes forward, he says, neither to accuse nor to defend; the issue, "if we are sensible men," is not "their justice" but "our good counsel" (3.44.1). "For though I should pronounce them ever so unjust, I would not for that bid you kill them, unless it would be advantageous to do so: nor, though they had some claim to indulgence, would I recommend it, unless it appeared to be for the good of [Athens]" (44.2).

---

[6] On Diodotus' indebtedness to Cleon in formulating a response to Cleon, see Bodin *REA* 42 (*Mélanges Radet*) (1940) 36–52; Ebener *WZUH* 5.6 (1956) 1085–1166; Schram *AntRev* 35.1 (1965) 126–29; Macleod *JHS* 98 (1978) 68–78.

[7] The statement is all the more remarkable in view of the fact, noted by Macleod *JHS* 98 (1978) 75 n.47 on the authority of Aristophanes *Thesmophoriazusae* 356–60, that each meeting of the assembly opened with a solemn curse of deceitful speakers.

[8] See, for example, Bury *Ancient Greek historians* 137–39; Cochrane *Thucydides* 103–4; J. H. Finley *Thucydides* 177; Romilly *Imperialism* 137–49, *Phoenix* 28 (1974) 97–98, and *Douceur* 151–53; Grene *Greek Political theory* 29; Wassermann *TAPA* 87 (1956) 29; Stahl *Thukydides* 121; von Fritz *GGS* 1:688; De Ste-Croix *Origins* 13; Kagan *Archidamian war* 159–60; Walzer *Just and unjust wars* 9–10; Pouncey *Necessities* 86–87; Proctor *Experience* 61; Connor *Thucydides* 84–91; Heath *Historia* 39 (1990) 388–89; Coby *CJPS* 24 (1991) 85–89. Cohen *QUCC* 45 (1984) 52–53 follows Kagan and Connor in recognizing that it is for rhetorical reasons only that Diodotus forgoes an appeal to justice; it remains to be seen how cleverly Diodotus contrives to deal with this problem.

Diodotus is notorious for thus elevating interest above justice. The first to do so, however, was Cleon: even if unjust, his decree is necessary. Diodotus stands this on its head: even if just, the decree is idiotic. This is a brilliant stroke. Cleon, who has promoted a "justice" that is mere vengeance, now looks softheaded for having bothered with justice at all.

There are four stages to Diodotus' self-styled argument from interest. After sketching them, I will show how they also comprise an argument from justice. The interest at issue is that of deterring revolts. Diodotus therefore begins his attack on the decree with a blanket deprecation of the deterrent power of the death penalty. Although death dogs many offenses far less grave than rebellion, still, individuals and cities dare to offend, blindly confident in the soundness of their schemes. "All are by nature prone to transgress, whether acting individually or as peoples, and there is no law that can prevent it" (3.45.3).

In support of this view, Diodotus evokes the earliest times. It is "likely"—he does not say certain—that in those days the penalties for the greatest crimes were lighter (ibid.). Not that these times were a golden age. Offenses abounded then as now—they are, after all, endemic to our nature—and punishments soon grew more severe. Nor does he argue that those in authority were wiser then; they were as naive as inexperience could make them. Experience brought ever harsher punishments, as lighter ones failed to contain human nature. This process of learning culminates in the insight of Diodotus himself. Where the lawmakers of old had supposed that even mild punishments would suffice to deter transgressions, Diodotus sees that none does, however terrible. His somber wisdom stands at the furthest remove from the hopefulness of antiquity. Yet the two concur to this extent: neither innocence nor wisdom resorts to harshness as the remedy for crime.

Diodotus claims no special access to the truth about the earliest times. Strikingly, neither the traditional authorities—the poets—nor the researches of Thucydides himself (1.1–23, 2.29, 2.102, 3.96.1) support Diodotus' version of those times. The poets speak of a true golden age, Thucydides of universal penury and violence. It is as if Diodotus has borrowed his crimes from the latter and his punishments from the former. Can he plausibly assert this combination as "likely"?

There is only one assumption that makes sense of Diodotus's account: from the dawn of punishment, its unique and unwavering purpose has been the deterrence of future offenders. Not retribution (justice) but only deterrence (interest) has ever moved human beings to punish. Only thus could we support the inference that only with the passage of time have even the gravest offenses incurred corresponding penalties.

How "likely" an account of punishment this is will appear from the case at hand. Neither in wrath nor in doubt have the Athenians given one thought to deterrence. As their first impulse had been to crush the transgressors as they deserved, their second had been to wonder whether all those consigned to destruction deserved it. Diodotus' deadpan account of punishment ignores just those aspects of it most prominent in the case before him. By sketching the "history" of punishment as if it were a matter of deterrence only, he unobtrusively nudges his listeners toward acquiescing in this perspective. In thus implying the primacy of interest to justice, he develops one side of Cleon's argument—in order to turn the tables on Cleon.[9]

A policy of self-interest divorced from justice may appear ruthless. It implies harshness without scruple whenever this serves a useful purpose. Conversely, however, it condones harshness only when it serves a useful purpose, that is, one other than retribution. In the case of punishment the indicated use is deterrence. Yet Diodotus minimizes the power of punishment to deter. His argument may even seem to imply the abolition of punishment. Explicitly, he wisely leaves it at suggesting that to kill the Mytilenians in particular, while just, would serve no useful purpose. By adopting Cleon's harsh insistence that interest is prior to justice, Diodotus gets away with attacking Cleon's harsh decree—without yet questioning its justice.

Thus far Diodotus has maintained that however just Cleon's policy, it would not advance Athenian interests. He now proceeds to argue that it would harm them. While failing to deter rebellions, Cleon's policy would deter surrenders (3.46). As of now, a revolted ally that finds itself hopelessly beleaguered will yield as Mytilene did, hoping to extenuate an untimely revolt with a timely surrender. To kill the Mytilenians would be to proclaim the same fate alike for those who capitulate early and for those who will not do so at all; it would thus drive all cities to resist to the bitter end. Having impoverished herself with long sieges, Athens would regain only ruined towns, unable to pay either damages or tribute.

The third stage of the argument at first seems almost parenthetical. Its link to the second is the general reflection that the Athenians should look to their interests (i.e., to their tribute) rather than sit as strict judges of justice.

> Presently, however, we do the opposite, and if we have defeated some free people which, ruled by force, has risen (as is reasonable) for its independence, we suppose that we must punish them harshly. We ought, however, not chastise free men to excess after they have risen, but watch them to excess before they rise, and forestall their having a mind to do so; having overpowered them we should put the blame on as few as possible. (3.46.5–6)

The last clause of this passage leads naturally to the fourth stage of the argument: by acting as Cleon advises the Athenians would delight their enemies. At present the demos in each of the subject cities is well disposed

---

[9] For a different reading see Strauss *City and man* 234–35.

toward Athens and, if forced to revolt by the oligarchs, forms an Athenian fifth column.[10] If, however, the Athenians kill the Mytilenian people, "who took no part in the rebellion, and as soon as they acquired arms, of their own free will surrendered the city," not only will they be "guilty of the injustice of killing their benefactors," but they will gratify oligarchs everywhere. Henceforth, even when the people have been compelled to rise by hated rulers, they too will hold out to the end, Athens "having served notice that the same punishment awaits those who are guilty and those who are not" (3.47.3). Indeed, Diodotus concludes, even if the demos at Mytilene were guilty, Athens ought to overlook that fact, rather than lose the one ally remaining to her elsewhere (47.4).[11]

Diodotus has moved from the expediency of distinguishing lesser from greater offenders—the Mytilenians from rebels who refuse to surrender—to that of distinguishing between the wholly blameless and the starkly guilty. This last discrimination is one to be made among the Mytilenians.

Both of these arguments—as well as the intermediate sally on the superiority of prevention to cure (3.46.6)—implicitly define expediency in the matter as deterrence. Diodotus proves not to deny the power of punishment as a deterrent. A properly calibrated scale of penalties could be counted on to achieve the desired effects: deterring halfway offenders from going the rest of the way and the innocent from throwing in their lot with the guilty. Cleon's scheme too would deter, and infallibly—but, as we have seen, in the wrong direction.

This clear emphasis on the deterrent force of punishment—obviously including capital punishment—might seem to clash, both logically and rhetorically, with the first stage of the argument. For there Diodotus has minimized that very power of punishment he is now so keen to exploit. In fact Diodotus has nowhere asserted that the fear of punishment deters no

[10] Cogan *Human thing* 55–65 argues that Diodotus' speech inaugurates a new "ideological" phase of the war. Cogan overstates, however, the novelty of the policy of supporting the demos in the subject cities against the few. Diodotus presents the friendship of the demos for Athens as an established fact, and Ps.-Xenophon *Constitution of Athens* 2.10–11, presumably dating from the same period as the actual Mytilenian debate, presents favoring the demos in the subject cities as the established Athenian policy. The main argument against Cogan's thesis, however, is that no speech (and no action) reported by Thucydides suggests that anyone in Athens sees the war as a struggle of democracies against oligarchies, and democracy elsewhere as a principle for which Athens is fighting (as opposed to an instrument useful for maintaining the empire). This would form a minimum condition for regarding this (or any) stage of the war as ideological. On the general question of the "ideological" character of the war cf. Fliess *Bipolarity* 127–37.

[11] Diodotus recommends however, not that [all] "culpable democrats be spared punishment" (Coby *CJPS* 24 [1991] 88), but merely that Athens spare the Mytilenian people, who either were guiltless or can readily be cast as such (3.47). He implies not that Athens ought not punish even a flagrantly rebellious demos, but that she should punish *only* a flagrantly rebellious one.

rebellions: he has merely stressed that it will never serve to deter all of them. When he moves from the psychology of revolt to that of surrender, his more hopeful assessment of the power of deterrence probably does not strike his listeners as jarring.

Diodotus' true difference with Cleon is not over whether punishment deters, but over how reliably it does so and how to manage it so as to enhance its reliability. Diodotus argues that Cleon exaggerates the likelihood of deterring the commission of what is, after all, a crime of passion. Rebels, feckless and hopeful at the outset, will find the prospect of punishment more daunting once they can see that they are cornered. Diodotus would exploit the power of fear at the juncture when the mind is most defenseless before it. While it may be ineffectual at deterring revolts, it can succeed in curtailing them and greatly reducing their costliness to Athens.[12]

This argument seems persuasive enough. When, however, Diodotus proceeds from the question of how to encourage surrenders (3.46.1–4) to that of how to discourage popular participation in revolts (47.1–4), a contradiction appears. The suggestion of the earlier passage appears to be that all the Mytilenians ought to be spared for having surrendered promptly. The later passage argues, however, that the few (being guilty) ought to be punished and the many not. Are the guilty in fact to be offered clemency as an inducement to future rebels to surrender early, thus enabling Athens to recover rebel cities without ruining them? Or are they to be punished harshly (while the people are spared) as an inducement to peoples to remain aloof from future revolts? Diodotus appears to avoid this problem by now attributing the alleged early surrender of the city to the people alone, acting against the wishes of the few (47.3).[13] The distinction between more and less obdurate rebels collapses into that between rebels and alleged loyalists. Despite his success at obscuring it, the problem itself remains.

The difficulty may be stated as follows: if a revolt will typically arise from a ruling oligarchy, then usually it will be for them to decide whether and when to abandon it. (We recall that even in Mytilene it was the few who finally made this decision.) Only if the Mitylenian few, and not merely the many, find indulgence will their example serve to encourage their peers elsewhere to surrender sooner rather than later. (Otherwise Diodotus' policy will no more encourage early surrenders than Cleon's.) Yet such indulgence seems incompatible with so treating them as to cement the loyalty of the commons elsewhere. Does not the kindly treatment of the people emerge precisely in contrast to the severe treatment of the few? Must not an example be made of the guilt of the few precisely in order to make an example of the innocence of the many? Ultimately, Diodotus may agree with Cleon that light punish-

---

[12] For further elaboration, see Coby *CJPS* 24 (1991) 83–84.

[13] Cf. Macleod *JHS* 98 (1978) 76–77, which also elaborates on the doubtfulness of this interpretation of the events.

ment of the guilty merely encourages offenses (3.39.7): why not revolt if, when worst comes to worst a timely surrender can be counted on to save you from the worst? If the policy appropriate to encouraging surrenders also tends to encourage revolts, which ought Athens to choose?

While, then, the threat of harsh punishment might not suffice to deter all revolts, it may be needed to deter any of them (and even to avoid encouraging them). At 3.46.6 Diodotus confirms that he no less than Cleon is concerned with forestalling, not only popular participation in rebellions, but the rebellions themselves. There he implicitly concedes that sanctions may deter revolts, but suggests that what deters is less the harshness of a sanction than the relative certainty of incurring it. To dissuade offenders, one must flaunt one's power so as make them feel cornered from the beginning. To this end, he implies a policy of preemptive surveillance. The best deterrents are bright streetlights, a cop on the beat, and the infallible punishment of past offenders.[14] Diodotus clearly concedes here that punishment may serve to deter offenses, even where that meditated is revolt. But granted that more certain punishments will deter more effectively than less certain ones, will not more certain and harsher punishments deter more effectively than more certain and lenient ones? If so, it looks as if Diodotus himself concedes that the punishment of the captive oligarchs must be harsh. His final word is not that these deserve clemency (rather he has gone on to credit the demos with handing over the city) but that the Athenians should deal with them as they please.

Diodotus' argument from interest is thus complex and problematic. He flirts with suggesting that punishment as such accomplishes little and that a lenient punishment of both oligarchs and demos would accomplish more than a harsh one. He concludes, however, by bolstering the Athenians' own second thoughts, endorsing harsh punishment of the oligarchs but none at all of the demos.

Diodotus offers, moreover, more than just an argument from interest. He presents what he more than once denies, an appeal to justice. At the climax of the speech, where it matters most, this appeal finally breaks the surface. There he states outright that to kill the demos would be more than a stupidity; it would be a crime (3.47.3). This is not an aberration, a *cri de coeur* that escapes him in spite of himself. In fact we cannot follow his self-styled argument from interest without at the same time imbibing a sense of the injustice of the decree.

For maximum clarity I present two charts of the plan of Diodotus' argument. Its structure is ABA'B', interweaving two trains of thought, each of which unfolds in two stages. Chart 1 outlines these as arguments from interest, chart 2 as simultaneous underhanded appeals to justice.

---

[14] Cf. J. Q. Wilson *Thinking about crime*.

Chart 1

1. (A) (45) That harsh
   punishment will not prove
   expedient in the sense that
   Cleon pretends, because
   transgressors, including, above
   all, rebel cities striving for their
   freedom, simply cannot help
   themselves.

2. (B) (46.1–4) That it is
   expedient to punish the less
   guilty less harshly than the more
   so.

3. (A′) (46.5–6) That harsh
   punishments are not expedient
   in deterring free men from
   asserting their freedom; instead
   one must watch them carefully.

4. (B′) (47) That it is expedient to
   punish the guilty and not the
   guiltless.

Although the argument on the right side of the charts requires no further comment at this stage, a few words are in order concerning the one on the left. Its unity consists in two points, the recurrence of the mention of freedom as the end for which the Mytilenians had acted (3.45.6, 46.5–6), and the assertion that though guilty as charged, yet they acted only as they could not have helped acting (45.4–7, 46.5). The stages differ in that stage 2 emphasizes the first of these points in a way that transforms the import of the second. In having risen for the sake of freedom, as free men will inevitably do, the Mytilenians have a claim not only on the sympathy of the Athenians but on their admiration as well. Not only have they failed due to errors to which all men including Athenians are liable, but they have dared and failed for the sake of something that Athenians prize above all others.

Strauss notes that in the first stage of Diodotus' argument (A) he suggests that though guilty, the Mytilenians might deserve clemency.[15] He does this not by denying that their guilt is flagrant—it is too soon to challenge that presumption—but by implying that the flagrantly guilty are a class somehow worthy of sympathy. There is, he asserts, no circumstance of human

---

[15] Strauss *City and man* 234.

Chart 2

1. (A) (45) That though guilty in
    the usual sense of having done
    the deed, the Mytilenians are
    guiltless in having been driven
    by overwhelming compulsion,
    including the yearning for
    freedom and empire, two of the
    "greatest things."

2. (B) (46.1–4) That though
    guilty, they are not as guilty as
    they might have been.

3. (A') (46.5–6) That though they
    did rebel, in so doing they acted
    as befits free men.

4. (B') (47) That the people at
    least are entirely guiltless, that
    is, did not rebel, and, what is
    more, handed over the city.

life, from poverty, its daring nourished by necessity, to abundance, its craving for more (*pleonexia*) fed by arrogance and presumption, that is not in the
grip of some fatal and imperious passion. "Hope also, and longing (*erōs*),
the latter leading and the former following close behind," lure human beings to ruin, as does fortune, which by favoring a few deludes all (3.45.6).

Diodotus could hardly expect his audience to endorse the view that
transgressors of every sort are blameless. He avoids the onus of having aired
it by speaking openly only of interest, that is, of the problem of deterrence.
By evoking, however, the shadow of a doubt about punishing even flagrant
offenders, he paves the way for his next suggestion, that the Mytilenians
were not even flagrant offenders.

It is to this end also that Diodotus first mentions here the "greatest
things," freedom and empire, for which cities are only too prone to hazard
everything (3.45.6). Diodotus invokes these "greatest things" in explaining
why cities tend to err even more than individuals, bent as they are on such
glorious prey. He also thereby dignifies, however, transgressor cities far
above their individual counterparts, the criminals within each city.

Freedom and empire are the ends that Athens too respects the most.
Diodotus reminds the Athenians that the rebels are their mirror image, not
only in their fallibility but in their aspirations. In seeking to revolt from

Athens they have done only what the Athenians themselves would have done.[16]

It is to this last suggestion that Diodotus returns when he lectures on how to treat free men (A'). Having pointed out that though guilty of rebellion the Mytilenians had not proved obdurate, he intimates that rebellion itself evinces qualities that the Athenians admire. Having now implied that the Mytilenians have been swept by irresistible forces (A) to commit a less than flagrant version (B) of what is hardly an injustice (A'), Diodotus concludes that of even this offense, so hedged about with extenuations, the *demos* is innocent (B').

Every step of the argument from interest thus bears an implicit appeal to justice. Diodotus responds to the fix in which Cleon has placed him by appealing to the people's pity and fairness while reassuring them that he speaks only to their shrewdness and toughness (3.48).

Even so, the vote is a close one (3.49.1). Cleon has changed more minds than Diodotus has changed back. The penultimate act of the drama unfolds. A second ship is dispatched and hastens to overtake the first. It just barely succeeds—and only because the first ship had dawdled on its "horrid business" (49.4). We can picture the Athenian oarsmen plying ever more slowly as rage yields to doubt and doubt to remorse. This is a nice touch. It reminds us that the story hinges on a spontaneous change of heart of the Athenians. Had they not once again fallen prey to Cleon, they would not have needed Diodotus.[17]

From the depths of Diodotus' argument from interest, pipes the still, small voice of justice. In this seems to consist the deception that he has as good as promised (3.43.5).[18] Grave complications remain, however. The

[16] Romilly *Imperialism* 141 and n.1; Huart *Le vocabulaire* 484 n.1 and *Réseaux* 18 (1972) 30 n.25. Cf. Macleod *GRBS* 18 (1977) 245–46 with *JHS* 98 (1978) 75–76.

[17] On the anecdote of the two triremes, see Connor *Thucydides* 16–17, 86–87.

[18] With the exception of Strauss *City and man* 234, only Moraux *EC* 22 (1954) 22; Winnington-Ingram *BICS* 12 (1965) 79; Huart *Le vocabulaire* 484 n. 1 and *Réseaux* 18 (1972) 17–38; Macleod *GRBS* 18 (1977) 245 and *JHS* 98 (1978) 77; and Manuwald *Hermes* 107 (1979) 407–22, among the commentators on this passage prior to my discussion in *APSR* 78 (1984) 485–94, had discerned in it one or the other element of the appeal to justice that I have emphasized. None, however, had presented the structure of the argument as a whole as implying such an appeal or had argued that each stage of the case from interest appealed to our sense of justice. It was Strauss who, by noting that the treatment of deterrence at 3.45 raised questions not of expediency only, suggested to me that the speech as a whole called for the kind of interpretation that I have attempted. See also Bruell *APSR* 68 (1974) 11–17; Corsi *APSR* 68 (1974) 1679–80; Bruell ibid. 1680–81.

Macleod *JHS* 98 (1978) 76–77 argues that Diodotus' deceit consists in recommending a policy that is no more in the interest of Athens than Cleon's. But this critique supposes that Diodotus encourages the Athenians to rely on the spontaneous goodwill of the people to deter revolts and encourage surrenders—which, as I understand the speech, he does not. Macleod takes too seriously Diodotus' initial dismissal of the power of deterrence and so is deaf

justice he settles for seems to fall short of the standard implied by the bolder reaches of his argument. And the problem of reconciling interest and justice thus recurs at a deeper level of the speech.

Diodotus asks only that the Athenians spare the Mytilenian demos while trying at their leisure the thousand ringleaders (3.48.1). He must anticipate that they will kill these latter at least, as they shortly do on the motion of the ubiquitous Cleon (50.1).[19] Diodotus leads the Athenians back to acting as their own second thoughts had suggested (36.4); they had never questioned the guilt of the oligarchs. Indeed he makes the innocence of the people emerge by contrast with the guilt of the rich (47). Can Diodotus, however, regard the rich as guilty?

There are, as we have seen, two strains to Diodotus' appeal, one that invokes common sense notions of justice (BB'), and one that calls them into question (AA'). Diodotus' genius lies in subordinating the second of these strains to the first. An argument absolving the flagrantly guilty serves in practice merely to further the plea that some of the accused are innocent, an implicit defense of rebellion, to gain a hearing for the claim that some of the defendants took no part in it. Rhetorically, this makes sense; it raises, however, some troubling questions. What must Diodotus think—what are his most attentive listeners to think—of the justice of killing the oligarchs?

Attentive listeners will recognize Diodotus' arguments as variations on the theme of the Athenian thesis. What earlier Athenians have offered as a defense of their empire he invokes as equally an excuse for rebellion against it. So, for instance, he adds freedom to empire as one of the "greatest things" that nature bids cities pursue. This indeed is implicit in the thesis. If all cities would rule if they could, it follows that none would be ruled and that freedom is a sort of mean between the two conditions. If human nature is such that Athens cannot but strive to rule, it is such that her subjects cannot but resist being ruled, and if the thesis exculpates rulers, by the same token so must it exculpate rebels (cf. 1.77.4–5, 4.61.5). The thesis thus proves, on reflection, to imply the sympathy of the strong for the very resolve of the weak to oppose them.

---

to his subsequent proposals for manipulating this power more adroitly than suggested by Cleon.

[19] Apropos of this mass execution, Connor *Thucydides* 86–87 notes that the pleasing tale of the two ships that precedes it provides only false closure to the narrative; Thucydides quickly jolts us back to earth. Gomme *HCT* 2:325 plausibly questions whether there could have been a thousand ringleaders; the Athenians appear to have killed the whole of the city's governing class. Connor further notes that the Athenians proceed to inflict a cleruchy on Mytilene (a mass confiscation of the land for the benefit of Athenian colonists, to whom those who till it must pay rent): it is not as if the people of the island escape unscathed. I am not persuaded, however, by Connor's argument (87 n.19) that the cleruchy must have figured in Diodotus' proposal to repeal the original decree.

Secondly, Diodotus extends the compulsion to transgress to a tendency to err in so doing. This he does the more easily in that one Greek word denotes both (*hamartanein*, "to miss one's mark," "to go astray").[20] He thus deepens the pathos of the lot of failed rebels, whose errors are to be assigned to the same overwhelming forces that drove them to venture. And by casting blundering not as contemptible but as a symptom of universal human weakness, he forges yet another bond of sympathy between victor and vanquished.

Lastly Diodotus extends the thesis from cities to individuals. For this too there is an evident practical reason. Wishing to convey that the Mytilenians, although flagrant transgressors, might yet deserve sympathy, he must suggest that all transgressors have some claim to it. He begins, therefore, with the most striking case, not of extenuating circumstances, but of the want of any: that of common criminals. He then argues how much worthier of solicitude is a rebel city (3.46.5–6).

These differences notwithstanding, the intention of Diodotus in propounding the thesis is formally the same as that of the others who do so. He seeks to extenuate alleged transgression as so deeply rooted in the character of the actor that indignation is an inappropriate response to it. This defense, however, as appears from its extension to all, rests neither on individual pathology nor (as so often today) on allegations concerning environment. It accuses not the aberrations of this or that individual or society, but human nature itself.[21]

Anticipating Machiavelli, Hobbes, and Nietzsche, Diodotus casts transgression not as an aberration but as the fundamental human fact and bids us reflect on the consequences. The first of these is the real difficulty of reconciling justice and interest. Here Diodotus' original assertion is not misleading, even if its truth lies deeper than is at first apparent. In the case of the demos, to be sure, both justice and interest appear to be served by leniency. Athens has no choice, however, but to punish the oligarchs severely: she can hardly absolve flagrant rebels and hope to preserve the empire. Yet flagrancy, according to the deepest stratum of Diodotus' presentation (A and A'), is no more culpable than innocence.

In the world as Diodotus describes it, there are and must be many who incur punishment, but there are no transgressors as piety understands that term. The crucial "compulsion," according to him, and the one to which all others point, is the compulsoriness for human beings of their apparent good. The poor strive for necessities, the rich for superfluities: the latter extenuate no less than the former. All yearn for the "greatest things"; for

---

[20] Cf. Bodin *REA* 42 (1940) 41; Romilly *REG* 78 (1965) 564–66; Stahl *Thukydides* 121; Hunter *Past and process* 156 n.4. For other examples of the ambiguous use of ἁμαρτάνειν and its cognate noun ἁμάρτημα, see 3.56.5; Antiphon 1.4; 4.8; Pindar *First Olympian* 64.

[21] Cf. Reinhardt *Vermächtnis* 197.

cities, this means freedom and empire and all that these entail of dignity and devotion,[22] nobility, indignation, and cruelty. Diodotus does not enter the absurd claim that law never deters, that none ever conform their actions to it and are thus far capable of resisting transgression. Yet insofar as it is indeed through deterrence that the law restrains most of us most of the time, we are not more just than those who transgress, only more fearful. And even if some of us are more just than others, none, he suggests, is immune to seizure by an unjust eros and, once seized by it, to being swept on to ruin by hope. This is what Diodotus means by the inability of law to restrain nature (3.45.7). While we may dispute the notion of the good on which offenders act, we cannot blame them "morally" for acting as their good beckons. Whoever "sees the good (sc. of self-restraint) but cannot do it," he is all the less culpable, inability not being a crime; whoever seeing some illicit good abstains from it, is determined by some other reason, some other good to be sought or evil to be averted.[23]

Diodotus' speech thus cures us alike of our indignation at others who disregard our good in favor of theirs and of our qualms at preferring our good to theirs. Yet it is nothing if not a plea for taking an enlightened view of one's good. If he shares the "Athenian thesis" with several other speakers, he carries it a step further than they, and that makes a very great difference. What is elsewhere an assertion of the priority of one's own good to justice becomes in his mouth also a general teaching of human weakness or irrationality. He offers us a glimmer of the negative orientation Hobbes thought to discern in Thucydides. While he speaks of freedom and rule over others as the "greatest things" for individuals and cities alike, these figure in context less as the greatest goods than as what drives men to inflict the greatest evils whether upon themselves or others. Freedom and rule are the greatest goods in the sense of the most overpowering (cf. 1.75–76). Diodotus stresses not the grandeur but the danger and poignancy of empire;

---

[22] Cf. Strauss *Natural right and history* 133–34.

[23] No one simply chooses to act whether justly or unjustly, regardless of whether it seems good to do so; we choose to act as we do because we perceive it as good. Eros is longing for some good; the most powerful, least resistable erōs is evoked by the greatest goods. Those who withstand the blandishments of these do so either because they shrink from the evils that lurk along the way or because they happen to possess knowledge of a more compelling good (cf. Plato *Republic* 366cd, 485c–486b). Insofar as all choice is with reference to some consideration or appearance of good and bad (and hence is somehow determined by it), the notion of choice as morally free (and so of certain choices as deserving punishment) involves us in an infinite regress. Stated anachronistically, Diodotus implicitly denies the unconditionality of the "good-will," and hence its unconditional goodness. To exalt human freedom and responsibility (i.e., to take the side of "Sparta") is to reduce to arbitrariness a pattern of conduct that is natural and intelligible; it is (in contradiction to the fundamental insight of the Athenian thesis) to treat human conduct as supernatural (cf. 1.76.3). Such, at any rate, is one way of making sense of Diodotus' argument which honors its indebtedness to the Athenian thesis.

the vaster the undertaking, the more likely the misplaced confidence in success.

Ultimately in assessing Diodotus' position we must consider what he says not only about Mytilene but about the process of deliberation in Athens and all other cities.[24] (Pericles, who in the Funeral Oration stresses the virtues of Athens, insists on her difference from other cities; Diodotus, whose painful task it is to reprove her for her vices, presents most of these at least as vices of cities as such: in this he goes even beyond Cleon, who presents them as vices of democracy.) Diodotus first appears as the champion of full and free deliberation and so, apparently, of a rational political process of the sort praised by Pericles (cf. 2.40). Reflection, however, confirms Gomme's remark that Diodotus "comes perilously close to questioning the utility of free discussion."[25] More precisely, he indicates his doubts as to the possibility of free or rational discussion.

Diodotus defends deliberation as the only means of reaching sound decisions (3.42). Those who would deny this, he insists, are fools or more likely rogues, who, "wishing to persuade of something disgraceful and doubting their ability to speak well in a base cause, . . . slander well so as to cow both their opponents and their listeners." Worst of all are those (like Cleon) who accuse their adversaries of corruption. For these latter are then suspect even should they prevail and, should they fail, are reputed not only unintelligent but unjust. "And such goings-on are no favor to the city, for fear deprives it of advisers."

Diodotus seems to agree with our civil libertarians that deliberation is indispensable for unearthing useful truths. He differs with them, however, over the conditions favorable to it. Indeed he begins where they leave off, with ostensibly free public discussion. The problem he points to, as will appear from his lines just cited, is that free debate proves a contradiction in terms. There is a Gresham's law of speakers: the bad, if not silenced, will drive out the good. They will do so by fomenting distrust, thus driving the good to despair of persuading of their goodness. "The prestige of Diodotus cannot well coexist with the prestige of Cleon."[26] The deliberative marketplace is unfree because bounded by considerations of trust, which diverge widely from those of reason.

Diodotus suggests, however, that we can at least imagine a radical change in this state of things. "[The city] would prosper best if . . . citizens of this [slanderous] sort . . . were incapable of speaking" (3.42.4). This sounds like a prayer: in what actual city has the power of speech ever deserted those who

[24] Cf. my earlier treatment of this question, *American Scholar* 53 (summer 1984) 313–25; for a response and elaboration, see Coby *CJPS* 24 (1991) 86–87. On the generality of Diodotus' analysis of deliberative assemblies, see Romilly *La construction* 127.

[25] Gomme *HCT* 2:314.

[26] Strauss *City and man* 232.

would abuse it? And if heaven is unlikely thus to provide, can the city do anything for itself? Diodotus suggests that it can.

> As for the good citizen, he ought not intimidate those who speak against him, but to show himself a better speaker on the up and up; and while the moderate city will not confer additional honor on the man who advises it well, neither should it subtract from what he already has, and as for him whose judgment happens not to prevail, not only should it not punish him: it should not even show him disrespect. For then it would happen least that a successful speaker, hoping to achieve still greater esteem, would speak against his better judgment in order to please, and that an unsuccessful one, also aiming to please, would court the multitude by resorting to these same means. (3.42.5–6.)

The course prescribed to good citizens here depends on that prescribed to the city. Under current conditions, high-minded abstention from slander has proved no match for indulgence in it, or the bad citizens would not have managed to silence the good ones. For now, then, speaking no evil cannot define the part of even best citizen, who by practicing it would be placed in danger without thereby helping the city. At most, Diodotus here indicates how the good citizen would speak if all speakers were good citizens— that is, if the city somehow deterred bad citizens from speaking. Such is precisely the aim of the reform that Diodotus suggests to the city.

With this proposed reform, we reach the heart of Diodotus' articulation of the problem of deliberation. He offers it as dryly as if it were an amendment to Robert's Rules of Order. In fact it implies a radical transformation of political life. It is utopian, by which I mean that it offers a spurious solution meant to clarify a genuine problem.

There are two reasons for regarding Diodotus' proposal as utopian. The first is the downright impossibility of implementing it. Anyone with deliberative experience knows that to heed advice *is* to honor the adviser: the honor lies in the heeding. Most assemblies, after all, observe a Diodotean etiquette: every member is equally the "honorable," the "distinguished" solon from wherever. This cannot obscure the fact that the members are of most unequal influence. When some rise to speak, the mind wanders, while others command its utmost attention. Inevitably, to persuade someone of the wisdom of your position is to gain in that person's esteem, and to fail to do so is to lose in it. The habitually persuasive enjoy great repute (which in turn enhances their persuasiveness), while those who go always unheeded get none. This is true by nature, not law, and no law can hope to oppose it.

As for tangible political honors, these are primarily offices, positions of trust and responsibility. (The Greek word *timē* means both honor and office.) How are we to allot offices if not according to perceived integrity and wisdom? Yet nothing so confirms our good opinion of people in these regards as that we regularly follow their advice. It is as effective speakers that people first attract political notice and that all politicians must retain such notice. Here, as before, it proves beyond the pale of possibility to abolish all incentive to successful speaking.

The second sense in which Diodotus' proposed reform proves utopian is this: entirely superfluous for some societies, it would be completely futile for the rest. A wise society (were there one) would have no need of this reform. It would see through Cleons and so would need no other means of deterring them. Having failed as speakers, they would soon subside. Such a society would be eager to obtain the advice even of those who spoke only to acquire reputation—for the only way to impress it would be to advise it wisely.

Diodotus' proposal is relevant, then, only to unwise societies (such as he appears to take all actual societies to be). We recall that he has described the city that would proceed as he advises not as "wise" but as "moderate." It is moderate in confessing its lack of wisdom, in seeking to deter bad advice that it knows might persuade it if given.

On reflection, however, this "moderate" city proves an impossibility. The same lack of perfect deliberative wisdom that necessitated such moderation would undo it. Let us suppose what cannot be supposed, that a society could succeed at refraining from honoring successful speakers and dishonoring the unsuccessful and could thereby silence the honor-loving while drawing out those with pure intentions. Since it would be unreasonable to expect unanimity even from these on complicated life-or-death issues, such a society would still have to pass on the conflicting advice before it. The "moderate" city, however, lacking wisdom itself and therefore unable to recognize it reliably in others, could not but fall back on heeding the speakers that it trusted. The assembly would continue to be swayed by considerations of trust that it mistook for those of reason, and skill at inspiring trust would remain the crucial art of speakers—of wise, patriotic speakers no less than others.

So long as audiences fall short of wisdom—so long as they are in need of advice—wisdom will be neither sufficient nor necessary to a given speaker's success at persuading them.[27] This is the real point of Diodotus' utopian suggestion, and its ramifications are very great.

The trouble with the Athenians, moreover, is not just that they cannot recognize good advice. Where they suspect the motives of the speaker, they will reject his counsel even though they can find no fault with it (3.43.1). They would rather ignore good advice than risk having something put over on them.

From this it follows that plain good advice, in the absence of the art of fostering trust, remains at the mercy of the calumnies of opposing speakers.

---

[27] Cf. Keynes *Revision* 1–3.

Diodotus' prescription for Mytilene, however beneficial to Athens, cannot prevail among suspicions that he speaks disloyally. Candor is not transparent and so cannot suffice to dispel suspicions of craft. Craft alone can do that, by contriving a persuasive sheen of candor.

Such considerations explain the most astounding stroke in Diodotus' speech, his explicit avowal of the necessity of deception in public life. His insistence that the city cannot be served either badly or well except through lying to it (3.43.3) seems, on the face of it, ill suited to dispel the distrust of him stirred by Cleon. Such, however, must be its intention: to convey a frankness so complete as to persuade of the honesty of the speaker, even though he is proclaiming the necessity of deception. It is hard to suspect the candor of anyone so candid about his lack of it.

It also helps that here, as throughout Diodotus' discussion of deliberation, he speaks in such denunciatory tones. He seems to demand of the people that they mend their ways and at last give simple honesty a hearing. He sketches the status quo as so defective that we are unlikely to reflect that he denounces the way of the world as a means to succeeding according to it.

Diodotus concludes his discussion of deliberation with one last suggestion as to how cities might decide things more sensibly. He remarks that, as matters stand, even being heeded is risky for advisers: they and they alone are blamed should the outcome prove disastrous.[28] We note that Diodotus does not counsel, even in a utopian vein, against rejecting those advisers whose advice proves bad when taken (as opposed to merely seeming bad when given). He suggests only that the discredit be more equitably distributed (3.43.4–5). It is not, then, simply bad for the city to distinguish among its counselors if it does so in such a way as to offer them an incentive to advise it well. Diodotus' treatment of inducements for speakers resembles his treatment of deterrence of rebels: it is a question not of ceasing to employ these but of learning to do so judiciously.

Deceit may be necessary, but is surely not sufficient, to insure abiding success in politics. For that, it must serve to persuade of good advice rather than bad. To this extent, at least, the good of even an unprincipled statesman converges with that of the city. Diodotus is presumably confident that his advice on handling the allies is good. There remains the necessity of deception. We have discussed his subterfuges in the matter of Mytilene, forced on him in part by the unseemly tactics of Cleon. Still to discuss is his resort to those unseemly tactics.

Diodotus denounces the procedure of Cleon as unworthy of a good citizen. In so doing he also adopts it. In blaming Cleon for impugning the integrity of his opponents, he impugns Cleon's integrity. While presenting imputations of corruption as prima facie evidence of the corruption of the

[28] 2.61.1, 64.1; Ps.-Xenophon *Constitution of Athens* 2.17.

accuser, he manifestly engages in them—and thus seems to stand convicted of corruption out of his own mouth. That he gets away with this tactic attests not his probity but his cleverness: to sow distrust of someone for sowing distrust is the most ingenious way of sowing distrust of someone.[29]

Distrust of their leaders, aggravated by a fear of being too trusting of them, mingled with a longing for a leader they can trust: such, according to both Cleon and Diodotus, is the natural temper of the led. The people give a hearing only to opinions of speakers they trust; trust itself does not issue from a careful hearing. Hence the permanent necessity—even in a direct democracy where decisions are in the hands of the people assembled—of what we call "image politics." Considerations of trust shape and limit all deliberation, and in practice Diodotus agrees with Cleon that trust accrues to those who are best at exploiting distrust. He presents aspersions as too important to be left to the unscrupulous.[30]

But what of Diodotus himself? If the city could see through Cleon, it would not trust him; would it trust Diodotus?[31] We have already noted that Diodotus presents the vices of Athens as peculiar neither to her nor to democracy, but as incident to cities as such. Whether in his discussion of foreign policy or of the pitfalls of deliberation, he appears (once we have penetrated his clouds of rhetoric) to gaze down on Athens from an Olympian height. We could hardly expect any city to trust a citizen who saw it as so much less than it saw itself; the city, in its majesty, declines to be surveyed from an Olympian height. Nor is it surprising that the vastness of the gulf between Diodotus' understanding of the city and its own will appear only on considerable reflection, that is, only to those listeners whose understanding is already at some remove from the city's.[32]

---

[29] Cf. Aristotle *Rhetoric* 3.15; Pseudo-Aristotle (Anaximenes?) *Rhetorica ad Alexandrum* 39; Moraux *EC* 22 (1954) 17–21; Winnington-Ingram *BICS* 12 (1965) 78.

[30] Cf. Ps.-Xenophon *Constitution of Athens* 1.7, 2.19.

[31] Cf. Banfield *Here the people rule* xv: "The intellectual . . . has nothing in common with the politician and, except as he may sometimes be used by the politician, plays no role in American politics. . . . It sometimes happens that an intellectual is also a politician: Lincoln is a good example. . . . The combination does not occur very often, however, and when it does the individual finds it expedient to keep his intellectuality out of public view."

[32] Cf. Thucydides' own statement that he writes not for a popular audience but only those few whose primary concern is the truth (1.20–22). On Diodotus as the speaker in the work who rises to the greatest level of generality (and thus of proximity to Thucydides himself), see Romilly *Construction* 96, 118–19, 127, 128. Cf. Hunter *Past and process* 156–57. Müri *MH* 4 (1947) 251–75 and Stahl *Thukydides* esp. 122–28 offer "Diodotean" interpretations of Thucydides but have little to say about our issues. The clearest Thucydidean parallels to Diodotus' argument concerning human nature are 3.82–83; 4.58–64 (discussed just below); 4.65; 4.108.4; 5.84–116; 6.24 and 54–59 (the role of eros in the Sicilian expedition and in the downfall of the old Athenian tyranny). For others, cf. Müri and Stahl.

Some have recently deplored the manipulative character of Diodotus' speech, which by arguing on the basis of expediency rather than justice further lowers the tone of public dis-

The Speech of Hermocrates at Gela

The speech of Hermocrates at Gela (4.59–64) is at the same time one of the slyest and one of the wisest in Thucydides. Perhaps only that of Diodotus rivals it in either respect.[33] Thucydides accords it extraordinary emphasis: events in Sicily, hitherto marginal in the work, now for the first time seize center stage, and where we would expect an antilogy we receive just one authoritative speech which (after the fashion of Pericles and Brasidas) sweeps all before it.[34] Of greatest interest to us is that Hermocrates here becomes the only non-Athenian in the work to state the Athenian thesis. Like Diodotus, however, Hermocrates offers it not merely as an apology for imperialism, but as the ground of a general political outlook.

In representing Syracuse at the pan-Sicilian conference at Gela, Hermocrates confronts a complex situation. Sicily is divided among Greek and barbarian (cf. 6.2–5), and the Greeks are divided among themselves, not only into many cities, but into two "races," Dorian and Chalcidian (Ionian) (cf. 6.76–87). These are "hostile by nature" (4.60.1) and natural allies of Sparta and Athens, respectively (cf. 3.86). Even the Dorians, however, are divided among themselves, for all Sicilian cities fear Dorian Syracuse, the most powerful among them. Hence the allure of an Athenian connection, of an outside protector against a homegrown menace. After years of intermittent war, the cities are now tired of it. It has gained them nothing; none, however, has abandoned its original war aims. Beyond the parties having

---

course in Athens. See Macleod *GRBS* 18 (1977) 245–46 and *JHS* 98 (1978) 72–77; White *Words* 75–77; Connor *Thucydides* 86–91 (somewhat ambivalently); Euben *Tragedy* 180–83. It must be noted that Diodotus has no choice but to respond to Cleon in the only vein that promises success, that he appeals to justice in the most effective way open to him (that is to say surreptitiously), and that according to his own analysis (in agreement with Cleon's) public speech in democracy is never pristine; there is no possibility of a democratic "community of discourse." As for the speeches of Pericles, Thucydides presents these as highly artful and full of aspersions of his rivals. If the Mytilenian debate marks a decline in Athens, it does so by reminding us that she no longer boasts any single speaker as artful and, therefore, as predominant as Pericles. (At any rate, there are none who, unlike Diodotus, aspire to a leading role in the city and have hence gone to the necessary lengths to establish their trustworthiness.)

[33] Reinhardt *Vermächtnis* 197 rightly associates the two speeches. Useful is Landmann *Friedensmahnung*, a German dissertation that discusses the speech at Gela line by line. Edmunds *Chance and intelligence* 3, 17, 184–85 opposes Hermocrates' understanding to that of Pericles, concluding that the former exemplifies Dorian moderation in the face of the uncertainty of fortune. Hammond in Stadter ed. *Speeches* 49–59 argues that the generalities in the speech express Thucydides' mature understanding. Best is Connor *Thucydides* 119–26, who recognizes Hermocrates' privileged status and the great resonance of the speech for the work as a whole.

[34] Connor *Thucydides* 119–22, which also notes that the speech proves the dramatic pivot of Book Four and of the whole Archidamian War: "[I]t marks the transition from Athenian success at Pylos to the setbacks . . . related in the later portions of the book."

assembled, then, there has been no tangible progress toward peace prior to Hermocrates' speech. He proves the great peacemaker in Thucydides, the only speaker then to merit a Beatification (". . . For they shall be called children of God" Matthew 5.9). The deity whose name Hermocrates bears is, however, the god of thievery and stealth.

Each of the preceding speakers has urged the claims of his particular city (4.58). Hermocrates, however, begins by noting that Syracuse is not the city suffering most from the war (59.1). Indeed, he never discusses what she in particular stands to gain from a peace; the implication is that as the strongest city and the one having the least to fear from war, so she stands to gain the least from peace that would be invidious to her rivals, that is, no more than the benefits common to peace, in which all cities will share equally. He pronounces war an evil—as befits a peacemaker—but rather spoils the effect by presenting this as a truism known to all deterring none. "No one is constrained to undertake war in ignorance [sc., of its evils], any more than he is deterred from it by fear if he supposes that something is to be gotten by it. For to the latter party, the gain appears greater than the terrors, while the former would rather stand the risk than give so much as an inch" (59.2). The claim is not that war, as an evil, must be shunned: its benefits may predominate. When, however, its evils ensue while the expected gains do not, the parties may agree to cut their losses.

In order to show that the cities have warred unseasonably, Hermocrates distinguishes between their particular interests and that common to all Sicily. Although the cities contest the division of the island's ample pie, they risk losing the whole to Athens (4.60). Hermocrates does not dispute the primacy of particular interests; a city need concern itself with broader ones only insofar as its own interests demand it (59.3, 61.1). As we have seen, he describes the Sicilian cities as "hostile by nature" (60.1); although his primary reference seems to be to the ethnic cleavage between Dorian towns and Chalcidian ones, his argument seems further to imply that every city is by nature the foe of every other. Accordingly, in enjoining the cities to practice moderation (61.1), he calls on them not to set aside their respective interests for the sake of some broader one, but merely to pursue the former in an enlightened fashion, summoning only allies genuinely useful to that end.

No sooner, however, has Hermocrates thus vindicated the cities' concerns with their several interests, than he insists that they will be guilty of stasis if they continue to contend on the basis of these interests (4.61.1). "We must be reconciled, individual with individual, and city with city, and try in common to save all of Sicily" (61.2). What has transformed the Sicilian cities from natural enemies into a single community whose very division into cities can be likened to stasis? Only the advent of Athens. The common good or interest, which Hermocrates began by promising to address (59.1), is not distinct from the particular goods of the cities but is their aggregate

(61.3: *en tēi Sikeliāi agathōn . . . ha koinēi kektēmetha*). It is common to them only vis-à-vis an external threat. The menace of a common enemy constitutes a common good.[35]

In the rest of 4.61 Hermocrates debunks the Athenian claim to have come to Sicily in order to aid the Ionian cities against their "enemies by nature" the Dorians. Their real aim, he contends, is to use the Ionians to defeat the Dorians and then to reduce the former, thus becoming masters of all Sicily. Far from decrying this mendacity, however, and the imperialism of which it is the instrument, he entirely excuses them. "That the Athenians should covet and scheme for these things is only too pardonable, and I blame not those who wish to rule but those who too readily serve. For it is ever men's nature to rule those who submit, just as it is to resist those who attack" (61.4). The only non-Athenian to state the Athenian thesis, Hermocrates blames not a lust for the good things of others but merely a lack of vigor in defending one's own. He exhorts the erstwhile allies of Athens to emulate her energy, and to bestir themselves to protect their freedom just as she does to deprive them of it.

Having expounded the exigencies of the moment, Hermocrates proceeds to praise peace even apart from such considerations (4.62). Now he proclaims a unanimous agreement that peace is excellent in its own right. He dilates in some detail on its blessings and the corresponding risks of war. But has he not just minutes ago dismissed such things as universally known and universally irrelevant? As either ineffectual or superfluous? It makes good sense, however, that, having suggested to his fellow connivers of their own good that peace is timely, he should seek to console them for renouncing the objects each had sought to gain through war. He therefore reminds each that, the fortunes of war being unpredictable, each stood to lose as much as he stood to gain; better just to agree to retain what they presently have. To this end he offers an argument of truly Athenian generality, while affirming the apparently "Dorian" point of the supremacy of fortune in the world.[36]

Hermocrates begins 4.63 by returning to the matter most nearly at hand: the undefined fear of the unknown future should join with apprehensions about Athens to push the cities to make peace. He explicitly offers these meditations as excuses each city can offer for renouncing its original war aims; he takes it for granted that willingness to do so will depend not on

---

[35] Cf. Landmann *Friedensmahnung* 15. Connor *Thucydides* 123–26 ignores this point and so regards the use that Hermocrates makes of the Athenian thesis as more paradoxical than it is. If "the so-called law of the stronger [here] becomes an injunction for the weaker to unite," it also remains a justification for the stronger to crush the weaker—as Hermocrates intends for Syracuse to do as soon as the coast is finally clear. From the pan-Sicilian coalition against Athens will arise a new Syracusan empire (cf. 6.33.5–6).

[36] See Edmunds *Chance and intelligence* 89–142 on Thucydides' association of the Dorians with deference to the sway of chance.

reflections on the human condition but on present frustrations, which cry to have a good face put on them. Indeed, even *after* having argued forcefully for the blessedness of peace and the riskiness of war, he feels it necessary not only to advert to these urgent (and nonrecurring) grounds for a truce, but to stress that should they make peace now the cities will certainly war among themselves again in the future (63.1–2). The cities evidently welcome assurances that they will not groan under the blessings of peace forever, assurances, that is, that they are being called on to defer their war aims but not to abandon them. As Hermocrates has suggested that no one is deterred by the evils of war, so he does not believe he has persuaded his listeners of the desirability of permanent peace.

In 4.64, his conclusion, Hermocrates begins by applying his argument to his own case, "as the representative of a very great city, more used to attacking others than to defending [itself]" (64.1). Again stressing the pitfalls of going to war and thus entrusting oneself to fortune, he declares himself ready to make concessions and calls on the rest to follow suit. Briefly returning to the issue of Dorians and Ionians, he again presents their common plight and name (as Sicilians) as a more potent consideration still. And again he consoles them for the necessity of making peace by reminding them that the future will hold opportunities for war, but war conducted ("if we are moderate" 64.3) without the participation of foreign adventurers.[37]

Hermocrates succeeds in persuading the cities arrayed against Syracuse to accept her offer of a compromise and to send Athens packing (4.65.1–2). We must wonder, however, just how he has managed this. Assuming only ordinary wariness in these cities long harried by Syracuse, must they not see through Hermocrates? He as much as confirms that no sooner will they have repelled the alleged Athenian threat than they will face a Syracusan one— and that not only the Ionian cities will face it but the other Dorian ones also. He not only condones imperialism (4.61), but winks at (even as he unmasks) the ethnic argument as a cover for it: Syracuse is wont to use just that argument. (Hermocrates himself will use it at Camarina [6.76–80].) He stresses that peace will be short-lived, that the Sicilian wars will certainly resume but next time without an Athens to sustain the foes of Syracuse. He clearly implies that there is no common ground among the Sicilians save that posed by the outside threat; that in its absence Syracuse, "a very great city, and one more used to attacking others than to defending itself," will pursue her own imperial aims. What is this if not to speak, with glaring

---

[37] In this chapter, Hermocrates speaks of the Sicilian Chalcidians (Ionians) as kinsmen (ξυγγενῶν) of each other, but the Athenians (equally the kinsmen of these) as ἀλλοφύλους ἐπελθόντας ("interlopers of alien stock"). Ἀλλόφυλος, while a standard word for foreign, means literally "of another tribe"; as we have seen, Hermocrates seeks to replace ancestral notions of friendship or kinship with political or circumstantial ones. An ironic echo of this usage is to be found at 6.9.1.

ineptitude, at cross purposes with himself? What is it but to remind the allies of Athens (and not just these) why they should maintain her presence in Sicily? And yet the enemies of Syracuse agree to send Athens away. Are they fools?

No. Neither is Hermocrates. He makes it easy to see through his speech. He also suggests, however, as if inadvertently, how those who fear Syracuse can have their cake and eat it. For the Athenians, always so ready to intervene "even when uninvited" (4.60.2), can always be invited to return, and those who look to them for protection can plan to manipulate this threat in order to check Syracusan aggression. Let the Leontines send Athens away, confident that they can always ask her back.[38] In the meantime, they can enjoy the advantages of the Athenian connection without the hardships of war.

Hermocrates is the only Thucydidean speaker to ply his listeners with the heady pleasure of having seen through his efforts to put one over on them. Is he even thus putting one over on them? Yes and no. Hermocrates sees that the moment is not ripe for Syracusan expansion; better for her to bide her time, while promoting a grand coalition against Athens. Should Athens come to grief, the defeat of her empire will pave the way for the rise of the Syracusan one—out of that very coalition (cf. 6.33.5–6). Hermocrates casts Athens as the new Mede, Syracuse as the new Athens—and himself as the new Themistocles.

Although not a monument to the justice of the speaker, Hermocrates' speech does procure a reasonable facsimile of the common good of the Sicilian Greeks. In addressing exclusively the particular interests of his listeners—in elaborating a notion of the common according to which nothing can be common but an enemy—Hermocrates honors the Athenian insight into the weakness of justice. At the same time he stresses the power of justice—as a basis of false hopes and an incitement to folly.

Let us return to his argument for the blessings of peace (4.62). It reminds us of Diodotus (3.45–46): to err is human, but the error once felt, it is equally human to be at least briefly amenable to reason. Hermocrates catches his fellow Sicilians just at the point at which Diodotus had argued that the Athenians should apply pressure to revolted subjects, on the downswing of their fortunes and the consequent upswing of their reasonableness. This Diodotean premise of qualified human reasonableness is not simply hopeful; once the Sicilians have composed themselves, the cycle of error and hindsight will begin anew.

It follows that peace in particular can never be more than temporary, and Hermocrates makes this explicit. As surely as cities sometimes make peace

[38] Eventually they do; or more precisely, the Athenians come to their assistance "uninvited" [by them] but allegedly to succor them, at the behest of the Egestaeans: see, for example, 6.6.2, 6.8.2.

and reject war as an evil, so they will in time war again regardless. Hermocrates identifies two delusions that commonly entice cities to their ruin (4.62). Both remind us of Diodotus. The first recalls his emphasis on the tendency of actors to exaggerate their relative strength (3.45.5–6). Hermocrates presents this as a tendency to underestimate the power of fortune; a strong city's vulnerability to that power increases through its very conviction that its strength exempts it.

The second of the delusions exposed by Hermocrates reminds us of another remark of Diodotus: cities, because they can always cite cases of others who have succeeded with fewer resources than their own, forge blithely onward, relying on fortune to favor them also. This might seem to imply not an underestimation of the power of fortune, but an overestimation of its friendliness. Hermocrates, however, does present it as a kind of disregard of fortune's power. Parallel to cities' overconfidence in their strength is their overconfidence in their justice. When a city has suffered a setback and therefore deems itself wronged, it is likely to venture beyond its strength, in a misplaced confidence that justice is strength—notwithstanding that the setback has rather exposed the city's weakness.[39]

Hermocrates' speech thus supplements that of Diodotus by extending the latter's account of the delusions that tempt cities to venture. The human presumption of the favor of fortune turns out (not surprisingly) to rest on a presumption of the power of justice. Not only does the prospect of doing injustice fail to restrain cities from encroachment, but the fact of having suffered it inflames them to run foolish risks. People's professions of justice are not merely hypocritical; their actions confirm their faith in its power. They are such virtuosi of self-deception, however, that this faith is highly selective. Hollow as a prop to moderation, justice is a potent stimulus to folly. We might restate the Athenian thesis as follows: cities not only venture to the limits of their strength, but tend to come to ruin by venturing far beyond these limits—and that a sense of their justice compounds their errors by further inflating their sense of their strength.

Is a sense of one's justice inseparable from unreasonable confidence in the power of that justice to protect the bearer? In this crucial respect, what Thucydides shows us appears to confirm what Hermocrates tells us. The Melians; the Spartans (cf. especially 7.18.2); the Corinthians, confronted with the insolent ingratitude of their Corcyrean colonists (1.26.3–4); Nicias—all of these examples confirm that a conviction of one's superior justice nourishes the expectation that one's desert will be somehow rewarded. Might this syndrome afflict Athens as much as any? It is not only that most of her citizens are much less "enlightened" than their boldest

---

[39] Cf. Aristotle *Rhetoric* 2.5.21.

spokesmen. It is also that these very spokesmen, for all their breathtaking and questionable candor, appear to cling to some conviction of their (relative) justice. (We recall that even the envoys to Melos seemed, in the end, reluctant to relinquish this notion.) Can it be that the standard Athenian deprecation of the power of justice is very much a half measure, because it exists side by side with an unrecognized hope that justice (i.e., the superior justice of Athens) will nonetheless prevail in the world? Can the envoys dismiss the expectations of the Melians less because they hold in their hearts that all such hopes are vain than because they reject the Melian claim to superior justice? Athens, which prides herself on her superior justice, must hold that she practices justice for its own sake (1.77), even while questioning whether so to practice it makes any sense. Can it be that, unbeknownst to herself she resolves this difficulty in the usual manner? To recall again Strauss's words, "there is something reminding of religion in Athenian imperialism."[40] There is nothing reminding of it in the speeches of Diodotus and Hermocrates.

Neither right nor might need prevail in human affairs: each is equally liable to failure. And the disappointment is equal for each, because as the just were confident in their justice, so too were the unjust confident in their strength. We must remember, however, that Hermocrates' rhetorical task is to deter both equally. Fortune is the most useful thing to him as a speaker and allegedly to Sicily only inasmuch as it offers an equal inducement to peace for every city, large or small, strong or just. It does not follow that he in fact presumes that power and justice are equally ineffectual. Indeed his overall analysis of the Sicilian situation ascribes no weight to justice and all weight to relations of strength. Even so, it may benefit the strong to remember that they are not omnipotent, that justice (or more correctly, fortune) sometimes triumphs in the world. This might induce them to remain within the limits of their strength.

The incalculability of the future (*to astathmēton tou mellontos*), although the most powerful and dangerous of all things, is also thereby the most useful (*chrēsimōtaton*) (4.62.4), since all are equally vulnerable to it and so can equally benefit from the salutary restraint of fear of it (*dediotes*, 62.4; *deos dia ton astathmēton*, 63.1). "Against hope, Hermocrates invokes fear."[41] Fear, insofar as it lessens our hopes, is itself a beacon of hope; it is, as Hobbes would later say, the passion to be reckoned on. As our most powerful incentive to act with foresight (*promēthia*, 62.4),[42] fear is the uniquely

[40] Strauss *City and man* 229. Cf. Landmann *Friedensmahnung* 58–63 on the "religious" character of the hopes in justice that Hermocrates punctures here.

[41] Connor *Thucydides* 124.

[42] "Προμηθία is a crucial word, unusual in Thucydides but used again by Hermocrates in 6.80.1. Like πρόνοια it refers to contemplation of the future, but the emphasis is not on what

reasonable passion; Hermocrates speaks not of *phobos* but of *deos*.[43] He invites us to fortify ourselves against fortune by granting our subjection—and reducing our exposure—to it.

Fortune, according to Hermocrates, thrives on our neglect of it. Is it altogether a case of human neglect? Such is arguably the view of Thucydides' Pericles.[44] If so, Hermocrates takes issue with him, as he does (before the fact) with atheistic modernity. While agreeing that no superhuman force supports justice, he refuses to suppose human intelligence capable of conquering chance. There is neither a grace that perfects nature nor (as the moderns would argue) a political art or science that can do so.[45] Hermocrates is less hopeful than Hobbes, whom he so seems to resemble, because he agrees with Diodotus that human beings are not (even potentially) rational and therefore fearful creatures but irrepressibly hopeful ones. (This explains his concession that the effectiveness of any argument from fear is merely seasonal, dependent on fresh wounds to be licked.) Most of us are dominated by present concerns, which are almost always hopeful ones: our reasonableness is never more than intermittent and circumstantial. Our natural hopefulness limits the hopes that we may reasonably place in fear.[46]

Hermocrates' argument is not that life is so incalculable that everything is up in the air and nothing can be accomplished. While invoking *to as-tathmēton*, he has also implicitly confined its sway; that Athens will divide and conquer he has presented as fully calculable, as it is that the Sicilian cities, having made peace, will fall again to warring among themselves. The fundamental contradiction of his speech (on which, as so often with speeches, its success depends) is that he presents a dire outcome as certain unless the warring cities come to terms on the basis of the insight that no outcome is certain. Still, his true position may be merely that unless Sicily

---

can be known about the future and hence on prediction, but on what cannot be known—the element of unpredictability or immeasurability, here τὸ ἀστάθμητον." (Connor *Thucydides* 124)

[43] On the significance of this distinction between "good" (i.e. reasonable) and "bad" fear, see Romilly *ClMed* 17 (1956) 119–22. She describes (121) Hermocrates' speech as a praise of "bonne crainte," the advantages of which "correspondent aux inconvénients de l'elpis."

[44] See Edmunds *Chance and intelligence* 7–88. Cf. Democritus fr. 119.

[45] On the substitution in Hobbes of art for grace, see Manent *Dix leçons* 54–58, 72–74.

[46] Romilly (*ClMed* 17 [1956] 124) rightly remarks that Thucydides differs from Hobbes in denying that the effect of fear is to lead to "la création d'un ordre stable et consenti." "Dans le monde décrit par Thucydide, la crainte n'est créatrice que de puissance"—and power is always unstable. I would add only that a principal reason for its instability is what we might describe as the hopefulness of power. Of course, we must remember that whereas Hobbes considers primarily relations among individuals, Hermocrates and Thucydides consider primarily relations among cities; not even Hobbes holds out the prospect of fear as grounding stable relations among the latter. On Thucydides' view of the role of fear in domestic politics, see chapter 8 and Romilly ibid. 124 n.2.

unites an Athenian conquest is highly likely. Surely this would justify a rhetorical claim that such a result is inevitable.

The elements that Hermocrates presents as predictable are permanent aspects of the political situation, grasping which will enable us better to cope with it. These elements include both the instability of fortune and the human tendency to presume upon its favors. That statesman is likely to succeed best who keeps these factors always in mind: to err is human; to anticipate and avoid that error, politic. It should go without saying that success is never guaranteed. For Hermocrates as for Diodotus, to achieve a rational comprehension of the world is to achieve an understanding of the weakness of reason in the world.

Chapter 8

DOMESTIC POLITICS

THUCYDIDES is little known as a theorist of domestic politics. His failure to articulate the best regime contrasts with the elaborate constructions of Plato and Aristotle, hence his habitual exclusion from the canon of political philosophers.

The question of the best or most choiceworthy regime points to the priority in domestic life of choice over compulsion. In foreign affairs even the best cities do as they must, which is often the very opposite of justly (*Republic* 422a–423a). (Neither Plato nor Aristotle even raises the question of the best international order.) The question of the best regime also presumes, therefore, the priority of domestic over foreign affairs, or the freedom of the city from such externalities as would crimp its domestic policy. In tracing the democratization of Athens to defects in the city's music education, Plato's Athenian Stranger conspicuously abstracts from those outside pressures that forced this process on her: he discounts the necessity of a navy to Athens and hence of her having enfranchised the demos.[1] In fact Plato and Aristotle are well aware of the obstacles to strict justice at home posed by the presence of powerful neighbors. The best city must be so situated as to be able to dispense with foreign affairs or to fob them off on others.[2] Such good fortune is not to be presumed and is rarely (if ever) obtained. This is one reason the best city is "to be prayed for," that is, why its actualization is (to say the least) not wholly within human power to contrive.[3] The "best regime" serves these authors as a pattern for the best human life (i.e., as a means of expounding that life) rather than as a blueprint for any actual city.

Thucydides does not exaggerate even provisionally the scope of choice in domestic affairs. He certainly offers no hope that human beings will ever find themselves free to actualize a just political order. This is in part due to his frank emphasis on the exigencies of foreign policy in a world ruled by the Athenian thesis. His Corinthians urge the Spartans to accept the primacy of

---

[1] Plato *Laws* 698a–e; 700a–701c; 707a–c; cf. Strauss *City and man* 237–38.

[2] Plato *Republic* 422a–423a and *Laws* 704a–707d; Aristotle *Politics* 7.2 (1324b22–1325a5), 7.3 (1325b23–32), 7.5–6.

[3] Plato *Republic* 450cd, 456b, 499a–d, 540d; Plato *Laws* 687cc, 709cd, 736d, 757e, 841c; Plato *Alcibiades 1* 135bd; Aristotle *Politics* 7.11 (1330a34–38) and 7.13 (1332a28–31).

foreign affairs over domestic ones (1.68–71): that regime is to be preferred which is best suited to successful contention with other regimes.

The problems of foreign and domestic affairs are linked not only practically but theoretically, via the Athenian thesis and the variations on it that characterize the thought of Diodotus and Hermocrates. As we have seen, the Athenian thesis corrodes the basis of domestic trust. It raises the specter that tyranny and treason, necessarily anathema to the city, are rationally defensible nonetheless, or that the erstwhile tyrant seeks to suppress the citizenry with no less right than that with which it seeks to thwart him. So too Diodotus and Hermocrates imply in their different ways the problematic status of the common good in a city the members of which are so unequal in wisdom.

In the world as Thucydides displays it, moreover, cities face more pressing concerns than pursuing a phantom of perfect justice. Much like his Diodotus, Thucydides stresses not the heights of sweet reasonableness to which cities threaten to rise, but the depths of chaos into which they are never far from plunging. The articulation of the best regime he leaves to his characters (Pericles, Archidamus, Athenagoras); the description of the political nadir he jealously reserves for himself.

The collapse of the city is the subject of the two longest passages of exposition that Thucydides offers in his own name. Each of these treats of the irruption into the city of natural compulsions that law is powerless to contain. The theme of these passages is not, however, the tension between law or right and compulsion as such. For law, after all, is itself compulsion, which is effective insofar as it threatens evils the avoidance of which its subjects regard as compulsory. As has been well observed, the leitmotiv of Thucydides' presentation of political pathology is the inversion of all sound principles of human conduct.[4] This inversion reflects another one, that of the compulsions to which human beings are normally subject. Common civility proves to depend on certain constraints the primacy of which becomes visible only through their absence. Thucydides teaches us to discount the seeming spontaneity of decency.

In this chapter we will consider these two extreme cases, which clarify the character of the normal ones, and conclude with a discussion of the question of the regime.

PLAGUE

The plague of Athens descended on the city in the second spring of the war and raged unabated for two years. Having discussed the obscurity of its

---

[4] In particular, see Edmunds *HSCP* 79 (1975) 73–92.

origins, the course of its symptoms, and its impact on beasts, Thucydides turns to its effects on the private lives of the various classes of sufferers (2.47–51). Most of these it reduces to solitary wretches, alone in their prostration and indifferent to all wider concerns.

Thucydides next discusses the consequences for the plague of the Athenian political situation. The most lethal aspect of that situation is the wartime overcrowding of the city due to the influx from the countryside (2.52). Because of it death rages uncontrollably, and the public places of the city, both profane and sacred, are strewn with heaps of the homeless, unattended dead and dying. It is from this in turn that the laws of the city are first disturbed (2.52.4), beginning with the laws of burial, which the survivors, overwhelmed by the calamity, can or will no longer observe. Thucydides begins his discussion of lawlessness, then, with those laws the flouting of which follows most directly from the specific character of the disaster; it is notable that these are sacred laws.[5]

Thucydides' emphasis thus shifts from the consequences of the political situation for the plague to those of the plague for the political situation.

> And moreover it was the plague which first fostered greater lawlessness in the city in other respects. For people now blithely ventured what before they would have done covertly and not just as they pleased, seeing the sudden changes and how, some rich person dying suddenly, another who before possessed nothing now instantly owned what had been the first man's. And so they decided to spend quickly and for the sake of enjoyment, holding their bodies and their wealth alike to be but things of a day. No one was keen to persevere in what had been reputed noble (or honorable, *kalon*), holding it uncertain whether he would survive to achieve it. Instead the pleasurable and whatever procured it were established as both noble and useful. Fear of gods and law of men deterred no one, for as to the former, people judged it all the same whether they revered [the gods] or not, seeing that all died regardless, and as for crimes none expected to stay alive long enough to come to trial or pay the penalty, holding that a much heavier sentence had been pronounced against them, and that before it fell, it was only fair (*eikos*) to enjoy life a little. (2.53)

Here, as throughout his account of the plague, Thucydides looks back to the Funeral Oration, which immediately precedes it. Pericles had praised the Athenians for eschewing private display, instead regarding their wealth as a resource for public action (2.40.1) in keeping with their dedication to the city and the endless glory that it conferred. Under the impact of the plague the Athenians forsake that graceful restraint extolled by their leader. Indifferent indeed to amassing wealth, but equally so to employing it for any public or distant object, their sole concern is to spend it before death wrenches them from it.

---

[5] Cf. our discussion of Thucydides' treatment of the theme of piety within the context of the plague, above pp. 87–90.

The transition from the reckless squandering of one's own to criminality in the usual sense occurs by way of a sentence on the *kalon*, the honorable or noble or fine. The kalon, by definition something difficult, requires perseverance, which in its turn makes sense only with an eye to its goal; the contraction of the human horizon of action is therefore fatal to the kalon as previously conceived. Moderation, severed from any prospect of reaping the anticipated benefits, appears mere bondage to outworn constraints. Even in their desperation, however, the Athenians do not simply abandon the noble in favor of the pleasant, the former losing its hold on them. Instead they assimilate the two, with the noble sharing the fate of the useful (*chrēsimon*), that other, grayer barrier to losing oneself in the delights of the moment. Both noble and useful collapse into present pleasure and whatever procures it, so that these last are now accounted honorable as well. The appeal of (and to) the noble persists, but to the confusion of all decency and of that proud self-restraint which in better times expresses nobility of soul.

Lastly Thucydides records the crime wave for which this corruption of the noble paves the way. Absent fear of disgrace, the restraints of last resort are fear of gods and human law. If the gods, however, cannot or will not protect their worshippers, why would they punish transgressors? As for human law, it commands only where it can punish; it is effective only where it succeeds in mimicking necessity. Relieved of fear of punishment by their fear of the plague, people take whatever they can and can even believe that they have it coming. Whatever the dejection (*athymia*) that overwhelmed those actually struck by the plague (2.51.4), those still waiting for the ax to fall display spirit of a sort. Sentence having been pronounced on them, they balk at perishing with their books unbalanced, without a crime to fit the punishment.[6]

The plague, "harsher than human nature can bear" (2.50.1), overwhelms the Athenians utterly. Even so, both the noble and the "only fair" retain their power over them. Rather than efface these the plague inverts them, honor becoming an inducement to debauchery and moral indignation a spur to crime, in defiance of an outrage from which the city can offer no protection.

Stasis

Thucydides' schematic statement on stasis (civil discord) follows his account of a particular instance of it, at Corcyra in the fifth year of the war (3.70–81).[7] That account, a masterpiece of Thucydidean narrative,[8] begins with

---

[6] Cf. Xenophon *Apology of Socrates* 28.

[7] Kagan *Archidamian war* 175–81; John Wilson *Athens and Corcyra* 87–106. Pouncey *Necessities* emphasizes the interaction of war and stasis throughout Thucydides' work: as the war arises from an instance of stasis in Epidamnus, on the fringes of the Greek world, so it culminates in Athens herself falling into stasis. Cf. Loraux *QS* 23 (1986) 98–102.

[8] Cf. Connor *Thucydides* 95–100.

disagreement between the few and the many over Corcyra's allegiance in the war, leading to perversion of the laws of the city (both sacred and profane) in the service of factional ends, then to a bloody oligarchic coup d'état, and finally to desperate class warfare spurred by the intervention of both Sparta and Athens.

These events evoke Thucydides' longest comment on any aspect of the war (3.82–83), a comment also unique in echoing his initial statement of the purpose of his work (cf. 3.82.2 with 1.22.4; cf. 3.82.1 [*èkinèthè*] with 1.1.2 [*kinèsis*]).[9] Of all the enduring possibilities of which Thucydides apprises us, stasis is that one the permanence of which he most emphatically calls to our attention.

For Thucydides the war that is his comprehensive theme subsumes the excesses of stasis; these while hardly unknown in peacetime are next to normal in wartime. While he sees no need to invoke domestic pathology to explain the prevalence of war among states, he stresses that the rigors of war aggravate domestic pathology.

> In times of peace neither side had the excuse or the willingness to call in the two great powers, but when the war was on, alliances were easily obtained by those on both sides who, plotting a new order of things, sought through calling in outsiders both to harm their opponents and to acquire power for themselves. . . . In times of peace and prosperity both cities and individuals have minds of a better cast, from not falling subject to overwhelming necessities. But war, filching away the easy provision of the everyday, is a violent teacher, which brings most men's tempers level with their fortunes. (3.82.1, 2)

Society thrives on the rhythm of daily life—the whir and hum of the insistent, recurrent needs of the body. For as long as these needs are smoothly greased, most of us will abide the status quo and will even appear devoted to it. War disrupts society by throwing us back on our bodies, on that aspect of our lives that is most our own or in respect of which we are most "individuals." It peels away our veneer of easy sociability.

This may sound surprisingly modern, as if Thucydides accepted the primacy of economics over politics or of prosperity over virtue. He surely sees that most people lack virtue in adversity and that few care for the body politic half so much as they do for their own. He does not, however, anticipate modern thought by promoting prosperity as an effective hedge against

---

[9] Stahl *Thukydides* 117–18 and n.42; Farrar *Origins* 135 n.18. I follow most commentators in rejecting 3.84 as a later interpolation (see most recently Hornblower *Commentary* 488–89). As the passage is difficult and renderings of it vary widely, the reader may wish to consult, in addition to the versions by the translators of the work as a whole, the efforts of Gomme *HCT* 2:383–85, Grene *Greek political theory* 9–12, and Pouncey *Necessities* 33 and n.5. Useful discussions include Strauss *City and man* 146–47; Edmunds *HSCP* 79 (1975) 73–92; Macleod *ProcCamPhilolSoc* 205 (1979) 52–69; Cogan *Human thing* 149–54; Connor *Thucydides* 95–105; Loraux *QS* 23 (1986) 95–134; Euben *Tragedy* 187–94.

stasis: prosperity, presupposing peace as it does, is for that very reason wholly unreliable. Thucydides moreover regards prosperous societies as no less inclined to war by their wealth than poor ones are by their poverty (cf. 3.45.4 with 8.24.4).

Thucydides therefore does not suggest that physical deprivation is the sole or even the primary germ of stasis. Rather, it figures as what disposes men to follow those who "plot a new order of things, who . . . seek both to harm their opponents and to gain power for themselves." Thucydides never suggests that these political passions—the ambition to rule and the thirst to avenge fancied wrongs—spring from or mask economic ones. In times of peace, these factional leaders would less readily gain a hearing (perhaps even with themselves); in wartime they feed on the prevailing anxiety.

The most celebrated aspect of Thucydides' presentation of stasis is his discussion of the debasement of language.[10] "And they scrambled, in their judgments, the usual estimations of actions as expressed by the words for them" (3.82.4).[11]

[10] The current celebrity of this aspect owes a good deal to fashionable theories according to which language (i.e., a particular language shared by members of a particular group) is what constitutes a given political community, the minds of its members, and thereby the members themselves, so that stable political community is a matter above all of a stable political language. Whatever the merits of these theories, which their adherents understand to originate in Heidegger, one must take care not to ascribe them to Thucydides. Such a view construes human beings as radically historical (and so conventional) beings and political dissolution as internal to the realm of conventions or "culture." For Thucydides, by contrast, the gravest problems of politics (including and above all that of stasis) attest to the power of *nature* in human life, opposing and overwhelming that of convention. It is the natural frailty of the human body and the natural ambition and vindictiveness of the human soul which combine to nourish stasis; this explains why it remains a permanent possibility, independent of considerations of "culture." The political task accordingly remains the suppression of nature (in part through the enlisting of its power). On the relation between nature and convention cf. 3.45.7. For intelligent examples of the approach that has evoked these reservations, see White *Words* 3–4, 66–67, 75–80; Euben *Tragedy* 167–201. Cf. chapter 2, note 22.

[11] Cf. Hobbes's translation: "The received value of names imposed for signification of things was changed into arbitrary." On the proper construction of this difficult and controversial sentence, see most recently Proctor *Experience* 204; John T. Hogan *GRBS* 21 (1980) 139–50; John Wilson *CQ* NS 32 (1982) 18–20; Loraux *QS* 23 (1986) 104–6. Hogan, noting (139) that "scholars have usually taken this as an assertion that the political partisans changed the *meanings* of the words they used, and by this is understood the denotations of the words, their referents," goes on to propose that not only might a mindless daring have come to be considered comradely courage, and caution bred of forethought an excuse for cowardice, but that the first of these qualities might have come to be praised, and the third to be blamed, under their usual names. This I find unpersuasive and unsupported by Thucydides' elaboration of his meaning. Wilson, rejecting Hogan's suggestion, rejects also the usual rendering of this sentence as something like "words changed their meaning," which phrasing implies (according to him) precisely that irrational daring became a term of praise and prudent hesitation one of blame. Whatever the proper meaning of "meaning," what scholars have meant and readers have read by "words changed their meaning" is a change in "the denotations of words, their referents," and, as Thucydides proceeds to make clear, that is what in fact occurred—with some necessary qualifications (cf. Strauss *City and man* 147 n.8).

A mindless daring was held to be the courage of a loyal comrade, caution bred of forethought an excuse for cowardice, good sense a cloak of unmanliness, and an intelligent grasp of all sides of a question inability to act on any. (3.82.4)

Thucydides' treatment of the structure of virtue foreshadows that of Aristotle,[12] while lending useful rigor to the notion of political extremism. "Extremism" in a strict sense defines the mentality of stasis. The excess of a disposition comes to be admired in place of its mean, and the mean comes to be despised as the deficiency of this excess. Having supplanted the mean as the standard, moreover, the extreme continuously feeds on itself: it enjoins a striving for ever fresh extremes, a frenzied struggle to exceed one's rivals at excess itself.

The way is thus open to the equation of rage with manliness and of brutality with trustworthiness. And so it is also open to placing a premium on plots and counterplots, while whoever contrives to avoid the necessity for either, by restoring a measure of trust between the parties, is reviled as disloyal and cowardly. "In a word, to thwart him who intended evil was praised, and likewise to suggest [it] to him who was contemplating none"(3.82.5). The distinction between foiling and fostering transgression has dissolved; there is no community of the lawful warding off the attacks of the lawless, but a general recourse to lawlessness with no distinction made between defending and assailing.

There follows a sketch of the collapse of the three pillars of Greek society: kinship, human law, and divine law.

And so even the bond of kinship became more extraneous (*allotriōteron*) than that of faction, because of the greater readiness of the latter to dare no matter what. For such associations aimed not at advantage[13] within the established laws, but at self-aggrandizement in defiance of them, and the faith of the members in one another drew its strength not so much from the divine law [sc., of oaths] as from their common complicity in lawlessness. Fair words from opponents met with precautionary deeds, not sincere acceptance (*gennaiotēti*), if [those who received them] had the upper hand.[14] To retaliate against another stood in higher regard than to avoid harm to oneself. Oaths of reconciliation, if any there were, were sworn by the two parties only with a view to an immediate perplexity, because they found themselves otherwise powerless.[15] When oppor-

[12] Aristotle *Nicomachean ethics* 2.5–9. On the phenomenon described by Thucydides, cf. *Rhetoric* 1.9.28–29.

[13] Reading, with Dionysius, Valla, Stahl, and Poppo, ὠφελίᾳ (dative of purpose and so parallel with πλεονεξίᾳ at the end of the sentence) for ὠφελίας (genitive) of the MSS.

[14] Or, "fair words from opponents (if they had the upper hand) evoked precautionary deeds, not sincere acceptance." The Greek is ambiguous.

[15] Or, "Oaths of reconciliation, if any there were, were sworn by the two parties only with a view to an immediate perplexity, and derived their power (i.e., their authority) from no other source." Again the Greek is ambiguous.

tunity offered, he who first made bold to seize it by taking his opponent unawares held it sweeter thus to avenge himself by imposing on the other's trust than openly, reckoning not only on the safety of this course, but that by prevailing through treachery he might carry off the prize for intelligence. (3.82.6–7)

Standing by one's kin was the true north of the Greek moral compass, the bedrock of social relations.[16] Politically speaking, the blood tie is ambiguous, for it limits devotion to the common good and so is liable to denunciation as the primal spring of corruption and injustice.[17] Here, however, it appears in a more honorable light. The effectual truth of such political zeal as overwhelms attachment to the family is not impartial justice but the brutality of faction. Kinship makes excuses; faction does not accept any (cf. 3.80.5).

From the decay of subpolitical restraints we proceed to that of political ones. The erosion of law is identical with that of the common good. This last here figures not as a lofty substantive good transcending those available privately, but as the confinement of the struggle for private good within common bounds. By hedging these bounds with evils—the punishments that the laws prescribe for transgressors—the city enforces on the citizens a salutary moderation. In restricting the advantage of each, the laws serve that of all; the greatest evil that laws avert they avert simply by being laws.[18] Unhappily, this truth becomes clear to all only with the breakdown of law.

From human laws, finally, we pass to the divine. However necessary to a decent society, piety, like kinship, figures here only as a prominent victim of stasis, not as any sort of bulwark against it. In the stasis at Corcyra, piety is very early perverted for factional ends (3.70.4–6), after which we hear only of lying oaths and breaches of asylum, to say nothing of carnage in holy places. Politically, piety mattered to the Greeks above all as the foundation of oaths, so it is on these that Thucydides dwells. Amid conditions of stasis, oaths are hollow, figuring only as means of the very deceit they are supposed to preclude.

In expounding the weakness of oaths, Thucydides notes that stasis leads men to prefer revenge to safety. (A concern with safety is one source of the power of oaths.) In a strange but familiar paradox, men become heedless of their lives in their very rage at those who threaten these. To this thirst for vengeance every usual scruple cedes. Once intelligence parts company with decency, nothing gains a reputation for the first like a deed that would formerly have shocked the second. Even in normal times men cherish clever-

[16] Plato *Republic* 332a–b; Connor *Thucydides* 99.

[17] Cf. 2.35–46 (and the discussion in the Prologue to the present book); Plato *Republic* 461e–465c.

[18] This is different from saying that the greatest good that any laws achieve they achieve merely by being laws.

ness to the detriment of virtue (3.82.7); now, the foulest murder counts as the sweetest.

The cardinal calamity of stasis is that trust disappears from society, thus dissolving society itself. Stasis destroys the infrastructure of civil trust. Seem as it might that trust among citizens must depend on their treating one another decently, in fact it is rather their decent behavior which proves to depend on their mutual trust. This is not to deny that the truly virtuous would trust each other or that virtue is the soundest basis for trust. It is to say that in actual cities the basis for trust is much shakier. What passes for virtue depends on trust, which in turn depends on mutual interests, which as such foster mutual restraint. It is not decency which holds most people in check, but such extrinsic constraints as make decency pay.

> To blame for all of which was the craving for rule[19] from motives of rapacity (*pleonexia*) and ambition (*philotimia*), from which sprang the zeal (*to pro-thymon*) of the parties once embroiled in contention. The leading men in the cities, on both sides, each with fine-sounding names, the one party extolling "equality before the law for the multitude" and the other "moderation through the rule of the best," made prizes of those common concerns to which they paid devoted lip service (*logōi therapeuontes*). Stopping at nothing in their contest to subject each other, they dared the most terrible things, and pushed their re-venges further still, not deferring to justice and the advantage of the city, but on both sides restraining themselves only as pleased them at the moment. (3.82.8)

Thucydides here anticipates, and rejects, the claim of the "stasismonger" to have acted out of zeal for the public good: the hotter the zeal and the grander the professions, the greater the indifference to the public good.[20] "Justice and the advantage of the city" give way so completely before private ambition as to leave only ruins behind for it to conquer.[21]

This long chapter on stasis is followed by a brief but climactic one. We must try to grasp how it is climactic: how what it describes is the crowning evil of such a throng of evils.

---

[19] Ἀρχή = ἐπιθυμία τοῦ βούλεσθαι ἄρχειν. (Scholiast)

[20] Some today stress "ideology" as the spring of the worst political evils, in Thucydides' time as in our own. Cf. Cogan *Phoenix* 35 (1981) 1–21 and *Human thing* 149–54, which ascribes the extremism of the partisans to "the abstractness of [their] ideological orientation." See also Müri *MH* 26 (1969) 65–79. But cf. Hunter *Past and process* 153: Thucydides does not ascribe stasis to "idealism, altruism, or even adherence to a professed political program."

[21] In this respect Thucydides' treatment of stasis is "Diodotean." Cf. Democritus fr. 249 (Diels/Kranz). I thank Eve Grace for calling my attention to a defect in this regard in my earlier account, Orwin *JPol* 50 (1988) 831–46. Cf. also Slomp *HistPolTht* 11 (1990) 577–78. On the self-contradictoriness of the ambitions of the party chiefs, see White *Words* 76; Euben *Tragedy* 189.

Thus every form of malignancy took root among the Greeks as a result of the stasis, and ingenuousness *(to euēthes)*, in which innate nobility *(to gennaion)* plays so great a part, was laughed into oblivion; while the frame of mind that everywhere prevailed was that of two armies confronting each other with distrust. There was no word binding enough, no oath terrible enough to reconcile them, and all alike, when they got the upper hand, calculating that no lasting security was to be expected, rather than bring themselves to trust others, did what they could to protect themselves. The meaner minds were most likely to prevail, for fearing their own failings and the wits of their adversaries (lest they be overmatched in argument and the others, in the resourcefulness [*ek tou polytropou*] of their wits, contrive to preempt them), they boldly resorted to deeds. Their opponents, on the other hand, in their contemptuous confidence that they would anticipate them and that they themselves had no need to obtain by deed what was theirs for the taking by wit, tended to be caught off guard and destroyed. (3.83)

To euēthes is an ancient term for simplicity and integrity—so ancient that it usually occurs in classical Greek only in its ironic sense of simpleton.[22] *To gennaion* is the old aristocratic term for human worth, the root of which implies that it is inborn.[23] Thucydides here uses old-fashioned terms to designate old-fashioned virtues. These have never looked better than as the negations of the qualities prized by the factions.

As for *to polytropon*, Thucydides' term for the wiliness feared but finally vanquished by the meaner minds, this is its sole occurrence as a noun in classical prose. As an adjective, it had supplied Homer's famous epithet for Odysseus, "of many turns," or resourceful. It too is an old-fashioned term, although the man whom it denotes takes pride in adaptability. It is easy to think of characters of Thucydides to whom the word might apply, such as the Athenian general Demosthenes, or even the Athenians collectively. Thucydides locates this man of *to polytropon* at the opposite extreme from him of *to euēthes* and *to gennaion*—the former is the man most dreaded by the factious intriguers, the latter the man most scorned by them.

And yet the extremes meet. The man of *to euēthes* is moderate without necessarily being intelligent; for him of *to polytropon*, intelligence is all. But for intelligence to sever itself from moderation is for it to enter on a fool's game, which it can win only by assimilating itself to folly.[24] The ambitions that fire stasis are futile; they are self-contradictory and self-devouring. The most straightforward of men and the most devious, this latter-day Ajax and

---

[22] Cf. Thucydides' only other use of it at 3.45.7.
[23] Cf. the uses at 1.136.4, 2.41.5, 2.97.3, 4.92.7.
[24] Cf. Macleod *ProcCamPhilolSoc* 205 (1979) 59–60.

Odysseus, have thus a common interest in avoiding stasis, and Thucydides by so warning them shows himself impartially a friend to both.

PLAGUE, STASIS, AND THE PERICLEAN VISION

Plague and stasis offer opposite routes to the disintegration of the city: they are the extremes between which all normal politics lies, which, as such, help clarify the conditions of political normality. Stasis displays the consequences of the radical "politicization" of life; the plague, those of its depoliticization. I bracket "politicization" because although the partisanship of stasis is political, it destroys politics,[25] precisely by subverting all restraints on it: justice and the common good prove to be deeply indebted to the private. In the case of the plague, on the other hand, the common withers away, ceasing to command obedience or even attention.

Both accounts call attention to the body, the mute substratum of political life, out of sight when out of mind, but profoundly dangerous when troubled. In the case of stasis, the real or anticipated threat to the body is itself of political origin: the interruption of daily supplies as a result of the vicissitudes of war. The response is therefore political: a struggle for mastery in the city which, by unleashing the harshest political passions, breeds heedlessness of that very survival the insecurity of which spurred stasis in the first place. In the case of the plague, the enemy is nonhuman—divine or natural but mysterious (cf. 2.64.2)—and does not lead to strife among human beings except incidentally. Rather than poison civic relations it overwhelms them. Yet even here such "political" concerns as attachment to the noble and the just do not disappear but are perverted.

Stasis and plague concur in suggesting that there is no greater political misfortune for human beings than to be freed from the constraint posed by their bodies. Both phenomena thus comment on the Funeral Oration. Pericles eulogizes citizens who, while retaining their individuality, have emancipated themselves from their bodies and live in anticipation of a glorious immortality for which, as it were, they exchange their bodies. The Funeral Oration, despite or because of its genre, consistently abstracts from death and the body. The plague, by contrast, brings home both the primacy and frailty of the body—as well as its centrality to actual political life in Athens as elsewhere.[26]

Society proves to depend more fundamentally on our hopes and fears for our bodies than (as Pericles would appear to wish) on our capacity to overcome these. In fact, people cease to fear for their bodies only when they

---

[25] I am indebted for this suggestion to J. Peter Euben.

[26] Strauss *City and man* 194–95, 229 n.92. Cf. Reinhardt *Vermächtnis* 214; Flashar *Epitaphios* 463–64. For a collation of the numerous close parallels (and contrasts) between the Funeral Oration and the plague, see Konishi *AJP* 101 (1980) 29–41.

lose all hope for them, as in the case of the plague, and there the consequence of their ceasing to fear for their bodies is a headlong rush to indulge
them. The plague discloses the abyss that yawns when citizens can no longer
see the city for their bodies. In stasis, on the other hand, the combatants
continue to fear but despair of solid security. Here, too, the weight of their
bodies ceases to restrain their most destructive passions and even serves as a
goad to them. In an ugly parody of the course commended by Pericles to the
Athenians in their dealings with foreign enemies (2.42.4),[27] the parties, not
out of free and noble choice but swept away by the torrent of violence, come
to prefer vengeance to safety.

Society, then, owes its stability largely to the ballast provided by our
everyday concerns for the body and our ability to satisfy those concerns, and
most of all to our fear of death, coupled with the hope of postponing it.
Thucydides thus corrects the Funeral Oration and implies a more moderate
position. So long (and only so long) as the city commands our concern with
the preservation and comfort of our bodies, it may reasonably hope to keep
our other passions in check.[28] The city that succumbs to "overwhelming
necessities" (*akousious anankas*, 3.82.2)[29] loses the means of enforcing its
own. In normal times society mediates between its citizens and necessity: on
the one hand, it protects them from it; on the other, it represents it to them.

Thucydides shows us that the chasms that yawn beneath us in politics are
deeper than the peaks that beckon us are high. No regime that he shows us
approaches the heights limned by Pericles: not Athens, not any other. The
evils of anarchy, on the other hand, prove only too real and near at hand.
Hence his sympathy for the Spartan regime, which, as we have seen, aimed
less at achieving the political best than at avoiding the political worst—
vulnerability to the threat posed by its Helots. The passage on stasis reveals,
I think, better than any other in the work, how deeply mindful is
Thucydides of the benefits of Spartan sobriety. He notes that stasis con-
vulsed, "so to speak," all of Hellas; in fact it engulfed Athens but not Sparta
(cf. 1.18.1 with 2.65.11–12, 6.53–61, 8.47–98).[30] Nothing bespeaks
Sparta's greatness like the evils that her regime averts, evils the reliable
absence of which outweighs all other political goods. Being negative, however, this achievement is inconspicuous, like the power of Sparta generally
(1.10):[31] Athens abounds in brilliant spokesmen like Pericles and Alcibiades, to say nothing of spectacular deeds, but the case for Sparta needs
Thucydides himself to do justice to the horrors of civil war.

[27] Cf. Loraux *QS* 23 (1986) 100–102.

[28] Cf. the Talmudic tractate *Pirke Avot (Sayings of the Fathers)* 3.2: "Reb Hanina, the deputy
high priest, said, 'Pray for those in authority, for if it were not for fear of the government, men
would eat each other alive.'"

[29] Literally, "necessities that deprive [human beings] of willing."

[30] Herter *RhM* 93 (1949) 142.

Thucydides may thus appear to share with his great student Hobbes a "negative" political orientation. We ought to take our political bearings not from what attracts us as best, but by what repels us as worst. For Hobbes, that than which nothing is worse is the state of nature or of anarchy; in this he and Thucydides are at one. No reader of the two writers will fail to note the similarities of their accounts of anarchy, which is for both the definitive human evil. Stasis is a war of all against all, in which no one can trust anyone, the preemptive strike is de rigueur, and those who might seem superior to others fare, if anything, even worse than they.[32]

Yet Thucydides' orientation is not simply negative. True, at 3.83 he anticipates Hobbes's critique of pretensions of political superiority by drawing our attention to the dire consequences of stasis for those who claim to be importantly better than others. His tone, however, is not captious and debunking like Hobbes's remarks on this subject. Instead, he registers, apparently with equal sympathy, the fates of two kinds of excellence that appear incompatible: a noble guilelessness and a ruthless wiliness. "Moral" and "intellectual" virtues are equally the prey of stasis; the plague, too, discriminates against the better men (2.51.5). The crowning evil of both calamities is not that they menace all, but that they menace the better citizens most, to whom in these worst of situations their very superiorities are fatal.

This concern with the fate of excellence explains why Thucydides is not simply "conservative," why Sparta must share his admiration with Athens. Each city achieves its distinctive superiority: Athens rises higher to fall lower. Yet the men of virtue figure as a class in Thucydides only in the contexts of plague and stasis, and this underscores a sobering reality. The annihilation of virtue is only too real a possibility; its political ascendancy is not. What is highest in the city is incomparably more fragile than what is lowest. Thucydides shows the better citizens how much they have to lose if politics spins out of control; he opposes their tendency to take their standing in the city for granted. He reminds them that even the most "Athenian" of types depend on "Sparta"; whenever life's fragile steadiness is shattered, the dregs will likely rise to the top.[33] In normal times, this much at least can be avoided, which is not to say that the good have clear sailing. But we have already seen that for Thucydides the depths of politics are far more daunting than the heights. It is in this light that we must assess his silence on the question of the best regime.

---

[31] Cf. Orwin *RevPol* 51 (1989) 349.

[32] Cf. Hobbes *Leviathan* chap. 13.

[33] On the "Athenianness" of the tendencies that culminate in stasis, see Strauss *City and man* 147: "It would seem to follow that the fully developed contrast between Sparta and Athens is that between the city at peace and the city in the grip of civil war." Cf. Euben *Tragedy* 190.

THE QUESTION OF THE REGIME

As we have seen throughout, the protagonists of Thucydides' work are regimes. The issue of *the* regime figures only as it presents itself to *these* regimes as well as to the others whose deeds he records. The question of the regime does not present itself to the Spartans (although cf. 4.126.2). It comes in Book Eight to preoccupy Athens (8.47–98) as well as her subject cities (48, 63–65, 72–75).[34] In just this context, however, Thucydides calls our attention to characters who deprecate the importance of this question.[35] While these characters argue for different (and even contrary) policies, they unite in rejecting allegiance to a particular regime in favor of unity at home and empire and freedom vis-à-vis other cities.

In keeping with this general approach, Thucydides himself questions the claims of the prevalent regime principles of his day: democracy and oligarchy. Brief formulations of these claims figure in his account of stasis: there he dismisses them as mere slogans masking boundless private ambition (3.82.8). In addition, he provides us with the case for democracy in the mouth of one of its partisans and the case against oligarchy in the mouth of one who (oddly enough) will soon become its dogged adherent. Democracy proves to fare as poorly at the hands of its supporter as oligarchy does at those of its (erstwhile) opponent.

The prime eulogist of democracy in the work is the Syracusan demagogue Athenagoras (6.38–39). (Pericles praises not democracy but Athens, which "is called" a democracy [2.37.1] but which he lauds for what distinguishes it from other democracies.) Athenagoras might seem equal to the task, for his praise of democracy is impressive. He begins by appealing to the leaning toward democracy implicit in the very fact of the *polis*. For if a city is *one*, if it comprises a genuine community, ought not all its members enjoy one and the same privileges (6.38.5)? Athenagoras proceeds to refute the objection that "democracy is neither intelligent nor equitable."[36]

---

[34] For more adequate discussions of the complicated action of this book and its implications for the question of the regime, see Connor *Thucydides* 210–30 and Forde *Ambition to rule* 116–75.

[35] Consider Phrynichus at 8.48.4–7 and Peisander at 53.3 (which gains emphasis as the only fragment of direct discourse in the book), Alcibiades at 86.6–7, Thucydides the Pharsalian at 92.8. Phrynichus deprecates the question of the regime in opposing the change to oligarchy; Peisander in advocating it; Alcibiades and Thucydides in mediating between oligarchs and democrats.

[36] Literally οὔτε ξυνετὸν οὔτ' ἴσον, "neither intelligent nor equal"; the regime of ἰσο-νομεῖσθαι, of the equal subjection of all to the same laws (6.38.5), is here taxed with inequality by Athenagoras' hypothetical objector. The challenge implies that true equality consists of equal treatment for equals and unequal treatment for unequals (cf. Aristotle *Politics* 3.9; Xenophon *Education of Cyrus* 1.3.17).

But I say first of all that the term people identifies the whole, oligarchy but a part, and that if the wealthy are excellent stewards of property, and the intelligent are best at advising, then the many, having listened, excel at deciding,[37] and all these alike, taken separately and all together (*xympanta*), enjoy equal shares in democracy. Oligarchy, on the other hand, shares the dangers with the many, but not merely cheating these of [their fair share of] the benefits, grabs and keeps them all (*xympanta*). (6.39)

Athenagoras talks an excellent game. Considering the context of his remarks, however, Thucydides could hardly have presented the case for democracy more disparagingly. Athenagoras is both a fool and a scoundrel. His speech is a response to Hermocrates' assertion that the Athenian armada is on its way to Syracuse (6.33–34). In his judgment of the plausibility of this claim as well as of the danger that such an invasion would pose, he is further off the mark than any other speaker in Thucydides.[38] At this crucial juncture, when his city faces unprecedented peril, he urges it to devote itself not to diplomacy and rearmament but to stasis. As the champion of democracy, he wields the banner of *isonomia* only as a weapon against his political rivals, whose chastisement he proposes for crimes that even he admits they have yet to commit (38.4). In particular he seeks to subvert all trust in Hermocrates, by far the most able Syracusan (72.1; cf. 4.58) and crucial to their hopes of mounting a successful defense. To sum up, his claim that democracy comprises a regime of the whole advances an agenda that could hardly be more partisan, imprudent, and unjust.

Athenagoras is not identical with Syracuse or her democracy: the unnamed general who follows him to the podium, likewise a democratic official, does what he can to undo the damage caused by the speech (6.41). His attack on calumny strikes a Diodotean note. Like the Athenian people then, that of Syracuse now displays its superiority to its worst impulses. Still, enough of Athenagoras' mud and folly stick so that the city takes no effective measures of defense.[39]

However dubious Athenagoras' case for democracy, his criticisms of oligarchy ring true. These find confirmation from an unlikely source, the

---

[37] On the respective roles of the intelligent and the many, compare 2.40.2 and 3.36–49. On the case for the people as the best deciders, cf. Herodotus 5.97 with Aristotle *Politics* 3.11.

[38] Cf. Pouncey *Necessities* 14. In one respect only is Athenagoras correct in his assessment of the strategic situation: in stressing the impediments the Athenians will face due to their want of cavalry (6.37.1).

[39] On this debate, see Cogan *Human thing* 100–106; Frank *Prudentia* 16 (1984) 99–107; Yunis *AJP* 112 (1991) 186–90. The imbroglio at Syracuse also serves to comment on the one at Athens in the same year. Athenagoras' claims for democracy and his own public-spiritedness parallel those of the rivals of Alcibiades; the alleged oligarchic plot of Hermocrates corresponds to that alleged of Alcibiades; and the witch-hunt the general averts at Syracuse proceeds with frenzy at Athens.

Athenian general Phrynichus, who soon after stating his case against oligarchy becomes the most unwavering partisan of the oligarchy newly established at Athens (cf. 8.48.4–7 with 8.68.3). This he does partly (as we shall
see) for compelling personal reasons. Yet he can also claim public grounds
for his change of allegiance, the same ones indeed that he had originally
urged against oligarchy. If domestic harmony is the crucial consideration for
Athens in her crisis, and if Alcibiades is not a man for any regime, oligarchic
or democratic (48.4), then whatever regime may be counted on to exclude
him becomes the best advised as offering at least a chance of cohesiveness
and a consistent foreign policy.

The arguments for establishing oligarchy had been two: that only thus
could Athens obtain the restoration of Alcibiades and so obtain help from
the Persian king, and that to install oligarchies in the subject cities would
secure their loyalty to Athens. It is in contesting this second claim that
Phrynichus echoes Athenagoras. Oligarchy is a part of the city posing as a
whole, and the masquerade has become quite threadbare.

> And as for the allied cities to whom oligarchy was now offered, he well knew
> that this would not make the rebels come in any the sooner, or confirm the loyal
> in their allegiance; for the allies would never prefer slavery, whether with oligar-
> chy or democracy, to freedom under the regime they actually possessed, to
> whichever type it belonged. Besides, the cities thought that the so-called gentle-
> men (*kalous k'agathous onōmazomenous*) would prove just as oppressive as the
> people, as being those who originated, proposed, and for the most part bene-
> fited from the acts of the people harmful to the allies. Indeed, if it depended on
> the better men, the allies would be put to death without a trial and violently,
> whereas the people was their refuge and the moderator (*sōphronistēs*) of these
> men. (8.48.6–8)

Whether the oligarchs in the subject cities maintain their present independence (i.e., remain in rebellion, either under an oligarchy or with the
design of establishing one later) or whether they accept the gift of oligarchy
now with the intention of rebelling later, the offer will not wed them to the
empire. As for the peoples in the cities (most of which are presently democracies), they would find an oligarchy imposed from without doubly odious,
and anticipation of any such fate would merely confirm them in the fact or
intention of rebellion. Both classes, moreover, will balk at the prospect of an
oligarchy in Athens. They now know better than to trust the so-called
gentlemen there.

Phrynichus thus impugns with Athenagoras and with Thucydides, at
3.82.8, the myth of the moderation of the upper classes. These eschew not
the acquisitiveness (*pleonexia*) of the people but merely the scruples or
confusions that soften the people's indulgence of it. Phrynichus refrains
from explicit comment on the claim of the gentlemen to govern within their

respective cities. In describing, however, the people as the "corrector" or "moderator" (*sōphronistēs*) of the "so-called gentlemen," he takes up an oligarchic slogan and flings it back at his colleagues (cf. 3.65.3).[40] The "gentlemen's" "correction" of the many merely masks their oppression of them: the actual harshness of the few requires correction by the relative gentleness of the many.[41]

In the end Phrynichus himself falls victim to the countermovement in Athens (urged along by Alcibiades) toward the restoration of the democracy (8.92.2). In the meantime, however, events have confirmed his prescience in the matter of the allies.

> Exactly what [the upper class at Thasos] most wished befell them, the reform of the city with no risk to themselves and the deposition of the people which would have opposed them. Thus affairs . . . turned out contrary to [the hopes of] the Athenian oligarchy, as also . . . in the cases of many other subjects. For no sooner had the cities received moderation[42] and a certain room for maneuver than they continued on to outright freedom without being gulled by the hollow "autonomy" dangled by the Athenians. (8.64.3–4)

The rulers in the subject cities have learned that to form the regime is not enough; whichever regime you form, the substance of freedom is to be preferred to its shadow. This in itself points in the direction not of a surrender to one's domestic rivals, but of a compromise at least to the extent required to present a united front to outsiders. Of those who would cling to power for themselves at the expense of their city's freedom, Thucydides suggests with Livy that *et humiliter serviebant et superbe dominabantur.*[43]

We must then conclude with Connor that in this matter of the regime "Thucydides . . . has managed to lead his reader beyond clichés and conventionalities."[44] He leads us to see each party as the other sees it, qualifying thereby the claims that it makes for itself. Neither regime is conceded a clear superiority in justice to its rival; each is exposed as mounting a merely partial claim. In this Thucydides' treatment of oligarchy and democracy anticipates

---

[40] The third and last usage of σωφρονιστής in Thucydides, that of Euphemus (6.87.3), must reflect his awareness of the force of the term for his Dorian, oligarchic audience.

[41] On this relative gentleness of the people cf. Aristotle *Athenian constitution* 40; Plato *Seventh letter* 324d, 325b; Thucydides 8.73.6 (Samos, following however the extreme vindictiveness of the earlier democratic victory at 8.21). The Chian regime that practices such restraint at 8.24.6 appears to have been some sort of mixed regime: the Spartans impose an oligarchy on the city at 8.38.3. See Kagan *Fall* 43–45.

[42] Thucydides here appears to employ another oligarchic slogan, this one to describe regimes more restrictive than democracy (cf. 3.82.8). The irony here is that for once the oligarchs actually do act with moderation in preferring true independence to sham.

[43] "So proudly did they dominate, even as they so humbly served." Livy 24.25.8.

[44] Connor *Thucydides* 229–30. Cf. Stockton *Classical Athenian democracy* 167–68; Pope *Historia* 37 (1988) 276.

those of Plato and Aristotle. To be sure, they go beyond Thucydides in articulating a "best regime." As already noted, however, each presents this regime as exceedingly unlikely of actualization and therefore as supplying only indirect guidance for any program of political action. Each thinker proposes moderation as the compass of political life, promoting loyalty to tolerably decent regimes, whether democratic or oligarchic, and the reform of each in the direction of the other.

Thucydides' intentions are similar. As we have seen, his Diodotus suggests that the crucial reform of the city—its achievement of a "moderation" that is more than merely a partisan slogan—is not to be anticipated. It follows that its approximation is the practically crucial political achievement. By deflating the pretensions of the rival regimes in favor of harmony and self-determination, Thucydides encourages the decent partisans of each to compromise with those of the other. He thus points the way to a regime without a name, which Aristotle will later dub "polity" (or the "generic" regime [*politeia*]).[45]

Thucydides' view further emerges from his presentation of the career of Phrynichus. Of the host of notable characters in Book Eight, only he vies with Alcibiades in arresting the attention of the reader. The fates of the two are intertwined: the great adversary of Alcibiades, Phrynichus is the only one who succeeds at beating him at his own kind of game (8.50–51). His eventual fate is both comical and sad, but it is also symptomatic.[46] In his first appearance he impresses by his shrewd and resolute devotion to the cause of Athens. With rhetoric so reminiscent of the envoys to Melos as to be uncanny if merely coincidental, he deters his fellow commanders from an act of foolish bravado that would imperil the safety of the empire and city (27; cf. 5.111.3). In his second episode, he similarly holds out against his colleagues, now on political questions rather than a military one, but evincing the same blend of intelligence and patriotism (48.4–8). This time, however, he does not prevail, and, having disclosed his opposition to the recall of Alcibiades, he finds himself in a parlous situation. From his early peak of devotion to the city, his career degenerates into desperate shifts the one clear principle of which is to save his own neck. Indeed, in the space of just a few sentences, he passes from impressive loyalty to Athens to apparent treason.[47] By the time of his murder he is definitely contemplating treason, if

---

[45] Aristotle *Politics* 3.7, 4.7–9.

[46] For a recent survey of the career of Phrynichus and the controversies that it has evoked, see Grossi *Frinico*.

[47] It is possible to interpret as treasonous Phrynichus' behavior at 8.50–51, when he negotiates with the Spartan enemy and even offers to betray Samos to it (see Pouncey *Necessities* 132–34; Forde *Ambition to rule* 137–39). Another view is also possible. True, Phrynichus himself describes his decision to denounce Alcibiades to Astyochus as harmful to the interests of Athens, but then he could hardly have presented it to Astyochus in any other light. We must

only as a last resort (91). The irony is that because he begins by opposing any change of the democratic regime at Athens (and this for reasons that are nonpartisan), he ends up a victim of his loyalty to the oligarchy that has come into being despite him. Having incurred the ire of Alcibiades by opposing his restoration, he supports the oligarchy as staunchly for reasons of his own preservation as he had originally opposed it for reasons of the preservation of the city.

Be this as it may, Phrynichus' conduct foreshadows that of his sometime colleague Theramenes (cf. 8.68.4), that of "acting the good citizen under all regimes."[48] Thucydides' judgment on him may likewise foreshadow the favorable one of Aristotle on Theramenes. In times of the utmost crisis, whatever regime promises cohesion is superior to those that do not. If Phrynichus is right about the crucial importance to the city of excluding Alcibiades, then he is just as right to oppose the oligarchy that intends to restore Alcibiades (and which begins by persecuting Phrynichus in order to endear itself to the exile, 54.3) as he is to cling to it with unsurpassed staunchness (68.3, 90.1) once it becomes clear that it will not do so. Unhappily for Phrynichus, the oligarchy in its final stages again gives ear to the blandishments of Alcibiades. It also falls into disarray through its own chiefs (89), who basely begin to vie for the favor of the people, the recall of Alcibiades, and a return to democracy. Had these men held firm to the policy of oligarchy at home and vigorous prosecution of the war abroad, they would not have driven those who had held firm to it to intrigue with Sparta to preserve both the oligarchy and their skins. As to whether Phrynichus is right about Alcibiades, it seems fair to say that Athens is incapable of living either with him or without him.

The oligarchy proclaims moderation (8.53.3) and, through the childish rivalry of its leaders, brings Athens to the brink of civil war (89–94). Its comedy culminates in the advent of the Five Thousand, that fleeting offspring of inadvertence. Originally a council existing only in the slogans of

---

put ourselves in Phrynichus' place. He is convinced, as he has claimed (and as future events will confirm), that the King will never come over to the side of Athens and therefore that the recall of Alcibiades will not bring the city Persian gold but only renewed dissensions. If he can persuade the enemy to dispose of Alcibiades, he rids himself of a dangerous enemy and Athens of a no less dangerous friend. As for Phrynichus' behavior after Astyochus betrays him in turn to Alcibiades, we hardly need construe it as a genuine plot to convey Samos to the enemy; more likely he intends it for what it turns out to be: a successful gambit to retrieve his own reputation while diminishing that of Alcibiades, at no real risk to Samos or the empire. (Note that Thucydides describes Phrynichus as surprised at the outcome of his first letter to Astyochus but not at the outcome of the second, which is, after all, predictable on the basis of the outcome of the first.) Phrynichus here vindicates Thucydides' description of him at 27.5. He deserves high marks for outwitting the wily Alcibiades; unfortunately for him, his is not the last laugh. Cf. Kagan *Fall* 127–29.

[48] Aristotle *Athenian constitution* 28.5.

Peisander and his fellow plotters in order to veil from the public their intention of establishing an oligarchy (65.3–66.1), it comes to perform the opposite function, as the slogan of the renegade oligarchs who wish to veil from their colleagues their intention of restoring the democracy (92.11). It in fact paves the way for this restoration. As the only Athenian regime of Thucydides' time neither democratic nor oligarchic, it serves like the career of Phrynichus as a touchstone for his judgment on regime questions.

> And now most of all, for the first time at least in my lifetime, the Athenians appear to have enjoyed a good regime (*ouch hēkista . . . eu politeusantes*).[49] For there was a judicious blending (*metria xynkrasis*) of the few and the many, and this is what first enabled the city to raise itself out of its wretched circumstances. (8.97.2)

Thucydides' respect for Pericles notwithstanding, he endorses the Five Thousand as a better regime than the democracy that Pericles guided, despite its likely incompatibility with the ascendancy of a Pericles or any other single leader.[50]

We know that the Five Thousand, which comes into being in the last pages of Thucydides, lasted for only a few months. At 2.65, moreover, where he sketches the fate of Athens, this regime he praises so highly rates no mention: it was not able to resolve the fundamental problems of Athens.[51] The Five Thousand may look like a triumph of the public interest conceived in a nonpartisan manner, achieved through a compromise between democracy and oligarchy, fleet and city, such as Alcibiades has urged from Samos in order to preserve freedom and empire. In fact it comes into being out of sordid intrigue and as a merely transitional phenomenon. The Five Thousand arises from oligarchy as a stage of a movement away from it: there is no reasonable prospect that this movement will stop short of democracy.[52]

[49] I am accepting Connor's bold construction of an extremely difficult sentence. Connor *Thucydides* 228 n.234; for a discussion of the problems, see Andrewes *HCT* ad loc.; Donini *Posizione* 4–12. For the verdict, cf. Aristotle *Athenian constitution* 33.2.

[50] The oligarchic elements of the regime would tend powerfully against the ascendancy of any one citizen, for the notables are more jealous than the people are of the preeminence of any one of their number (cf. 8.89).

[51] On the duration of the Five Thousand, see Aristotle *Athenian constitution* 34.1; cf. 41.2 for a silence parallel to that of Thucydides 2.65.

[52] The Athenian people had agreed in principle to oligarchy only in order to obtain the restoration of Alcibiades and the Persian subsidies that he was expected to bring (8.54.1–2). In the event, the oligarchy had imposed itself against their will and stained itself with their blood (65–70). The issue, as framed in the struggle between the fleet at Samos and the Four Hundred at home, was that of democracy versus oligarchy (76.1): the oligarchy having been routed, the fleet, once reconciled with the city, would not have accepted half measures. As for the people back home, having deposed the Four Hundred, recalled Alcibiades, and routed the foe at Cynossema, it promptly regained its old confidence (106.5): this was a democratic confidence.

The Five Thousand thus functions less as a model than as a heuristic device.[53] Thucydides' treatment of the question of the regime remains true to his somber emphasis on the horrors of plague and stasis. While he praises particular statesmen and cities, he finds little to praise in either democracy or oligarchy as such. The loftiest claims of each serve only to mask its worst excesses; we may conclude that the glory of a *metria xynkrasis* lies in its avoidance of these excesses. Regimes of neither type are reliably moderate save under compulsion: every city needs a saving equivalent of the servile menace at Sparta and Chios. Each of the regime principles is most tolerable when restrained by the other; by embracing both, the Five Thousand restrains both.

As we have stressed, the question of the regime appears in Thucydides not primarily as that of democracy versus oligarchy, but as that of Athens versus Sparta. The one is recognizably oligarchic (4.126.2), but its excellence transcends oligarchy; the same may be said of Athens and democracy. The two communities instantiate permanent polarities, toward one or the other of which other cities tend, although none has realized them as fully.[54] Athens and Sparta thus serve to clarify the prospects and limits of other regimes. In closing, we will only repeat that while stability is Thucydides' primary concern in assessing regimes, it is not the only one; he shares with Athens its typical aspiration to great heights, purged of its equally typical immoderation. He practices a daring in the realm of thought not appropriate to that of action.[55]

Nor could the Five Thousand have survived its decision to recall Alcibiades. For, as he viewed the city, there was him and then there was everyone else, the man of destiny and the throng of followers he could mobilize to prosecute his vast ambitions. He was hostile to any regime that limited the franchise, thus fostering collective leadership and precluding direct appeals to the people. The man "who was suitable for no regime" (8.48.4) required a democracy. Cf. McGregor *Phoenix* 19 (1965) 27–46.

[53] Cf. Connor *Thucydides* 228–30.

[54] Cf. 6.69; 7.21, 55–56, 66–68; 8.96 (Syracuse); 8.24 and 40 (Chios).

[55] Cf. Strauss *City and man* 229–31; Edmunds *Chance and intelligence* 143–203; Euben *Tragedy* 191–99.

Chapter 9

RECAPITULATION AND CONCLUSION: THE HUMANITY OF THUCYDIDES

Woe unto the world because of offences! for it must
needs be that offences come, but woe to that man by
whom the offence cometh!
—Lincoln, Second Inaugural Address,
quoting Matthew 18.7

THUCYDIDES shows us the self-revelation of the cities of Athens and Sparta, the poles and peaks of "Greekness" or of evolved political life; the significance of the war lies above all in this process of self-revelation. The unfolding of the question of blame and exculpation is a leading aspect of this process. Sparta takes her official stand on the primacy of justice and piety in human affairs. She insists on their obligatoriness and accepts no excuses for deviation from them. She treats all adversaries (and even neutrals) as if these merited punishment for not having chosen to fight on her side (2.67.4; 3.32.1–3; 3.68). Rather than extenuate her own conduct she denies any need to do so. For the same reason that they are reluctant to admit their own injustice, the Spartans prosecute the war with vigor only when fully persuaded of the injustice of their foe; when confronted with serious reverses, they interpret them as chastisement for past wrongdoing (7.18.2; cf. 1.128.1). Thus they implicitly deny that cities are ever compelled to resort to injustice; they thus suppose the rule of just gods who shelter human beings from necessity.

The spokesmen for Athens, abroad if not at home, stress rather the power of necessity to encroach on justice and piety. What is novel in their argument is not the claim that human beings are subject to compulsions that extenuate what would otherwise be crimes. It is rather their attempt to extend the sway of necessity (and so of alibis invoking it). Without denying the presumptive injustice of imperialism, they present all of the usual motives thereof—honor and profit no less than safety—as compulsory and thus extenuating. The effective Spartan denial of the force of necessity thus confronts the unwonted Athenian expansion of it. In the absence of a resolution of this question, it is impossible to assign aitia or blame for the war: ironically, the Spartan view of justice, if applied to the facts as the narrative presents them, tends to exculpate Athens (while inculpating

Sparta); the Athenian view tends to exculpate Sparta (although without inculpating Athens).

This "Athenian thesis" notwithstanding, the Athenian outlook remains ambiguous (and so does the opposition between her and Sparta). Most (and the most authoritative) spokesmen for Athens continue to insist on a realm sheltered from necessity. Precisely the most famous statement of "Athenianism," Pericles' Funeral Oration, presents her empire as a free project, untainted by baseness or necessity. The Funeral Oration appears thoroughly godless; even so, this most beautiful testimony to the glory of Athens agrees with the "Spartan" outlook in its abstraction from the force of necessity. In his final speech, by contrast, delivered under the impact of siege and plague, Pericles defends his war policy as the child of duress. He proceeds, nonetheless, to rise to a mighty crescendo of nobility. Similarly, the envoys to Sparta, while insisting on an expanded notion of duress as justifying the fact of the empire, also defend it in terms of justice. Athens is compelled to rule; within the bounds of compulsion, she rules with impeccable justice. She therefore continues to deserve full marks for virtue, in justice as in other respects; natural necessity stops well short of crushing human freedom and virtue. Even the envoys to Melos, so often decried as brutal exponents of realpolitik, express their pride in Athens for that noble daring which is a condition of justice.

As those envoys to Melos remind us, it is not only the Athenian position which is ultimately ambiguous. Sparta, the exponent of piety and of human responsibility to act justly, proves in fact to be deeply mired in necessity. If, unlike Athens, Sparta never faces this issue, that is because necessity itself so shackles her that she lacks the freedom for such reflections. In practice the Spartans equate justice with the advantage of Sparta, that is to say, with whatever is required to meet the necessities that anchor their regime. Despite her pretensions to remain at rest as befits her sobriety and justice, Sparta is alternately restrained from and impelled to action by the exigencies of maintaining an invisible empire.

Neither Sparta nor any other city known to Thucydides affords an example of genuine tranquility: none can sustain the claim that it refrains from ruling other cities despite a capacity for so doing, merely out of justice, moderation, or piety. The first round of the argument belongs to Athens. This victory proves dubious, if not Pyrrhic. It cannot disconcert the Spartans, who remain entirely deaf to it. It does rebound on Athens; most practically and immediately, on her internal politics. Alcibiades applies to domestic affairs the Periclean rhetoric of foreign affairs, with its implied acceptance of the Athenian thesis. He presents the city as but an arena for competition among citizens, as foreign affairs writ small. In effect, he preaches perpetual stasis, suspended for the time being only because of the alleged unique congruence between his lofty ambitions and the petty ones of the people. This not only feeds the popular suspicions of tyranny that Alcibiades naturally inspires, but also justifies his antagonists in their Cleonian policy of manipulating distrust of him so as to curry trust in themselves. Civic unity cannot survive without a notion of the common good as a basis of trust among the citizens. The truly pious Nicias, having unwisely taken the lead in fomenting distrust of his ambitious rival (6.12.2), thus finds himself in sole charge of that grand expedition on which he never wanted to embark in the first place.

In practice, then, the introduction of the Athenian thesis into domestic affairs proves disastrous. What, however, of its applicability in theory? If foreign affairs is the realm of necessity, domestic life would appear to be that of freedom and so, potentially, of justice and piety. Certainly Thucydides does not deny the importance of these in fostering trust among the citizens. In revealing, however, the fearsome power within the city of extraordinary compulsions and the daily decisiveness of ordinary ones, his accounts of plague and stasis go some way to confirm (and to extend) the Athenian thesis. Among citizens as among cities, not virtue but necessity is the force to be reckoned on. For most human beings the ultimate exigencies are those of the body, and the city's success in normal times depends on enlisting these in its behalf. When a crisis denies it this resource, it learns the weakness of those left to it. That regime is most solid which has succeeded in rendering virtue most necessary, Sparta then rather than Athens (cf. 1.84.4 with 2.38), with a deep bow to the Helots. The "common good" emerges in opposition to a common enemy.[1]

On Thucydides' showing, then, it is not so clearly true that the Athenian thesis is inapplicable to domestic life as that no city dare admit its applicability. The good of the city demands a healthy dose of that hypocrisy so scorned by the noblest Athenians and by Alcibiades in particular.[2] In this hypocrisy Sparta excels every other Greek city, just as she does in virtue (5.105.4). The Spartans' virtue is inseparable from their misfortune: they are no more free to neglect it among themselves than they are to practice it toward outsiders. The virtue of the Athenians is less a matter of harsh education and consequently is less reliable inside the city; that of Sparta is less reliable outside it. Sparta pays a heavy price in individual or natural excellence for the high average standard that she attains among her rank and file; Brasidas, a man of rare virtue even by Athenian standards, is nothing short of a miracle at Sparta. Miracles aside, the triumph of Sparta (as at Mantineia, 5.57–75) is the triumph of the ordinary Spartan. Athens rises higher than her rival, only to sink lower.

More generally the truth of the Athenian thesis raises the nagging ques-

---

[1] 3.9–14, 4.59–64, 4.80, 8.1–3, 8.40.2, 8.64.5.
[2] Cf. Forde *JOP* 54 (1992) 387–89.

tion of where (and if) one may draw the line between the demands of
necessity and the realm of human virtue and choice. This question the
Athenians, with their longing for a noble politics, must find particularly
troubling; they can hardly ignore it, since it is they who in their noble
candor have raised it.

Again and again the representatives of Athenianism contradict themselves, rejecting on the one hand the possibility of acting against "necessity"
conceived as advantage, and claiming on the other to do so. From the
envoys to Sparta, who, while proclaiming the tyranny of the three compulsions, insist also that Athens, in the mildness of her imperial rule, defies
these compulsions at least enough to lodge a claim of virtue; to the dispu-
tants in Boeotia, who struggle to apply this line of thought to piety; to the
envoys to Melos, whose pointed affirmation of the noble as distinct from
and superior to the advantageous subverts their attempt to reinterpret it to
the Melians in terms of advantage—the Athenians grapple recurrently with
the dilemmas of their thesis. How combine the extensive sway they insist on
according necessity with the primacy they wish to assign to virtue or the
noble? Not by claiming, as they begin by doing, to practice genuine justice
but only in secondary matters. If justice is only worth such small sacrifices of
safety, honor, and profit, why practice it at all? If it is worth greater sacrifices,
then how pride oneself on such small ones? "*Fiat justitia*—where it costs
little" cannot be the authentic voice of justice.

A second problem is that in invoking the "greatest things" in extenuation
of empire, the envoys to Sparta appeal to a prominent feature of the anat-
omy of justice. It is that there are situations in which we may justly neglect
the usual demands of justice (cf. 4.98; Plato, *Republic* 331c–d). There are
things that all human beings, even very just ones, must be pardoned for
preferring to justice. Of such cases we say not that we are permitted to act
unjustly, but that our departure from the rule is itself justified. We assimilate
the exception to the rule, thereby saving both. On reflection, however, these
exceptional instances of justice imply a powerful challenge to it.

The envoys to Sparta assert that the range of these exceptions is much
wider than is usually admitted. Interpreting what is said in the light of what
is done, they suggest that nature compels every human society to cherish at
least three goods more deeply than justice. It provides an alibi that our very
sense of justice bids us honor. By focusing our attention on the exceptions
rather than the rule, the Athenians mire the rule in so many exceptions as to
strip it of all power as a rule. At the very least their position discloses a real
problem with conceiving justice in terms of rule and exception.

The Athenians, moreover, inevitably raise the question of whether justice
is itself a good. When the envoys to Sparta suggest that fear, honor, and
profit are compulsory, they mean that maximum provision against the former and for the two latter is irresistibly good for a city. So has it always been,

and so it is for Athens. So, too, according to the envoys in Boeotia and on Melos, empire and its maintenance in the face of the risks of losing it are goods that override all others, even in the eyes of the gods. Justice if good is not a good of this stripe. It is at most resistibly good; one is excused for abandoning it to the extent dictated by these more powerful goods, praised for adhering to it more than these goods require (1.76.3). In this lies its superior nobility. But is justice good at all for the one who is just? Or is it merely praised by those who hope to benefit from it because it is advantageous to them (cf. 1.76.2)? The Athenians do not clearly raise this question. Their arguments, however, compel us to do so.

There remains the possibility that justice is good because it is honored by the gods, that is, as an aspect of piety. Of the foremost proponents of this view—the Spartans, the Melians, and Nicias—only the Spartans avoid disaster. Their success, however, appears to owe no more to their reliance on piety and justice than to their unavowed departures from these. As for the Melians and Nicias, their fidelity to their hopes from the gods are clearly elements of their undoing. Yet equally undone, in Sicily and finally in the war as a whole, are the Athenians; does this imply a partial vindication of piety?

The defeat of the Athenians, in Sicily and the wider war, Thucydides ascribes not to their impiety but to their factionalism (2.65.11; cf. 6.15). Yet the two issues prove closely connected—if not always as we would expect. Certainly Thucydides connects the trust that prevails at Sparta with the prevalence of domestic justice and piety. Athens pays grievously for the absence of such trust, whether among her leaders or between them and the people. And it is a crucial defect of residual Athenian piety that rather than mitigate factional strife it aggravates it, as above all in the case of the frenzy over the Herms. Yet if we analyze the precise connection between this frenzy and the failure of the Sicilian project, we must again confront the questionableness of piety as such. If the Athenians were going to persist in their Sicilian undertaking, they should have left Alcibiades in charge of it. "But Alcibiades' . . . presumed impiety made it necessary for the Athenian demos to entrust the expedition to a man of Melian beliefs whom they could perfectly trust because he surpassed every one of them in piety." "Not indeed the gods, but the human concern with the gods without which there cannot be a free city, took terrible revenge on the Athenians."[3] Piety is good and even necessary because it lends support to domestic justice. The truth divined by the pious is that of the qualified necessity of piety, "without which there cannot be a free city" because it is necessary to the mutual trust on which free cities depend.

The blindness of the pious is to the fact that the necessity of piety is

---

[3] Strauss *City and man* 209.

qualified. Thucydides teaches both the benefits of piety and the necessity of statesmen proceeding beyond it precisely because cities cannot; he therefore also teaches the necessity for statesmen of appearing to remain with it. In this light not only the speeches of Alcibiades but those of Pericles appear highly questionable. As for impiety which is to say injustice abroad, it is harmful because it tempts men to foolish ventures and because it threatens to corrode justice at home. Sparta averts this last threat through her hypocrisy.

The case for the goodness of justice cannot, then, be made persuasively on the basis of piety. We therefore return to the problem of squaring justice with compulsion. The Athenians would honor Pericles' injunction to become lovers (*erastai*) of Athens; they would regard her—and so, by reflection, themselves ("for that for which I have praised the city is only the virtuous deeds with which these and their like have adorned it," 2.42.2)—as supremely beautiful. They wish to leave deathless monuments of their nobility and virtue. Their candor is an aspect of their nobility. Yet the city as object of eros does not jibe with the city as thrall of safety and profit. (As for honor or *timē*, it appears problematic; the speakers at Sparta present it as a compulsion and those at Melos as a frivolity. Neither position is friendly to its nobility.) The Athenians' noble longing to know and to tell the truth about themselves and their city brings to light ever greater objections to understanding the city as simply noble.

For this reason among others compulsion weighs increasingly heavily on the Athenians as the war proceeds. The envoys to Sparta, who offer the three compulsions as extenuations of an imperial policy then at its zenith, evince no sense of them as crushing fatalities. These compulsions have so far exacted few sacrifices in the realm of virtue and nobility. (That they have exacted great sacrifices of other kinds attests to the Athenians' nobility.) The virtues other than justice shine through the empire with a dazzling light, as does justice itself in the sense of the devotion of the citizens to the good of their city. Even in foreign relations, so largely the realm of necessity, the envoys claim that Athens has practiced justice to an unprecedented degree. By acting successfully on the three compulsions a city can go on to practice a nonhypocritical virtue; the necessities to which Athens is subject merely serve to illuminate her justice. For the time being necessity justifies while hardly chafing (at least in the decisive respect of virtue): it constrains the Athenians but it does not oppress them.

Pericles too, in his final speech, exhorts the Athenians to bow to the exigencies of their situation thereby demonstrating their virtue. Finding his audience profoundly oppressed by the necessities of war, he contends that such privations, while not to be sought, are nonetheless to be welcomed. While not acquiescing in war except insofar as it is necessary, the wise city will console itself with the thought that by so acquiescing with resolve and dedication it incurs an imperishable reputation for virtue. It freely chooses to bear up under necessity; the fame that it reaps justifies this choice.

Later exponents of the Athenian thesis present the prize for acquiescence in necessity as less shining. That such acquiescence is both excusable and advisable remains as true as before. That it manifests resplendent virtue or even leaves room for it is less clear. The Athenians in Boeotia deny that their occupation of the sanctuary is impious; those on Melos, that their empire deserves reproach. The former do not allege the superior piety of Athens (except in contrast to the gross impiety of the Boeotians in refusing to return the corpses). The latter, having disclaimed all pretense of justice and having barred the Melians from advancing any, even so enter a claim to the superior daring of Athens and therewith her superior openness to the noble and the just. In context this claim seems wistful and even slightly ludicrous: in investing Melos, Athens purports to be acting out of fearful caution, and she enjoins this same caution on the Melians themselves. In the light of the sequel, it is shocking, for although the slaughter of the Melians does not follow from the principles of the envoys, still it is Athens which commits it.

The deepest problem with the envoys' claim of the superior nobility of Athens emerges from their very lectures to the Melians on what true nobility demands. In their "enlightened" understanding the noble appears to split asunder. On one hand is the shadow of the old aristocratic notion, a competition in manly virtue (*andragathia*) characterized by its spontaneity and independence from necessity. Of this only a vestige remains (5.101), as a luxury for those who can afford it. Then there is another notion, which, unlike the first, has inherited the seriousness of the original, but which, unlike the original, avows its subordination to necessity (5.111.3). In this view the noblest (or at any rate least ignoble) course of action is the most prudent, that is, best advised with regard to safety or profit. This notion of the noble as deferring to safety or profit is more than just new: it is paradoxical, representing, as the envoys indicate, an inversion of the prevalent understanding. It is hard to reconcile either passage with that in which the envoys state the kinship of the just and noble, suggesting that both keep company only with daring.

All such Athenian speakers, then—including the Pericles of 2.60–64—while stressing the long reach of necessity, display their wish for an ultimate triumph over necessity. In this the Funeral Oration is indeed a cardinal statement of "Athenianism," which proves to have something in common with piety. To understand this crucial common ground between the exponents and opponents of the Athenian thesis, we must turn to a third class of speakers: those who analyze political life in terms of longings and hopes.

"The very least one would have to say is that there are different kinds of compulsion."[4] These range from what one must do to avoid the worst at the hands of others to what one must do to achieve the best for oneself (cities being allegedly compelled by nature to pursue the latter no less than to avoid the former). *Ananke* figures in political discourse primarily as a ground of excuse; it cannot, therefore, be severed from the question of justice. In its least ambiguous sense (that employed by Thucydides himself at 7.57–58), compulsion is both external and direct: the constraint exerted by stronger cities on weaker ones that are at their mercy. Nothing else is *as* clearly compelling and therefore as clearly extenuating. Other putative compulsions are implicit in the circumstances that face cities and individuals—*ta anankaia* in the sense of *ta deonta*, objective requirements that must be met because their actual well-being demands it. These may be obvious, or they may present themselves only to the minds of the prudent. One such compulsion is the necessity for imperialism where it is in fact a necessity (as it was for Athens after 480 B.C.). Lastly, there are some "compulsions" by which individuals and cities feel themselves gripped which ignore the distinction between rational necessities and superfluities; they correspond to no external exigency but habitually drive us to defy these. They do not procure a city's happiness so much as they imperil it.

The Athenian thesis as formulated by its political advocates does not sufficiently attend to the distinctions among these kinds of necessities. It follows from these distinctions that preeminent among the necessities discernible by the prudent are bulwarks against the pseudonecessities just described. The most effective (also the rarest) such contrivance is a sound regime after the manner of Sparta or Chios. (While the most effective it is of course not foolproof.) In another category is Pericles' accomplished stewardship of an otherwise shaky regime at Athens; in yet another is the unknown Diodotus' lone intervention in the affairs of his city.

Diodotus and Hermocrates, the wisest speakers in the work, join the other exponents of the Athenian thesis in asserting the primacy for each city of its own good, as well as in preaching acquiescence in necessity. Yet whereas those other exponents proclaim such acquiescence to be universal and ineluctable, these stress the tendency of both citizens and cities to resist it. For necessity determines the conduct of human beings only insofar as they themselves recognize it as such. And their vision is notably unreliable.

This whole argument of Diodotus and Hermocrates does not contradict the Athenian thesis so much as it expands it. The envoys to Sparta had extended, apparently already impermissibly, the boundaries of the necessary or compulsory: it came to cover all the usual motives of the injustices of cities. Even so, they had implicitly accepted the distinction between the necessary or irresistible motive and the optional or resistible one: nature

---

[4] Strauss *City and man* 210.

allows us a crucial leeway (1.77). Diodotus, however, while distinguishing between the poor who are customarily unhinged by necessity and the rich who are undone by superfluities, means equally to exonerate both. Everything depends on circumstance or station: to those who possess what they need, the superfluous beckons as insistently as the needful does to those who lack the needful. The superfluous is no less inflammatory than the necessary—and so no less extenuating.

The realm of choice or of rational action for human beings is thus even smaller than the other exponents of the thesis have foreseen: most human beings are unfree even to acquiesce in necessity. We see necessities where none exist, ignore them where they do. The wish is father to the thought (*autokratōr logismos*, 4.108.3): human experience is necessarily mediated by hope and longing. Wishfully and longingly magnifying our power to obtain the good for ourselves, we chronically overstep the bounds of that power. Not only does our subjection to necessities excuse our errors and offenses, but so does our incessant, all-too-human disregard of that subjection.

We can now do justice to what was both most intriguing and most questionable in the original presentation of the Athenian thesis, the claim that honor and profit were no less compulsory (and so no less necessary) for cities than safety. As we have seen, Thucydides follows Diodotus in indicating his rejection of this view: the profitable at least (as well as the just) is to be distinguished from the compulsory (7.57). We may now correct the assertion of the envoys to Sparta as follows: without being as compulsory as safety, honor and profit are equally or even more alluring. Again and again individuals and especially cities risk their safety for the sake of honor and profit; again and again they minimize the risks of so doing.

In this context justice too demonstrates the power of its hold over human beings, for a city's supposition of the justice of its cause is one of the chief factors leading it to venture (4.62), as it is the chief one leading it to punish when punishment is not even in its interest (3.36–49). So easily are human beings persuaded of the justice of their desires that they trust indifferently (and with equal fecklessness) in that justice or in their human strength (4.62), that is, in divine support where they need it and in divine nonintervention where the need for such support is their neighbor's. So great are our capacities for self-deceit that pious hopes will dog the protagonists of even the least just ventures: the Athenian many expect the gods to favor the Sicilian expedition (6.32, 8.1.1). "Punitive" justice, similarly, brands as injustice whatever obstructs our happiness (in effect, the self-concern of our rival): it thirsts to avenge such injustice. "Justice" of either of these usual kinds itself requires extenuation; what provides it is the same consideration that mitigates other more obviously errant behavior: our natural weakness and folly.

The question of compulsion is further complicated by that of chance.

What cities face are almost never compulsions strictly speaking, for the course of political life does not admit of sure predictions of the outcome of a given course of action. Cities are called on to act not on certainties but on probabilities. This very fact fosters the human proclivity for entrapment by improbabilities.[5] What ought to make us cautious in venturing, the unpredictable fickleness of fortune, instead lures us onward. Conversely, those who enjoy prosperity and strength will almost certainly presume on these, disregarding the power of chance to upset even the best-laid plans. We will have it both ways, presuming on fortune or dismissing it—itself a form of presuming on it—as our hopes suggest. Thucydides surely does not mean to suggest the possibility of conquering fortune.[6] Be this as it may, by neglecting fortune's power to harm us, we collaborate to magnify it.

Fortune is ascendant, moreover, within us as well as without us, "subjectively" as well as "objectively." Eros obeys no necessities just as hope acknowledges none. While they may buffet us with the force of necessity, the gusts that sweep the human soul are ultimately a matter of chance. Every human station is subject to such gusts (3.45.2–7; 4.62); none is proof against them. In this sense as in the other, there is no certain bulwark against chance.

This perfected Athenian thesis is superior to the original also in accounting for the reluctance of cities to embrace the thesis; this reluctance is not to be ascribed to hypocrisy alone. Every city lives by hopes incompatible with the thesis, even Athens whose spokesmen proclaim it. The very authority of the city supposes its dignity, and its dignity depends absolutely on its claim to act freely, nobly, and with justice. Every city necessarily exaggerates its mastery of its fate; each presumes far too much upon its freedom and virtue (however it may conceive this last) and looks to the world to reward these. The hopes aroused by Pericles thus resemble, in the decisive respect, those older ones cherished by the Spartans, the Melians, and Nicias; civic piety is still piety and involves (to say the least) no less an embellishment of the world than traditional piety.

We are now in a position to return to the question of the wisdom of piety. Nicias understands transgression as inevitable, without concluding from this that it is strictly speaking necessary (7.77.3–4). He seems then to accept the premise of the Athenian thesis (that "transgression" is ubiquitous) while rejecting the conclusion (that being ubiquitous it is compulsory and therefore cannot be understood as transgression). In counseling moderation, piety counterfeits wisdom. Unfortunately, the fears that it fosters are insep-

---

[5] 3.45, 4.62, 4.65.4, 4.108.3–4, 5.103.

[6] Cf. Reinhardt *Vermächtnis* 195: "Machiavelli war der Meinung, als Weib lasse sich Fortuna gern von Jünglingen bezwingen. Thukydides scheint anderer Meinung." ("Machiavelli was of the opinion that Fortune, like a woman, willingly submits to being forced by the young. Thucydides appears to be of a different opinion.") Cf. Edmunds *Chance and intelligence* 143–203.

arable from immoderate hopes. Even the fearful Spartans display these hopes: their excessive confidence in inaction depends at least in part in their exaggeration of the saving power of avoiding injustice (1.71; 7.18.2–3). For Nicias as for the Spartans, the Melians, and the plague-stricken people of Athens, the acknowledgment of transgression as such vouches for the possibility of avoiding it—for the possibility, then, of human dignity and worthiness of divine protection.

Thucydidean wisdom agrees with piety that "transgression" is inevitable without it following from this that any given case of it is strictly necessary. But what piety sees as a *hamartēma* in the sense of transgression, wisdom sees as one in the sense of error or missing the mark. While piety denies the sway of necessity, wisdom sees in a *hamartēma* a failure to acquiesce in it. Where piety sees sin wisdom sees the hopeful fecklessness of eros. Again we must stress that this last understanding is not itself hopeful: it does not promote a shallow rationalism, nor does it underestimate the depth of the roots of evil in the human soul. For Diodotus, if for anyone, *tout comprendre est tout pardonner*; "transgression" is "error"; vice is ignorance and virtue wisdom. Yet he has pondered deeply human perversity, including the terrible crimes routinely (and sincerely) committed in the name of justice. It is just one such crime that he strives to prevent. The inclinations of men are misguided from their birth;[7] they will always act on notions of their good that are destructive both to themselves and to others. Diodotus announces a more terrible truth than that human beings are evil; namely, that they are not.

Thucydidean wisdom thus perceives folly, willfulness, and perversity as the rule for human beings, and as volcanic in their power when aroused. Where piety sees transgressions of sacred law, wisdom sees nature bursting the bounds of convention (3.45.7, 3.82–83). Wisdom concurs with piety that even the offenses of the most powerful are likely to incur chastisement in the end: by the gods, as the pious hold; according to the wise, by the consequences of overreaching or through the corrosive effect of injustice abroad on justice at home. Whereas piety therefore views the discomfiture of offenders as certain, wisdom views it as merely likely. Whereas piety presumes a retribution proportionate to the offense, wisdom regards such hopes as incoherent. Human beings will do what they will do, and they will suffer what they will suffer. And where piety looks with hope toward the reward of virtue, wisdom foresees none (save for avoidance of the risks peculiar to injustice): while nature at least tends to punish the overweening, it evinces no corresponding solicitude toward the guiltless.[8]

---

[7] Cf. Genesis 8.21.

[8] "Thucydides' theology—if it is permitted to use this expression—is located in the mean (in the Aristotelian sense) between that of Nikias and that of the Athenian ambassadors on Melos." Strauss *Studies* 101.

This qualified convergence of the perfected Athenian thesis with piety brings us face to face with one of the greatest paradoxes of Thucydides' work. In its genesis Athenian thought appears inseparable from Athenian practice: it originates in daring and represents the crown of that daring. Yet what is daring about it is its unfettered and unflinching rationalism, and this proves not entirely friendly to daring on the political plane. Confusedly in the envoys to the Melians, more clearly in the thought of Diodotus, Athenian rationalism implies political moderation—even as it comes to grips (confusedly in the envoys, clearly in Diodotus)—with the imposing obstacles that our nature poses to such moderation. Such moderation, however, is (to say the least) better sustained by Spartan ancestral piety than by that daring of the Athenian people which is inseparable from its relative (but highly qualified) rationality. For reasons that are wholly rationalistic, Thucydides rejects "rationalism in politics."

Athenian thought, properly understood, thus issues in an endorsement of Sparta—an endorsement qualified by its gratitude to (and sympathy with the aspirations of) the regime that fostered it. Thucydides achieves in thought (the only plane on which it can be achieved) a synthesis of the Spartan manner and the Athenian one.

Diodotus stands apart from the other exponents of the Athenian thesis because he has reflected on it more deeply. According to him, only due to the universal propensity of cities to exaggerate their strength do they regard themselves as masters of themselves and their policy. The rational spontaneity that Pericles had ascribed to Athens in his Funeral Oration is far too much to presume of her or of any city. Tossed on the tempest of collective passion, prey to volcanic hopes and rages, cities learn too late that they were blindest when most certain that they saw. The city as plaything of eros (cf. 3.45 with 6.24), as prone to gusts of base or noble longing, of ambitions as vast as they sometimes are witless, is incompatible with the city as object of eros, as ultimate focus of human longing (2.43; cf. 2.64). The city as Diodotus presents it ceases to command our reverence even as it ceases to provoke our indignation. It remains capable of evoking our pathos.

We have already noted that in Diodotus' speech the compulsions to which human nature is subject assume their most sinister guise. We would wish ourselves coolheaded, free of their delusive allure. Not freedom or empire, but the wisdom to pursue them with discrimination looms as in practice the greatest good for cities and individuals alike.[9] Is such wisdom possible for us? In his bid to evoke sympathy for the Mytilenians, Diodotus stresses, as he must, universal human frailty. But does he do justice to himself? Diodotus too is (only) human. He displays, however, an awesome firmness, a

---

[9] Cf. Farrar *Origins* esp. 135–37, 142–44, 187–91 for an analysis that in some respects parallels this one.

confidence in his capacities tempered by a precise awareness of the limits of rhetoric, and a sovereign mastery of the intricacies of his situation. He clearly implies at both 3.43.3–4 and 45.6 that some individuals enjoy a tighter grip over themselves than do cities; the only people qualified to advise their city are those who do not lose their head to it (cf. 1.70.6). Surely Diodotus does not. In him, more than in any other character, the rationalism of Athens achieves its peak, a peak which necessarily rises above Athens.

Obviously Diodotus does not despair of his city. In the wake of just such a gust of passion as he decries in his speech, he moves boldly to recall Athens to its better self. Cities (like Athens here) are capable of second thoughts; at least some of the time they can be brought to listen to reason. Indeed cities are capable of learning lessons of the first importance (8.62). There is room in the city for those who like Diodotus understand politics *sub specie aeternitatis*. Yet effective intervention depends on conditions beyond the power of the statesman to assure; the errors of cities are more easily corrected than avoided, and their correction unavoidably sets the stage for their repetition. Diodotus and Hermocrates stand at some distance from Pericles and his confidence in the power of intelligence to subdue chance; their understanding, however, is no less "Athenian" than his. If anything, it is more so, if what is most Athenian is the rationalism whose characteristic expression is the Athenian thesis. For in their speeches reason "overcomes itself" by achieving self-consciousness of its limits.

Diodotus' perilous intervention is not without possible benefit to himself: consider the evil to someone like him of life in a city dominated by Cleonian hatred of reason.[10] Nor, however, must we conclude that he is without regard for Athens in suggesting a policy that preserves alike its reasonableness, its interest, its dignity, and its humanity. Is the susceptibility of even the sage to eros and other vicissitudes of mood or temper (*orgē*) a possible ground of his benevolence toward the rest of us? Does wisdom confer some degree of immunity to these, but without severing the bond of sympathy between himself and those to whom the malady may still prove fatal (cf. 2.51.6)? Thucydides himself suffered from the plague and, even while suffering from it, recorded its symptoms with an eye to benefiting future patients; the plague is partially analogous with Athenian imperialism (cf. 1.70.9 with 2.49.6).[11] Was he himself once similarly afflicted by Athenianism, that noble political fever future outbreaks of which his book may help to cure at least in a few sufferers (those who in their concern for truth most resemble himself)? Is his desire to leave a *ktēma es aei* thus motivated by humanity as well as (or instead of) a thirst for a posthumous succès d'es-

---

[10] See Bolotin in Strauss and Cropsey *History* 30–31.

[11] On the parallels between Thucydides' presentation of the plague and of his project as a whole, see Romilly *La construction* 120–24.

time? And if this enters into his motives, why not into those of Diodotus, who is called on to make a far lesser effort (albeit at a much greater risk)?

In interpreting any great thinker one finally reaches such a stage of "per-hapses." Within the limits of my understanding of Thucydides and of the issues, I have tried to show that his humanity is accessible to all readers who will follow the thread of his argument and make it fully their own.

Appendix 1

THUCYDIDES 1.22.1–3

THUCYDIDES' procedure in the speeches has been the subject of much debate. His statement of it is as follows.

As for what different men uttered in speech, on the one hand, both as they were preparing for war and once they were actually engaged in it, it was hard to *remember* (*diamnēmoneusai*) *the exact words* (*tēn akribeian*) of what was spoken, both for me when I heard them myself, and for those who brought me reports from elsewhere. *As it seemed to me* (*hōs d'an edokoun emoi*), therefore, that the several speakers would have expressed, *concerning the matters at hand in each case* (*peri tōn aiei parontōn*), *what best met the needs of the occasion* (*ta deonta malista*), so have I set it down, while keeping as closely as possible to *the whole outline* (*tēs xympasēs gnōmēs*) of what was actually spoken. As regards the deeds done in the war, on the other hand, I did not think it worthy of myself to record them on the authority of the first comer, *nor as seemed* [*most likely*] *to me* (*oud' hōs emoi edokei*), but whether I was present myself or whether I had to rely on others, only after having strived for the greatest possible *exactitude* (*akribeia* again).[1] The discovery of which cost me much labor, for those present at the various deeds did not relate the same things in the same way, but as favor for whichever side or as *memory* (*mnēmē* again) suggested. (1.22.1–3)

For the deeds Thucydides claims accuracy;[2] for the speeches, accuracy to a point.[3] The problem is to locate that point, and to grasp Thucydides' proce-

---

[1] The discussion that follows focuses on Thucydides' statement on speeches. His statement on deeds is also difficult and highly contentious. My translation follows the persuasive exegesis of Schepens *L''autopsie'* 94–146, 188–91.

[2] Grosskinsky *Programm* 28–58; Pearson *TAPA* 78 (1947) 39–60; Strauss *City and man* 164–65; Schepens *L''autopsie'* 94–146.

[3] Cf. Egermann *Historia* 21 (1972) 575–78 and Jebb in Abbott ed. *Hellenica* 252–53, which suggests what Thucydides might have written here had accuracy been his standard for the speeches. For the argument that Thucydides has aimed at the maximum feasible accuracy for the speeches, see Grene *Greek political theory* 20–23; Gomme *EGHL* 156–89 and *HCT* 1:138–39; Kagan *YCS* 24 (1975) 75–77; Cogan *Human thing* x–xvi. In my opinion these arguments pay too little attention to the contrast between Thucydides' statements of his handling of speeches and of deeds, as well as slighting the significance of the δέοντα clause.

This position is far more credible, however, than the opposite one: that the speeches owe next to nothing to their originals and even that Thucydides has fabricated them out of whole cloth, inventing speeches where none were given. Cf. Schwartz *Geschichtswerk* 105 and *Gnomon* 2 (1926) 73–80; Jaeger *Paideia* 1.396; Romilly *Imperialism* 242; Flashar *Epitaphios* 5–6; M. I.

dure beyond it. "The conditions for a satisfactory interpretation . . . are that equal weight be given to each part of [the] statement and that [as] so interpreted [it] square with Thucydides' practice . . . in the speeches."[4] We must reconcile Thucydides' professed reliance on his own opinion as to the requirements of each situation (*ta deonta*) with his professed adherence to the speech as really given—and both with his actual practice.

We must stress that Thucydides does promise for the speeches accuracy to a point. He declares his fidelity to the *xympasa gnōmē* of what was actually spoken. This should mean the "whole scheme"; that is, the whole argumentative structure, of the speech as actually spoken. *Xympas* normally conveys in Thucydides the whole of a thing as opposed to just a part of it. That is the obvious way to take it here, as intensifying the professed allegiance to the gnōmē.[5] What Thucydides means by *xympasa gnōmē* is, moreover, anchored in what was actually spoken on a given occasion, and it is something to which he has "[stuck] as closely as possible." He means a train of thought or sequence of arguments, something in what was actually said that must be closely followed if it is to be accurately conveyed.[6]

As for the term *gnōmē*, Thucydides uses it in narrower and broader senses, ranging all the way from an "intention," whether merely harbored or openly expressed (*gnōmē* as "motion proposed"), to someone's comprehensive assessment (stated or unstated) of the situation confronting him. His usage suggests, however, that the narrower sense implies the broader: an intention or proposal is an aspect of, and depends on, the proposer's grasp of the whole situation. In some places where gnōmē figures primarily in the first of these senses, Thucydides expands it to include the second.[7] The gnōmē is the reasoning underlying a given decision, and so, by extension, that decision itself. In fact *gnōmai* (the plural form) in the broader sense just cited, as extended accounts of the proposals or intentions of agents, may read much like the outlines of speeches. Where they are accounts of proposals (as with

---

Finley *Use and abuse* 32; Erbse *Agora* 339. To this the proper response is Kagan *YCS* 24 (1975) 77: "The fact is that no one has shown that there is a single speech in Thucydides . . . that could not have been given in something like its Thucydidean form." So too Gomme *EGHL* 156–89 and Adcock *Thucydides* 28–33; cf. Grant *CP* 15 (1965) 261–66.

[4] Edmunds *Chance and intelligence* 166, following Luschnat *RE* suppl. 12 (1971) cols. 1167–79.

[5] John Wilson *Phoenix* 36 (1982) 97–98.

[6] Grene *Greek political theory* 22. John Wilson *Phoenix* 36 (1982) 99 suggests that "keeping as closely as possible to" "gives far too specific a sense to the middle voice of ἔχω," and that while Thucydides claims to "take the complete γνώμη into account" in composing a speech, he does not claim to stick closely to it. This seems an odd interpretation of "keeping as closely as possible to." We might add that elsewhere in Thucydides where the middle voice of ἔχω takes γνώμη as its subject, its sense is clearly "hold fast to" (1.140.1, 8.81.1.)

[7] 1.44, 45.1; 2.20; 3.92; 6.47.1; 6.50.1; 6.71–72.1; 7.48.1 (ἐγίγνωσκεν); 7.52.3, 4; 8.87.2, 6.

Demosthenes at 6.52), rather than of intentions left unspoken (as with Tissaphernes at 8.87), they amount to reports of speeches presented in indirect discourse—and as such recall Thucydides' several other such reports.

Thucydides' treatment of the speeches that he presents in indirect discourse provides a final clue to the meaning of *xympasa gnōmē*. These appear to represent such reports of speeches, whether garnered first- or secondhand, as serve Thucydides elsewhere as the bases of his reconstitutions of speeches. These summaries seem to vary with the length and complexity of their originals. All, however, recount not only the speaker's proposal or conclusion, but his supporting arguments. In this they are identical to the reports just discussed, which Thucydides describes as *gnōmai*. Very likely they are also examples of xympasai gnōmai, the raw material of Thucydidean speeches.[8] If so, the xympasa gnōmē would include all the arguments advanced by the speaker, something like an outline of the actual speech, "the points made in" it.[9]

While such is, in my view, the most plausible interpretation of the xympasa gnōmē clause, it remains to reconcile it with the other clause of Thucydides' statement. His speakers speak as "they, each in turn addressing the matters successively at hand, seemed to [Thucydides] to say *what best met the needs of the occasion (ta deonta malista)*."[10] The meaning of *ta deonta* is not in doubt. They are "the things needful," "the requirements of the case which are there to be fulfilled"; "with [this term and its cognates] one passively submits to the exigencies of one's situation."[11] That ta deonta are required is, of course, not to say that they are always perceived. To do "the needful" (as I will now call it) is the work of the citizen (1.70.7); to command it is that of the officer (5.66.3); to expound it can be a lengthy matter, even for a laconic Spartan (4.17.2); to discern it consistently is reserved to the greatest statesmen (1.138.3). To have discerned it in the given case is the claim of every deliberative speaker (2.60.5). We must not minimize the task that Thucydides sets himself of furnishing "the needful" to his speakers. This means not what the speaker must say because he cannot possibly avoid it ("what anyone would have to say under the circumstances") but rather what he must say to speak well.[12]

---

[8] Cf. Hudson-Williams *CQ* 42 (1948) 76–81.

[9] John Wilson *Phoenix* 36 (1982) 99.

[10] A reader has questioned whether μάλιστα here possesses true superlative force, noting that in Thucydides it sometimes means "approximately," "more or less." In fact μάλιστα rarely conveys this latter sense in Thucydides except in certain expressions of number, and it clearly possesses true superlative force in the other three cases where it modifies cognates of δέοντα: 3.13.7, 4.5.2, 4.92.3.

[11] Benardete *Glotta* 93 (1965) 293, 295 n.2.

[12] See Forbes *Thucydides Book One* ad loc.: "'what was wanted,' what was appropriate to each occasion, what to the best of Thucydides' own judgment the circumstances called for . . . ;

Speaking well includes speaking persuasively. According to Pericles, who should know, discerning the right course for the city is but one of the virtues of a speaker, along with integrity and the ability to expound his case (2.60.5; cf. 3.37–38, 42–43). Lacking even one of these, the others are useless; without rhetorical astuteness, wisdom and patriotism are vain. Every deliberative speech is both "about" and "to."[13]

Still, we must bear in mind the strict limitation announced in the "sticking as closely as possible" clause. Thucydides fortifies each speech with "the [rhetorically] needful," but never beyond what is compatible with the actual structure of the argument. Each speech is thus a joint endeavor of Thucydides and the original author—and so contrived that it is possible to distinguish only partly their respective contributions.[14] For since the very structure of the argument of a forensic speech aims primarily at persuasion, no clear distinction can be drawn between this structure and the elements in the speech conducing to persuasion. Whatever in a speech is not needful but inept must stem from the original speaker; whatever is needful Thucydides may have added to the speech—but he also may have found it there. How much he contributes to a speech will depend on how needy it was when he found it. Presumably he works with some very good speeches and some very bad ones; in no case does he improve them beyond what the xympasa gnōmē will bear.

The speeches are not necessarily more truthful by virtue of Thucydides' contribution of deonta. He will not enhance a speech with more of the truth than conduces to its success as a speech. (It also follows that he may enhance it with alluring falsehoods.) The speeches do emerge from his hands, however, as truer to the demands of their respective occasions. And by answering better to the needs of the speakers, so do they also to those of the reader. The more we reflect on the speech, the more the occasion comes alive for us. Merging with the original audience, faced with a crucial decision and a speaker who presumes to guide us, we are moved, if we are good readers, to scrutinize each speech with the utmost care. Is the argument consistent? Are the premises and the inferences compelling? What is missing, and why? Of a pair of speeches, which best rebuts or anticipates the claims of the other?

---

the best arguments for peace and war, or for severity or mercy to revolted allies, the most appropriate praise or blame for Athens or Sparta, Thebes or Plataea . . . on any given occasion." So too Marchant *Thucydides Book One* ad loc.: "the best arguments that could be found to support the ξύμπασα γνώμη of the speaker." Cf. Maddalena *Thucydidis . . . liber primus (tomus I)* ad loc.

[13] Cf. Macleod *Historia* 23 (1974) 52: "Partly [τὰ δέοντα] refers to the content of a speech which gives the 'necessary' advice in the given circumstances. . . . But in 1.22.1 it applies rather to those elements of a speech which make it coherent and persuasive, the valid presentation of a 'case.'"

[14] Aron *History and Theory* 1 (1960–61) 109; Winnington-Ingram *BICS* 12 (1965) 70–71.

The debates become our debates, for which we too must assume responsibility.[15]

It is to further these deliberations of ours that Thucydides assures (to a point) the rhetorical competence of his characters. Each case receives its day in court, presented as forcefully as its nature allows, and none, such as it is, fails by default. Because the scheme remains as it was, we may join the original listeners in judging it—and we may judge their judgment of it.[16] By furnishing the speech with what is "needful" while remaining true to the "whole structure of the argument," Thucydides contrives to combine fidelity to the essential elements of the historical situation with fidelity to his object in recording it, namely our political education.[17]

Thucydides' speakers thus offer no interpretation of a situation which must not itself be interpreted in light of that situation. From the assertion of something we can conclude neither that Thucydides nor that the speaker thinks it true, but only that one or both deem it useful. Thus are the speeches, as Hobbes discerned, "of the contexture of the narrative," and such that the reader "must draw out [their] lesson[s] unto himself." We must look from speech to deed and from deed to speech, as each sheds light on the other.[18]

Thucydides, then, improves the speeches, but he does not perfect them. In fortifying each with the "needful," he does not mend its defects as a guide to action. He thus preserves them as the speeches of his characters rather than his own, as political speeches rather than as impartial analyses. He makes only such contributions to them as serve the rhetorical aims of his speakers. This is not to say that his contributions may not elucidate the situation directly; a given statement may be persuasive as well as true, or even persuasive because it is true. In fact this policy allows Thucydides great leeway in commenting on events, whether those at hand in a specific situation or those at some distance from it, and so it allows also for establishing ironic and other contrasts.[19] Above all, it offers him scope for generalities, for every rhetorical task requires some.[20]

---

[15] Hobbes *EW* 8:vii–viii; Aron *History and Theory* 1 (1960–61) 110; Dewald in *Greek historians* 57–58; Macleod *Historia* 23 (1974) 53: "The speeches thus invite . . . critical scrutiny, the result of which may be a sense not only of enlightenment, but of tragedy. For they move . . . by their fallibility no less than they illumine . . . by their penetration."

[16] Cf. Adcock *Thucydides* 45–46: "The dialectical methods of Thucydides are at the disposal of either side in a debate, and so are used impartially to reinforce either. . . . The dialectical skill put at the disposal of a speaker will raise his actual arguments to a higher power. Thus the reader will best judge the case for either side, and so appreciate the validity of either thesis."

[17] Cf. Girard *Essai* 41–48.

[18] Cf. Stahl in Stadter ed. *Speeches* 62; Farrar *Origins* 133–34.

[19] The speeches abound in interplay that cannot have figured in the originals. See Romilly *Histoire et raison*; Strauss *City and man* 163–74; Wallace *Phoenix* 18 (1964) 251–61; Pouncey *Necessities* 13–15; Rawlings *Structure*; Connor *Thucydides*.

[20] Aron *History and Theory* 1 (1960–61) 104.

Thucydides may also furnish a speech, always agreeably to its practical intention, with deonta of a more exalted sort—those apt for conveying a deeper understanding of the war as a whole or of war in general,[21] or most generally (and also most particularly) the speaker's own comprehensive grasp of the situation that confronts him (*ta paronta*). (For this too may figure in the speaker's practical intention.) A speaker may refrain from saying everything that he thinks—a reticence the necessity of which may follow from the very urgency of his immediate practical task. Thucydides is hardly the only speaker in his work aware of the gulf between the mass of listeners (whom the deliberative speaker, unlike Thucydides, must persuade) and those few whom he hopes to educate.[22]

Like the poets (his critique of whom furnishes the context for his statement), Thucydides embellishes the truth; he "orders things for the better" (1.21.3). Not all things, however. He undertakes only such improvement on truth as serves truth. In the first place, he does not perfect deeds. Embellishing deeds, poets and logographers obscure them, or leave them as obscure as they found them (1.21.1; cf. 6.2.1). He for his part relates deeds without embellishment. Speeches he perfects, but only within limits. While embellishing them with "the needful," he recreates the speaker's case and the occasion as they were. He sharpens each speech as an exposition of that case and a mirror of that occasion, but without depriving it of its primarily practical character. He spurs our thought, but always within the limits of the project of the original speaker: we must always, then, reflect first on that project, and so on the situation it addresses.

Thucydides' improvement of the speeches serves our comprehension of the unadorned facts; this is why I call it an improvement on truth that serves truth. Homeric adornments, gods and heroes, cede to chaste Thucydidean ones, *deonta* that serve both the fleeting turn of the speakers and the lasting one of author and reader.[23]

[21] J. H. Finley *Thucydides* 95–99; Edmunds *Chance and intelligence*, 166–68; Tasolambros *In defense* 132–33; and others have argued for the distinction between the δέοντα suitable to political speeches and those suitable to "historical" ones, that is, those intended not to sway a crowd but to inform posterity, and have argued that the δέοντα that Thucydides provides are of this latter sort. On my reading of 1.22, if he provides the "needful" in the "historical" sense it is only within the bounds imposed by the "needful" in the "political" one.

[22] The most impressive examples of speeches that communicate with listeners (and readers) on more than one level are that of Hermocrates at Gela (4.59–64), Pericles' famous Funeral Oration (2.35–46), and the debate between Cleon and Diodotus (3.36–49). All of these speakers practice carefully nuanced communication while also indicating (albeit and necessarily only by means of such communication) the necessity of practicing it.

[23] Cf. Thibaudet *Campagne avec Thucydide* 49.

THUCYDIDES' USE OF *PROPHASIS* AT 1.23.5–6

THERE ARE GOOD reasons to doubt that Thucydides here uses *prophasis* in a "scientific" sense of "objective cause." The first is that such a usage would imply stark opposition between *tēn alēthestatēn prophasin* and the "grievances" or imputations of blame, while in fact Thucydides offers no such opposition.[1] He begins by raising the question of why the two sides broke the treaty then in force between them and suggests that precisely his account of the grievances will resolve it; it is *this* account—that of the grievances— that he offers so that no one need ever again seek "from what" (*ek hotou*) so great a war arose. The next sentence, the one featuring the "truest *prophasis*," begins with the particle *gar* (roughly "for"). Far from implying an opposition with the sentence preceding, the suggestion is that this one follows from it: in the course of examining the grievances, we will encounter the truest prophasis, Thucydides' mention of which is parenthetical. The passage implies two contrasts (conveyed by the particles *men . . . de*), one between the truth of the prophasis in question and its inconspicuousness in speech, and the other between this last and the conspicuousness of certain of the grievances. Thucydides implies first that his account of the grounds of complaint and points of difference among the parties will serve to acquaint us with the truest prophasis; next, that the latter stands in contrast to the former in that while they are conspicuous it is very little so. There is, however, no contradiction here; after all, he says not that the "truest prophasis" was immanifest in speech (i.e., in the articulation of the grievances) but only that it was much less so than the grievances themselves. It is there in the speech of the combatants, but we will have to be on the lookout for it. Crawley's translation concocts an apologetic air ("Still it is well . . .") for Thucydides' second avowal of his intention of relating the grievances, but no apology is required (or present in the original). In fact Thucydides proceeds to devote by far the greater part of Book One to just these "grievances alleged." Indeed he reminds us throughout the book that such is what he has done and is doing.[2]

[1] Cf. Heath *LCM* 11 (1986) 104–5.

[2] Walker *CQ* NS 7 (1957) 27–38. Heath *LCM* 11 (1986) 104–5 argues against the claim that Thucydides contradicts himself by asserting that the truest prophasis was least manifest in speech and then presenting an account that includes speeches dominated by it. In fact the truest prophasis, although not wholly invisible (which Thucydides never claims it to have been), is less visible in the speeches than is the issue of injustice (i.e., of infractions of the treaty). For

The second reason for questioning the "scientific" interpretation of this passage concerns the meaning of *prophasis*.[3] Later in the evolution of the Greek language the term indeed came to mean "cause" in the objective sense. And it was indeed already current in the medical writings, from which Thucydides allegedly borrowed it. (Thucydides even uses it in a medical context at 2.49.2.) It is looking increasingly doubtful, however, that the sense of *prophasis* even in the medical writings of the time was a precise technical one. The medical usage seems rather to have mirrored that of everyday life. The prophasis of an ailment was the "reason given" for it, whether by doctor or patient, which, like all reasons given, might be true or false.[4]

---

examples of the approach that Heath is disputing, see Romilly *Imperialism* 16–57 and Rhodes *Hermes* 115 (1987) 154–65.

[3] The term is a verbal noun derived either from πρόφημι (the root of which is "speak") or προφαίνομαι (the root of which is "show" or "appear"). πρόφημι means "foretell," whereas πρόφασις never means "foretelling"; this argues for a derivation from προφαίνομαι, "to show forth." The fact that the alpha in the word is long, on the other hand, may argue for a derivation from πρόφημι (see Sealey *CQ* NS 7 [1957] 3, but cf. Browning *Philologus* 102 [1958] 60–74). In recent years, the argument has been made that there were in fact two different πρόφασις lexemes (one from each of these two roots), that the one derived from πρόφημι meant an alleged reason and the one derived from προφαίνομαι meant an actual one, and that Thucydides uses both, the one at 1.23 being the "objective" version (Lohmann *Lexis* 3 [1952] 5–49; Rawlings *Prophasis*). On the Lohmann/Rawlings theory, see Pearson *TAPA* 103 (1972) 390–94; Lynn S. Wilson *Aitia and prophasis* and in Gerber ed. *Greek poetry and philosophy* 319–36.

[4] Pearson *TAPA* 83 (1952) 210–11 and 103 (1972) 388–90. See at 2.49.2.

Appendix 3

THUCYDIDES' PRESENTATION OF THE DEMAND
FOR THE REPEAL OF THE MEGARIAN DECREE

KAGAN *Outbreak* 321–25 argues that at least the first of the demands ascribed to the Spartans at 1.139—that Athens revoke the Megarian decree—represented a serious attempt to reach an accommodation. He notes that for Sparta to have posed this lone demand as a sufficient condition of peace implied a repudiation of the concerns of Corinth and so may have reflected the temporary restoration to grace of the Spartan peace party, which was willing to call Corinth's bluff over the latter's threat to bolt the alliance. (Kagan concedes that the later and final Spartan demand—that "Athens leave the rest of Greece independent"—was indeed merely an attempt to contrive *hoti megistē prophasis*, which confirms that the Spartan war party, following the rebuff of the ultimatum over Megara, was once again firmly in the saddle.)

Kiechle *Gymnasium* 70.4 (1963) 292–94 and Rhodes *Hermes* 115 (1987) 161–63 go still further in asserting the centrality of this decree, the latter even claiming that Thucydides deliberately downplays its significance so as to conceal the responsibility of Athens and Pericles for the war.

These alternative interpretations help clarify Thucydides' reasons for minimizing the significance alike of the Megarian decree, the Spartan demand that Athens repeal it, and the Athenian refusal to do so. True, Megara was an ally of Sparta, so the Athenian decree concerning her, whatever its content (and even if not a violation of the treaty), may well be construed as "laying hold of [the Spartan] alliance" (1.118.2). Megara was weak, however, and although of great strategic importance because she commanded the passes of Geraneia (the chokepoint for Spartan invasions of Attica), had no choice but to cling to the protection of a larger power, whether Sparta or Corinth. Neither of these latter, however, would have gone to war over the decree (or the plight of Aegina, about which Sparta also remonstrates at this time). Corinthian solicitude for Megara is seen to depend on the fact that Corinth's own fish are in the fire: Megara serves her merely as a further means by which to goad Sparta and her other allies to war so as to relieve Poteidaea. If, similarly, the crucial issue for Sparta was the possible defection of Corinth (which defection alone might also have entailed that of neighboring Megara), we can understand why Thucydides consigns the outcry over the Megarian decree to *hoti megistē prophasis tou polemou*. For then

Sparta could not possibly have delivered this ultimatum to Athens except with the approval of Corinth, that is, except on the understanding shared by both allies that Athens was certain to reject it. Kagan, while contending that this rejection was not a foregone conclusion, admits that Pericles urged it with all his power, that he was firmly in control of Athenian policy on the eve of the war, and that the Peloponnesians had by now every reason to grasp this fact (having recently failed to diminish his influence by means of their invocation of the curse of the Goddess).

In Thucydides' analysis, then, the Megarian decree and the uproar over it, however noisy, had much to do with why the Peloponnesians claimed to go to war but little to do with why they went. The distinction between the *aitiai kai diaphorai* of 1.23.5–6, on the one hand—the Corcyrean and Poteidaean affairs—and the expostulations intended to obtain *hoti megistē prophasis tou polemou*, on the other, remind us that the former, unlike the latter, were anything but mere justifications of a decision already taken: they were reasons why it was taken.

We may also note that insofar as Thucydides' emphasis in Book One is on clarifying the question of right, neither the demand to revoke the Megarian decree nor the demand that the cities (such as Aegina) be left independent is relevant in the primary sense. Neither involves a plausible breach of the letter of the treaty on the part of Athens; neither, therefore, sheds much light on the question of aitia. Who bears aitia for the war continues to depend on the correctness of the Spartans' prior determination, at 1.88, that Athens has broken the treaty.

BIBLIOGRAPHY

Adcock, F. E. Thucydides in Book I. *Journal of Hellenic Studies* 71 (1951) 2–12.
_____. *Thucydides and his history*. Cambridge: Cambridge University Press, 1963.
Allison, June W. Sthenelaidas' speech: Thucydides 1.86. *Hermes* 112 (1984) 10–16.
Alter, Robert. *The world of biblical literature*. New York: Basic Books, 1991.
Amit, M. The Melian dialogue and history. *Athenaeum* 46 (1968) 216–35.
Andrewes, A. *See also* Gomme, A. W., K. J. Dover, and A. Andrewes.
_____. Thucydides on the causes of the war. *Classical Quarterly* NS 9 (1959) 223–39.
_____. The Mytilene debate. *Phoenix* 16 (1962) 64–85.
Aron, Raymond. Thucydide et le récit des événements. *History and Theory* 1 (1960–61) 103–28.
Bahr-Volk, Marie. A note on the figurative words denoting posture and position in Thucydides' Melian dialogue. *Classical Bulletin* 52 (1976) 59–60.
Banfield, Edward C. *Here the people rule. Selected essays*. 2d ed. Washington, D.C.: American Enterprise Institute Press, 1991.
Barbu, N. I. Remarques sur le droit chez Thucydide. *Studii Clasice* 8 (1966) 35–44.
Barel, Yves. *La quête du sens: Comment l'esprit vient à la cité*. Paris: Editions du Seuil, 1987.
Bartoletti, Vittorio. Il dialogo degli Ateniesi e dei Melii nella 'Storia' di Tucidide. *Rivista di filologia e d'istruzione classica* 67 (1939) 301–18.
_____. Potenza della Sicilia e ardore degli Ateniesi in Tucidide. *Studi italiani di filologia classica* 14 (1937) 227–35.
Barton, A. T., and A. S. Chavasse, editors. *The fourth book of Thucydides*. London: Longman, Greens, 1890.
Bayer, Karl. Athenische Realpolitik: Zu Thukydides VI:76–88. In *Festschrift für Franz Egermann*, edited by Werner Sürbaum and Friedrich Maier, 57–65. Munich: Institut für Klassische Philologie, 1985.
Benardete, S. G. *Dei* and *chrē* in Plato and others. *Glotta* 93 (1965) 285–97.
_____. Leo Strauss' *The city and man*. *Political Science Reviewer* 8 (1978) 1–20.
Bloedow, Edmund F. Sthenelaidas the persuasive Spartan. *Hermes* 115 (1987) 60–66.
_____. The speeches of Archidamus and Sthenelaidas at Sparta. *Historia* 23 (1981) 129–43.
Bluhm, William T. Causal theory in Thucydides' Peloponnesian War. *Political Studies* 10 (1962) 15–35.
Bodin, Louis. Diodote contre Cléon. *Revue des études anciennes* 42 (*Mélanges Radet*) (1940) 36–52.
Bolotin, David. Thucydides. In *History of political philosophy*, edited by Leo Strauss and Joseph Cropsey, 7–31. 3rd ed. Chicago: University of Chicago Press, 1986.
Bowersock, Glen W. The personality of Thucydides. *Antioch Review* 35.1 (1965) 135–46.
Bradeen, D. W. The popularity of the Athenian empire. *Historia* 9 (1960) 257–69.

Browning, Robert. Greek abstract nouns in -*sis*, *tis*. *Philologus* 102 (1958) 60–74.

Bruell, Christopher. Thucydides' view of Athenian imperialism. *American Political Science Review* 68 (1974) 11–17.

———. Reply to Corsi. *American Political Science Review* 68 (1974) 1680–81.

———. Thucydides and Perikles. *St. John's Review* 32, 1 (1981) 24–29.

Brunt, P. A. Spartan policy and strategy in the Archidamian war. *Phoenix* 19 (1965) 255–80.

Burckhardt, Jacob. *Force and freedom: Reflections on history.* Edited by J. H. Nichols. New York: Pantheon Books, 1943.

Bury, J. B. *The ancient Greek historians.* New York: Macmillan, 1909.

Cagnazzi, Silvana. *La spedizione ateniese contro Melo di 416 a.c.: Realtà e propaganda.* Bari, It.: Adriatica editrice, 1983.

Cagnetta, Mariella. Gli agoni intrecciati nell'opera di Tucidide. *Rivista di filologia e d'instruzione classica* 111 (1983) 422–31.

———. Platea: Ultimo atto. *Quaderni di storia* 19 (1984) 203–12.

———. Riforma della dialettica agonale nel dialogo dei Meli. *Quaderni di storia* 32 (1990) 159–62.

Cajani, Guglielmino. La tranquilità dei Meli. *Prometheus* 6 (1980) 21–28.

Canfora, Luciano. Per una storia del dialogo dei Melii e degli Ateniesi. *Belfagor* (1971) 409–26.

———. *Totalità e selezione nella storiografia classica.* Bari, It.: Laterza, 1972.

Cawkwell, George. Thucydides' judgment of Pericles' strategy. *Yale Classical Studies* 24 (1975) 53–70.

Chatelet, François. *La naissance de l'histoire. La formation de la pensée historienne en Grèce.* Paris: Editions de Minuit, 1962.

Cicciò, Michela. Guerre, *staseis* e *asylia* nella Grecia del V secolo A.C. In *I Santuari e la guerra nel mondo classico,* edited by M. Sorti, 132–41. Milan: Università cattolica del Sacro Cuore, 1984.

Classen, J., and J. Steup, editors. *Thukydides.* 5th ed. 4 vol. Berlin: Weidmann, 1919.

Clay, Jenny Strauss. The generation of monsters in Hesiod. *Classical Philology* 88 (1993) 27–38.

———. *The wrath of Athena. Gods and men in the Odyssey.* Princeton: Princeton University Press, 1983.

Coby, Patrick. Enlightened self-interest in the Peloponnesian War: Thucydidean speakers on the right of the stronger and interstate peace. *Canadian Journal of Political Science* 24.1 (1991) 67–90.

Cochrane, C. N. *Thucydides and the science of history.* London: Humphrey Milford, 1929.

Cogan, Marc. *The human thing: The speeches and principles of Thucydides' History.* Chicago: University of Chicago Press, 1981.

———. Mytilene, Plataea, and Corcyra: Ideology and politics in Thucydides. *Phoenix* 35 (1981) 1–21.

Cohen, David. Justice, interest, and political deliberation in Thucydides. *Quaderni urbinati di cultura classica* 45 (1984) 35–60.

Collingwood, R. G. *The idea of history.* Edited by T. M. Knox. Oxford: Clarendon Press, 1946.

Conflenti, Giuseppina. *Tucidide.* Rome: n.p., 1963.

Connor, W. R. "Sacred" and "secular." *Hiera kai hosia* and the classical Athenian concept of the state. *Ancient Society* 19 (1988) 161–88.

———. A post modernist Thucydides? *Classical Journal* 72 (1977) 289–98.

———. Narrative discourse in Thucydides. In *The Greek historians: Literature and history. Essays presented to A. E. Raubitschek*, 1–17. Stanford: Stanford University Department of Classics/ANMA Libri, 1985.

———. *Thucydides*. Princeton: Princeton University Press, 1984.

Cornford, F. M. *Thucydides mythistoricus*. London: Edward Arnold, 1907.

Corsi, Jerome R. Communication. *American Political Science Review* 68 (1974) 1679–80.

Cox, Richard H. Thucydides on Themistocles. *Politikos* 2 (1992) 189–97.

Crane, Gregory. Power, prestige, and the Corcyrean affair in Thucydides I. *Classical Antiquity* 11 (1992) 1–27.

Creed, J. L. Moral values in the age of Thucydides. *Classical Quarterly* NS 23 (1973) 213–31.

De Sanctis, Gaetano. Postille tucididee, 1: Il dialogo tra i Meli e gli Ateniesi. *Rendiconti della Reale Accademia dei Lincei* (Classe di Scienze Morali) ser. 6, vol. 6 (1930) 299–308.

De Ste-Croix, G.E.M. Notes on jurisdiction in the Athenian empire, 1. *Classical Quarterly* NS 11 (1961) 94–112.

———. The character of the Athenian empire. *Historia* 3 (1954) 1–41.

———. *The origins of the Peloponnesian war*. London: Gerald Duckworth, 1972.

Détienne, Marcel. *L'Invention de la mythologie*. Paris: Gallimard, 1981.

Dewald, Carolyn. Practical knowledge and the historian's role in Herodotus and Thucydides. In *The Greek historians: Literature and history. Essays presented to A. E. Raubitschek*. Stanford: Stanford University Department of Classics/ANMA Libri, 1985.

Diels, Hermann, and Walther Kranz, editors and translators. *Die Fragmente der Vorsokratiker*. Rev. ed. 3 vol. Berlin: Weidmann, 1952.

Diller, Hans. Freiheit bei Thukydides als Schlagwort und als Wirklichkeit. *Gymnasium* 69 (1962) 189–204.

Donini, Guido. *La posizione di Tucidide verso il governo dei Cinquemila*. Turin, It.: Paravia, 1969.

Donnelly, Jack. Thucydides and realism. Paper presented to the International Studies Association, Vancouver, March 1991.

Dover, K. J. *See also* Gomme, A. W., K. J. Dover, and A. Andrewes.

———. *Thucydides*. Oxford: Clarendon Press, 1973.

Ducrey, Pierre. *Guerre et guerriers dans la Grèce antique*. Fribourg, Switz.: Office du Livre, 1985.

Eatough, Geoffrey. The use of *hosios* and kindred words in Thucydides. *American Journal of Philology* 102 (1971) 238–51.

Ebener, D. Kleon und Diodotos. *Wissenschaftliche Zeitschrift Universität Halle* (Ges.-Sprachw.) 5.6 (1956) 1085–1166.

Edmunds, Lowell. *Chance and intelligence in Thucydides*. Cambridge: Harvard University Press, 1975.

———. Thucydides' ethics as reflected in the description of *stasis*. *Harvard Studies in Classical Philology* 79 (1975) 73–92.

Egermann, Fritz. Thukydides über die Art seiner Reden und über seine Darstellung der Kriegsgeschehnisse. *Historia* 21 (1972) 575–602.

Engeman, Thomas S. Homeric honor and Thucydidean necessity. *Interpretation* 4.2 (1974) 65–78.

Erbse, Hartmut. Zwei Fragen zur Geschichtsbetrachtung des Thukydides. In *Agora: Zu Ehren von Rudolph Berlinger. Neues Jahrbuch* 13 (1987) 331–46.

——. Über das Proimion des thukydideischen Geschichtswerkes. *Rheinisches Museum für Philologie* NF 113 (1970) 43–69.

Euben, J. Peter. *The tragedy of political theory: The road not taken*. Princeton: Princeton University Press, 1990.

Farrar, Cynthia. *The origins of democratic thinking. The invention of politics in classical Athens*. Cambridge: Cambridge University Press, 1988.

Ferrara, Giovanni. La politica dei Meli in Tucidide. *Parola del Passato* 11 (1956) 335–46.

Finley, John H., Jr. The unity of Thucydides' history. [1940] In Finley, *Three essays on Thucydides*, 118–69. Cambridge: Harvard University Press, 1967.

——. *Thucydides*. Cambridge: Harvard University Press, 1942.

Finley, M. I. Thucydides the moralist. In Finley, *Aspects of antiquity*, 44–58. New York: Viking Press, 1968.

——. Myth, memory, and history. In Finley, *The use and abuse of history*, 11–33. London: Chatto and Windus, 1975.

——. Sparta. In *Problèmes de la guerre en Grèce ancienne*, edited by J.-P. Vernant. Paris and The Hague: Mouton, 1968.

Flashar, Helmut. *Der Epitaphios des Perikles. Seine Funktion in Geschichtswerk des Thukydides*. Rev. In Flashar, *Eidola: Ausgewählte Kleine Schriften*, edited by Manfred Kraus, 435–81. Amsterdam: B. R. Grüner, 1989.

Fliess, Peter J. War guilt in the history of Thucydides. *Traditio* 16 (1960) 1–17.

——. *Thucydides and the politics of bipolarity*. Baton Rouge: Louisiana State University Press, 1963.

Forbes, W. H., editor. *Thucydides Book One*. Oxford: Clarendon Press, 1895.

Forde, Steven. *The ambition to rule. Alcibiades and the politics of imperialism in Thucydides*. Ithaca, N.Y.: Cornell University Press, 1989.

——. Thucydides on the causes of Athenian imperialism. *American Political Science Review* 80 (1986) 433–48.

——. Varieties of realism: Thucydides and Machiavelli. *Journal of Politics* 54 (1992) 372–93.

Frank, Daniel H. The power of truth (Thucydides 6.37–42). *Prudentia* 16 (1984) 99–107.

Freeman, Kathleen. *Ancilla to the pre-Socratic philosophers*. Cambridge: Harvard University Press, 1962.

Funke, Hermann. Poesia e storiografia. *Quaderni di storia* 23 (1986) 71–93.

Galpin, Timothy J. The democratic roots of Athenian imperialism in the fifth century B.C. *Classical Journal* 79 (1983–84) 100–109.

Garlan, Yvon. *La Guerre dans l'antiquité*. Paris: FAC Fernand Nathan, 1972.

Garst, Daniel. Thucydides and neorealism. *International Studies Quarterly* 33 (1989) 3–27.

Gillis, Daniel. The revolt of Mytilene. *American Journal of Philology* 92 (1971) 38–48.

_____. Murder on Melos. *Rendiconti dell'Istituto Lombardo* (Classe di Lettere) 112 (1978) 185–211.

Girard, Jules. *Essai sur Thucydide*. Paris: Librairie Hachette, 1884.

Gomme, A. W. The speeches in Thucydides. In Gomme, *Essays in Greek history and literature*, 156–89. Oxford: Clarendon Press, 1937.

Gomme, A. W., K. J. Dover, and A. Andrewes. *A historical commentary on Thucydides*. 5 vol. Oxford: Clarendon Press, 1945–72.

Gomperz, Theodor. *The Greek thinkers*. Translated by Laurie Magnus. 2 vol. London: John Murray, 1901.

Grant, J. R. A note on the tone of Greek diplomacy. *Classical Quarterly* NS 15 (1965) 261–66.

_____. Toward knowing Thucydides. *Phoenix* 28 (1974) 81–94.

Grene, David. *Greek political theory*. Original title, *Man in his pride*, 1950. Chicago: University of Chicago Press, 1965.

Grossi, Gianni. *Frinico tra propaganda democratica e giudizio tucidideo*. Università degli Studi di Padova. Pubblicazioni dell'Istituto di Storia antica. Rome: "L'Erma" di Bretschneider, 1984.

Grosskinsky, August. *Das Programm des Thukydides*. Berlin: Junker und Dünnhaupt, 1936.

Grote, George. *A history of Greece*. 12 vol. New York: Harper and Brothers, 1857.

Gundert, Hermann. Athen und Sparta in den Reden des Thukydides. *Die Antike* 16 (1940) 98–114.

Hammond, N.G.L. The particular and the universal in the speeches in Thucydides. With special reference to that of Hermocrates in Gela. In *The speeches in Thucydides*, edited by Philip A. Stadter, 49–59. Chapel Hill: University of North Carolina Press, 1973.

Heath, Malcolm. Justice in Thucydides' Athenian speeches. *Historia* 39 (1990) 385–400.

_____. Thucydides 1.23.5–6. *Liverpool Classical Monthly* 11 (1986) 104–5.

Herter, Hans. Freiheit und Gebundenheit des Staatsmannes bei Thukydides. *Rheinisches Museum für Philologie* 93 (1949) 133–53.

_____. Pylos und Melos. *Rheinisches Museum für Philologie* 97 (1954) 316–43.

Heubeck, Alfred. *Prophasis* und keine Ende (zu Thukydides 1.23). *Glotta* 58 (1980) 222–36.

Hoffmann, Stanley. *Justice beyond borders*. Syracuse, N.Y.: Syracuse University Press, 1981.

Hogan, J. C. Thucydides 3.52–68 and Euripides' Hecuba. *Phoenix* 26 (1972) 241–57.

Hogan, John T. The *axiosis* of words at Thucydides 3.82.4. *Greek, Roman, and Byzantine Studies* 21 (1980) 139–50.

Hornblower, Simon. *A commentary on Thucydides*. Volume I. Books I–III. Oxford: Clarendon Press, 1991.

_____. *Thucydides*. Baltimore: Johns Hopkins University Press, 1986.

Huart, Pierre. L'idée de justice chez Thucydide (à propos de deux épisodes du livre III). *Réseaux* 18 (1972) 17–38.

———. *Le vocabulaire de l'analyse psychologique dans l'oeuvre de Thucydide*. Paris: Klincksieck, 1968.

Hudson-Williams, H. Ll. Conventional forms of debate and the Melian Dialogue. *American Journal of Philology* 71 (1950) 56–69.

———. Thucydides, Isocrates, and rhetorical composition. *Classical Quarterly* 42 (1948) 76–81.

Hunter, Virginia. Thucydides, Gorgias, and mass psychology. *Hermes* 114 (1986) 412–29.

———. *Past and process in Herodotus and Thucydides*. Princeton: Princeton University Press, 1982.

Hussey, Edward. Thucydidean history and Democritean theory. *History of Political Thought* 6 (1985) 118–38.

Immerwahr, Henry R. Pathology of power and the speeches in Thucydides. In *The Speeches in Thucydides*, edited by Philip A. Stadter, 16–31. Chapel Hill: University of North Carolina Press, 1973.

Jaeger, Werner. *Paideia: The ideals of Greek culture*. Translated by Gilbert Highet. 2 vol. 4th ed. Oxford: Basil Blackwell, 1954.

Jebb, R. C. The speeches in Thucydides. In *Hellenica*, edited by Evelyn Abbott, 244–95. London: Longmans, Green, 1898. Reprinted in Jebb, *Essays and addresses*, 359–445. Cambridge: Cambridge University Press, 1907.

Johnson, Laurie M. *Thucydides, Hobbes, and the interpretation of realism*. DeKalb: Northern Illinois University Press, 1993.

Jordan, Borimir. Religion in Thucydides. *Transactions of the American Philological Association* 116 (1986) 119–47.

Kagan, Donald. *The Archidamian war*. Ithaca, N.Y.: Cornell University Press, 1974.

———. *The fall of the Athenian empire*. Ithaca, N.Y.: Cornell University Press, 1987.

———. *The outbreak of the Peloponnesian war*. Ithaca, N.Y.: Cornell University Press, 1969.

———. *The peace of Nicias and the Sicilian expedition*. Ithaca, N.Y.: Cornell University Press, 1981.

———. *Pericles of Athens and the birth of democracy*. New York: Free Press, 1991.

———. The speeches in Thucydides and the Mytilene debate. *Yale Classical Studies* 24 (1975) 71–94.

Kennedy, George. *The art of persuasion in ancient Greece*. Princeton: Princeton University Press, 1963.

Keynes, John Maynard. *A revision of the treaty. Being a sequel to The economic consequences of the peace*. London: Macmillan, 1922.

Kiechle, Franz. Ursprung und Wirkung der machtpolitischen Theorien im Geschichtswerk des Thukydides. *Gymnasium* 70 (1963) 289–312.

Kirkwood, Gordon M., Jr. Thucydides' words for cause. *American Journal of Philology* 73 (1952) 37–61.

Konishi, Haruo. The composition of Thucydides' history. *American Journal of Philology* 101 (1980) 29–41.

Lacey, W. K. Thucydides 2.45.2. *Proceedings of the Cambridge Philosophical Society* 10 (1964) 47–49.

Landmann, Georg Peter. *Eine Rede des Thukydides. Die Friedensmahnung des Hermokrates*. Kiel: Lipsius und Tischer, 1932.

Lateiner, Donald. Nicias' inadequate encouragement. *Classical Philology* 80 (1985) 201–13.

———. Heralds and corpses in Thucydides. *Classical World* 71.2 (1977) 97–106.

Lavagnini, Bruno. *Saggio sulla storiografia greca*. Bari: Laterza, 1933.

Legon, Ronald P. Megara and Mytilene. *Phoenix* 22 (1968) 220–25.

Levi, Mario Attilio. In margine di Tucidide. *Parola del Passato* 7 (1952) 81–112.

———. Il dialogo dei Meli. *Parola del Passato* 8 (1953) 5–16.

Liebeschuetz, W. The structure and function of the Melian Dialogue. *Journal of Hellenic Studies* 88 (1968) 73–77.

Lincoln, Abraham. *Speeches and writings, 1863–1865*. New York: Library of America, 1989.

Lloyd-Jones, Hugh. *The justice of Zeus*. Rev. ed. Sather Classical Lectures. Berkeley: University of California Press, 1983.

Lohmann, J. Der Verhältnis des abendländischen Menschen zur Sprache. *Lexis* 3 (1952) 5–49.

Longo, Oddone. Strage a Micalesso (e altrove). *Studi in onore di Adelmo Barigazzi*. *Sileno* 10 (1984) 1, 363–77.

Lonis, Raoul. *Les usages de la guerre entre Grecs et Barbares*. Paris: Les Belles Lettres, 1969.

Loraux, Nicole. *The invention of Athens: The funeral oration in the classical city*. Trans. Alan Sheridan. Cambridge: Harvard University Press, 1986.

———. Thucydide et la sédition dans les mots. *Quaderni di storia* 23 (1986) 95–134.

Luschnat, Otto. *Die Feldherrnreden im Geschichtswerk des Thukydides*. *Philologus*, Suppl. 34, Heft 2 (1942).

———. Thukydides der Historiker. *Real-Enzyklopädie*. Suppl. 12 (1971) 1085–1354.

Macleod, Colin (C. W.) *Collected essays*. Oxford: Clarendon Press, 1983.

———. Thucydides and tragedy. In *Collected essays*, 140–58.

———. Rhetoric and history (Thucydides 6.16–18). In *Collected essays*, 68–87. First published in *Quaderni di storia* 2 (1975) 39–65.

———. Thucydides' Platean debate. *Greek, Roman and Byzantine Studies* 18 (1977) 227–46.

———. Form and meaning in the Melian Dialogue. *Historia* 23 (1974) 385–400.

———. Reason and necessity: Thucydides III 9–14, 37–48. *Journal of Hellenic Studies* 98 (1978) 64–78.

———. Thucydides on faction (3.82–83). *Proceedings of the Cambridge Philological Society* 205 (1979) 52–69.

Maddalena, Antonio. *Thucydidis Historiarum Liber Primus (Tomus I)*. Florence: La Nuova Italia, 1951.

Manent, Pierre. La vérité, peut-être. *Débat* 72 (1992) 170–78.

———. *Histoire intellectuelle du libéralisme: dix leçons*. Paris: Calmann-Lévy, 1987.

Manuwald, Bernd. Der Trug des Diodotus. *Hermes* 107 (1979) 407–22.

Marchant, E. C. *Thucydides Book One*. [1905] Bristol, Eng.: Bristol Classical Press, 1982.

Marinatos, Nanno. Thucydides and oracles. *Journal of Hellenic Studies* 101 (1981) 138–40.

——. *Thucydides and religion.* Königstein, Czech.: Hain, 1981.

McGregor, Malcolm F. The politics of the historian Thucydides. *Phoenix* 10 (1956) 93–102.

——. The genius of Alcibiades. *Phoenix* 19 (1965) 27–46.

Méautis, Georges. Le dialogue des Athéniens et des Méliens. *Revue des études grecques* 48 (1935) 250–78.

Meiggs, Russell. *The Athenian empire.* Oxford: Clarendon Press, 1972.

Melzer, Arthur M. *The natural goodness of man. On the system of Rousseau's thought.* Chicago: University of Chicago Press, 1990.

Mikalson, Jon D. *Athenian popular religion.* Chapel Hill: University of North Carolina Press, 1983.

——. Religion and the plague in Athens, 431–423 B.C. In *Studies presented to Sterling Dow on his 80th birthday*, 217–25. Durham, N.C.: Duke University Press, 1984.

Milosz, Czeslaw. *The Witness of poetry.* Cambridge: Harvard University Press, 1983.

Moraux, Paul. Thucydide et la rhétorique. *Etudes classiques* 22 (1954) 3–23.

Müri, Walter. Beitrag zum Verständnis des Thukydides. *Museum Helveticum* 4 (1947) 251–75.

——. Politische Metonomie (zu Thukydides 3, 82, 4–5). *Museum Helveticum* 26 (1969) 65–79.

Nestle, Wilhelm. Thukydides und die Sophistik. *Neue Jahrbücher für das klassische Altertum, Geschichte, und deutsche Literatur* 17 (1914) 649–85.

Nietzsche, Friedrich. *On the genealogy of morals and Ecce homo.* With 75 aphorisms from other works. Translated by Walter Kaufmann. New York: Vintage Books, 1966.

——. *Thus spoke Zarathustra.* In *The portable Nietzsche.* Trans. Walter Kaufmann. New York: Viking Press, 1954.

Orwin, Clifford. Machiavelli's unchristian charity. *American Political Science Review* 72.4 (1978) 20–30.

——. The just and the advantageous in Thucydides: The case of the Mytilenaian debate. *American Political Science Review* 78 (1984) 485–94.

——. Piety, justice and the necessities of war: Thucydides 4 97–101. *American Political Science Review* 83 (1989) 383–88.

——. Democracy and distrust. *The American Scholar* 53 (summer 1984) 313–25.

——. Thucydideses (review essay on W. R. Connor, *Thucydides*). *The American Scholar* 55 (winter 1985–86) 128–30.

——. Justifying empire: The speech of the Athenians at Sparta and the problem of justice in Thucydides. *Journal of Politics* 48 (1986) 72–85.

——. *Stasis* and plague: Thucydides on the dissolution of society. *Journal of Politics* 50 (1988) 831–47.

——. Thucydides' contest: Thucydides 1 22 in context. *Review of Politics* 51 (1989) 345–64.

Ostwald, Martin. *Ananke in Thucydides.* American Classical Studies 18. Atlanta: Scholars Press, 1988.

———. Diodotus, the son of Eucrates. *Greek, Roman and Byzantine Studies* 20 (1979) 5–13.

Palmer, Michael. Love of glory and the common good. *American Political Science Review* 76 (1982) 825–36.

———. Alcibiades and the question of tyranny in Thucydides. *Canadian Journal of Political Science* 15 (1982) 103–24.

———. *Love of glory and the common good. Aspects of the political thought of Thucydides.* Lanham, Md.: Rowman and Littlefield, 1992.

Parker, Robert. *Miasma: Pollution and purification in early Greek religion.* Oxford: Clarendon Press, 1983.

Paronzi, Virginia. Etica e politica nella concezione tucididea della storia. *Aevum* 20 (1946) 217–31.

Parry, Adam. Thucydides' historical perspective. *Yale Classical Studies* 22 (1973) 47–61.

Pearson, Lionel. Review of Kurt von Fritz, *Die griechische Geschichtsschreibung. American Journal of Philology* 90 (1969) 347–52.

———. Thucydides as reporter and critic. *Transactions of the American Philological Association* 78 (1947) 39–60.

———. *Prophasis* and *aitia. Transactions of the American Philological Association* 83 (1952) 205–23.

———. *Prophasis:* A clarification. *Transactions of the American Philological Association* 103 (1972) 381–94.

———. *Popular ethics in ancient Greece.* Stanford: Stanford University Press, 1962.

Pohlenz, Max. Thukydidesstudien I. *Göttingische Gelehrte Anzeigen* (1919), 95–138.

Pope, Maurice. Thucydides and democracy. *Historia* 37 (1988) 276–96.

Pouncey, Peter R. Disorder and defeat in Thucydides, and some alternatives. *History of Political Theory* 7 (1986) 1–14.

———. *The necessities of war: A study of Thucydides' pessimism.* New York: Columbia University Press, 1980.

Powell, C. A. Religion and the Sicilian expedition. *Historia* 28 (1979) 15–31.

Pritchett, W. Kendrick. *The Greek state at war. Part 4.* Berkeley: University of California Press, 1985.

———. *Studies in ancient Greek topography. Part 3.* Berkeley: University of California Press, 1980.

Proctor, Dennis. *The experience of Thucydides.* Warminster, Eng.: Aris and Phillips, 1980.

Quinn, T. J. Political groups in Lesbos during the Peloponnesian war. *Historia* 20 (1971) 405–17.

Rahe, Paul A. *Republics ancient and modern: Classical republicanism and the American revolution.* Chapel Hill: University of North Carolina Press, 1992.

Rawlings, Hunter R., III. *A semantic study of prophasis to 400 B.C.* Wiesbaden, Ger.: Hermes Einzelschriften, 1975.

———. *The structure of Thucydides' history.* Princeton: Princeton University Press, 1981.

Regenbogen, Otto. Thukydides als politischer Denker. In *Kleine Schriften,* edited by

Franz Dirlmeier, 217–47. Munich: C. H. Beck Verlag, 1961. (First published in *Das humanistische Gymnasium* 44 [1933] 2–25).

Reinhardt, Karl. Thukydides und Machiavelli. [1943] In *Vermächtnis der Antike. Gesammelte Essays zur Philosophie und Geschichtsschreibung.* 2d ed., revised and enlarged, edited by Carl Becker, 184–218. Göttingen: Vandenhoeck und Ruprecht, 1966.

Rhodes, P. J. Thucydides on the causes of the Peloponnesian war. *Hermes* 115 (1987) 154–65.

Richardson, John. Thucydides 1.23.6 and the debate about the Peloponnesian war. In *"Owls to Athens": Essays in classical studies presented to Sir Kenneth Dover*, edited by E. M. Craik, 155–61. Oxford: Clarendon Press, 1990.

Romilly, Jacqueline de. La thème du prestige dans l'oeuvre de Thucydide. *Ancient Society* 4 (1973) 39–58.

———. La crainte dans l'oeuvre de Thucydide. *Classica et Mediaevalia* 17 (1956) 119–27.

———. *La construction de la vérité chez Thucydide.* Paris: Julliard, 1990.

———. *La douceur dans la pensée grecque.* Paris: Editions "Les belles lettres," 1979.

———. *Histoire et raison chez Thucydide.* Paris: Editions "Les belles lettres," 1956.

———. [*Imperialism.*] *Thucydides and Athenian imperialism.* Translated by Philip Thody. Oxford: Basil Blackwell, 1963.

———. Fairness and kindness in Thucydides. *Phoenix* 28 (1974) 95–100.

———. L'optimisme de Thucydide et le jugement de l'historien sur Périclès. *Revue des études grecques* 78 (1965) 557–75.

———. Les prévisions non vérifiées dans l'oeuvre de Thucydide. *Revue des études grecques* 103 (1990) 370–82.

———. *Thucydide et l'impérialisme athénien.* Paris: Plon, 1947.

Rousseau, Jean-Jacques. *Emile, or of education.* Introduction, translation, and notes by Allan Bloom. New York: Basic Books, 1979.

Rusten, J. S., editor. *Thucydides [The Peloponnesian war] Book Two.* Cambridge: Cambridge University Press, 1989.

Saxonhouse, Arlene W. Nature and convention in Thucydides' History. *Polity* 10 (1978) 461–88.

Schadewaldt, Wolfgang. *Die Geschichtsschreibung des Thukydides.* Berlin: Weidmann, 1929.

Scharf, Joachim. Zum Melierdialog des Thukydides. *Gymnasium* 61 (1954) 504–13.

Schäublin, Christoph. Wieder einmal *prophasis. Museum Helveticum* 28 (1971) 133–44.

Schepens, G. L'*autopsie*' dans la méthode des historiens grecs du V siècle avant J.-C. Brussels: Koninklije Akademie, 1980.

Schneider, Christoph. *Information und Absicht bei Thukydides. Hypomnemata* 41. Göttingen, Vandenhoek und Ruprecht, 1974.

Schram, John M. Prodicus' "fifty-drachma show-lecture" and "the Mytilenian debate" of Thucydides: An account of the intellectual and social antecedents of formal logic. *Antioch Review* 35.1 (1965) 105–30.

Schuller, S. About Thucydides' use of *aitia* and *prophasis. Revue belge de philologie et d'histoire* 34 (1956) 971–84.

Schwartz, Eduard. Review of Fritz Taeger, *Thukydides*. *Gnomon* 2 (1926) 73–80.

———. *Das Geschichtswerk des Thukydides*. [1929] Reprint. Hildesheim, Georg Olms Verlag, 1969.

Sealey, R. Thucydides, Herodotus, and the causes of war. *Classical Quarterly* NS 7 (1957) 1–12.

———. *A history of the Greek city-states, ca. 700–338 B.C.* Berkeley: University of California Press, 1976.

Shorey, Paul. On the implicit ethics and psychology of Thucydides. *Transactions of the American Philological Society* 24 (1893) 66–88.

Slomp, Gabriella. Hobbes, Thucydides, and the three greatest things. *History of Political Thought* 11 (1990) 565–86.

Sordi, Marta. Il santuario di Olimpia e la guerra d'Elide. In *I santuari e la guerra nel mondo classico*, edited by M. Sordi, 20–31. Milan: Università cattolica del Sacro Cuore, 1984.

Stahl, Hans-Peter. Speeches and course of events in Books Six and Seven of Thucydides. In *The speeches in Thucydides*, edited by Philip A. Stadter, 60–77. Chapel Hill: University of North Carolina Press, 1973.

———. *Thukydides. Die Stellung des Menschen im geschichtlichen Prozess. Zetemata* 40. Munich: C. H. Beck, 1966.

Stockton, David. *The classical Athenian democracy*. Oxford: Oxford University Press, 1990.

Strasburger, Hermann. Thukydides und die politische Selbstdarstellung der Athener. *Hermes* 86 (1958) 17–40.

Strauss, Leo. *The city and man*. [1964] Chicago: University of Chicago Press, 1978.

———. *Natural right and history*. [1953] Chicago: University of Chicago Press, 1978.

———. Preliminary observations on the gods in Thucydides' work. In *Studies in Platonic political philosophy*, edited by Thomas L. Pangle, 89–104. Chicago: University of Chicago Press, 1984. Originally published in *Interpretation* 4 (1974) 1–16.

———. Jerusalem and Athens: Some preliminary reflections. In *Studies in Platonic political philosophy*, edited by Thomas L. Pangle, 147–73. Chicago: University of Chicago Press, 1984. Originally published as *The City College Papers*, no. 6. New York: The Library of the City College of New York, 1967.

Tasolambros, F. L. *In defense of Thucydides*. Athens: Grigoris Publications, 1979.

Thibaudet, Albert. *En campagne avec Thucydide*. Paris: Editions de la Nouvelle Revue Française, 1922.

Topitsch, Ernst. *Anthropeia physis* und Ethik bei Thukydides. *Wiener Studien* 61–62 (1943–47) 50–67.

van der Valk, M.H.A.L.N. Zum Worte *Hosios*. *Mnemosyne* 3d ser. 10 (1942) 113–40.

Veyne, Paul. *Les Grecs ont-ils cru à leurs mythes? Essai sur l'imagination constituante*. Paris: Editions du Seuil, 1983.

von Fritz, Kurt. *Die griechische Geschichtsschreibung: Von den Anfängen bis Thukydides*. 2 vol. Berlin: Walter de Gruyter, 1967.

Walker, P. K. The purpose and method of the "Pentekontaetia" in Thucydides, Book I. *Classical Quarterly* NS 7 (1957) 27–38.

Wallace, W. P. Thucydides. *Phoenix* 18 (1964) 251–61.

Walzer, Michael. *Just and unjust wars*. New York: Basic Books, 1977.

Wassermann, F. M. The Melian dialogue. *Transactions of the American Philological Association* 78 (1947) 18–36.

———. Post-Periclean democracy in action: The Mytilenean debate. *Transactions of the American Philological Association* 87 (1956) 27–41.

Westlake, H. D. Thucydides 2.65.11. *Classical Quarterly* NS 8 (1958) 102–10.

———. The commons at Mytilene. *Historia* 25 (1976) 429–40.

White, James Boyd. *When words lose their meaning. Constitutions and reconstitutions of language, character, and community*. Chicago: University of Chicago Press, 1984.

Wilson, James Q. *Thinking about crime*. Rev. ed. New York: Basic Books, 1983.

Wilson, John. *Athens and Corcyra: Strategy and tactics in the Peloponnesian war*. Bristol, Eng.: Bristol Classical Press, 1987.

———. The customary meanings of words were changed—or were they? A note on Thucydides 3.82.4. *Classical Quarterly* 32 (1982) 18–20.

———. Strategy and tactics in the Mytilene campaign. *Historia* 30 (1981) 144–63.

———. What does Thucydides claim for his speeches? *Phoenix* 36 (1982) 95–103.

Wilson, Lynn S. On a second *phaino*-derived *prophasis* lexeme: some doubts. In *Greek poetry and philosophy: Essays in honor of Leonard Woodbury*, edited by Douglas E. Gerber, 319–36. Chico, Calif.: Scholars Press, 1984.

———. *Prophasis* and *aitia* and its cognates in pre-Platonic Greek. Ph.D. dissertation, University of Toronto, 1978.

Winnington-Ingram, R. P. *Ta deonta eipein*: Cleon and Diodotus. *Bulletin of the Institute of Classical Studies* (London) 12 (1965) 70–82.

Winton, R. I. *Philodikein dokoumen*: Law and paradox in the Athenian empire. *Museum Helveticum* 37 (1980) 89–97.

Yunis, Harvey. How do the people decide? Thucydides on Periclean rhetoric and civic instruction. *American Journal of Philology* 112 (1991) 179–200.

Ziolkowski, John T. *Thucydides and the tradition of funeral speeches at Athens*. Monographs in Classical Studies. New York: Arno Press, 1981.

INDEX

NOTE: This index contains names of Thucydidean characters, places, peoples (except for the ubiquitous Athenians and Spartans), and incidents, as well as ancient and modern authors cited and those modern critics who are mentioned in the text and/or most prominently cited in the notes. A complete listing of Thucydidean passages may be found s.v. Thucydides. Italicized page numbers identify the principal or thematic discussion of the topic or passage in question.